FROM READING TO WRITING
A Reader and Rhetoric

Second Edition

Laurence Steven
Laurentian University

Douglas H. Parker
Laurentian University

Prentice Hall Allyn and Bacon Canada
Scarborough, Ontario

Canadian Cataloguing in Publication Data

Steven, Laurence
    From reading to writing: a reader and rhetoric

2nd ed.
Includes index.
ISBN 0-13-780537-3

1. English language — Rhetoric. 2. College readers. I. Parker, Douglas H. (Douglas Harold),
    1942–   . II. Title

PE1408.S73   1999   808'.0427   C99-931800-1

© 1999 Prentice-Hall Canada Inc., Scarborough, Ontario
Pearson Education

Previous edition was published as *From Reading to Writing: A Reader, Rhetoric and Handbook*
Copyright © 1989 Prentice-Hall Canada Inc., Scarborough, Ontario

Prentice-Hall, Inc., Upper Saddle River, New Jersey
Prentice-Hall International (UK) Limited, London
Prentice-Hall of Australia, Pty. Limited, Sydney
Prentice-Hall Hispanoamericana, S.A., Mexico City
Prentice-Hall of India Private Limited, New Delhi
Prentice-Hall of Japan, Inc., Tokyo
Simon & Schuster Southeast Asia Private Limited, Singapore
Editora Prentice-Hall do Brasil, Ltda., Rio de Janeiro

ISBN 0-13-780537-3

Vice-President, Editorial Director: Laura Pearson
Acquisitions Editor: David Stover
Developmental Editor: Jean Ferrier
Associate Editor: Lisa Phillips
Copy Editor: Lu Cormier
Production Editor: Melanie M. Meharchand
Production Coordinator: Peggy Brown
Permissions/Photo Research: Susan Wallace-Cox
Cover Design: Lisa LaPointe
Cover Image: PhotoDisc
Page Layout: Arlene Edgar

16 17 18 DPC 09 08 07

Printed and bound in Canada.

Pages 285 to 288 constitute a continuation of this copyright page.

To the memory of Jack Lewis

Contents

5   An Anthology of Readings   111

Preface

In the first edition of *From Reading to Writing* we tried to be all things to all people: in addition to a rhetoric, we were a reader, a usage handbook, and a research paper primer. Our goal was laudable, but over the years comments from adopters have reinforced for us that the reader and rhetoric, and our linking of reading and writing, are the *raison d'être* of the book. Many instructors still use separate handbooks for what were for us, finally, peripheral subjects. Consequently, we have been able to shorten the book considerably by dropping both the handbook and the chapter on the research paper. Further, by integrating our discussion of the standard developmental strategies into the reading and writing occasions, we have been able to delete all the appendices from the first edition.

We have also reduced the number of complete essays from 42 to 33. Of these, 16 are new to this edition. Though the selection of essays from the first edition has stood the test of time (with regular users of the book pleading with us not to delete "that essay, please"), we felt that some change was in order, simply because the passing of a decade has given us a great deal more excellent Canadian prose. We wanted to share the new wealth.

With regard to the organization of the essays, we have put all of them together in one anthology chapter. Individual mode chapters have been replaced by one chapter introducing the four modes, with the discussion of each followed by a "Hands On: Reading into Writing Assignment." Here, students, using our "List of Readings, with Subject and Mode Classifications," work with three or four essays they draw from the anthology, essays sharing common mode and subject. Such an arrangement allows instructors more flexibility in assignments. All essays have equal emphasis, and all have appended questions.

As in the first edition, two passages for reading and writing analyses form the core of chapters 2 (The Reading Occasion) and 3 (The Writing Occasion). The first, which focuses on the Internet, is taken from Ross Laver's article "Plugging into the Future," and will appeal to students who are intrigued by a technology that is sweeping the planet and shows no signs of abating. The second passage, taken from Northrop Frye's *The Educated Imagination,* is a more abstract piece that proved popular in the first edition and whose subject—spiritual bankruptcy—will challenge students, drawing them into more theoretical reflection. What links the two pieces is the notion of culture, both the culture of technology and the traditional culture of humanistic thought and values. What separates the two pieces—indeed makes them ostensibly antagonistic to each other and therefore a fruitful source of classroom discussion and debate—is the long-standing ideological divide between humanistic study and science. A discussion that focuses on this divide might serve to show students that the opposition is more apparent than real. Because of the links between these two passages *or* because of their apparent differences, we hope that instructors will work their way through both of them with us.

There is a major difference in the degree of detail provided for the passages in chapters 2 and 3. The Laver passage on the Internet is examined in painstaking detail: the theory upon which this book is based *plus* its application forms the basis of our discussion. In addition, numerous exercises designed to test the student's comprehension of the book's theory are found in the Laver sections of both chapters. On the other hand, the Frye sections are much less theoretically detailed: they are largely stripped down to the practical aspects of reading, responding to, and writing about Frye's concerns. We chose to omit the majority of the theory here for two reasons: first of all, including it again after discussing it in detail in connection with the Internet and Laver would seem redundant; but secondly, and more importantly, we felt that students who had studied the theory in Laver might launch out on their own in examining the Frye passage and test the extent to which they had absorbed the principles found earlier. For those who flounder with Frye or need more help with him than they first thought they might, we have included page references to the appropriate theoretical discussion found in the Laver sections. And we also encourage students to try their hand at the exercises found in Laver even if they are dealing with Frye since these exercises are appropriate to both works.

Our revision of *From Reading to Writing* was helped immensely by two people: Geoffrey Parker and Kelly Smith. Geoff took time from his busy student schedule of assignments to write an essay about the Internet for us, and then we had the effrontery to revise it in public in these pages! Thanks Geoff, for your good humour and reliable word processor. Kelly Smith, secretary of the Laurentian University English Department, singlehandedly ferreted out the permissions for all readings used in this book—excerpts as well as complete essays. This is a painstaking job, requiring diligence and diplomacy. Kelly has both commodities in abundance, and we thank her sincerely. We appreciated, also, the constructive comments of reviewers who read our revised manuscript at various stages: Ingrid Hutchinson, Fanshawe College; Jon-Paul Henry, Douglas College; Susan Tiura, Lakehead University; Renate Eigenbrod, Lakehead University; and A.W. Plumstead, Nipissing University. Finally, to the editorial staff at Prentice Hall Canada: "Take a bow!"

L.S., D.H.P.

INTRODUCTION

No matter what you are studying at the post-secondary level—from the most esoteric of philosophy courses to the most practical of commerce offerings—there is one thing you can count on: your years of higher learning will require you to discipline your thought. Why else would the various branches of learning be called disciplines? Each has its body of knowledge and/or method of proceeding with which you are expected to become familiar, if not to master. And for the most part this learning is embodied in books. Though professors will lecture, and though labs, practicums, and exams will test your learning, a large part of learning any discipline will come through the *act* of reading for your courses. We stress the word act because fruitful reading demands active, rather than passive, readers. Third- and fourth-year students have not simply absorbed (like sponges) more material than their counterparts in first year; upper year students have learned to *think* more independently. They have wrestled the content of their discipline into a meaningful shape. This wrestling is exercise for the mind—and much of it entails reading, grappling with books. Reading seriously teaches us how to think. If we do not succumb to boredom or frustration (understandable responses to new and difficult reading) but persevere, we are forcing our minds to explore new landscapes. Most of us will agree that experience is an effective teacher; well, serious reading *is* experience.

The present text will help you discipline your reading. And disciplined reading will not only take you beyond your initial visceral or "gut" reactions and so enable you to determine the meaning of a piece of writing; it will also encourage you consciously to evaluate that writing. An analogous situation may illustrate the point more vividly. Imagine you are a rather traditional person beginning a two-hour bus trip. Just as you settle yourself into your seat, an apparition in battle fatigues and sporting wildly cropped purple hair sits down beside you. Your immediate gut reactions may involve panic, disgust, or curiosity. If you yield to the first two you effectively prevent any relationship from developing and deny yourself an

1

opportunity to learn something new. If, however, you act on your curiosity and ask, ever so inoffensively, why someone would want to wear purple hair, you open the door to a relationship. You are inviting your travelling companion to convey something of the meaning of his or her life to you. That meaning may confirm your fears about today's youth, or may correct misconceptions you have harboured; whatever the ultimate outcome of the encounter, the experience is a spur to thought and therefore to intelligent evaluation. Similarly, disciplined reading leads you to establish an informed perspective, or point of view, on the subject. And this perspective is the natural basis for your own writing.

About This Text

Our text demonstrates how good writing arises out of good reading. Part I deals with the reading and writing process; Part II constitutes an anthology of readings. In the Process chapters we take you step by step through a *reading occasion,* indicating what good readers do regularly, though often unconsciously. Here we encourage you to read actively, to see reading as an activity whose quality depends on how engaged with the piece you are. We then move to the *writing occasion*—the place where most process rhetoric texts begin and end. This text differs in that when you turn from the reading to the writing occasion, you take with you the raw material for your writing in the form of written responses you have made to your reading. Too often, in our opinion, rhetorics aimed at post-secondary students ignore the most obvious source of raw material for writing: the reading those students do.

Consequently, our anthology chapter provides 33 readings for students to respond to. Students are expected to read and respond to the various essays with a specific goal in mind: writing their own essays on the same general subject. There is only a small gap between reading and writing; students produce their essays the same way they do in most university courses: by reading, interpreting, and responding.

How to Use This Book

From Reading to Writing originated in our feelings, as teachers of composition, that we were not spending enough time on reading with our students. Readings were studied because they were good models of some particular writing feature we wanted to illustrate and not normally because of their subjects as such. We found ourselves either curtailing class discussion on the general questions a reading raised in order to meet the requirements of our course outline, or allowing the discussion to develop at the expense of the more formal presentation of rhetorical principles. In neither case was the intimate connection between good reading and good writing—where the latter is born of the former—demonstrated. The present text is our attempt to rectify the deficiency.

Part I–The Process: From Reading to Writing (Chapters 1–3)

Our process chapters provide a detailed, step-by-step procedure which guides you from your initial encounter with a carefully selected paragraph (in one demonstration example by Ross Laver on the Internet; in a second demonstration example by Northrop Frye on spiritual bankruptcy; and in a third "hands on" example by Patricia Hluchy on teenagers) through to a revised version of an essay you will write in response to the subject of that paragraph.

Chapter 2—The Reading Occasion—offers you a method for handling your reading in a systematic fashion. (Some instructors may find the procedure restraining and may choose to adapt it to their own and their students' needs. This is as it should be; we do not offer the approach as a straitjacket but as a framework which has proved helpful to our students in their encounters with assigned readings.) For each reading, then, we ask you to

1. *actively read* the piece;
2. make brief notes on *subject* (identifying the *thesis statement, topic sentence,* or, if neither of these appears, the *controlling idea*), *audience,* and *purpose;*
3. identify *developmental strategies;*
4. prepare a *summary* of the main points in a radically abbreviated form;
5. write a *response* (of at least 100 words) to the piece.

Chapter 3—The Writing Occasion—carries on directly from the reading occasion. In traditional process rhetorics the first stage is "invention," in which students are introduced to various strategies for engendering raw material for their writing. When we consider writing's intimate connection with reading, however, we see that much of our invention is implicit in active reading. Following the five-point framework for reading outlined above draws into consciousness many of the concerns students must face in their own writing. Your responses, in great measure, are the raw material out of which you will fashion your own essays.

Consequently, once students have arrived at responses for each of the readings under consideration, we ask that you

1. *examine the responses* to discover your personal stance toward the issue (or issues) presented in the readings as a whole;
2. through considerations of your own *subject, audience,* and *purpose,* refine that personal stance into a workable *topic* with its own clear *thesis statement, topic sentence,* or *controlling idea;*
3. determine effective *developmental strategies;*
4. write a *first draft;*
5. revise from large items to small.

You will have noticed that the reading and writing frameworks parallel each other to a large degree. The parallel formats are our way of acknowledging and stressing the similarities between the processes of good reading and good writing. Chapter 1—The Relationship Between Reading and Writing—presents these processes as mirror images having their roots in that central human act—interpretation.

In chapters 2 and 3, two complementary avenues reinforce the approach to reading and writing used in this book.

Demonstration

First of all, we demonstrate the procedure by reading and responding to paragraphs by Ross Laver on the Internet and by Northrop Frye on spiritual bankruptcy. We develop our responses to Laver's piece to the point of the thesis statement, then ask a student to write a draft essay on the subject of the Internet, which we then revise. In response to the Frye piece we produce our own essay, both draft and revision. At each stage of the process we provide a general discussion and a specific illustration of the principle involved.

Hands On

Here we present a paragraph on teenagers and TV for students to work on. For each step in the process we ask leading questions designed to focus your attention and help you get underway.

Our suggestion is that you read our demonstration of a particular step and work on your own exercise in a parallel fashion. You will probably get a better grasp of active reading, for example, if you (1) read what we have to say about it generally; (2) examine how we put theory into practice when we actively read two paragraphs; and (3) try it on your own.

Part II—Theory of Modes and Anthology of Readings (Chapters 4 and 5)

Readings in this text will normally be assigned as part of an essay assignment. The process initiated with one paragraph in Part I (chapters 2 and 3) is repeated in Part II (chapters 4 and 5) but with readings anywhere from two to ten pages in length. Chapter 4 contains an introductory discussion, plus a Hands On: Reading into Writing essay assignment, for each of the four major writing modes—narration, description, exposition, and argumentation. For each reading-into-writing essay assignment, students complete the five-step active reading process for three or four anthology essays, as well as answer the questions appended to each one. The responses thus generated form the basis of the student essay to be written predominantly according to the mode under consideration.

The 33 alphabetically arranged anthology essays that comprise chapter 5 are preceded by a chart offering notations on subject and dominant mode, as well as a list of possible subject groupings. Each essay is followed by questions on its subject, audience, and purpose, as well as its structure and style.

Part I

THE PROCESS: FROM READING TO WRITING

THE RELATIONSHIP BETWEEN READING AND WRITING

People who read only as a diversion from television surfing–or surfing the Internet–perhaps encourage us to believe that reading is passive. They view it as something that one does at the end of a hard working day, or during periods of leisure, or on one's holidays, or as an aid to sleeping. It is our view, however, that reading is a true activity, an endeavour that can be immensely pleasurable because it calls for the reader's complete intellectual and emotional involvement.

Whether we are aware of it or not, reading involves an unspoken agreement between writer and reader. The writer writes to communicate a view, to make a point, to win an argument, to show a position. The reader, on the other hand, gives the necessary time and attention to reading with the assumption that the writer is actually saying something important or worthwhile. In short, the writer's job is to say something effectively; the reader's job is to understand what is being said and to judge its value.

This relationship between writer and reader—this struggle to communicate on the one hand and to understand and assess the communication on the other—is one of the most important intellectual activities. It is also one of the most solitary. Writing is an activity comprising an encounter between the writer and the page. The active reader must also encounter the text, prepared only with intelligence, emotional make-up, common sense, and past reading experience. The basic requirements for both writer and reader are peace and quiet, adequate time for writing, reading and reflection, and perseverance. A reader must come to a text with a view to understanding and evaluating what it is a writer wants to communicate. Reading, therefore, demands as much serious attention as any skill or sport we are determined to learn. In addition it demands a degree of concentration, attention, and critical evaluation not normally associated with television or Internet surfing.

INTERPRETATION

Whether we are aware of it or not, interpretation is something that we do constantly during the course of our everyday lives. Reading an expression on someone's face is an act of interpretation; listening attentively to the words and sounds of a song is one too; so is reading a letter written to you by a loved one. The *activity* of interpretation is so central to all parts of our lives and often such an unconscious part of them that we are likely to take it for granted, much as we do breathing. Unless you are a complete misanthrope and live on an uninhabited island, you engage in the activity of interpretation and critical assessment every day of your life. And even if you do live on an uninhabited island, you'll find yourself forced to interpret or assess even at a very basic level: for example, in order to survive you may need to *read* signs which tell you about possible changes in weather, sea level, and the like.

Three central factors that are either consciously or unconsciously involved in interpretation or critical assessment are *subject, audience,* and *purpose,* terms that make up the reading and writing *occasion* and that will appear in this book time and again as the terms upon which both active reading and writing hinge. Briefly, writers must make clear the *subject* on or about which they are writing, the *audience* for whom the work is intended, and the *purpose* of the writing. The critical and active reader, in order to participate fully and intelligently, must pick up the clues that the writer provides about *subject, audience,* and *purpose.* In short, *critical reading mirrors careful writing:* what the writer has in mind when writing, the reader has in mind when reading. The inevitable conclusion is that learning how to become a critical and active reader will help you become a better writer: reader and writer ask the same questions.

SUBJECT, AUDIENCE, AND PURPOSE

Subject and the Reader

No matter what the occasion, everything you read must be about something: it must have a subject. If you are asked to read and assess a three-page essay on Canadian culture, you will have to decide, first of all, what aspect of the general subject the piece of writing is about. No one can hope to deal adequately with a subject as broad as Canadian culture in three pages. As a reader it becomes your responsibility to search for the controlling idea in the paper, the idea that narrows the general subject to a specific topic. This controlling idea is normally found in what is known as a *thesis statement.* Sometimes a thesis statement is more than a single sentence, so it is important to read through the entire essay first to determine where the controlling idea is. In our imaginary topic on Canadian culture you, as a critical reader, will know that the topic has to be narrowed and that you should search for the sentence or sentences that narrow it. One of a number of such narrowing sentences might be, "If we can judge from the declining subscriptions to the Hummingbird Centre over the last three years, Canadian culture is in a sad state." Note how the writer has narrowed the topic effectively: subscriptions are said to be declining in one locale only, not in concert halls in general. The period under consideration is limited: the essay will concern declining subscriptions in one locale over a three-year period.

Subject and the Writer

Writers have an obligation to narrow their subjects in accordance with the audience they are writing for, the purpose for writing, and the length constraints with which they may have to work. In other words, writers have to take a general subject and choose a controlling idea. There may be literally thousands of such ideas. Writers must choose the one that best satisfies their purpose and appeals to the audience they expect to reach.

Audience and the Reader

For any piece of writing the reader must ask who is being addressed. If you were reading a speech on the Internet that was prepared for a group of people wanting to learn the technology, you would expect to read something entirely different from what you would read if it were a talk on the Internet for a group of computer science students. The former piece of writing could take very little for granted about the Internet; the latter a good deal. The reader must at all times be conscious of who is writing, and for whom.

Audience and the Writer

Make certain that, as a writer, you know whom you're addressing. A clear understanding of your audience can help you narrow your subject and formulate an effective and appropriate thesis statement or controlling idea. Using terms like "Web site" and "on-line" without explanation to an audience that knows very little about computer technology or the Internet could leave them gasping with incomprehension. Worse, they might do the last thing you want them to do: stop reading what you thought would interest them.

Purpose and the Reader

Determining why a writer wrote something is a particularly important interpretative task for a reader. More often than not, finding the writer's motive for writing involves a consideration of the writer's subject and intended audience. For example, the purpose of a store owner worried about legislation on Sunday shopping may be to convince the public that the opportunity to shop seven days a week is a great convenience. What the reader should also know, however, is that the store owner's stated purpose might not be the same as the real purpose: it may be that the store owner is less concerned about the convenience to shoppers than about the likely increase to business of a seven-day shopping week. In other words, readers must be aware that stated purposes may not be the same as real intentions. Passages that appear in most respects to be expository—wanting only to show or explain—may in fact be argumentative, as might be the case in our example of the shop owner.

Purpose and the Writer

Writers must know the purpose for putting pen to paper. If the purpose for writing a particular piece is unclear to the writer, chances are the focus or controlling idea (i.e., the specific subject or thesis) of that piece will be unclear, shifting, or non-existent. If, for example, you are a conservationist writing to other conservationists about industrial pollution, there is a good chance that you do not need to convince anyone of anything. You may simply follow an expository line and explain the implications of the latest industrial accident. If, on the other hand, your audience is a group of industrialists, you may have to follow an argumentative line to convince them that an accident is as serious as you believe it to be. Making a thoughtful decision about purpose early on will make your writing easier, and keep your readers on track: *the track you want them on.*

THE READING OCCASION

DEMONSTRATION

In the Introduction we outlined five steps that we feel will help you get maximum value from your reading. They were as follows:

STEP 1: *Actively* read the piece.

STEP 2: Make brief notes on *subject* (including thesis statement, topic sentence, or controlling idea), *audience, and purpose.*

STEP 3: Identify *developmental strategies.*

STEP 4: Prepare a *summary.*

STEP 5: Write a *response.*

To encourage regular practice of steps 2 through 5, we suggest that you maintain a *reading workbook* in which you do the note-taking for these steps for each reading you encounter in the course. The notes need not be extensive, but even brief notes will help fix your active reading in your mind. Referring to the reading workbook will bring a piece of writing and your reactions to it back to your consciousness quickly; it will also give substance to class discussions of your reading.

Step 1: Active Reading

Whenever possible read with a pencil in your hand and use it to make brief notations in the margin or to underline or circle significant words in the text itself. Marking up your own text of a reading brings the dimension of engaged thought to your reading (be careful not to mark up library copies—photocopy these and work with the photocopy).

Use margins to record thoughts, observations, disagreements, or difficulties you might be having with the text. If you see changes in thought in an expository or argumentative text note these in the margin.   *explain.*

Underline and circle words or ideas that might seem foreign to you so that you can follow up on them and give them greater attention either through dictionary study or further contemplation.   *thoughtful observation*

Use your pencil to link main points, or ideas that repeat with variation. Note developments in ideas by drawing linking lines between the main idea and its other manifestations.

READING OCCASION ONE: ROSS LAVER ON THE VALUE OF THE INTERNET

In the following pages we will demonstrate the principles of active reading by going through each step of the reading occasion for one sample paragraph written by Ross Laver and taken from an article entitled "Plugging into the Future," *Maclean's,* 29 January 1996, pp. 28–31:

underlined
technical
language
contributes
to

Applets? Java? Thirty-two-bit Web browsers? Yes, once

tone?
ironic?
satiric?

again, legions of techno-nerds are whipping themselves

A large number

into a virtual frenzy over the latest developments in cy-

berspace, jabbering in some strange, impenetrable di-

alect and dreaming of the day when the much-ballyhooed

information superhighway reaches into homes of good

convince
or
persuade

consumers everywhere. Of course, most of those very

through
illustration,

same consumers could hardly care less about Java and

slang?
why?

its applets, whatever the heck they are. Internet fever

cause & effect,
comparison,

may have taken North America's media by storm in 1995,

definition

but for the majority of Canadians the on-line universe is

still the exclusive playground of the electronic elite—the

estimated five to ten per cent of the population who own

both a computer and a modem fast enough to surf the

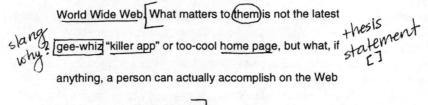

World Wide Web. What matters to them is not the latest

slang *why?* gee-whiz "killer app" or too-cool home page, but what, if   *thesis statement* [ ]

anything, a person can actually accomplish on the Web

that is of any practical value.

Step 2 (a): Subject

The question we ask most commonly when someone recommends a book or a movie to us is, "What is it about?" All of us who read, go to films, look at pictures—whether so-called works of art or even simple family photographs—search for the subject since it is subject that, initially at least, allows us to "enter" a book, a movie, or a photograph and encounter its meaning.

Looking for the subject should be your first task when you confront a piece of prose. Oftentimes the subject of a passage will be obvious and jump right out at you. Other times it might be more difficult to locate and you may experience a number of false starts before you discover it. Sometimes the subject will appear as the first sentence; other times it will be in the middle of a passage or even at its end.

The subject in the Laver passage does not jump right out at you. Indeed the initial sentences of the paragraph seem to fly in the face of meaning through their diction and their form. First of all, the first three sentences probably take us by surprise because we are used to reading paragraphs that begin with declarative sentences. In this paragraph, these sentences are in the form of questions, and none of them is a complete sentence. Two of the three are *choice of* *use of words* *in writing* made up of only one word, both of which are probably foreign to us, and the third—lacking a verb as do the first two—uses an equally foreign multi-word phrase. Rather than providing us with a comforting and meaningful context, the first three "sentences" tend to wrong-foot us because of the diction used by the author and his violation of grammatical rules. *pursue* On a quest for subject, we can't even find meaning.

Sentence four is more reassuring since it behaves at least like a normal English sentence with subject, verb, and modifiers; however, its diction—words like "techno-nerds," "cyberspace," and "information superhighway"—makes some of us feel as if we are still on the outside of meaning looking in.

We soon begin to learn, however, that the author wants us to feel confused about both the strange language and the bizarre grammatical structures he has been using because he is introducing us to a subject about which some of us know nothing or, at least, very little; namely, an area of high technology known as the Internet, a technology with its own highly specialized diction and grammar—in essence a foreign language. And it is foreignness that the author has made us feel throughout a large part of this paragraph until we reach sentence six where the notion of "Internet fever" is first mentioned.

Having reached this point and solved the mystery that the first few sentences introduce, we might be tempted to conclude that the subject of this passage is "Internet fever," but we probably would be wrong to jump to this conclusion. The author is less concerned with "Internet fever," which is a disease caught by "techno-nerds" who know the meaning of "applets" and "Java," than he is with its "practical value," a notion not introduced until the final sentence of the paragraph. The subject of the paragraph, reserved for its final sentence, is, therefore, the practical value of the Internet: "what, if anything, a person can actually accomplish on the Web."

Once you have found the *topic sentence* (if you are reading a paragraph), or the *thesis statement* (if your reading is longer than a paragraph), or the *controlling idea* (if an unequivocal topic sentence or thesis statement is not apparent), you should expect to find supporting details for it in the remaining or, in this case, the earlier parts of the piece. You should be able to see the logic and coherence in the writing even though you may not agree with what the author is saying. In the Laver passage the sentences that precede the final one where the subject is finally stated all work to show the closed, mysterious, and inaccessible nature of the Internet for the majority of people. This inaccessibility is emphasized largely through the mysterious diction which forms a part of the Internet's language, a language which is foreign "for the majority of Canadians" even though it is comprehensible to "legions of techno-nerds."

Reading Workbook Notes: Subject

> What is there in the Internet world that is of practical value to the majority of Canadians who are not yet part of the electronic elite?

Practice Reading: Subject

Actively read the following paragraphs, focusing on clues to subject. After you have completed your textual notations and marginalia, prepare reading workbook notes on subject for each one comparable in length to ours just above.

> When I first became curious about sex, I'd sneak fancy dirty books like John Cleland's classic, *Fanny Hill: or Memoirs of a Woman of Pleasure,* from my father's library, dog-ear the carnal bits, and hide them under tomes on Michelangelo. I always felt furtive, but that was understandable—I was 12, and steamy books were the scratch-and-sniff poor cousins of literature.
>
> Over the past decade or so, things changed. What was once dismissed as smut has suddenly become respectable as erotica. Librarians will tell you which erotic books gave them the greatest pleasure. On my last trip to Coles, I saw erotic books piled high alongside cookbooks and the classics—and the majority of them were written by women. I skimmed the shelves and found titles like *Slow Hand, Fever, Touching Fire.* The offerings were not only by famous writers such as Alice Munro and feminists like Susie Bright, but also insurance agents, farm women, and teachers, all with provocative tales to tell.
>
> In the past, erotic books and films were a man's world. Men produced them; men read them and watched them. So why are so many women jumping into the fray?

Eve Rockett, "Some Like It Hot," *Chatelaine,* May 1996: 75–76, 116, 120.

Sleep is not dispensable, regardless of the attempts in today's society to treat it as if it were merely unproductive "down time." The desire to get more sleep is not a sign of laziness, nor does it represent a lack of ambition. The need for sleep is real, and the idea that one can go without sleep is wrong. Perhaps it is time for policy makers, health workers, and all the rest of us to wake up.

Stanley Coren, "Sleep Sliding Away," *Saturday Night,* April 1996: 19–22.

Step 2(b): Audience

All writing is addressed to a literate audience, but having said this we have to acknowledge that there are various degrees of literacy and, therefore, various audiences to whom authors can address themselves. In the Laver passage, the author seems to be addressing himself to those Canadians who are not yet computer literate or adept in the mysteries of the world of the Internet. Happily, Laver also includes himself in this category. For although he uses highly technological and specialized language such as "applets," "Java," "Thirty-two-bit Web browsers," "cyberspace," and "information superhighway," he questions the meaning of some of these terms (notice the question marks), refers to those who understand this language as "the electronic elite," and tells his audience in good, down-home slang that he doesn't know himself what "the heck" some of these terms mean. In addition, one can detect a note of satire in his description of this group of electronic elites. He refers to them unflatteringly as "techno-nerds" who whip themselves into "a virtual frenzy" over their subject, and who spend their time not talking, but rather "jabbering in some strange, impenetrable dialect."

The audience Laver wants to speak to and be a part of is people who know little or nothing about the Internet. But one might also argue that in mocking the enthusiasm of the "techno-nerds" and even by insulting them through unflattering diction, he also wants to get their attention so that they might learn something from him, an area to be discussed under Purpose below.

Reading Workbook Notes: Audience

Those who, like the author, are impatient with the techno-nerds and who wish to know the practical value of their talents; but also the techno-nerds themselves.

Practice Reading: Audience

Actively read the following paragraphs, focusing on clues to audience. After you have completed your textual notations and marginalia, prepare reading workbook notes on audience for each one, comparable in length to ours just above.

It is the medium we most love to hate. The glowing black cube, the cathode-ray Cyclops lodged in our living rooms. We regard it with fascinated horror, feel powerless before it, sucked into its evil vortex. We use it, in the resonant phrase of the critic Neil Postman, to amuse ourselves *to death*. Television: bane of our lives, the hardest of hard drugs.

Except it isn't.

Mark Kingwell, "The Goods on the Tube," *Saturday Night,* March 1996: 69–70.

Ultimately, the undergraduate experience is a rite of passage, profound and transformative. Day to day, it's an adventure. Knowledge comes in many forms, and, no matter how taxing your existential and academic struggles, the following questions are guaranteed to confound you along the way: Is Kraft Dinner one of the four basic food groups? Can you make a can of tuna last more than three consecutive meals? Does the weekend begin on Thursday after class or Friday at noon? If your paper is four weeks late, should you plead illness in the family or tell the truth?

Ann Dowsett Johnston, "Introduction," *The Maclean's Guide to Universities*, 1996: 5.

Step 2(c): Purpose

Every author has a purpose in mind when writing. Successful writing communicates that purpose; unsuccessful writing does not. We are not here speaking of the effectiveness of the communication, but of whether the purpose is communicated at all. Before we can evaluate an author's purpose, we must know what it is. Authors may want to tell a story (narration), describe an event, person, or phenomenon (description), explain or demonstrate something (exposition), or convince someone of something (argumentation). Or they may want to do a little of each within the same piece of writing. Whatever choice they finally make carries certain implications for the presentation of their writing: its tone, its diction, its range of reference, its audience. For example, an author who begins an article for the public on the safety of nuclear power with a detailed, specialized exposition of how the Pickering, Ontario, reactor functions has misconceived the primary purpose of such an article, which is to convince an uneasy populace. Though the expository account of the workings of the reactor will have to be included to make the argument a convincing one, it should not usurp the dominant purpose. Further, the author should adjust the diction and range of reference to a level that can reasonably be expected of the audience implied by the dominant purpose.

Now that we have defined purpose, can we see the purpose of Laver's paragraph? Laver places himself in the camp of Canadians who are not part of the "electronic elite," and his purpose may very well be to convince these "techno-nerds" that their knowledge has very little meaning for those outside their small privileged circle. Hence, Laver argues this position by highlighting some of the group's arcane language—its "impenetrable dialect"—to draw the group's attention to its privileged, if largely irrelevant, status. He shows (exposition) them to themselves in the way others might see them in order to convince (argumentation) them of the true worth of their endeavour. The perspective is admirably captured by Laver through the use of such down-putting terms as "frenzy" and "jabbering."

Laver's purpose, therefore, is both to show and, by showing, convince "the electronic elite" to put their cyberspace knowledge to good effect by presenting its practical value to the rest of us. In short, Laver challenges the "techno-nerds" to speak a language we can all understand, appreciate, and apply to our lives.

Reading Workbook Notes: Purpose

To encourage those whom he mocks to recognize that their knowledge should be shared and communicated in a practical way with those who make up the majority of the Canadian citizenry.

Practice Reading: Purpose

Actively read the following paragraphs, focusing on clues to purpose. After you have completed your textual notations and marginalia, prepare reading workbook notes on purpose, comparable in length to ours above.

> *Water.* We all use it. We all need it. That is why Black's developed System Crystal, to protect the purity of water. This unique system purifies and reuses water in a continuous closed loop process, reducing the annual water usage at Black's Photofinishing Plant by 97%. With System Crystal, we have also eliminated water and chemical discharge into the municipal sewers. So the next time you have pictures developed at Black's, you will receive big, beautiful prints and help us all help the environment.
>
> An advertisement for Black's Photography published in *This Country Canada,* 1:1 (1992): 14.

> A North American supermarket is market place, temple, palace, and parade all rolled into one. It is both the expression and the symbol of the goals and the means of North American civilization, physically embodying the culture's yearnings for size, availability, freedom of choice, uniformity, variety, abundance, convenience, cleanliness, speed, and the reduction of hierarchy to quantity: money and amount. It both tempts and constrains us: lets us loose inside but controls and defines us even as it exacts its toll at the exit. Buying a bag full of groceries at a North American supermarket is as essential for a traveller attempting to understand this culture as taking an evening stroll would be in Spain or Italy, or eating in a popular restaurant in France.
>
> Margaret Visser, *Much Depends on Dinner,* Toronto: McClelland & Stewart, 1986. 22.

Step 3: Developmental Strategies

Developmental strategies are techniques that authors use to help them express their purposes. Whether the mode of writing is narration, description, exposition, or argumentation, certain techniques are used again and again to develop the thought. Essentially there are six developmental strategies:

1. Comparison and Contrast
2. Cause and Effect
3. Classification and Division
4. Illustration
5. Definition
6. Process Analysis

Comparison and Contrast

Comparison and contrast are two aspects of the same exercise. The one sees similarities between things, the other differences. In your writing these two elements are normally combined and you should show both similarities and differences between items, although you probably will try to stress one over the other depending on the nature of the items being assessed, your purpose in writing, and the length of the assignment.

Comparison and Contrast Steps and Guidelines

(a) Limit comparison and contrast to two items.

(b) Remember that to compare means to show both similarities and differences.

(c) Emphasize the main point of the comparison.

(d) Choose a topic that lends itself to comparison.

(e) Plan your essay by lining up the comparisons and contrasts and deciding on the order of presentation.

(f) Be sure you follow a method of presentation: for example, should you proceed by discussing the items one at a time (the so-called "chunk" method) or feature by feature (the "slice" method)?

Cause and Effect

Cause-and-effect thinking appeals to humanity's deepest instincts; in a profoundly mysterious world human beings want to know the answer or answers to the question *why*. Effects are no less important in our lives; if causes give us *reasons for,* effects provide us with *results of.* Generally, it is easier to write a convincing cause-and-effect paper—either expository, argumentative, or a combination of both—if the subject you choose is impressionistic and subjective rather than scientific or polemical. People are less likely to quibble with your causes or effects if the experience you are detailing has a highly personal element built into it.

Cause and Effect Steps and Guidelines

(a) Limit your discussion to causes or effects.

(b) Start with an effect and try to explain its cause or start with a cause and try to determine or predict its effect.

(c) Make certain that causes and effects are true and legitimate.

(d) Acknowledge the possibility of several possible explanations.

(e) Establish a large enough sample group in cause-and-effect papers that argue a point or establish a hypothesis.

Classification and Division

Classifying, categorizing, or sorting helps us deal with the plethora of activities, experiences, and information to which life exposes us every day. Classifying helps us to organize items in terms of a larger whole. Division lets us examine or analyze phenomena once they are sorted or classified. Division and classification are primarily used to inform or explain—they are standard expository strategies.

Classification and Division Steps and Guidelines

(a) Classification focuses on similarities within a common field (think of classification as the many different television sets that General Electric makes).

(b) Division focuses on differences within a common field (think of division as the many different components within a particular General Electric television model).

(c) Normally classification and division work together.

Illustration

Communicating with illustrations is such a commonplace occurrence that we may have to prod ourselves to bring techniques for using them into conscious awareness. Illustrations are tied to generalizations. When we make a general point, examples or illustrations become relevant.

Illustration Steps and Guidelines

(a) Be certain that you provide sufficient illustrations to support a general assertion.

(b) Make your illustrations comprehensible.

(c) Do not feel the need to support with an illustration every assertion that you make.

(d) Do not allow the illustration to take on a life of its own.

Definition

The dictionary is what most people think of when the word "definition" is mentioned, and certainly a well-worn dictionary is a good friend. But dictionary definitions only go so far; they are a good initial step but they rarely provide us with more than the formal definition of words. Types of more interesting definitions are examples, comparisons, and even narratives. Each of these tends to bring to life or demonstrate the idiosyncrasies contained within the concept or word whose meaning—within the context of your essay—you are trying to capture.

Definition Steps and Guidelines

(a) Dictionary definitions provide formal, analytical definitions, not personal, contextually based ones.

(b) Be aware of the existence of specialist dictionaries.

(c) Make certain that the word you define has a specific enough focus to make the meaning clear and relevant.

Process Analysis

Process writing, like comparison and contrast, cause and effect, definition, illustration, and classification and division, is often used in the service of exposition. <u>First and foremost,</u> *First of all* expository writing explains, shows, or presents something to a reader. Process writing, more particularly, explains, shows, or presents by showing *how to:* for example, how to do, find, discover, learn, examine, understand, build, work out, elucidate, decipher, improve, change, or perform something.

Process Analysis Steps and Guidelines

(a) Be certain of all of the steps in the process.

(b) Be certain that you put all of the steps in the correct order.

(c) Do not get sidetracked on parts of the process.

Laver's most obvious developmental strategy is illustration. The whole passage, through its use and parody of technical language, *shows* us as well as the "techno-nerds" themselves that their technology is not reaching all of us who might profit from it. Implied in this illustration, therefore, is a comparison-and-contrast relationship and a cause-and-effect one as well. *We,* that is the majority of Canadians, including the author, are set against *them,* the "electronic elite." *They* might have something to teach *us,* if only *they* saw the benefits of speaking *our* language. *They* are the group that makes up an exclusive 5 to 10 per cent of the population; *we* make up the rest of it. The *effect* of their attitude manifested in their specialized vocabulary and, incidentally, in the fact that they have the money to purchase the necessary equipment is to alienate us from them and make us sceptical about the real value of the technology that whips them "into a virtual frenzy."

The overlap of strategies in this passage is natural and common. Laver's piece is an interesting mix of illustration, comparison and contrast, and cause and effect. Indeed, one might even argue that Laver employs yet another strategy, namely, definition, in his altogether idiosyncratic explanation of who comprises "the electronic elite." All of these strategies intertwine and yet add their own distinctive qualities to the reading. Do not feel that you must subordinate some strategies to find one that colours the whole piece. Strategies are tools: writers use them where they are appropriate. Carpenters do not limit themselves to a screwdriver if the job at hand calls for a hammer and drill as well.

Reading Workbook Notes: Developmental Strategies

1. <u>Illustration</u>: The whole paragraph illustrates how the world of high tech, specifically the Internet, leaves the majority of Canadians cold and far behind.
2. <u>Definition</u>: The author defines "electronic elite" in an unflattering way by focusing on its language and enthusiasm.
3. <u>Comparison and Contrast</u>: This strategy is implied in the passage as the author sets up a "them and us" situation.
4. <u>Cause and Effect</u>: We see the effects of "techno-nerd" language on the majority of Canadians, namely, incomprehension and, as a result, uninterest.

Step 4: Summary

Learning to summarize your reading will give you practice in recognizing what is essential and what is peripheral to a piece of writing. In addition, being able to summarize through paraphrasing something that you've read will let you know whether or not you really understand the piece of writing. In your summary do not comment on the author's attitude but simply try to capture the essence of the argument in your own words. The thesis statement, topic sentence, or controlling idea will provide a focus for your summary. The length of a summary will vary with the length and complexity of the source. But the rule of thumb is that a summary is radically shorter than the original.

In the Laver passage the topic sentence is the final one, and the earlier sentences all build toward the claim the author makes in the final sentence.

Reading Workbook Notes: Summary

Those who are knowledgeable about the specialized language and workings of the Internet must realize that many Canadians really want to know the practical value of a technology that, at the moment, engages only about five to ten per cent of the population.

Step 5: Response

Having completed the preceding 4 steps conscientiously, you will probably have a solid understanding of the reading in question. You can now—and only now—make an informed response to the piece, deciding, for instance, whether you agree, disagree, or are neutral to the thesis that Laver puts forth. In your summary you need not give a sentence-by-sentence critique of the passage and you must not, at this stage, merely summarize what the author says since summary is not the same as critical response. Your response should be considerably longer than your summary.

Reading Workbook Notes: Response

Based on what Laver says, and on my own observation of the techno-babble world in which we live, I would agree that the Internet and its devotees have not yet convinced us that there is anything of any real practical value in this relatively new technology. This is not to say that the Internet is not worthwhile; it is only to say that we have not yet been told, in a language that we can understand, whether or not this technology holds anything for the majority of Canadians. At the moment, the Internet appears to be an expensive toy that only a few can afford and understand. Laver's focus on the private language of "the electronic elite" is only one example of the ways in which speakers of the same tongue—in this case English—are increasingly cut off from areas of new knowledge by code grammars and languages that disenfranchise the majority for the sake of entertaining a privileged minority. If technology in general is to help us live our lives better, it needs to move into the mainstream of life by moving out of the realm of play and techno-babble.

READING OCCASION TWO: NORTHROP FRYE ON
SPIRITUAL BANKRUPTCY

The second of the two demonstration readings designed to help you understand how active and critical reading works is an excerpt from Northrop Frye's book *The Educated Imagination*. Students can choose to work on this passage rather than Laver's or to work on it after having mastered the techniques outlined in the Laver section. The theoretical discussion of active reading principles and paradigms found in our discussion of Laver's work apply equally well to the following passage from Frye.

Step 1: Active Reading

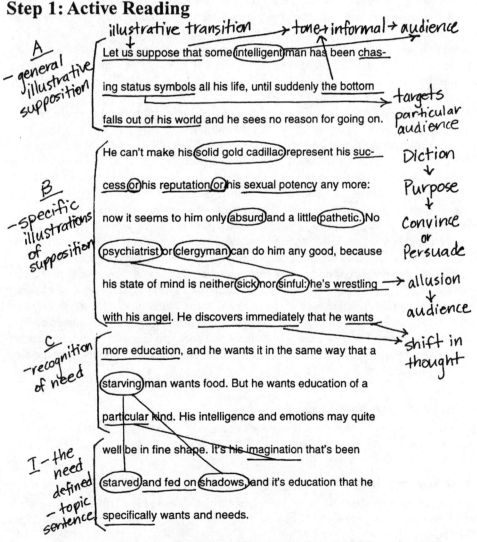

Text of the passage, with handwritten annotations:

illustrative transition → tone → informal → audience

A — general illustrative supposition

Let us suppose that some intelligent man has been chasing status symbols all his life, until suddenly the bottom falls out of his world and he sees no reason for going on.

→ targets particular audience

B — specific illustrations of supposition

He can't make his solid gold cadillac represent his success or his reputation or his sexual potency any more: now it seems to him only absurd and a little pathetic. No psychiatrist or clergyman can do him any good, because his state of mind is neither sick nor sinful: he's wrestling with his angel. He discovers immediately that he wants

Diction ↓ Purpose ↓ Convince or Persuade

→ allusion ↓ audience

→ shift in thought

C — recognition of need

more education, and he wants it in the same way that a starving man wants food. But he wants education of a particular kind. His intelligence and emotions may quite well be in fine shape. It's his imagination that's been

I — the need defined — topic sentence

starved and fed on shadows, and it's education that he specifically wants and needs.

Northrop Frye, *The Educated Imagination*, Toronto: CBC Enterprises, 1963. 65.

Step 2(a): Subject

As was the case with the Laver passage, the subject of this Frye passage does not jump right out at you. Rather, you have to read and re-read, think and re-think to find the controlling idea. Notice how the paragraph begins. The "Let us suppose" indicates that the author is presenting an illustration of something—and that *something* is the subject we are looking for. The intelligent man whose world has fallen apart is *not* the subject; he is only an example or illustration of it. To find the subject we need to keep reading. Sentences two and three give more specific details about this man and his predicament—but they do not state what the predicament is. In sentence four, however, we get a shift in direction: the man "discovers" something. Sentences five and six define the limits of the discovery, and in so doing they gradually bring the subject into focus. As the paragraph moves toward its conclusion, it moves further away from illustration and closer to generalization until in sentence seven—the topic sentence—the subject is finally found. Although it is tempting to locate the topic sentence in sentence four where the notion of education is first mentioned, this would be a hasty judgement since it is not until sentence seven that we learn that the man in the passage is longing for a particular type of education, namely, of the imagination.

In the paragraph under examination we can see the logic and coherence in the writing even though you may not agree with what the author is saying. We can see how sentences one and seven (the first and last of the paragraph) sandwich between them the particular details that each calls for. We hear in sentence one in a general way of what happens to "some intelligent man" who "has been chasing status symbols all his life." Sentence seven concludes the passage by indicating that such symbols are only "shadows" that starve the imagination. What falls between these two general statements is illustration: a reference to a particular status symbol, the "solid gold cadillac," and references to what the symbol stands for: "success," "reputation," and "sexual potency." The starvation that the man now feels (sentence seven) is illustrated in his pathetic feelings (sentence two) and in the fact that a psychiatrist and a clergyman cannot help him (sentence three). The notion of starvation in sentence seven finds an echo in the simile of a starving man wanting food in sentence four. (Notice how we have linked these items in our active reading.) In short, the passage is a fine example of how the subject or the *what* is articulated and illustrated throughout. There is a sense of orderly and coherent interplay between general statement and detail. The former frames the passage; the latter is found between the two framing sentences.

Reading Workbook Notes: Subject

The need for an educated imagination to give meaning to a materially full but imaginatively empty life.

Practice Reading: Subject

Turn your attention once more to the passages entitled "Some Like It Hot," *Chatelaine,* May 1996 (p. 13 above) and "Sleep Sliding Away," *Saturday Night,* April 1996 (p. 14 above).

Step 2(b): Audience

One of the most reliable clues in determining the audience for a particular piece of writing is the author's use of diction. A careful examination of our passage from Northrop Frye reveals that the author eschews colloquialisms, street talk, slang, and dialect. He opens by saying "Let us suppose," not "Y'all give a listen now to this here example." Frye designates the man's materialism as "absurd and a little pathetic" rather than as "dumb and a little silly." Frye speaks of "psychiatrists," not "shrinks," and "cadillacs," not "caddies"; the central figure of the illustration is an "intelligent man," not a "smart guy," an expression which in our own time might have more than one signification. At the other extreme, Frye makes no use of diction belonging to a particular, specialized discipline or of language requiring special knowledge. His intelligent man *has* been "chasing status symbols all his life, until suddenly the bottom falls out of his world"; he *has not* been "conspicuously consuming all his life, until suddenly his purview undergoes a radical negative transformation." Frye uses the concrete image of the "solid gold cadillac" rather than a vague phrase such as "proliferating acquisitions." The man is said to be "wrestling with his angel" rather than "engaged in a psychological debate between his id and superego."

Because Frye is careful to pitch his diction in the middle of the range between informal and highly formal, there is no reason to believe that the general reader could not understand what is being said. But general audiences are made up of individuals, and though the audience may generally understand, there will be some readers who will not know what Frye means by "status symbols" or by "wrestling with his angel." Others may not realize that the "solid gold cadillac" is a figurative way of summing up all the man's material wealth—his status symbols. Some people may just not be able to afford the luxury of Frye's educated imagination; they may be too busy struggling to pay the rent to find time to chase status symbols or wrestle with angels. These people would not form part of Frye's audience. The target audience for his piece needs to be in a position to comprehend the crisis the "intelligent man" is going through; they need, probably, at least a middle-class income, if not a higher one. They need a certain level of intelligence themselves.

Beyond these characteristics for Frye's ideal reader, we should ask ourselves about another one brought about through the changing social movements of recent years. In discussing the passage we have followed Frye's lead in speaking of the intelligent "man," rather than "person" or other alternative. Although we feel sure that Frye had people in general in mind and intended nothing invidious by his masculine references, his language (and ours insofar as we followed his lead) may alienate some readers sensitive to feminist issues who otherwise meet the criteria of income and intelligence that we have spoken of. In brief, Frye may have limited the number of receptive readers of his passage more than he wanted to. The point is worth generalizing: in addressing yourself to an audience, keep in mind the human sensitivities (whether of sex, race, religion, or social class) that may have a bearing on the language you use.

Reading Workbook Notes: Audience

Intelligent middle- or high-income people who either are, or have the potential to be, chasers of status symbols, and who, consequently, can comprehend—if not appreciate—the predicament Frye has outlined.

Practice Reading: Audience

Turn your attention to the passages entitled "The Goods on the Tube," *Saturday Night*, March 1996 (p. 14 above) and "Introduction," in *The Maclean's Guide to Universities*, 1996 (p. 15 above).

Step 2(c): Purpose

Whether consciously or unconsciously, perceptive readers pick up the clues to purpose that careful writers provide explicitly or implicitly for them. The opening of the Frye passage— "Let us suppose"—signals an illustration of some point; it is *showing* us something. We are right to detect an expository element in Frye's purpose. But exposition is not all there is to it. The first sentence supposes "that some intelligent man has been chasing status symbols all his life." Though Frye is not explicit about his purpose, he has deliberately chosen a phrase—"chasing status symbols"—calculated to make middle- and upper-income readers in western capitalist society reflect on their material pursuits. The phrase carries connotations of triviality, banality, and self-interest that a more neutral phrase like "acquiring material possessions" does not carry to nearly the same extent. Without explicitly doing so, Frye has introduced an argumentative element into the passage. Readers will feel the need—even if slightly—to defend themselves against the charge of being status-symbol chasers. And this is exactly where Frye wants them. He can go on to *explain* the need for an educated imagination through illustration and definition while at the same time choose the diction and range of reference that brings one set of standards—status symbols, solid gold cadillacs, success, reputation, sexual potency—into an implicitly *argumentative* conflict with another—wrestling with angels, educated imagination. This overlap of purposes, or modes, is what you will find in most writing. Those of you who read and studied the Laver passage on the Internet will readily see that it, as well as the Frye passage, judiciously mixes modes to emphasize the purpose of the passage.

Reading Workbook Notes: Purpose

> To induce his audience to reflect on their possible need for an educated imagination by implicitly convincing them of their predicament, while explicitly explaining the phenomenon to them.

Practice Reading: Purpose

Turn your attention to the advertisement for Black's Photography published in *This Country Canada*, 1992 (p. 16 above) and the passage from *Much Depends on Dinner*, 1986 (p. 16 above).

Step 3: Developmental Strategies

Review these strategies found on pages 16–19.

The most obvious strategy in the Frye passage is illustration. The whole passage is one large illustration or example of the need for an educated imagination. The piece begins with "Let us suppose," clearly signalling that an illustration is forthcoming, and the opening sentence sets the scene. Sentences two and three are specific illustrations of the more general opening supposition where the status symbols are identified. The intelligent man's seeing no reason for going on is given credence when we learn that psychiatrists and clergymen can do nothing for him.

Sentence four shifts from specific illustrations to definition. For the rest of the piece, Frye gradually defines the need for an educated imagination by narrowing the possibilities of what the need is. It is a need for education, but education of a particular kind, and so on. This strategy of definition began earlier but worked in a negative fashion: Frye defined the need by what it was not. In sentence four we simply get a shift from negative to positive definition. And it is not until sentence seven that the full definition comes.

Although illustration and definition are the clearest strategies employed by Frye, the passage also embodies an implicit cause-and-effect structure. Because the man chases status symbols, Frye implies, "the bottom falls out of his world and he sees no reason for going on." That is one cause-and-effect relationship (though not developed). A second one arises out of the first: because he sees no reason for going on in his conventional lifestyle, he casts about for other avenues to meaning. The effect of this searching is that he "discovers immediately that he wants more education."

Reading Workbook Notes: Developmental Strategies

1. Illustration: The whole paragraph is an illustration but it embodies more specific illustrations within it.
2. Definition: The illustrations define what the man's malaise is not. They are followed by more positive statements which work to define what the malaise is.
3. Cause and Effect: The passage carries an underlying implication that chasing status symbols caused the bottom to fall out of the man's life. A major effect of such a change was that the man began to recognize his need for education.

Step 4: Summary

Review the advice on summary found on page 20.

Reading Workbook Notes: Summary

After suddenly awakening to the fact that his materially successful life is meaningless, an intelligent man finds that he "wants and needs" to educate his imagination.

Step 5: Response

Review the advice on response found on page 20.

Reading Workbook Notes: Response

It seems all too clear when we look around us that Frye is correct in his feeling that we are materially successful but spiritually poverty-stricken. Increasingly in Canada we seem to be importing our values from the USA. We are avid consumers, but the more we consume of US culture the less Canadian we become. Is our problem that we are a young country? We need to develop our imaginations, as Frye says, but how can we do this when television culture deadens them. Even the CBC has fallen on tough times, and it has traditionally been the promoter and protector of Canadian culture. Frye may imply that we need to wrestle with our angels, but how soon will it be before we cannot be awakened to that need?

HANDS ON: READING

In this section *you* put theory into practice by completing reading workbook notes for a passage taken from a review of a television series. You should do each step here in conjunction with your reading of the same step in the Demonstration section of this chapter. Following the model may give you more confidence as you launch out on your own active and critical reading. This is your first "hands-on" assignment in this text. By the time you have finished the Hands On: Reading into Writing section of chapter 3, the work you are about to do now will have blossomed into your first essay prepared wholly according to principles presented in this text. Take the time to answer our leading questions conscientiously. They will guide you into fuller observations of the reading passage and thereby into fuller responses. The fuller your responses are, the more solid will be the foundation of your writing occasion. The questions in the anthology chapter assignments are not so systematic or thorough; consequently, it is in your best interest to pay close attention to the questions here.

READING

Teenagers are the true existentialists. They make their absurd daily slog from math class to mall to MuchMusic, only to find themselves back in trigonometry the next morning. Blindly groping through a thick hormonal fog, they know all about fear and loathing. Convinced that no one has ever been as weird as they are, they feel terribly alone. Not even fully grown, they are obsessively morbid. Television has mostly refrained from visiting the teenage wasteland, opting instead to routinely dish up adult fantasies of adolescent life (the now-defunct *My So-Called Life* being a rare exception). *Straight Up,* however, tells it like it is. Created and produced by Adrienne Mitchell and Janis Lundman, the team that made the teen-girl documentaries *Talk 16* and *Talk 19,* the series of half-hour dramas is fresh, uncompromising, wry, disturbing—just like a real teenager. For adults, the show is a pungent reminder of how alienating adolescence can be. The question is whether young people themselves will watch this … reflection of their lives.

Patricia Hluchy, "Teenage Wasteland," *Maclean's,* 19 February 1996: 64–66.

Step 1: Active Reading

1. Circle the words in the passage that describe the author's sense of the teenager's situation.
2. Where in the passage does the author move from general description to particular application of this description?
3. What marginal notation should you place beside the author's reference to *My So-Called Life*?
4. What word in sentence one sets the stage for the description of teenagers that follows in the next five sentences?

Step 2(a): Subject and Thesis Statement, Topic Sentence, or Controlling Idea

1. How does the author's title, "Teenage Wasteland," contribute to her subject?
2. Pick out the paragraph's subject as found in its topic sentence.

Step 2(b): Audience

1. Who is the author's audience and might there be more than one audience? What evidence is there in the passage that leads you to your conclusion?
2. What audience assumptions does the author make? Can you draw an audience profile based on these assumptions?

Step 2(c): Purpose

1. Is the author's purpose primarily expository or argumentative? On what do you base your answer?
2. What can you determine about the author's purpose based on the sentence, "*Straight Up*, however, tells it like it is"?

Step 3: Developmental Strategies

1. Outline and justify the various developmental strategies in this paragraph.
2. How do these strategies work together to produce a convincing paragraph?

Step 4: Summary

1. Provide a brief summary of the author's main point or points in this paragraph.

Step 5: Response

1. Do you support or oppose the author's general picture of teenagers?
2. Do you support or oppose the author's view of the television portrayal of teenagers in general?

3

THE WRITING OCCASION

DEMONSTRATION

As we made clear in the first chapter there is a close relationship between the reading and writing processes, a relationship that we will explore in this chapter, where we discuss the writing occasion. Steps 1 through 5 of the reading occasion, discussed and exemplified in chapter 2, will help you become informed about how to read carefully and critically. Steps 1 through 5 of the writing occasion continue the informing process so that you can begin to feel confident when you put pen to paper. The writing occasion steps are as follows:

STEP 1: *Examine the responses* you made to your reading to determine your personal stance to the broad subject.

STEP 2: Consider your own *subject, audience,* and *purpose* to refine that personal stance into a workable topic with a clear *thesis statement, topic sentence,* or *controlling idea.*

STEP 3: Determine effective *developmental strategies.*

STEP 4: Write a *first draft.*

STEP 5: Revise the first draft and turn it into a *final draft.*

Just as we recommended in chapter 2 that you maintain a *reading workbook* in which you keep a record of your various thoughts about the work you read, so here, with the writing occasion, we recommend that you keep a *writing journal* for materials you accumulate during the various steps. The following examples of writing journal entries based on Ross Laver's article on the Internet and Northrop Frye's passage on spiritual bankruptcy that we read in chapter 2 are not meant to be seen as rigid directives but rather as general guidelines to help you understand the way in which a writing journal *might* take shape.

ESSAY ON THE INTERNET: RESPONDING TO LAVER

Step 1: Examination of the Response to Laver

Traditionally, the technique known as *brainstorming*—freely jotting down whatever comes into your mind as you consider the subject—has been used to generate ideas. The purpose of brainstorming is to write quickly and without concern for quality of ideas: you just want to accumulate material for later perusal. This technique of generating ideas, combined with actively reading our already written response to Laver's comments, will help you generate ideas about the subject.

What follows is (1) our active reading of our response to Laver's passage; and (2) two examples of brainstorming based on two items from that active reading.

Response to Ross Laver

Based on what Laver says, and on my own observation

~~the~~

of techno-babble world in which we live, I would agree

that the Internet and its devotees have not yet convinced

us that there is anything of any real practical value in this

relatively new technology. This is not to say that the

Internet is not worthwhile; it is only to say that we have

not yet been told, in a language that we can understand,

whether or not this technology holds anything for the ma-

jority of Canadians. At the moment the Internet appears

to be an expensive toy that only a few can afford and un-

derstand. Laver's focus on the private language of "the

electronic elite" is only one example of the way in which

speakers of the same tongue—in this case English—are

increasingly cut off from areas of new knowledge by code

grammars and languages that disenfranchise the major-

ity for the sake of entertaining a privileged minority.

If technology in general is to help us live our lives better,

it needs to move into the mainstream of life by moving   ⑦

out of the realm of play and techno-babble.

Active reading jottings:

1. A world of techno-babble
2. The practical value of the Internet
3. Its "language" (i.e., the language used to "explain" it) stands in the way of understanding
4. An expensive toy for those with money
5. Other examples of code language
6. The privileged minority
7. Technology designed to improve our lives, not merely to entertain

   The amount of raw material you generate from your written responses to your reading will depend largely on the length of those responses. Brainstorming with a view to generating more ideas can be very helpful in providing additional raw material which you may use in your writing assignment. What follows is the result of a one-minute brainstorming session based on only one active reading jotting (*4. An expensive toy for those with money*):

* Computer prices too high for everyone to afford
* Internet games
* What do we really learn from the technology?
* Information versus knowledge
* Trivia disguised as knowledge: high-tech "Trivial Pursuit"
* False intimacy based on technological companionship
* A dangerous toy that invades privacy
* The toy's addictiveness

   And here is the result of another brainstorming session, based on *7. Technology designed to improve our lives, not merely to entertain.*

* Technology often initially expensive
* After a few years, generally affordable; e.g., digital watches and VCRs
* The technology of space exploration providing us with valuable spin-off assets in the areas of medicine, for example
* Even entertaining technology can be useful; e.g., television
* Many high-tech items we now take for granted; e.g., telephone, car, laser technology

As you can see from this preliminary examination of our responses, there are numerous avenues waiting to be explored. Of course, you will not be able to use all of the areas that brainstorming and active reading responses open up, but providing yourself with a myriad of choices will give you a broad range of material to select from as you prepare to move toward the final step in the writing occasion, the polished final draft of an essay.

Step 2: Subject, Audience, and Purpose into Topic, and into Thesis Statement, Topic Sentence, or Controlling Idea

After establishing a list of possible areas of exploration through brainstorming and actively reading your own written responses to the reading, it's now time to pull back and ask yourself *what* you want to say *(subject), who* your reader is *(audience),* and *why* you are writing *(purpose).* Before you even select a topic and begin framing it into a thesis statement, topic sentence, or controlling idea, you need to ask yourself the what, who, and why questions so that you have a firm idea before you begin writing of the direction in which you will be travelling. Answering the what, who, and why questions—questions that you posed during active reading exercises in chapter 2—will give you a good grasp of what is known as the *rhetorical context* for your particular writing occasion.

Step 2(a): Subject

This section of the writing occasion corresponds to *Step 2(a): Subject* of the reading occasion in chapter 2.

For any writing project that involves prior reading, *a general subject area* is a given. If you choose to write a paper on computers, for example, you have already narrowed your subject to a point where reading about fly-fishing or women's fashion is not going to contribute in any obvious way to advancing your views on the subject. Although you now have a subject area, you do not as yet have a central focus—a necessity for all writing. To sit down to write a paper on computers without sharpening the focus will result in an unsatisfactory piece of work since the paper will not have a central idea to serve as its structuring principle. How long is the essay to be? To whom is it addressed *(audience)?* Why are you writing it *(purpose)?* These questions will help you determine the central focus of your essay, a focus that will manifest itself most tangibly in your essay's topic, title, and thesis statement.

For example, in Laver's demonstration passage and our response to it, the general subject area is the Internet, but not the Internet in general. Laver's passage and our response show that the more particular areas of concern are whether the Internet is a tool of entertainment for a select few or a tool of practical value for humankind in general. In addition, Laver has some important things to say about the English language as a means of communication, and our response develops this aspect a bit further. What neither Laver nor our first response to him imply, but what our brainstorming notes on our response suggest, is that there are positive aspects to technology.

Read the following paragraph and write a comment or two on what you determine to be its subject:

> We, the Inuit here in Labrador, still follow the traditional ways of our forefathers. Right
> to this day, we eat what our forefathers used to eat, food with no price tags on it, food

created for us ever since the Earth was created. People have different foods according to their land. This I was not aware of in the past. Some eat only what is grown in gardens; others eat whatever food they can get their hands on; and we, the Inuit, have a different diet because we are people of a cold land.

Martin Martin, "We, the Inuit Are Changing," This Country Canada, 1:1 (1992): 30–31.

Step 2(b): Audience

This section of the writing occasion corresponds to *Step 2(b): Audience* of the reading occasion in chapter 2.

Determining who your reader is, is essential in your writing process: it contributes to a strong focus, a definite diction, and a consistent tone and range of reference. Try drawing a profile of the audience for your essay. Consider such things as age, gender, financial status, level of education, ethnic background, occupation, religion, and location. In Laver's passage on the Internet, a number of audience pointers are evident: the passage could be addressed to the "electronic elite" or to those who are not in this select group, or perhaps more correctly, to both groups—the privileged minority and those still outside the technology looking in. Our response to Laver displays these audience pointers as well, but our brainstorming notes suggest another possible audience. When we note that technology usually gets cheaper after a few years, and that there have been beneficial spin-offs, aren't we beginning a defence of computer technology aimed at those who are not sure about it?

Read the following brief paragraphs and write a comment or two on the audience to whom they are directed:

> In Montreal these days, readers and book lovers have become spectators at a fight, the pages of *The Gazette* having been transformed into an arena for that diverting exchange of jabs and cross-hooks that is the Mordecai Richler-Mark Abley slugfest.
>
> The match-up has been classic. In one corner, Richler—novelist, essayist, satirist, all-round pesky gadfly. A generation older than Abley, he still has about him the aura of mouthy street fighter, his vague dishevelment and unabashed penchant for fine scotch and good cigars providing brusque counterpoint to his opponent's clean-cut image.
>
> Abley, in the other corner—a *Gazette* feature writer and former Books editor—is a poet and essayist whose style is graced with an elegant and frequently heartstopping delicacy. A soft-spoken man with a warm, sensitive demeanor, he is, I would venture to say, no cigar-chomper.

Janice Kennedy, "L'affaire Richler-Abley: A Classic Confrontation," The Ottawa Citizen, 14 July 1996: C12–C11.

Step 2(c): Purpose

This section of the writing occasion corresponds to *Step 2(c): Purpose* of the reading occasion in chapter 2.

Knowing *what* you want to write about and *who* you want to direct it to, will help you articulate *why* you want to write—what your purpose is. Writing to university or college students will mean that we need to explain certain pieces of information, but can assume other information will be readily understood. With the subject of the Laver passage, we might want to write an *expository* essay in which we try to explain the workings of the Internet; or taking our lead from Laver himself, we might want to write an *argumentative* essay in which we claim that for the Internet and computer technology in general to be more accessible to everyone, it must justify its universal applicability and be expressed in a language that has meaning for all of us. Given the brainstorming notes we made which suggested benefits of technology, we might even want to argue against Laver, and say that he's over-reacting, that all technology starts out expensive and hard to understand, but as it takes hold it becomes cheaper and comprehensible. Whatever the case, when we contemplate approaches based on either exposition or argumentation we are thinking about our essay's purpose.

Read the following paragraph and write a comment or two on what you consider to be its purpose. Note: Because the following passage is only one paragraph from a much fuller essay, it may not be possible for you to decide definitely on the purpose. But there is no harm in speculating:

> When I mentioned to an American that I was now more interested in the development of Canadian culture than I was in his, and that I intended to write something about it, he said: "What are you, a god-damned fascist?"—which shows how the cultural invader can be as paranoid about this subject as the threatened. The only way I can justify nationalism is to see it as a way of regulating what goes in and what goes out. I would like to see a balance in this exchange, nothing more. But it is a sign of how in control foreign interests are in Canada—I mean *mentally* in control—that every time we call for an accounting they accuse us of tribalism pointing towards another holocaust.
>
> R. Murray Schafer, "Canadian Culture: Colonial Culture," *Canadian Forum,* March 1984: 14–19.
> [See the entire essay in the anthology section of this book.]

Step 2(d): Topic and Thesis Statement

Your topic provides a focus for and should reflect your subject, audience, and purpose. In our case, the broad subject—the Internet—needs to be narrowed down to a workable size. Our reflections on subject, audience, and purpose in this chapter have helped establish our rhetorical context—the "ballpark" for our essay. But we still need a specific focus. This is where the question of topic enters the picture. Clearly, as suggested earlier, an essay with a limited length couldn't possibly deal with the vast subject of the Internet in a satisfactory or detailed manner. Entire books have been written on the subject, and even they have to declare a topic by being aware of their *own* subject, audience, and purpose. Therefore, a suitably narrowed *topic* on the Internet—taking into account our considerations of *our own* subject, audience, and purpose—might be the following:

The value of the Internet for Canadians

And an appropriate *thesis statement* developed from such a *topic* might be

Although at its present state of development, the Internet seems to be an expensive toy whose specialized language and cost are designed with a very small portion of the population in mind, the potential value of this technology for all Canadians resides in the amount of information it can generate and disseminate, its speed, and its relatively low cost.

As you will notice from the above thesis statement, your topic becomes a thesis when you make some *claim* about it. It is this claim—attitude, point of view, or position—that will control the direction of your essay and that your readers will rely on to keep them oriented. Using the above thesis statement, it is clear that the subsequent essay will begin by acknowledging that there are certain drawbacks to the Internet (drawbacks that Laver mentioned in his paragraph). But the majority of the essay will focus on the positive strengths of the Internet, and three strengths in particular. A well-developed thesis statement actually structures your essay for you and serves as a general outline letting you know what you will say in your essay and the order in which you will say it.

A final word about thesis statements concerns rigidity. At this stage of the writing occasion do not allow the thesis statement to become a straitjacket; it may change as you write and revise your draft. You may find, for example, that you want to change the order of the points you want to make, or even add new ones. This is fine. Your thesis statement will get you into a written draft, but second thoughts or the discovery of new material may force you to change direction and revise the thesis statement accordingly.

Read the following paragraph and write a comment or two on what you consider to be its thesis statement:

> Samuel Johnson's circumspection is not to be doubted, for on the subject of patriotism, he professed vastly different points of view. He once wrote that only the hearts of the most unenviable of men would not swell with patriotic pride at the sight of the battle of Marathon. That same year he remarked to his friend James Boswell that "patriotism is the last refuge of a scoundrel." It was as if Johnson were marking out the two extremes of a sentiment that, 200 years later, would still confound mankind in general and Canadians in particular. For if you think being a patriotic Canadian is a simple matter, consider for a moment the controversy that currently surrounds a single tree in downtown Toronto. People call it the Alexander Muir Maple.

> David Macfarlane, "On Days of Yore," *This Country Canada*, 1:1 (1992): 78–79.

Step 3: Developmental Strategies

This section of the writing occasion corresponds to *Step 3: Developmental Strategies* of the reading occasion in chapter 2.

Effective writing is planned writing. In the reading process you could ascertain the developmental strategies after finding the thesis statement. When you are writing you can determine the developmental strategies either before or after you have decided on a thesis statement, depending on whether you feel more comfortable working on a thesis statement first or the strategies first. As we made clear in chapter 2, when discussing developmental strategies, it is not necessary, nor is it always possible or desirable, to fix on only one strategy in your writing assignment. More often than not, several work together to produce an effective piece of writing. Recall that in our active reading of the Laver paragraph we isolated four examples of strategies—illustration, definition, comparison and contrast, and cause and effect—within the space of only six of Laver's sentences. Having argued for the flexibility of developmental strategies, it is, however, important for us to add that when beginning an essay it is helpful to have one or two strategies in mind. A quick look at the brainstorming notes we made on our response to Laver's passage is very revealing of potential strategies:

"information versus knowledge" and "trivia disguised as knowledge" suggest comparison/contrast

"high-tech items" suggests illustration

"spin-off assets" suggests cause and effect

Read the following paragraph and write a comment or two on its developmental strategy(ies):

> Canadians live under the remarkable illusion that we are technologically advanced people. Everything around us denies that assumption. We are, in many ways, a Third World country, selling our natural resources in exchange for the high technology of the industrialized world. Try going through your home and looking at the country of origin of your clothes, electrical appliances, books, car. The rare technological product that does have Canada stamped on it is usually from a branch plant of a multinational company centred in another country. But we differ from traditional Third World countries. We have a majority population of Caucasians and a very high level of literacy and affluence. And we have been able to maintain our seemingly advanced social state by virtue of an incredible bounty of natural resources.
>
> David T. Suzuki, "A Planet for the Taking," *Canadian Forum,* February 1985: 6–8.
> [See the entire essay in the anthology section of this book.]

Step 4: First Draft

One of the most difficult parts of the writing process is the point at which you actually start to put words on paper. A natural temptation that all writers face is to avoid the business of writing by convincing themselves that their topic needs more thought or research. There comes a time, however, when the writing must begin. One can always introduce new issues, directions, or items into a topic in the revision stage.

You will recall that while our *brainstorming* notes suggested other ways to view the technology question, our *response* to Laver's paragraph on the Internet was positive; in other words we agreed, more or less, with the concerns he expressed about the technology and its as yet unproven value for the majority of Canadians. Our draft essay might have reflected and developed the scepticism we expressed in our response to Laver's equally sceptical paragraph. However, we decided to try an experiment with the first draft by asking a first-year civil engineering student with a passionate interest in the Internet to write an essay on this subject, calling into question its value. However, he expressed interest in writing an essay which *defended* the Internet against the charges brought against it. After he told us what he felt was valuable about the Internet, we provided him with the thesis statement and nothing else, and turned him loose on the topic. We think you'll agree that he did a respectable job, but as our revision to his draft shows, his work could have been better had he known about the importance of subject, audience, and purpose in writing a good essay. It may very well be that you do not agree with his point of view and the arguments he marshals to support it. If this is indeed the case, you should actively read his essay and respond to it, perhaps developing Laver's concerns about the Internet, in an essay of your own, which takes into account subject, audience, and purpose.

First Draft on the Topic of the Internet.

I ——— The Internet, which has been around since the 1970s,

has become increasingly popular over the last 20 years,

and has recently witnessed a surge in the number of   *awk*

people who are active "surfers" of the Net. This surge is

in large part due to increased publicity of the on-line ser-

vices as well as to better and faster connections to the

ante   Net, which have allowed the Internet to become an in-

?

creasingly graphical experience. Although some may

argue that, at its present state of development, the

Internet seems to be an expensive toy whose specialized

language and cost are designed with a very small portion

of the population in mind, the potential value for all

Canadians of this technology resides in the amount of in-

formation it can generate and disseminate, its speed and   *wdy*

its relatively low cost. But before one attempts to analyze

dic   this value, a clear definition of what the word "Internet"

tense   represents is useful.   *dic*

II ——— The Internet is presently the world's largest computer   *see boxes on next page*

network. What this means is that, essentially, thousands

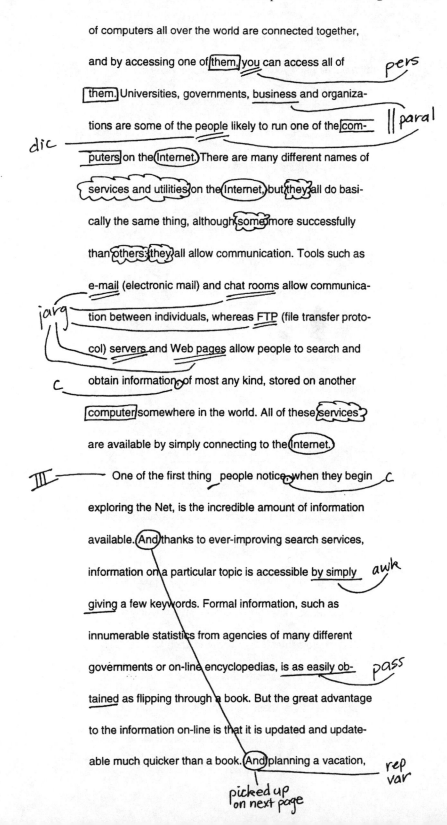

of computers all over the world are connected together, and by accessing one of them, you can access all of them. Universities, governments, business and organizations are some of the people likely to run one of the computers on the Internet. There are many different names of services and utilities on the Internet, but they all do basically the same thing, although some more successfully than others: they all allow communication. Tools such as e-mail (electronic mail) and chat rooms allow communication between individuals, whereas FTP (file transfer protocol) servers and Web pages allow people to search and obtain information of most any kind, stored on another computer somewhere in the world. All of these services are available by simply connecting to the Internet.

One of the first thing people notice when they begin exploring the Net, is the incredible amount of information available. And thanks to ever-improving search services, information on a particular topic is accessible by simply giving a few keywords. Formal information, such as innumerable statistics from agencies of many different governments or on-line encyclopedias, is as easily obtained as flipping through a book. But the great advantage to the information on-line is that it is updated and updateable much quicker than a book. And planning a vacation,

picked up on next page

*picked up fr.
prev. page*

a home renovation, or just about any other task is often

pers   much easier once you access one of the many companies

that now have "pages" on the World Wide Web. Finding

out whether a book is available round the street, or even   **dic**

at most any library around the world, is an exceedingly

simpler task than calling up each one. Another great

strength to the Internet is that it provides access to not-so-

formal information. Indeed, with little effort, one can find

the opinions and thoughts of anyone ranging from a lead-   **agr**

ing expert in their field, to the uninformed, and yet highly

opinionated Joe. As long as the segment of the population

you want to talk to has access to a computer hooked up

**faulty
logic**   to the Net, you are able to hear from them. And, as ac-

cess to the Internet becomes increasingly easy and inex-

pensive, so too does the number of people who use it.   **mod**

IV ———— Indeed, in Canada, Internet access is available with

c   little effort, and few costs. Universities and colleges all

across the nation provide students with the opportunity to

use the Internet, either from home or from the university

or college's computer laboratory, and often for free. Many

large corporations also offer free Internet access to their

**rep
var**   employees. And for those who do not get accounts either

from work or school, commercial Internet providers

charge as little as $10 a month for full access. So anyone

*picked up
on next page*

from prev. page

who has a computer, and even many who do not, can

easily use the Internet. If $10 seems a bit pricey to you,

it's because you do not yet know of the quantity of infor-   *pers*

mation that you presently obtain from another pay-for

source. News (updated in some sites every 30 minutes!),

weather maps, topological maps, quotes from the stock

market and much, much more are easily obtained in sec-

onds. Another great cost-saver in the everyday Canadian

household is the fast, free communication provided along

with the Internet access you purchase. E-mail, delivered

within seconds of being sent, does not require a stamp to

be stuck on the envelope like "snail-mail" does. And the

quickness of it allows it to easily provide the same infor-

mation as a long-distance phone call would, without the

expense. And many corporations across North America

now have teleconferences, rather than face-to-face con-

ferencing, which not only saves large amounts of money

previously spent on air travel and staying in a hotel, but   *paral*

also allows quicker and more frequent meetings.

V.———— Speed is also one of the key reasons for the

Internet's success. Part of this is due to ever-improving   *ref*

rep   *dic*
technologies, and part of it due to the vast amount of

people who currently use the Internet. The technology

awk that has within a few years raised the average user's access speed more than tenfold, <u>has allowed</u> an explo-   *awk*

sion of increasingly visual, audio, and interactive informa-

tion to be available within seconds. One can access

anything, from satellite pictures, to musical segments of a   *pers*

new album, to a video clip of your favourite television

show, in small amounts of time. And the other key to the

Internet's speed, the vast amount of people on it, is   *pers*

awk   equally as important. If you need someone's opinion on

where to eat, want to buy or sell your house, car, or any-

thing else, or need an answer or tip to an obscure ques-

tion (often a company is not willing to answer, even on

their telephone service line or 1-800 number), all you

need to do is post an article to a newsgroup. And any-   *rep*
                                                          var

where from minutes to hours later, depending on how

much interest your article has gathered, you'll receive e-

mail to answer your need. So, for instance, a high school

student conducting a survey of 500 people can, in a day

or two, accomplish what would have required much more

effort and time. And people looking for a quote on the

c   price of a new or used car can obtain it in seconds.

VI   So, in summary, the Internet is one of the more use-

collo   ful tools in present-day Canada. And its usefulness,   *rep*
                                                               var

sometimes obscured by its novelty, is undeniable. The

wealth of information, coupled with the speed at which it

is available, make it not only a good substitute for most other sources, but also one which provides information and services not available through other services. In an age where over-specialization has substantially reduced

rep the general knowledge of people in general and re-searchers in particular, the Internet provides the communication between people necessary to compensate for this over-specialization. People who do not recognize the advantages of the Internet are quickly becoming a minority, and expend more time and energy accomplishing the same tasks Net users do in minutes. (And) as technology *rep* *var*

dic continues to improve the speed(s) at which information is available, the Internet assures itself a definite place in

sxt mankind's future.

Step 5: Revision and Final Draft

Effective revision demands a method, otherwise you will waste a lot of energy and time. You need to concentrate on one aspect of your essay at a time. A common revision practice is the top-down approach, which breaks the revision into five stages. One version is as follows:

1. Large Items
   (a) Beginning
   (b) Closing
   (c) Overall coherence
2. Paragraphs
   (a) Units of thought
   (b) Transitions
   (c) Topic sentence and development
   (d) Coherence

3. Sentences

   (a) Variety

   (b) Passive and active voice

   (c) Wordiness

   (d) Awkward constructions and grammatical problems

4. Diction

   (a) Clichés

   (b) Jargon

   (c) Sexist language

   (d) Spelling

5. Effective Punctuation—A Matter of Choice

   What follows is an analysis of the first draft of the Internet essay, based on the above revision stages.

Large Items

Beginning

Let's look at the opening paragraph to see where it might be improved. The opening sentence provides us with a statement on the age and growing popularity of the Internet and, as such, serves as a good introduction to the broad subject of the essay. Sentence two briefly explains why the technology is so popular. Then follows the thesis statement, where the three major components of the subject (information, speed and cost) are mentioned for the first time. The paragraph closes with a sentence that alerts us to an upcoming definition of the term "Internet."

   Let's look more closely at the thesis statement, especially its placement in this first paragraph and its "although" clause. As mentioned earlier, thesis statements can come anywhere in the opening paragraph. In this paragraph of four sentences, the thesis statement appears third, and does not seem out of place in that position. The "although" or qualifying clause in the thesis statement might present a problem, however, depending on what the author does with it. If the "although" clause acknowledges (as this one does) that there is a point of view other than the author's, then the alternate point of view (i.e., that the Internet is an expensive toy, that it uses specialized language, and that it is costly) needs to be developed *briefly* somewhere in the paper.

   Is there a clear sense of who the audience is in this first paragraph? The subject seems clear, as does purpose: to *explain* (exposition) the Internet and *argue* (argumentation) its value. The author uses two examples of specialized language—"surfers" and "graphical experience"—which suggest that the essay might be addressed to an audience not entirely unfamiliar with the subject. However, the final sentence of this paragraph, with its promise of a definition, and the opening sentence, with its mention of the age of the Internet, suggest that the essay is being pitched to a non-specialist audience. Perhaps the sense of the audience for this essay should be sharpened in the final draft.

Closing

In paragraph six the author lets us know in the first sentence that the essay is drawing to a close by using the expression "in summary." A nice touch in this concluding paragraph is the way in which the author does not simply repeat the terms of the thesis statement, but instead lets us know *in other words* what the point of the essay has been. Sentence four introduces what some might see as a new thought—new thoughts should not be introduced when essays are drawing to a conclusion. We have to decide whether we can justify the inclusion of this sentence at this point or whether we should excise it.

Overall Coherence

If overall coherence refers to the way in which the essay hangs together and the way in which it develops the thesis statement, then we can perhaps find one problem in overall coherence in this draft. Although the thesis statement with its three principal areas of development and its qualifying "although" clause seem clear enough, the alternate point of view is not really mentioned again in the essay, and, some might argue, there is some overlap and repetition among the three areas of development. Moreover, the order of development is different from that expressed in the thesis statement. Notice that in paragraph four, devoted to the cost of the Internet, and paragraph five, devoted to the speed of the Internet, the author also discusses the type and amount of Internet information available. However, that subject was already dealt with in paragraph three. In addition, in the thesis statement, the author mentions the three components of his subject in this order: information, speed, and cost. However, in the essay he discusses these components in the following order: information, cost, and speed.

AUDIENCE Our discussion of audience needs to be extended to the entire essay. An essay must have a consistent view of its audience throughout. Although prepared to define the term "Internet" for the general reader with little or no expertise in the area, the author uses such specialized terms as "chat rooms," "file transfer protocol," "servers," and "Web pages," without defining them, thereby assuming that his general reader is aware of what they are. In the revision, we must constantly keep our not-so-well-informed audience in mind. While stretching readers is good, losing them is not. Furthermore, using undefined technical language validates the objection to the Internet as a technology whose vocabulary is incomprehensible.

PURPOSE The purpose of this essay—to argue the value of the Internet by showing its benefits in three areas—is evident throughout. However, as mentioned, the purpose would be better served if the author briefly explained technical or specialized language.

Paragraphs

Units of Thought

Just as an essay has a topic and thesis to which it adheres throughout its course, a paragraph should be a distinct unit of thought. All its sentences should contribute to the development of the topic of the paragraph as expressed in the topic sentence. This does not mean that different points cannot be expressed in the same paragraph. What it means is that these differing points must serve as supporting evidence for the controlling idea—usually, again, in the form of a topic sentence. If a point does not offer such support, it is irrelevant not only to the particular paragraph in which it appears but quite likely to the thesis of the essay as a whole.

Transitions

Transitions between paragraphs refer to the smooth movement from one paragraph to the next in an essay. The transition between paragraphs one and two is nicely done in the draft because the mention of "a clear definition" in the final sentence of paragraph one prepares us for the definition *per se* in paragraph two. Paragraph three introduces and develops the first of the three components of the thesis statement. Another helpful transition is found between paragraphs three and four. The mention of "inexpensive" in the final sentence of paragraph three introduces the notion of cost, the subject of all of paragraph four. The transition between paragraphs four and five could be clearer without being contrived or overly obvious.

Topic Sentence and Development

As stated earlier, the thesis statement in paragraph one, sentence three is that paragraph's topic sentence. The author's intention is to build up to it, but is it possible that sentence one of this paragraph competes with it? The opening sentence of paragraph two is that paragraph's topic sentence. It is a *general* statement of definition which is refined in the sentences that follow. Paragraphs three, four, and five begin with a general topic sentence and then provide specific detail to demonstrate the truth of the opening sentence. For the sake of variety, is it possible or desirable to use a different technique in one of those paragraphs?

Coherence

Just as an essay must have overall coherence (linkage between main points), paragraphs must also demonstrate a similar coherence. Notice our active reading notations on paragraph two of the draft. You can easily see how each sentence coheres to the ones around it through the repetition of key words, pronouns, or concepts. Such links, or transitions, assist the reader's understanding (Note: In paragraph two, words or concepts that are united to each other are indicated by circles, rectangles, or wavy lines).

Sentences

As we have mentioned on a number of occasions already, the subject of a piece of writing is bound up with the choice of developmental strategy. The more engaging your writing, the more your reader responds positively to your subject. Writing demonstrates a writer's personality; you want your reader to find you a person worth spending time with. One of the best ways to turn people off is to bore them. A series of plodding, monotone sentences—whether or not their content has intrinsic value—will lose your reader's attention as surely as yours is lost by the bore who imposes upon you in the cafeteria.

Variety

When we speak of sentence variety, we are referring to not only a judicious mix of sentences that are distinguished from each other by clausal structures (simple, compound, complex, and compound-complex) but also the use of sentences of different length. Failing to use a blend of different clausal structures often masks where you want the emphasis to fall in your sentences, paragraphs, and essays. And using only sentences of the same length—long or short—creates a prosaic paragraph with a boring rhythm.

Exercise

Using a good college dictionary, determine the meaning of simple, compound, complex, and compound-complex sentences. Once you have done so, find an example of each type in our draft on the Internet.

A sentence analysis of a paragraph or two of the draft may help clarify the importance of sentence variety. Of the four sentences in the first paragraph, the shortest—sentence four—is made up of 19 words. The other three sentences are very long, all in excess of 30 words, and one sentence—the third—in excess of 50. Although all sentences are grammatically sound, one feels slightly out of breath after having read the first three. The feeling of breathlessness might be avoided by making one of these sentences into two separate sentences or by breaking one of them with a semi-colon. The sentences of paragraph four are worthy of comment too. This long paragraph of 11 sentences is made up of a judicious balance of long and relatively short sentences placed to create a pleasant rhythm. There is also a good variety of sentence type. Let's look at the first seven sentences. Sentence one is a short simple sentence. Sentence two, a somewhat longer version of the same type. Sentence three is a very short simple sentence. Sentences four and five are relatively short complex sentences. Sentence six is a somewhat longer complex sentence. Sentence seven is a long simple sentence. Three of the four remaining sentences in this paragraph fall into the medium range for sentence length (about 20 words), and the final, long sentence is the only compound-complex sentence in the paragraph.

The author's forced cohesion of sentences in paragraph four needs attention. Notice how three of the eleven sentences begin with the coordinating conjunction "and." Beginning a sentence with "and" is not, as you may have been told in the past, a stylistic error. But beginning too many of them with "and" can be. The author has every right to use it to open the fourth sentence of this paragraph, but one has to wonder about the felicity of opening both sentences ten and eleven with "and." In fact, if you make your way through this draft, you'll see many instances where the author has used "and" in this way. Note them all and try to decide how you can make sentences cohere in other ways.

Two other sentence forms that will vary your sentence rhythm and help you achieve a certain emphasis are loose and periodic sentences.

Loose sentences are made up of a main idea followed by a number of clauses or phrases that create the effect of further thought adhering to the original idea. Sentence two in paragraph one is an example of a loose sentence.

In *periodic sentences*, the meaning is withheld until the end of the sentence, using anticipation to emphasize the main verb or activity. An example is the thesis statement of our draft.

Finally, four common sentence types found in most writing are the declarative, interrogative, imperative, and exclamatory.

Declarative sentences, or basic statements, are the ones we most commonly use. All of the sentences in our draft are declarative. *Interrogative sentences* ask questions. They may be genuine questions or rhetorical ones used to persuade. Do not overuse interrogative sentences in your writing. In many instances your reader will be looking for answers, not questions.

Imperative questions issue commands. Used sparingly they can give an effect of urgency and intensity to your writing. Overused, they simply irritate the reader.

Exclamatory sentences indicate shock, surprise, disgust, discomfort, or any heightened emotional reaction. Purely emotional reactions should not play a large part in your writing since they tend to overshadow discursive thought. And remember, to argue convincingly, you must argue rationally, not emotionally. The writer makes good use of one exclamatory phrase in paragraph four.

Passive and Active Voice

Excessive use of the passive voice saps energy from your writing. As a general rule, activity (the dog bit me) is better than passivity (I was bitten by the dog) in writing: It keeps the reader moving forward on the crest of the thought. Sentence four of paragraph one is an example of a passive construction, as is sentence three in paragraph three. Try making these sentences active and see which version you prefer. The rest of the essay makes use of the active voice to good effect.

Wordiness

Wordiness works against clarity and precision in writing. In our draft we have located an example of wordiness: In the thesis statement we can see two words used where one would suffice ("generate and disseminate"). Apart from this example, the essay is relatively free of wordiness.

Awkward Constructions and Grammatical Problems

One of the major problems with our draft is the number of awkward constructions and grammatical errors found within it. Awkwardly phrased sentences upset the rhythm of the passage and often cause the reader to stumble over unclear language. For example, in paragraph one, how, logically, can the Internet "witness a surge"? In the same paragraph, the expression "in large part" (sentence two) unnecessarily interrupts the verb "is due." In the same sentence, the antecedents for the word "which" are unclear. In the final sentence of paragraph one, the verb "is" is in the wrong tense. In paragraph two, sentence two, the writer defines "universities, governments, business and organizations" as "people." What's wrong with using the word "people" to describe these things? In the next sentence, what function does the expression "names of" serve? Would the sentence be better without this term? In sentence two of paragraph two, the writer refers to "you," but later, in the last sentence of the paragraph, the reference is to "people." This error is known as a shift in person. Find other examples of it throughout the essay. For further comments on awkward constructions and grammatical errors, consult our active reading notations on the draft itself.

Diction

Clichés

Clichés, or boringly predictable expressions, which, over time, have become empty of meaning, are not evident in our draft nor should they be in any good piece of writing. If you use clichés at all, you should do so in order to illustrate their emptiness.

Jargon

Jargon is a problem in this essay, as intimated earlier. The author uses language associated with a particular field—in this instance the technology of the computer and Internet—without providing readers with a simple meaning for these terms. Although willing to define the word "Internet," the writer does not define such difficult terms as "file transfer protocol," "servers," "Web pages," "World Wide Web," and so on. These terms, left undefined, might very well result in loss of reader interest because of incomprehension.

Sexist Language

Avoid gender-specific or sexist language in your writing. An example of it is found in the final sentence of the draft where the author refers to "mankind's future," rather than "humankind's" or "people's" future.

Spelling

Always verify the spelling of words that give you difficulty by consulting a good college dictionary. Additionally, if you use a word processor with a built-in spell check programme, you can verify the spelling throughout your text. However, while computer spell check programmes recognize most spelling errors, they will not alert you to homonyms and to misspelled words that are, in fact, legitimate words themselves (for example, if you type the word "is" instead of "it," the spell checker will not flag this as a spelling error since "is" is a real word). Furthermore, most spell check programmes are American; hence they are not programmed to recognize Canadian spellings as legitimate and may indicate that your Canadian-spelled word is an error.

Effective Punctuation

Writers often consider punctuation a mundane matter and therefore do not come to appreciate its potential for shaping the meaning of a piece. Though there are many punctuation rules that you must simply master, other aspects of punctuation are open to the writer's choice, depending on the desired effect. We have noted two instances of possible misuse of the comma in our notes on the draft.

Developmental Strategies: A Final Word

We will now look at the developmental strategies at work in our draft on the Internet. As we tried to make clear earlier, essays do not necessarily use only one strategy to either show or argue. More often than not, various strategies work together to create the author's desired effect based on subject, audience, and purpose. Our draft on the Internet provides us with a good example of the way in which strategies work together even when one predominates. A brief walk through the essay from beginning to end demonstrates the various strategies at work in the essay.

PARAGRAPH ONE: The second sentence uses cause and effect; the fourth sentence promises a definition.

PARAGRAPH TWO: All of the sentences provide the definition promised in the last sentence of paragraph one; the second and fourth sentences use illustration to define a term.

PARAGRAPH THREE: The second sentence is an example of cause and effect; the fourth and subsequent sentences use illustration.

PARAGRAPH FOUR: The entire paragraph after its initial topic sentence is illustration.

PARAGRAPH FIVE: Much of this paragraph is illustration.

PARAGRAPH SIX: Sentences three and five use cause and effect.

In summary, although we can detect at least three different strategies at work in this essay, the one that clearly predominates is illustration. The writer wants to argue the value of the Internet and does so by generating a series of topic sentences followed by pointed illustrations showing how the Internet works for the benefit of humankind.

Revised Version

What follows is our revision of the engineering student's draft, based on the analysis you've just read.

The Internet, a technology that has been available since the 1970s, has become increasingly popular over the last 20 years, a fact proven by the number of people who are now active "surfers" of the Net. In large part this popularity is due to the public's greater awareness of on-line services as well as to better and faster connections to the Net. Although some may argue that, at its present state of development the Internet seems to be an expensive toy whose specialized language and cost are designed with a very small portion of the population in mind, the potential value for all Canadians of this technology resides in the amount of information it can generate, its relatively low cost and its speed. But before attempting to comment on the Internet's value, it might be appropriate to define the term and some of its characteristics for those unfamiliar with this remarkable method of conveying information.

Quite simply, the Internet is the world's largest computer network. What this means is that through the Internet thousands of computers all over the world are connected together, and by accessing one of them, one can have access to all of them. Universities, colleges, governments, businesses, and other organizations, all with information to convey, are some of the groups likely to provide that information via the Internet. There are many different services and utilities on the Internet, but they all do basically the same thing, although some more successfully than others: they all allow communication. Tools such as e-mail (electronic mail) and chat rooms (dialogue groups or "virtual" coffee houses) allow communication between individuals. FTP (file transfer protocol) servers (electronic devices for transferring information from one site or person to another) and Web pages allow people to search for and obtain information of most any kind stored on another computer somewhere in the world. All of these services are available by simply connecting to the Internet.

Although initially subscribers to the Internet might see it as a new and intriguing toy, one of the first things they notice after exploring and becoming familiar with it is the incredible amount of information at their beck and call. Additionally, thanks to ever-improving search services, information on a particular topic is accessible by simply typing in a few keywords on a computer keyboard. Formal information—such as government statistics or on-line encyclopedias, world news, weather and topological maps, and quotes from the stock market—is more easily obtained in this manner than by flipping through books or reading newspapers. But the great advantage to obtaining the information on-line is that it is updated and updateable much more quickly than a book. Less formal information—for example, to plan a vacation, carry out a home renovation, or just about any other task—is often found more easily by electronically connecting to one of the many companies that now have "pages" on the World Wide Web. Finding out whether a book is available at a local library or even at most any library around the world, is a much simpler task than visiting the library or contacting it by mail. Another strength of the Internet is that potentially it provides access to a myriad of opinions and thoughts of anyone, ranging from a leading expert in a particular field, to the uninformed, and yet highly opinionated, Joe. As long as the source one wants to talk to has access to a computer hooked up to the Net, one is able to hear from that source. And, as access to the Internet becomes increasingly easy and inexpensive, more and more people take advantage of its services, disproving the view that the technology is elitist and expensive.

Indeed, in Canada, Internet access is available with little effort and few costs. Universities and colleges all across the nation provide students with the opportunity to use the Internet, either from home or from the university or college's computer laboratory, often for free. Many large corporations also offer free Internet access to their employees. And for those who do not have accounts either at work or school, commercial Internet providers charge as little as $10 a month for full access. So anyone who has a computer, and even many who do not, can easily use the Internet. Another great money-saver for the everyday Canadian household is the fast, free communication provided along with the Internet access you purchase. E-mail, delivered within seconds of being sent, does not require a stamp to be stuck on an envelope as "snail-mail" does; and the quickness of e-mail allows it to transmit the same information as a long-distance phone call would, without the expense. Additionally, many corporations across North America and around the world now have teleconferences, rather than face-to-face conferencing. Teleconferencing not only saves large amounts of money previously spent on transportation and accommodation, but also allows quicker, and more frequent meetings.

Speed is also one of the key reasons for the Internet's success. The rapidity of the transfer of information is due in part to constantly improving technology, which is in turn driven by the large number of people who currently use the Internet and the increasingly large number who will "log on" in the near future. The technology that, within a few years, has raised the average user's access speed more than tenfold, has given rise to an explosion of visual, audio, and interactive information available in seconds. One can access anything from satellite pictures, to musical selections from a new album, to a video clip of a favourite television show, in almost no time.

The other key to the Internet's speed, the large number of people on it, is equally important. Information on where to eat, how to buy or sell a house, car, or anything else, or responses to a troubling question (often a company is not willing to answer queries even on its telephone service line or 1-800 number) is often available through posting an article to a newsgroup. Anywhere from minutes to hours later, depending on how much interest the article has gathered, one might receive e-mail to answer the concern. So, for instance, a high school student conducting a survey of 500 people can accomplish in a day or two what would have required much more effort and time using traditional survey techniques. And people looking for something as simple and practical as a quote on the price of a new or used car can often obtain it in seconds.

In summary, the Internet is one of the most useful technological tools, not only for Canadians but for all peoples. And its usefulness, sometimes obscured by its novelty, is undeniable.

The wealth of information, coupled with the speed at which it is available and its relatively low cost, make it not only a good substitute for most other sources, but also one that provides information and services not available through other services. In an age where over-specialization threatens to underplay the importance of a good basic knowledge for people in general and researchers in particular, the Internet provides the communication between people that is necessary to compensate for this over-specialization. People who do not recognize the advantages of the Internet are quickly becoming a minority, and expend more time and energy accomplishing the same tasks "Net users" do in minutes. As technology continues to improve the speed at which information is available, the Internet assures itself a definite place in humankind's future.

Exercise

Actively read both first and final drafts, noting and commenting on all changes between the two versions. Decide whether you like the final draft better than the original and give clear reasons for your views. Of course, you may argue that the first draft, or parts of it, are better than the final version; but be certain to provide reasons for your opinions. For example, you may think the revisers should have deleted the small section on teleconferencing. After all, what has teleconferencing to do with the Internet?

ESSAY ON SPIRITUAL BANKRUPTCY: RESPONDING TO FRYE

Step 1: Examination of the Response to Frye

What follows is a further study of the Northrop Frye passage from the last chapter, with a view to generating a response to some of Frye's ideas. Remember that the theoretical discussion of the various steps in the active writing process applies to the Frye passage as well as it does to Laver's.

This brief active reading of our response to the Frye passage is followed by a list of brainstormed items generated from that response.

Response to Northrop Frye

It seems all too clear when we look around us that Frye is

correct in his feeling that we are materially successful but

①

spiritually poverty-stricken. Increasingly in Canada we

seem to be importing our values from the United States.

We are avid consumers (but) the more we consume of US (2)

culture the less Canadian we become. Is our problem (3)

that we are a young country? We need to develop our

(4) (imaginations,) as Frye says, (but) how can we do this when

(5)   TV culture (deadens) them? Even the (CBC) has fallen on

tough times, and it has traditionally been the (promoter (6)

and protector) of Canadian culture. Frye may imply that

we need to wrestle with our angels, (but) how soon will it

be before we cannot be awakened to that need? (7)

Active reading jottings:

1. Material success/spiritual poverty
2. Importing values from US
3. Losing our Canadianness
4. Canada's youth as a country—a problem?
5. TV culture deadens imagination
6. CBC cutbacks
7. Complacency increasing: can we be awakened?

A one-minute brainstorming session on one item from our response to Frye, item 5 in active jottings: *TV culture deadens imagination:*

* Canadian TV primarily American
* Even CBC TV is largely American
* Since 1950s, North America a TV culture
* Less reading about ourselves, about our past
* TV teaches us American culture and values
* We learn about acquisitiveness, competition, superficiality, rugged individualism
* TV cannot sustain serious thought
* Reality is turned into a commodity
* As a commodity, Canadian reality cannot compete—not glossy enough

Step 2: Subject, Audience, and Purpose into Topic, and into Thesis Statement, Topic Sentence, or Controlling Idea

Review the theory associated with topics and thesis statements on page 31.

Step 2(a): Subject

The subject area of the Frye passage might best be described in general terms as spiritual bankruptcy. The broad limits of any essay we write, then, are determined by this general subject. Given the broad subject of spiritual bankruptcy, what are we going to write about? When we look over our responses, and the material generated through invention techniques, we see some recurrent interests: (1) losing ourselves in materialism; (2) American influence on Canada; (3) the role of TV; (4) our youth as a country; and (5) life as a commodity. Based on these recurrent interests, it's clear that our concern is with the Canadian situation; we seem to be sacrificing our distinctiveness as a nation for the material success so evident south of the border. The subject we will want to develop, then, is spiritual bankruptcy in an affluent Canada.

Step 2(b): Audience

Avoid the temptation of writing for a "general" audience. The distinctive characteristics of your audience should be suggested by your responses to your reading and any subsequent inventing you have done. If you have taken some notes on your subject, these will help you as well. In our subject—spiritual bankruptcy in an affluent Canada—a number of audience pointers are apparent:

* Canadian
* Affluent, or with the potential to be so
* Relatively well-educated

If we consider the responses and inventing we did, we can add other possibilities:

* The generations that have grown up with TV
* Somewhat complacent
* Lacking substantial awareness of Canadian culture
* Regularly exposed to American media

Given these pointers to audience—pointers that indicate our areas of concern (though we may not have been conscious of them previously)—we can now identify three possible audiences that the pointers describe: entrepreneurs in their twenties or thirties; university students; and young professionals.

Because of our own bias as university professors writing a textbook, the most natural target audience for us will be university students. This does not mean that we will *explicitly* address university students; our decision simply means that as we are writing we will need to keep in mind that a university student reader (possibly a reader of a university paper) should be able to follow and respond to our essay.

Step 2(c): Purpose

We can ascertain, in part, the degree to which our purpose will be expository rather than argumentative by considering audience. Our decision to write about spiritual bankruptcy in an affluent Canada, however, reveals a negative evaluation of our spiritual state and thus a (possibly implicit) argumentative aspect of our subject.

Examine your responses to your reading and the inventing you have done. This will firm up your purpose, which may have its origins in unfocused anger, curiosity, or the simple desire to impart information. In your response, you will find not only subject matter but an attitude toward that subject matter. You need to ask yourself what that attitude implies. In our responses to Frye, for example, we express a concern about increasing complacency among Canadians and wonder whether we can be awakened to our spiritual poverty. Do we even recognize that there is a problem? Surely here we are revealing a purpose: we feel Canadians should be awakened. To awaken will involve more than simply showing and explaining—we imply that Canadians need a sound shake to wake them. In writing, that shake becomes argument or persuasion. We want to explain what spiritual bankruptcy means in Canada and how it comes about, but we also want to convince our audience that we need to change directions.

Step 2(d): Topic and Thesis Statement

Your topic provides a focus for, and should reflect, your subject, audience, and purpose. Clearly the subject—spiritual bankruptcy—is too broad and needs to be narrowed down to a workable size. As it stands, our essay could be about anything from declining church attendance, to exploitation of native sacred homelands, to loss of political idealism, to all these and more. When we examine our responses, however, and when we consider audience and purpose, we see that we are more concerned with causes of spiritual bankruptcy than with effects (though, of course, they go hand in hand). Audience and purpose indicate that we want to explain the causes of the situation to an audience that includes university students and, in so doing, convince them that the problem must be addressed. A suitably narrowed topic for the essay we propose to write on the subject of spiritual bankruptcy might be the following:

The major causes of spiritual bankruptcy in an affluent, complacent Canada

And an appropriate thesis statement developed from such a topic might be

Although Canada is one of the most affluent countries in the world, its very affluence, as well as its youth, its lack of culture, and its proximity to the United States, make it a potential victim of spiritual bankruptcy.

Step 3: Developmental Strategies

A quick look at some of the brainstorming notes we made on our response to Frye's passage is very revealing of potential strategies:

"Canadian TV primarily American" suggests classification and division

"Even CBC TV is largely American" suggests illustration

"TV teaches us American culture and values" suggests definition

Step 4: First Draft

What follows is the draft of our paper on spiritual bankruptcy. The marginalia and marks on the essay serve as the basis of Step 5, revision.

¶

— not relevant to topic

As we look around us in the latter half of the twentieth century, it is not difficult to see that society is in a state of dreadful confusion and instability. War and rumours of war threaten us every day; terrorism and political instability are commonplace; entire countries are being threatened by starvation while others luxuriate in seemingly endless wealth and resources; one country's god is another's devil as religious conflict abounds across the globe. The world seems full of strife, doubt, uncertainty, and hardship. Relative to the pain and suffering in the world, Canadians have it easy and no doubt find a great deal of satisfaction when they contemplate the fortunate state of their country. Yet social critics of our own country tell us that we are at a stage in our development where we need to take stock of what we consider valu-

wdy

able and important. Northrop Frye, for example, warns us of placing too much faith in material possessions at the expense of our inner life; similarly, Irving Layton argues that "cold" Canadians think too much of themselves and of what they possess and too little of others.

— does audience know these people ?

What both of these critics seem to be suggesting is that   *unsure* acquisitiveness is a habit of mind dangerous to the spiri-

tual life not only of individuals but of whole countries. In

our opinion, although Canada is one of the most affluent

countries in the world, its very affluence, as well as its

youth, its lack of culture, and its proximity to the United

States, make it a potential victim of spiritual bankruptcy.

unsure?

II   History seems to make it very clear that countries

that take their wealth for granted eventually suffer and

crumble as a result of an undue emphasis on material

well-being. The most notorious example of this principle

is, of course, the Roman Empire. The notion of Nero fid-

dling while Rome burned is a fine metaphor for the final

destructive influences of the pleasure principle. History

tells us that the Roman Empire was one of the most ad-

-good coherency provided by reference to Rome

vanced and developed empires of any age. And yet it fell,

almost overnight. In its final days, we are told, religious   *by whom?*

values declined, social programmes decayed, and indi-

vidual fulfillment and political corruption became the

order of the day. With the loss of its civic sense and the

increase in self-advancement came the gradual decay of

the entire society. Although Canadians are not Romans

why   and Canada is not Rome, there is a clear message here

for us. Daily we are bombarded through the media with   *pass*

images of what the good life is. All of these images seem   *unsure?*

to have one thing in common; that is, the importance of

acquisitions and possessions. We are regularly told that

we can buy happiness and contentment, and buy we do.

Canadians are among the world's greatest spenders and

consumers. They are also among the world's greatest

contributors to the pollution and garbage problems we all

face. In other words, Canadians buy things, use them as

best they can, and then discard them. This depressing

cycle of use and discarding should indicate to us how

fruitless it is to try and purchase happiness. This type of

"fulfillment" is as disposable and temporary as the various

goods that we jettison onto a growing heap of detritus, a

heap of useless commodities that in future may stand as

a monument to our own dissatisfaction with life. There is

a good deal to be said for increasing the standard of liv-

ing of any country, but if with this increase comes a de-

cline in the importance of spiritual values and inner

development, we should worry about the excessively high

price we are paying for our own material welfare.

As the adage has it, youth is a time of life that is all

too often wasted on the young. In order to become aware

of who or what one really is, it is necessary to learn

something about one's past so as to be able to determine

one's future. Although we should be careful about using

wdy

adages, and especially careful when we try to use them

to "solve" complex situations, it is, nevertheless, true that

young countries often seem to show a (lack of judgement

wdy

and consideration) that we often regard as characteristic

of young people themselves. In Canada, we have only

recently begun to consider our roots and, because our

roots do not go very deep, we are often in the position of

trying to determine from whom or from what traditions we

have sprung. Although it may strike some as a needless

waste of time to examine our past, such an examination

is central to discovering a sense of who we are and, as a

consequence, developing a sense of spiritual awareness.

Canada needs to know about its heroes, its struggles to

become, its origins. Such photographs of our country's

past do very much the same for a nation as an individual

photo album does for a family: it tells us about our ances-

try, it teaches us to respect our roots, it encourages us to

think about those whom we will one day leave behind.

A young country like Canada cannot afford to live only for

today if it expects to have a spiritual dimension of its col-

lective life and a vision of the future. To live for the pre-

sent, to "go for it" as the current philosophy would have it,

is to accept only the contemporary mythologies. And

those, like our disposable commodities, do not have

much depth or substance to them. For the sake of its

spiritual survival, Canada must not let its youth coerce it

into becoming merely a part of the "Pepsi generation."

IV

Another threat to Canada's spiritual well-being is its *good trans. signal*

—transition to new point is clear, but lacks strong coherency

apparent lack of concern with (nurturing and supporting)

what culture it does possess and its reluctance to en- *wdy*

courage the development of new cultural endeavours. *off topic*

The increasing study of Canadian literature in our

schools is a hopeful sign, which has put pressure on our

publishing industry to back Canadian authors. Yet if cul-

why is this neglect occurring?

ture is, in some sense at least, the repository of a coun-

try's soul and spiritual values, then Canada's reticence

because we live in a throwaway society influenced by US individualism and materialism

about cultural activity is a good indication of how it feels

about things of the spirit. Canadians regularly ignore their

artists; witness the financial difficulties that both the

Stratford Festival and Hummingbird Centre have recently

suffered through. Although we have a national arts

council that awards grants to struggling artists to help

them survive while they practise their craft, it is badly

underfunded. The recent financial cutbacks inflicted on

the CBC—traditionally seen as the only disseminator of *unsure?*

truly Canadian thoughts, ideas, and culture—suggest the

present government's attitudes towards culture as well.

All around us we seem to see the indicators that suggest *unsure and wdy* that culture doesn't pay. Perhaps the two most outstanding examples of this fact are found in our First Nations and Inuit peoples. Most Canadians choose to ignore these two ancient groups largely because they are different from the rest of us and live by a different code. But by ignoring them and letting them suffer in poverty and neglect we are also ignoring the significant cultural achievements that they have made to this country.

X

— transition clear, but argument would be tighter if points rose logically and irresistably out of prior paragraphs

The final detrimental influence on Canada's development of a spiritual dimension is its proximity to the United States. In our opinion, the US exerts a depressingly anti-spiritual influence over Canada which <u>we, as</u> <u>Canadians</u>, are all too ready to bow to. Perhaps we are intimidated by <u>its</u> size or perhaps by <u>its</u> success as the world's great super power. Whatever the reason, we are prepared to unquestioningly accept its many mindless magazines and television and radio broadcasts. But we suspect the real reason we are prepared and even willing

wdy

ref.

rep. of point in par. 2

to model ourselves on the United States is because, <u>as</u> <u>we have already suggested</u>, Canadians are enchanted and enthralled by the idea of material wealth. The US is undoubtedly the richest country in the world with the highest standard of living. <u>As we also suggested earlier</u>,

— need to avoid this repetition somehow

rep. again

there seems to be a correlation between wealth and cultural decadence. And this is as true for the United States as it is for Canada. Where else can we find so many activities meant to fill a spiritual void as in the United States? Fast-food restaurants, fun cities, pleasure palaces, and Disney universes abound. Where else but on American airwaves can one watch so many situation comedies, game shows, sports programmes, and cartoons. Canada, impressed by what the United States has achieved, is an all-too-willing consumer and emulator of this cultural mush. As a result she becomes increasingly interested in, and finally addicted to, wealth and the joys it apparently brings. Such joys, temporarily at least, win out over more legitimate concerns such as the country's need for a profound inner life.

We have not presented an altogether pleasant picture of Canada's spiritual situation, but we think it reflects, nevertheless, the reality of the situation in this country. It may very well be that for Canada to come to grips with its soul, it may have to deprive itself of many things that it now considers important. The question that Canadians must ask themselves, finally, is of what real worth is a wealthy but soulless nation.

Step 5: Revision and Final Draft

Exercise

Using as a guide the analysis of the first draft of the essay on the Internet (pp. 42–48), write a detailed analysis of the first draft of our essay on spiritual bankruptcy, ensuring wherever possible that you make use of the same general headings found in the analysis of the Internet essay.

What follows is the final draft.

A Vicious Circle: The Major Causes of
Spiritual Bankruptcy in Canada

It is easy for Canadians to be complacent: we have one of the world's highest standards of living; we have vast natural resources; and we have the military and economic might of the richest and most powerful nation on earth on our side—the lap of luxury has never felt so good. Yet even here, in the best of all possible worlds, there are occasional gnats—gadflies reminding us that while material affluence may gorge the stomach, it starves the soul. University of Toronto Professor of English and cultural critic the late Northrop Frye, for one, suggests that educating the imagination might help fill the void that faces an intelligent western person when, after "chasing status symbols all his life ... the bottom falls out of his world and he sees no reason for going on." The outspoken poet Irving Layton—Canada's self-styled gadfly if there ever was one—brings the argument home to roost: for him, the souls of Canadians are "miserable, nightmarish"; we are "isolated from one another by the fears and repressions engendered in a materialistic society almost wholly given up to the worship of money and status." Hard words, but true. Canada's material affluence—a direct result of American economic and, in turn, cultural influence on a young, impressionable country—precipitates Canada's spiritual bankruptcy.

History makes it clear that countries that take their wealth for granted eventually crumble. The image of Nero fiddling while Rome burned is a fine metaphor for the final destructive influence of the pleasure principle. Rome was one of the most advanced empires of any age. And yet it fell, almost overnight. Although Canada is not Rome, there is surely a message here for us. Daily the media

bombard us with images of the good life, all of which have one
thing in common: the importance of possessions. We are regularly
told that we can buy happiness—and buy we do. Canadians are among
the world's greatest consumers. We are also among the world's
greatest polluters. In other words, Canadians buy things, use
them, and discard them. Such a depressing cycle should indicate
to us how fruitless it is to try to purchase happiness. This type
of "fulfillment" is as temporary as the goods that we jettison
onto a growing heap of detritus, a heap that in future may stand
as a monument to our dissatisfaction with life. There is a good
deal to be said for increasing the standard of living of any
country, but if this increase comes at the expense of spiritual
values and inner development, we should worry about the excessively high price we are paying for our material welfare.

Canada's devotion to material affluence has been accelerated by
two intertwined factors: her relative youth as a country and her
location next door to the world's capitalistic dynamo. Young
countries often show a lack of judgement that is characteristic
of many young people, and Canada is no exception. Lacking the
solid sense of national vision which rises out of rooted historical traditions, Canada finds herself vulnerable to economic and
cultural influence from outside. And for us, outside means the
US. America exerts a depressingly anti-spiritual influence over
Canada which we, enchanted and enthralled by the idea of material wealth—so manifest south of the border—are all too ready
to bow to. Yet the cultural decadence that was attendant on
Rome's wealth also plagues the US. Where else can we find
so many activities meant to fill a spiritual void? Fast-food
restaurants, fun cities, Disney universes, and Crystal
Cathedrals abound. Where else but on American airwaves—which
is what Canadian TV largely consists of—can one watch so
many situation comedies, game shows, sports programmes, and
cartoons—and all of them punctuated by advertisements? Canada,
impressed by what the US has achieved, and lacking its own—and
different—standards of value, is an all-too-willing consumer
and emulator of this cultural mush. As a result, she becomes
increasingly interested in, and finally addicted to, wealth and
the joys it apparently brings. Such joys increasingly win out
over the country's need for a profound inner life.

Canada's adherence to the American materialist vision of success—the "throwaway society"—inevitably leads us to neglect
our own past and our own culture. Such neglect is potentially
tragic, since for people to be aware of who or what they
really are, it is necessary for them to know something about
their past. Canada needs to know about its heroes, its struggles to become, its origins. Such photographs of our country's
past do very much the same for a nation as an individual photo
album does for a family: it tells us about our ancestry, it
teaches us to respect our roots, it encourages us to think
about those people we will one day leave behind. To live for
the present, to "go for it" as the current philosophy would
have it, is to accept only the contemporary mythologies. And
those, like our disposable commodities, do not have much substance. If culture is, in some sense at least, the repository
of a country's soul and spiritual values, then Canada's adherence to the superficial contemporary mythologies is indicative
of how it feels about things of the spirit. To take the clearest example, the recent financial cutbacks on the CBC—traditionally seen as the only disseminator of truly Canadian
thought and culture—betray the government's attitude toward
the world of value.

Canadian affluence, on the American model, generates a vicious
circle which can only culminate in spiritual bankruptcy. Our neglect of our past and our culture leaves a vacuum in Canadian
life which American commercialism rushes to fill. And this commercialism encourages further neglect. It may very well be that
for Canada to come to grips with its soul, it will have to deprive itself of many things it now considers important. Yet of
what real worth is a wealthy but soulless nation?

Exercise
Actively read both first and final drafts, noting and commenting on all changes between
the two versions. Decide whether you like the final draft better than the original and give clear
reasons for your views. Of course, you may argue that the first draft, or parts of it, are better than the final version; but be certain to provide reasons for your opinions.

Supplementary Exercise
If you have studied the process whereby we generated an essay about the Internet, you
might like to compare the first and final drafts of that essay with the first and final drafts of
the essay on spiritual bankruptcy to decide which set of first and final draft seems more
successful to you. Feel free to define "successful" as broadly as you like.

HANDS ON: READING INTO WRITING

Here is where you move from reading to writing in your first essay assignment, begun in the Hands On: Reading section of chapter 2, as you actively read and responded to Patricia Hluchy's views of teenagers and TV (p. 26). At this point you need to take advantage of the questions we ask below. They will serve to remind you of the process you have read through in the demonstration section of this chapter, and will ensure that you do not neglect any significant observations.

Completing the planning checklist below is an effective way for you to put a check on your own writing process in its first three steps.

As well as acting as a check on work already completed, the planning checklist provides guidance on what you need to do as you begin. It will also help you to ensure that your preliminary work has, in fact, generated sufficient material for your draft. If you have followed the process conscientiously to this point in the book, you should have no trouble responding to these questions. If you do have trouble responding, the checklist will indicate specific areas for review by referring you to appropriate pages in this chapter. In any event, completing the checklist will force you to distance yourself from your material and to take stock of your project, and will in all likelihood convince you that you are ready to proceed.

The Planning Checklist

1. Responses and Invention

    (a) Have you examined your responses to the assigned readings to determine your concerns?

    (b) Have you fleshed out these concerns with invention techniques such as brainstorming and the basic journalist's questions: who, what, when, where, and why?

2. Rhetorical Context

    (a) Subject

    • Is your subject related, tangentially at least, to the general subject of your readings?

    • Does your subject reflect the concerns you identified in your responding and inventing?

    • Does your subject take into account your audience and purpose?

    (b) Audience

    • Does your audience reflect the concerns you identified in your responding and inventing?

    • Have you drawn up a profile of your audience?

    (c) Purpose

    • Does your purpose reflect the concerns you identified in your responding and inventing?

    • Does your purpose take into account your subject and audience?

    (d) Topic and Thesis Statement

    • Does your topic reflect, either explicitly or implicitly, the subject area, level of the audience, and considered purpose of your rhetorical context?

    • Does your topic reflect the limitations imposed by the writing occasion: your capabilities and your length constraints?

  • Does your thesis statement make a claim about your topic?

  • Does your thesis statement avoid editorializing?

  • Does your thesis statement reflect the concerns you identified in the earlier stages?

3. Developmental Strategies

   (a) Have you chosen one or more developmental strategies that reflect the concerns you identified in the earlier stages?

4. First Draft

5. Revision and Final Draft

Once you are ready to prepare your Final Draft (Step 5), the following questions will help you to make sure that your revision is thorough.

Large Items

   (a) Does your essay have a thesis or controlling idea which you clarify at the beginning?

   (b) Is your overall organization apparent? Have you employed appropriate developmental strategies?

   (c) Are all of your paragraphs related to your thesis?

Paragraphs

   (a) Does each paragraph have a clear topic sentence?

   (b) Are there clear transitions between sentences within paragraphs? Are there clear transitions between paragraphs?

   (c) Is each paragraph developed thoroughly with examples, illustrations, and details?

Sentences

   (a) Do your sentences vary in form and length?

   (b) Have you avoided wordiness by cutting away anything in your sentence that does not add directly to your paper?

   (c) Have you avoided using the passive voice?

   (d) Have you avoided basic sentence errors: comma splices, fused sentences, and fragments?

Diction

   (a) Have you avoided clichés and jargon?

   (b) Have you avoided unnecessary repetition?

   (c) Have you strengthened coherence through judicious repetition?

   (d) Is your diction appropriate for your audience?

Punctuation

(a) Have you considered how your punctuation shapes your meaning?

(b) Is all of your punctuation appropriate?

Before you hand in your revised version (Step 5) take care to answer the following questions:

(a) Have you proofread your work thoroughly for spelling, punctuation, and typographical errors?

(b) Did you adhere to proper format for presentation: cover page if necessary, margins, spacing?

Part II

Part

THEORY OF MODES AND ANTHOLOGY OF READINGS

詩之之连

THE FOUR MODES OF WRITING: NARRATION, DESCRIPTION, EXPOSITION, ARGUMENTATION

Chapter 4

The following discussion of the four modes of writing is designed to provide you with a convenient and largely theoretical summary of the various ways in which authors can give voice to their thoughts and ideas. It should be clear from the 33 essays that follow this discussion that although one mode may predominate in any piece of writing, usually modes work together to create a satisfactory finished product. In other words, it is not likely that you will find any piece of continuous prose that is *totally* indebted to only one mode for the effect it hopes to achieve. Our Contents and Analysis list of the 33 essays allows you to see how each essay blends modes to produce strong writing. As you work your way through these essays, you should note *how* and *where* authors make use of different modes within the same essay. In addition, you might like to decide whether our conclusions about which modes are used in what essays are always accurate and complete.

In the theoretical section which follows immediately, we discuss each of the modes in turn and provide you with examples drawn from writings by Canadian authors. At the end of each discussion there is a Hands On: Reading into Writing exercise which asks you—first of all—to critically read and respond to a selection of essays from the anthology that illustrates the particular mode under discussion. Once you have done so, you'll then go on to examine your responses and write your own essay on the same general subject.

NARRATION

Narration is, put simply, storytelling, and as such it is one of the oldest pastimes of humankind. Human beings, no matter what age they are, love telling and listening to stories. Well-constructed narratives appeal to our imagination and to our desire to know what happened. This urge to read on, to come to know more of the story, depends largely on the ability of the storyteller to capture our attention. One Canadian author argues that the beginning of the story is what makes or breaks it. He puts it this way:

> The most interesting thing about a story is not its climax or dénouement—both dated terms—nor even its style and characterization. It is its beginning, its first paragraph, often its first sentence. More decisions are made on the basis of the first few sentences of a story than on any other part, and it would seem to me after having read thousands of stories, and beginning hundreds of my own (completing, I should add, only about fifty), that something more than luck accounts for the occasional success of the operation. What I propose is theoretical, yet rooted in the practice of writing and of reading-as-a-writer; good stories *can* start unpromisingly, and well-begun stories can obviously degenerate, but the observation generally holds: the story seeks its beginning, the story many times is its beginning, amplified.
>
> The first sentence of a story is an act of faith—or astonishing bravado. A story screams for attention, as it must, for it breaks a silence. It removes the reader from the everyday.... It is an act of perfect rhythmic balance, the single crisp gesture, the drop of the baton that gathers a hundred disparate forces into a single note.
>
> Clark Blaise, "To Begin, To Begin," *The Narrative Voice*, Ed. John Metcalf, Toronto: McGraw-Hill Ryerson, 1972. 22.

In light of the foregoing quotation and keeping in mind that an author's intent is to capture our imaginations and interest early in a narrative, comment on how the following two passages from Canadian narratives do or do not succeed as examples of good storytelling:

> 1994 Halifax Harbor at night is a beautiful sight, and June usually finds the Macdonald Bridge lined with lovers and other appreciators. But in Halifax even June can turn on one with icy claws.
>
> A thermometer sheltered from the brisk wind would have shown a little below Centigrade zero. Norman Kent had the magnificent scenery all to himself.
>
> He was aware of the view; it was before his face, and his eyes were not closed. He was aware of the cold too, because occasionally when he worked his face, frozen tears would break and fall from his cheeks. Neither meant anything to him. He was even vaguely aware of the sound of steady traffic behind him, successive dopplers like the

rhythmic moaning of some wounded giant. That meant nothing to him either. On careful reflection Norman could think of nothing that *did* mean anything to him, and so he put one leg over the outer rail.

Spider Robinson, *Mindkiller,* New York: Berkley Books, 1983; Holt Rinehart, 1982. 1.

I was looking for a four-letter word for "narrow path," when I heard high heels on the stairs. High heels usually means business for me rather than for Dr. Bushmill, the chiropodist. With men on the stairs, it was only guessing. I put away the newspaper in time to see a fuzzy silhouette through the frosted glass of the door hesitate for a moment before knocking. I called "Come in already!" and she did.

She was the sort of woman that made you wish you'd stayed in the shower for an extra minute or taken another three minutes shaving. I felt a little underdressed in my own office. She had what you could call a tailored look. Everything was so understated it screamed. I could hear the echo bouncing off the bank across the street.

She took a chair on the other side of my bleached oak desk and played around with her handbag. It matched her shoes, and I thought that the car outside probably matched the rest of the outfit. Sitting in the sunlight, with the shadow of the letters of my sign caressing her trim figure, she looked about thirty, but I put part of that down to decent treatment, regular meals, baths and trips to Miami, things like that. When she raised her eyes to look at me, they were gray.

"You're Mr. Cooperman?" she asked.

"Would I lie to you?" I said, trying to help her over the awkward stage. The sign on the door told the truth too: BENJAMIN COOPERMAN LICENCED PRIVATE INVESTIGATOR. "What can I do for you, Miss...?" Her lips smiled suddenly, like a puppeteer had pulled the right string and then released it. Her eyes didn't change.

Howard Engel, *The Suicide Murders,* Harmondsworth: Penguin, 1985. 1–2. First published by
Clarke, Irwin, 1980.

The appeal to the reader's imagination that narrative fictional writing holds can be equally strong in nonfictional narrative. The most obvious difference between these two types of narrative, though by no means a hard and fast distinction, is that while fictional narrative is primarily concerned with telling a story, nonfictional narrative usually has a point to make. In other words, nonfictional narrative does more than simply tell a good story; it uses the story as the medium for further authorial commentary. This commentary coupled with the narrative might be used, for instance, to inform, convince, or persuade the reader.

Types of Narrative

Three types of nonfictional narrative that are very much a part of our daily lives are the personal narrative, the reportorial narrative, and the analytical narrative.

Personal Narrative

Personal narrative usually consists of a combination of event and commentary. Notice, for instance, the following passage from Farley Mowat's account of his reaction to the Second World War:

> On the second day of September, 1939, I was painting the porch of our clapboard house in the rural Ontario town of Richmond Hill when my father pulled into the driveway at the helm of his red convertible. He looked as if he might have had a drink or two—high-colored and exhilarated.
>
> "Farley, my lad, there's bloody big news! *The war is on!* Nothing official yet, but the Regiment's been ordered to mobilize, and I'm to go back in with the rank of major, bum arm and all. There'll be a place for you too. You have to sweat a bit for it, of course, but if you keep your nose clean and work like hell there'll be the King's Commission."
>
> He spoke as if he were offering me a knighthood or, at the very least, membership in some exceedingly exclusive order....
>
> My father's news excited me tremendously, for I had long been inflamed by his fulminations against the Russophobe French, British and U.S. politicians and industrialists who had connived at the growth and spread of fascism, concealing their real admiration for it beneath the public explanation that it was the only trustworthy "bulwark against communism." I shared my father's conviction that these men had betrayed democracy, and I took the debacle of Munich and the sellout of Czechoslovakia as proof of this. I believed that every healthy young man in the freedom-espousing countries was duty-bound to take up arms against the fascist plague and, in particular, the singularly bestial German brand.

Farley Mowat, And No Birds Sang, Toronto: McClelland & Stewart-Bantam, 1979. 3–4.

In this passage, Mowat begins with a narrative reminiscent of a certain day in 1939. He tells us what he was doing on this particular day and he quickly introduces dialogue to give the anecdote immediacy and a sense of drama. But the event soon gives way to a passage of extended commentary in which the author thinks about the effects that his father's news has on him. This personal narrative, then, is made up of a story *per se* plus commentary in the form of the author's reaction to the scene he has just presented. Both elements are central to this particular type of narrative since the story without the commentary would seem to have no point, and the commentary without the story would have no meaningful context.

Not all personal narratives, however, include commentary as explicit as that found in the foregoing excerpt. Notice the following passage:

> I will close on a memory, an important one. A different Florida when Venice was still un-
> derwater. There was a day years earlier in Fort Lauderdale. As usual, a Sunday, shortly
> after we had moved there from Hartley. A hurricane was a hundred miles off-shore and
> due to strike Fort Lauderdale in the next six hours. We drove from our house down
> Las Olas to the beach (Fort Lauderdale was still an inland city then), and parked a half
> mile away safe from the paint-blasting sand. We could hear the breakers under the
> shriek of the wind shaking the wooden bridge we walked on. Then we watched them
> crash, brown with weeds and suspended sand. And we could see them miles off-shore
> rolling in forty feet high and flashing their foam like icebergs. A few men in swimming suits
> and woolen sweaters were standing in the crater pools pulling out the deep-sea fish
> that had been stunned by the trip and waves. Other fish littered the beach, their bellies
> blasted by the change in pressure. My mother's face was raw and her glasses webbed
> with salt. She went back to the car on her own. My father and I sat on the bench for an-
> other hour and I could see behind his crusty sunglasses. His eyes were moist and
> dancing, his hair stiff and matted. We sat on the bench until we were soaked and the mu-
> nicipal guards rounded us up. Then they barricaded the boulevards and we went back
> to the car, the best day of fishing we'd ever had, and we walked hand in hand for the last
> time, talking excitedly, dodging coconuts, power lines, and shattered glass, feeling
> brave and united in the face of the storm. My father and me. What a day it was, what a
> once-in-a-lifetime day it was.

Clark Blaise, "A North American Education," *The Narrative Voice,* Ed. John Metcalf, Toronto:
McGraw-Hill Ryerson, 1972. 16.

In this long passage, the author clearly places the emphasis on the story itself. It is not until we reach the very end of it that we begin to see the commentary emerging. Until that point it is difficult to know exactly how the speaker feels about the experience he is living through. But in the second last sentence we begin to sense that it was an exhilarating experience for him. The final sentence makes the speaker's reaction very clear: the experience was so unusual and so charged with energy (a view that we can find within the narrative section itself) that he regards it as a "once-in-a-lifetime day."

Personal narratives are almost always written from the first person point of view, where the narrator refers to "I" or "me." The greatest effect of the first person viewpoint is immediacy and authenticity. We are generally more likely to believe someone who says "I was there, I saw it," or "It happened to me!" On the other hand, if a more distanced approach is called for, the third person point of view (he-him-she-her) is appropriate. While the third person is rare in personal narratives, it is the most common choice in both reportorial and analytical narratives.

Reportorial Narrative

Reportorial narrative offers information. Medical case studies are a good example of the reportorial type. They present events in the third person without additional commentary. The doctors involved use the case study as raw material from which they arrive at their own conclusions:

> Pierre and Marie, married four years, with a new house and savings in the bank, are eager to have children. Since Marie has already experienced two miscarriages, they are apprehensive when she becomes pregnant again, and they exercise great care to promote a full-term pregnancy. However, Marie miscarries for the third time. After unsatisfactory consultations with various health professionals, they hear of a physician noted for her success in fertility problems. She draws their attention to one precaution they failed to observe. They both continued to work at their regular jobs—Pierre as an anaesthetist spending many of his working hours in a poorly ventilated hospital operating room, and Marie as a scientist engaged in viral research in a government laboratory. Both jobs involve potential reproductive hazards for men and women. Can these two workers continue at their jobs without further damaging their ability to produce healthy offspring?

> Nancy Miller Chenier, *Reproductive Hazards at Work: Men, Women and the Fertility Gamble,*
> Ottawa: Canadian Advisory Council on the Status of Women, 1982. 1–2.

What we learn about in this passage are the details of a married couple's childless life together. The author tells us who they are, how long they've been married, what they work at, and some details concerning the wife's bad luck with her pregnancies. The problem (apparently involving the reproductive system of one or the other partner or perhaps of both of them) may be related to their jobs. The question with which the passage closes suggests a possible explanation for the problem, but clearly the entire situation is going to require far more investigation. The case study, then, gives the professional experts enough details to allow them to further investigate the situation and perhaps find an answer to the question that concludes the paragraph.

Factual news reporting provides other occasions for reportorial narrative:

Japan car sales

Foreign car sales in Japan rose 59 per cent from the previous year's levels to a record 9597 in July, a spokesman for the Japan Automobile Importers Association says.

West German car sales, which accounted for nearly three-quarters of July's import sales, were up 56 per cent from last year's levels. Although sales of US-made cars also rose sharply, they accounted for only 3.7 per cent of the total.

The monthly sales rise, which surpassed the previous record of 9504 sales set in June, reflected narrower price gaps between imported and Japanese cars and lower loan rates offered by foreign car makers, the spokesman said.

Sales of foreign cars in Japan in the first seven months of this year came to 54 053, a 42 per cent increase from last year's levels.

"Japan car sales," The Globe and Mail, 7 August 1987: B13.

This news report is devoid of authorial opinion or judgement. Its main concern is to present a disinterested and objective picture of an event. What we get, in short, are just the facts.

Plot summaries are also good examples of reportorial narrative. Normally we are told the events as they appear, with no additional commentary. Pick up any copy of *Coles Notes* to see how plot summaries work as reportorial narratives.

Writers of reportorial narratives are aiming for a certain objectivity; they do not want personal opinions clouding the issue or the facts. However, you should remember that complete objectivity is an unattainable ideal—simply our status as individual human beings means each of us will express personal, cultural, or political biases unconsciously, in the very style of our lives, despite our desire for impartiality. We must be wary of accepting blindly the reportorial narratives we read.

Analytical Narrative

In analytical narrative the author is more concerned to present an interpretation of events than to present the events themselves. In other words, the story serves as a point of departure for extended *commentary;* the events serve as the occasion for a discussion of wider issues:

Peaceful Toronto, Toronto the Good: I am on my way to the beer store near the corner when a small red Volkswagen cuts through the College and Bathurst intersection on a red light. It bounces off another car, swerves, skids, comes to rest pointing the way it had come! Another car follows it through the light, stops. Two men jump out. The teenage driver of the Volks sees the two men, pulls a gun from his pocket and begins to shoot. My journalistic integrity in shreds, I turn to run into an alley. But before I can move, the two men jump back into their car and drive straight at the kid, who gets off one more shot before he is flung into the gutter. The two men leap out again, seize him, throw him down over the hood of his car, and hold him there. I look around for the cameras. There aren't any. Those bullets were real. That accident was real. The screams of the people waiting at the streetcar stop were real....

The argument about gun control yields up the same emotional quotient as abortion or capital punishment. Defenders of the private ownership of guns occasionally declare that the "disarming of the citizenry" is part of the Communist conspiracy; whereas people who have never shot a gun in their lives (but who have seen *Godfather I* and *Godfather II* and will probably see *Godfather III* when it comes out) are convinced only depraved criminals or right-wing fanatics would ever want to do so. Amiable discourse, as you might expect, is absent. Everyone agrees on the hard facts, the statistics. But even in the moderate middle there is no agreement on how to interpret them.

Marq de Villiers, "Too Many Guns," *Toronto Life,* August 1975: 6.

The piece goes on in this vein looking at the issue of guns and gun control in Canada. Clearly, the introduction to this piece is written as narrative. It has the advantage of capturing and holding our attention as every good introduction should. But its purpose goes beyond this: it serves to bring to the reader's attention through anecdote the issue which the rest of the essay will analyze and comment on in great detail. Interpretive biography and history work in much the same way. They begin by introducing stories but quickly move on to the analyses of these stories; however, it is important to remember that even when the author's principal task is to analyze events or happenings, he or she must always maintain a secure hold on the narrative events which engender their respective analyses. To forget to answer the reader's question "What happened?" can be fatal to a work of biography or history—or any analytical narrative.

Before moving on, it may be worth noting that although chronological order is probably the most common principle of narrative organization, this is not a hard and fast rule. Your organization depends on what will create the best effect in your writing. Don't adhere slavishly to chronological order if your piece suggests that another method will yield better results.

Though narrative, as we have seen, is an independent mode with various classifications, it is often used in college and university writing as an aid to other kinds of writing. You will probably not often be asked to write narrative pure and simple. Rather, you will probably be asked to produce expository and argumentative writing to which narrative can be brought as an aid. Look back at the Marq de Villiers passage on guns that was quoted above. De Villiers is clearly more interested in the moral debate surrounding gun control than he is in the narrative events which introduce the analysis. However, he wins reader attention by beginning the analysis with a poignant and gripping story which leads naturally into the analysis itself. A clear understanding of how narrative works can help you write more effective non-narrative essays. The great beauty of narrative writing is that it brings into action more aspects of our human make-up than the discursive modes (i.e., exposition and argumentation). While narrative involves our usual reasoning faculties, it also makes appeals to the imagination, the emotions, and the memory, appeals which make our reading a more complete experience. Writers have not been slow to recognize this; just as authors know that robust diction carries more weight than cliché and commonplace, so they know that using narrative anecdotes and illustrations will give weight to their argument or exposition.

When you are writing narrative, either as the dominant mode of composition or in the service of some other mode, you will inevitably be faced with a decision about the degree of detail you want to include. In certain contexts too much narrative detail will only clog up the works, diverting attention from the main issue:

Changing a tire can be a simple enough task if you have the proper equipment and go at the job in a methodical way. One bright sunny morning at about 6:30 a.m. I decided that I would get up early and go golfing in order to beat the crowds of people who normally congregate at golf courses in good weather. I jumped into my car and proceeded in a carefree, breezy manner towards the golf course which is about six miles from my house. After having driven about three miles, I noticed that the road had suddenly become very bumpy and my car's steering very difficult to manage. Imagine my surprise when I realized that I had a flat right rear tire. After spending about forty-five minutes changing the tire, and another fifteen cleaning my hands, I arrived at the golf course only to have to stand in a long line of other eager golfers who had got out of bed after me, but who had, nevertheless, a better journey to the golf course than I had.

Although this small essay begins by suggesting that it is going to outline the steps one should take in changing a tire, it never fulfills its promise. Rather it gets sidetracked and talks more about the incidents leading up to the flat tire and the consequences of it than about the process itself. In other words, the narrative which is meant to lead into the process takes on a life of its own and abandons the essay's main goal.

In other contexts, however, a thorough presentation of narrative detail is necessary in order to make the analysis that follows comprehensible. Often writers move back and forth between summary and detailed presentation in an essay and even in a single paragraph. If you were assigned a process essay on how to change a tire, you might choose to begin with a paragraph-long anecdote from personal experience. In two or three sentences you could summarize the pleasurable events of the trip up to the fateful moment. Then you could switch into a more detailed presentation to describe your handling of the blowout itself, which would include the process part of the assignment. Vivid detail is a great asset to any writing, but remember that it needs a context that will give it significance. In the following paragraph the author judiciously combines both the process and the narrative. Note how the narrative segments do not compete with the process but rather enhance and personalize it:

The ideal rising temperature for bread dough is between 80 and 90 degrees Fahrenheit: if it is much cooler the rising is sluggish, if much hotter the yeast might burn itself out. If the thermostat in your home is set at 80 you can put your bowl of dough anywhere. If your temperature is normal, a warm spot or high shelf in your kitchen might do, or you could turn on the heat in your oven at its lowest setting for 5 minutes, then turn it *off* and put the dough in. A friend of mine puts her bowl of coffee-cake dough on a board on top of a radiator. I put mine on a sunny window ledge. In winter I put it on a shelf above an electric heating unit. While visiting at a summer cottage I found a perfect rising-place on a cool day was the seat of my car parked in the sun. And one shivery morning in September I mixed my bread dough at dawn and went back to my warm welcome bed. Like the slap of a frosty wet fish the thought struck me that dough won't rise well in the cold. I got up, brought the covered bowl to my bed and tucked it under the electric blanket. Of course I slept again. Of course the dough rose. Very quickly.

Edna Staebler, *Food that Really Schmecks*, Scarborough: McGraw-Hill Ryerson, 1968. 137.

When using paragraphs of narrative material in expository or argumentative essays, two methods of keeping a proper proportion of context and detail are deductive and inductive narration. In deductive narration the writer begins the paragraph by stating the main point—what is often called the topic sentence. The paragraph then develops this point through narrative event and detail. Inductive narration works in reverse. The narrative events and detail build up to a concluding topic sentence which expresses the main point of the whole. A good example of deductive development can be found in the Staebler passage above; the following is an example of inductive narration:

> When I received word that my first job interview would take place Monday morning at 9:30 I was ecstatic and found it extremely difficult to sleep for the whole preceding weekend. When Monday dawned at about 5:00 a.m. I jumped out of bed, showered for what seemed an endless period, and ate a very sparse breakfast, not wanting to have too much on my stomach. I then proceeded to get dressed in my very best clothes, certain in this case of the wisdom of the adage that clothes make the person. Even after this seemingly endless period of time I spent properly preparing myself, I discovered that it was still only 8 o'clock and that I still had an hour and a half to wait for my interview. In order to help pass the time I decided to walk to the office where the interview was to be held. However, I had not taken into account the fickleness of mother nature. No sooner had I reached the half-way point—the point of no return as it were—than it began to pour rain. I arrived at my interview sodden and sullen, my new dress looking very much as if it had just been thrown into a lake with me in it. Obviously even the best-prepared people must finally realize that there are certain factors which will always remain beyond their control.

HANDS ON: READING INTO WRITING

1. Using our subject and mode classifications (p. 111–114), choose three or four anthology essays that have a *narrative* component and share a *common subject*. Actively read these essays.

2. Answer the questions appended to each essay. Your careful responses to these questions should act as a spur to your thoughts and assist you when you complete the reading workbook entry.

3. Complete a reading workbook entry for each essay.

    (a) Comment on subject, audience, and purpose.

    (b) Identify thesis statement, topic sentence, or controlling idea.

    (c) Comment on developmental strategies.

    (d) Write a summary.

    (e) Write a response of at least 100 words.

4. Once you have finished dealing with the readings on an individual basis, you will have at least 300 to 400 words of informed response on the subject shared by the chosen essays. This body of material will serve as the basis for your own primarily *narrative* essay on the *same* subject, which should consist of three or four double-spaced, typewritten pages. Remember what has been mentioned time and again in this book: the techniques

that you learn as you actively read will be the ones that you put to good use when you write your own essay. Consequently, you need to follow the various steps we've outlined for the writing occasion:

(a) Examine your responses.

(b) Develop a workable topic and thesis in view of your subject, audience, and purpose.

(c) Determine effective developmental strategies.

(d) Plan and write a first draft.

(e) Revise.

DESCRIPTION

In general, in university or college writing, description, like narration, will come into play largely in the service of some other mode. Of course, this does not mean that description cannot stand on its own. Character sketches and technical descriptions are types of writing that need not form part of a larger context—though they normally do. Rarely is there such a thing as a descriptive passage that attains total objectivity. This is because every author will see the same scene with different eyes, will bring a different social, cultural, and sometimes even artistic background to bear on what is being described. Notice for example, the following description written by the Group of Seven artist A.Y. Jackson:

> A few days later, on 22nd August, we were four miles off Bathurst Island. It was snowing. Just before we rounded Cape Cockburn we ran for several miles alongside a floe of polar ice which we followed as though it were a canal bank. It was the largest ice floe Falke had ever seen. It was old, worn, and full of hollows filled with pools of fresh water which looked blue-green. We dubbed it the Harris ice pan. Up to that time we had not found anything named "Harris" in the Arctic. We got about halfway between Bathurst and Byam Martin Islands, where we were brought to a halt as there appeared to be no more open water. At midnight the landscape looked like an endless prairie covered with snow. Little pools of water here and there reflected the sun glow; to the east, the coast of Bathurst was blotted out by an approaching snow squall.
>
> A.Y. Jackson, *A Painter's Country,* Toronto: Clarke, Irwin, 1958. 130–131.

On the surface, this passage looks very much like an objective description of part of an Arctic voyage. We may be tempted to think that Jackson describes this scene very much like anyone else might. But notice how the personal and subjective do, nevertheless, find a place in this otherwise quite neutral and unspectacular description. In the third sentence of the passage Jackson describes the polar ice as if "it were a canal bank." This simile is a striking one and certainly not one that would come to the mind of just anyone seeing the same scene as Jackson. The second example is even more personal. Near the end of the passage Jackson dares to wax poetical and describes the landscape as "an endless prairie covered with snow." In this sentence Jackson brings his painter's eye to the cold and frozen Arctic and, through this very personal view of what he sees, emphasizes the size and apparent relentlessness of the Arctic landscape. Neatly tucked into this ostensibly objective description, then, are two examples of highly personal "seeing."

One can, of course, find descriptive passages where description and authorial comment or meditation on it are more obviously highlighted. In the following passage try to determine how Ludwig moves beyond Jackson not only in descriptive vividness, but also in the way in which he turns the scene over in his mind:

> Under canopies, in the few places one may sit and nurse a soft drink or beer without ransoming away an arm and a leg, the older folks stake claims to a seat, sip slowly, sagged and wilted. Arm in arm, leather-jacketed and blue-jeaned couples, parties, gangs, sweep through the crowd, in a great hurry to do it all before the chuckwagon horses change back to mice. Anyone dreaming of "one big break" must make his hit in the next few hours. So it's *hurry hurry, hurry scurry*, the rhythm on the midway, *click shuffle, scrape curse* in the casino, while in easy contrast, the young people space themselves out in front of the Sun Tree, make one joint service a dozen unhurried smokers while tired rock music ekes out its wobbly decibels. From time to time a pot-fogged dreamer floats off in the direction of food and foodlines—lines and lines here as elsewhere, sullen lines, giggly lines, crying lines (where the children wait for their last Stampede ride). The masses mass to pay out what was saved from bread to spend on circuses.

> Jack Ludwig, "The Calgary Stampede," *Maclean's,* July 1975: 24.

What one notices in this passage is not only a plethora of vivid and sometimes eccentric description, but an authorial commentary on the scene—an attitude if you like—issuing from the description itself. In other words, the author's careful choice of descriptive words lets us know how he responds to what he is describing.

The descriptive writer's greatest aid in achieving his or her end is an appeal to the reader's senses. Without this appeal, the notion of making a place, scene, or event come to life on the page is meaningless. We live in and by our senses; consider how often we use the following questions: "What does it look like?"; "How does it taste?"; "Does it feel good?"; "What's that smell?"; "Did you hear that?" These questions reflect how common primary sense experience is for us—to distance ourselves from the sensuous domain is to enter the realm of abstraction. Consequently, the writer who appeals to the reader's senses is appealing directly to the reader's experience. Writers of effective descriptions will involve as many or as few of the senses as are necessary to the impression being created.

Though we normally think of description as dealing with persons, places, or things external to us, we should not forget that we can also present our internal life—our feelings, emotions, thoughts—powerfully through description as well. Consider the following description of a train trip on Canada's "Rapido."

> ... 4:45 p.m., sharp, the station moves away from us ... leaving me exposed suddenly to the body of my city ... out the back corner of my eye that becalmed Beaux-Arts bulk, rising like a series of improved Buckingham Palaces piled atop each other—the Royal York, could only be she

> the long slit unended of Yonge Street—like all our streets—dissolved only by infinity

> with that wedding-cake turn-of-the-century prestige bank at the lower left-hand corner—Front Street corner: a kind of gaudy bodyguard for the longeststreetintheworldthatisYongestreet ending only in our Ontario Lake District. Bank of Montreal, at that!

with its back square upon me, the squat cube of our beer baron's art centre: O'Keefe

overtopping all these, the soft-nosed phallicity of Bank of Commerce—circumspect, uncircumcised—32 stories of Canadian self-satisfaction

the new National Trust tower, well below

& below again, prickly up these closed commercial shops, the spired incisions of the old City of Churches—Saint James & Michael & Metropole

Scott Symons, *Place d'Armes,* Toronto: McClelland & Stewart, 1967. 8.

In this passage Symons brings the various scenes that pass him by to life. He does this by creating a sense of speed in his prose (simulating the movement of the train), and by using descriptive imagery which gives a visual excitement to the scene. The description is highly idiosyncratic; the images are unusual; the pace of the passage rapid. The description in this passage captures the author's feeling for what he sees; the emotional impact of the entire scene is strong for him as he passes by it bit by bit. Not only do we discover the author's feelings for what he sees, but we ourselves are treated to a "new" view of a relatively old city. In short, in this passage Symons removes the veil of familiarity for us while at the same time allowing us to experience and "feel" the scenes that he passes.

The three quoted passages are obviously very different from each other and have different ends in view. It is of primary importance for writers of description to know where they stand at all times—both mentally, in terms of attitude, and physically, in terms of location. In the Jackson passage, the author's physical location is on a boat in the Arctic. What he describes rather sparingly are the scenes of the Arctic landscape that he sees from his vantage point. And his mental attitude reflects this touring stance: he describes scenes clearly, and on two occasions quite vividly; but he does not dwell on them, does not probe them for some hidden significance. His purpose is to give a brief description of a scene, and he remains securely on the surface of it. To present detailed descriptions of his own reactions and to launch into political and cultural meditations or diatribes would be to direct attention away from the scene and toward himself—the observer. We would have to question this confusion of attitude or stance.

The Symons passage goes to the other extreme. The author's physical location is inside a train. From his seat in a rapidly moving train he describes the scenes of Toronto life as he passes by them. But the nature of his description sets it apart from the largely "objective" stance that Jackson takes. Perhaps all of us have had the experience of sitting in a train observing the world pass by. But none of us would describe it in the highly personal and eccentric way that Symons does. Clearly Symons wants us to "re-see" a site that might already be familiar to us; he also wants us to understand how he feels about it. The scene, then, becomes the occasion for allowing us to learn more about the author's attitudes; the description of the scene is not an end in itself.

Coming between these two passages is Ludwig's. Ludwig is obviously more interested than Jackson in letting us know how *he* feels about what he sees. But his description is clearly not as impressionistic as that of Symons. Like Jackson, he wants us to be aware of the scene; however, unlike Symons, he does not treat the scene simply as a point of departure for the presentation of his own highly personal reflections on it.

In light of what we have just said, it is important to note that many discussions of descriptive writing speak of a spectrum stretching from objective description at one end to subjective at the other. Regularly we are told that objective description leans toward the scientific mode, presenting only the facts, what is there, while subjective description concerns itself with the emotions, with our personal perceptions and preferences. Yet the objectivity/subjectivity polarity begs questions. So-called objective descriptions cannot help but be selective. Authors must leave some things out—and their choices express personal judgements. Similarly, in the supposedly emotional/personal subjective description there is, in good prose at any rate, an attitude or stance presented which reflects substantial reasoning and therefore a certain authorial detachment.

For our purposes, a more useful distinction is between telling and showing, always keeping in mind that in most cases there is mingling and overlap. Descriptions that tell about, rather than show, the qualities of the subject in question are most useful in expository writing where explanation or overview is needed. The author keeps a certain distance from the item being described because there is usually a larger context of thought into which the description fits. The distance prevents the description from running away with the whole piece. In the following passage Ken Dryden describes the kind of heroism that is all too regularly imposed on the star hockey player. Dryden's point is that this heroic stature that many attain is the result of playing a game:

> It is the kind of special treatment professional athletes have grown accustomed to, and enjoy. It began with hockey, with teenage names and faces in local papers, with hockey jackets that only the best players on the best teams wore, with parents who competed not so quietly on the side; and it will end with hockey. In between, the longer and better we play the more all-encompassing the treatment becomes. People give, easily and naturally. And we accept. Slippers, sweaters, plant holders, mitts, baby blankets, baby clothes sent in the mail. Paintings, carvings, etchings, sculptures in clay, metal, papier-maché. Shirts, slacks, coats, suits, ties, underwear; cars, carpets, sofas, chairs, refrigerators, beds, washers, dryers, stoves, TVs, stereos, at cost or no cost at all. After all, a special person deserves a special price. A hundred letters a week, more than 3,000 a year—"You're the best," all but a few of them say. On the street, in restaurants and theatres, we're pointed at, talked about like the weather. "There he is, the famous hockey player," your own kids announce to their friends. In other homes, your picture is on a boy's bedroom wall. Magazines, newspapers, radio, TV; hockey cards, posters, T-shirts, and curios, anywhere, everywhere, name, face, thousands of times, flashed to an audience that waves into TV cameras, that writes to editors to have proud yellowed clippings in their wallets.
>
> Ken Dryden, *The Game,* Toronto: Macmillan of Canada, 1983. 158–159.

In this passage, Dryden is talking about hockey heroism and how it is attained. The passage, although important for the description of how heroism is, in some senses, forced on players, is nevertheless part of a larger case that Ken Dryden is making about the game of hockey itself. The movement of the piece is not toward the particular, but the general—Dryden is not discussing a specific hero but heroism in general as it applies to hockey.

Descriptions that *show* the qualities of their subject tend to move the other way, from the general to the particular. Call to mind again the Scott Symons passage quoted above. There we are not concerned with a general reaction to a scene by a representative human being; rather we are interested in the particular—some might even say peculiar—reaction of Symons himself. In this example, the author must get close to the scene to convey the details that will make this scene live. We get a greater range of diction and syntax in Symons's passage as he tries to convey the experience that *he* is having. The difference lies there: "telling" helps the author convey ideas (in Dryden's case, how hockey players come to think of themselves as heroes); "showing" helps the author convey experiences (in Symons's case, his "vision" of Toronto from a moving train).

Arrangement Strategies

Whatever else descriptive authors do, they must be sure to include only those features that contribute to the dominant impression the description is meant to achieve. All elements must work toward this impression—until you know what impression you want to create, you don't know what your organization or arrangement should be; you don't know where you stand. Once you are sure of the impression you are after you have a number of possible principles of arrangement to choose from: deductive and inductive, spatial, temporal, thematic and comparative.

Deductive and Inductive

As with narration, you may develop your descriptive paragraphs deductively or inductively. All of the passages quoted in this chapter proceed deductively, but both methods have much to recommend them, and your choice of which to follow will depend largely on the effect you want to create. Deductive development is appropriate when you want to present the main point up front and then flesh it out with descriptive sentences. Inductive development, by holding the main point or summary statement to the end, allows and, in fact, forces the reader to concentrate on the details as they are presented.

Spatial

Spatial arrangement is a useful way to keep the reader oriented at all times. You may describe an object from front to back, side to side, top to bottom, background to foreground, etc. You may go from wall to wall, room to room, or street to street in a spatial arrangement. Notice how in the Symons passage, the author moves from building to building.

Temporal

A temporal arrangement allows you to describe something as it changes (or does not change) over time. Whether your span is seconds or eons, the passing of time provides a natural principle of organization. Take, for instance, the Dryden passage. Dryden focuses on when the special treatment accorded sports figures began, when it will end, and what comes in between. The manifestations of heroism as described in the passage are ones that occur again and again. We get a sense that the ritual of hockey hero worship, like all rituals, is repetitive and never-ending. The final phrase "thousands of times" captures the feeling of constant repetition.

Thematic 氵莫糸

Thematic organization emphasizes the dominant impression, often by means of repetition. In the Ludwig passage, notice how many expressions reiterate the impression created by words such as "sagged" and "wilted."

Comparative

A final principle is arrangement by comparison. Symons, for example, as well as proceeding spatially, also makes use of metaphors and similes to enliven the description. Figures of speech extend the range of experience a description covers and so increase the readership it can appeal to. They also ignite our imagination to help us bring the subject to life.

HANDS ON: READING INTO WRITING

1. Using our subject and mode classifications (p. 111–114), choose three or four anthology essays that have a *descriptive* component and share a *common subject*. Actively read these essays.

2. Answer the questions appended to each essay. Your careful responses to these questions should act as a spur to your thoughts and assist you when you complete the reading workbook entry.

3. Complete a reading workbook entry for each essay.

   (a) Comment on subject, audience, and purpose.

   (b) Identify thesis statement, topic sentence, or controlling idea.

   (c) Comment on developmental strategies.

   (d) Write a summary.

   (e) Write a response of at least 100 words.

4. Once you have finished dealing with the readings on an individual basis, you will have at least 300 to 400 words of informed response on the subject shared by the chosen essays. This body of material will serve as the basis for your own primarily *descriptive* essay on the *same* subject, which should consist of three or four double-spaced, typewritten pages. Remember what has been mentioned time and again in this book: the techniques that you learn as you actively read will be the ones that you put to good use when you write your own essay. Consequently, you need to follow the various steps we've outlined for the writing occasion:

   (a) Examine your responses.

   (b) Develop a workable topic and thesis in view of your subject, audience, and purpose.

   (c) Determine effective developmental strategies.

   (d) Plan and write a first draft.

   (e) Revise.

EXPOSITION

Expository writing—along with argumentation one of the two main types of writing in college and university—is writing primarily designed to inform or explain. Its basic purpose is to provide information to an audience wishing to broaden its knowledge on a particular topic, or to help the audience better understand information it already possesses. Whichever of these purposes is chosen, the expository writer is normally more knowledgeable about the subject than the audience. People read expository writing to be informed and to learn; expository writers have something to teach. Whether you are explaining something as simple as how to make bran muffins or as complex as the differences in political philosophy between the Liberal and Conservative parties, you need to be aware that clarity and precision in writing are especially important in the expository mode. Being aware of the nature of your audience is also particularly crucial in exposition. If you are writing an essay in which you are explaining a photographic technique to a group of photographers, you can take much more for granted about photography than you could if you were explaining the same process to people who had just bought their first camera. Similarly, writing about the effects of a Canadian winter on wildlife to a group of Canadian naturalists would present a different explanatory chore from that of an essay on the same topic to a group of Floridians with a vague interest in animals. Simply handing over information would be more important in the former case, while improving understanding would matter more in the latter instance. However, whatever your topic and whoever your audience, you can be certain to have less difficulty writing an expository essay if you take into account the various developmental strategies at your disposal.

Before we turn to an examination of these strategies as they apply to exposition, it is important to state that regularly we find a combination of these strategies in a single essay. To take an absurd example, suppose you were writing an essay in which you were trying to explain the process of changing a flat tire to an audience of Bedouin camel drivers. In order to make your essay comprehensible to an audience whose knowledge of your subject would be slight or even non-existent, you might have to *define* both a car and a tire; explain the *cause* of flat tires and the *effects* of sharp objects penetrating rubber; give *examples* of sharp objects that can penetrate rubber; make *comparisons* between the functions that tires serve and the functions that camels' legs serve. Only at this stage might you be able to turn to the *process* of changing a flat tire. Look, for example, at the following excerpt from an essay on the historian Donald Creighton:

> D.G. Creighton was the greatest Canadian historian since, and perhaps even including, F.X. Garneau. In shifting, uncertain times his art celebrated and sought to inspire the survival of his nation.
>
> But this will be homage, not historiography. Unlike Garneau, who was a notary and a civil servant, Creighton made a profession of history. Of the many fine eulogies published since his death, none has dealt with his primary vocation—a curious omission especially in view of some newspapers' loudly proclaimed interest in teaching as opposed to research and publication. For fifty years D.G. Creighton taught in the History Department at the University of Toronto. How he taught deserves some comment.

I studied with him close to the end of his career when he might have been expected to slow down or coast on his reputation. Far from it. He continued writing at the same steady pace, producing four books and a collection of essays in recent years. He also continued to work at his teaching. I attended two of his seminars and for several years he supervised my thesis. I was constantly awed by his devotion to his calling, the conscious effort he put into teaching, and his fierce commitment to those he always referred to as *his* students. He was a great scholar and a great teacher.

Once, somewhat thoughtlessly, I burst into his office to ask for help with something that seemed important at the time. "Are you busy?" I asked. There he sat in the wicker chair off in the corner of the room. The chair creaked as he shambled to his feet, a little impatient with me I sensed. "Well, I have a seminar in an hour," he replied, "and I'm just finishing the reading." But he dealt graciously with my intrusion and I sped off dumbfounded that someone who had been through the material as many times as he had, who knew the subject as intimately as he did, would still, as retirement approached, do the reading for an undergraduate seminar. Now, as a busy teacher myself, I am even more amazed. He always referred to himself as a professional historian. He was also a professional teacher. But he made his own rules.

There was nothing spontaneous, improvised or casual about his seminar. At times it was stiff and awkward. It was always formal and correct. He took great care laying out the question to be discussed and the readings; he gave the paper giver specific guidance, and he expected the rest of us to return having mastered the literature, prepared to conduct an intelligent discussion of the topic. We were never expected to tear up the paper being presented in any vindictive, "American," hyper-critical way. Thorough, dispassionate discussion was the object. Certain points were expected to emerge from the discussion, however, and Creighton took pains to make sure these essentials were grasped during our amateurish deliberations.

H.V. Nelles, "Creighton's Seminar," *Canadian Forum*, 60:702: 5.

These few paragraphs about a famous Canadian are written largely in the expository mode. The author's subject is Donald Creighton, his thesis Creighton's talent as a teacher. What the author intends to *show, explain,* or *inform* us of is an aspect of Donald Creighton's life which he thinks has gone largely unacknowledged. Subject and purpose work together here as they must in all good writing; but what about audience? Presumably the audience that the author must have in mind is one that at least recognizes Donald Creighton's name; in other words, an audience that knows something—however slight—about Creighton and might like to know something more—in this case about his skill as a teacher.

It is interesting to note how various developmental strategies work together in these five paragraphs to help the author carry out his purpose. One could argue that the major developmental strategy is *definition*; after all, the author intends to provide further information about an already famous man, information that will make us more familiar with him. In a sense, then, he is defining a certain quality about Donald Creighton's life which many of us know nothing about. From one perspective, definition exemplifies the basic expository impulse—to make a thing clearer; in this case, Creighton's great teaching skills. But notice also the importance of other developmental strategies. In the second sentence of the second paragraph the author uses *contrast* to sharpen our sense of Creighton's personality as historian. The author also uses *illustration* or *example* to indicate Creighton's skill as a teacher. This is evident primarily in the fifth paragraph where he introduces the example of the seminar. Within the same paragraph we see the use of *process* development as Nelles outlines the steps by which Creighton created a successful seminar. Finally, perhaps to suggest the person behind the historian, Nelles introduces the *narrative mode* in paragraph four; this little story is based on an exchange that the author once had with the great man himself. To create a sense of immediacy, the author recalls part of the exact conversation for us. As this example of expository writing makes abundantly clear, good writing is made up of a skillful mix of strategies and rarely just one. In your own writing you should use various developmental strategies to help you deal with questions such as subject, audience, and purpose; you should never get to the point where you feel hemmed in by any one strategy even though one strategy normally predominates in each piece of writing.

Developmental Strategies

Process

Process writing is largely writing that tells people how to do something: how to change a tire; how to avoid paying income tax; how to lose 20 pounds; how to be successful at college or university. Each of the following examples of process writing deals with a different subject in a different way. The first is a simple recipe:

Oat Bran Cookies

175 ml (3/4 cup) butter or margarine

250 ml (1 cup) white sugar

125 ml (1/2 cup) brown sugar

1 egg (slightly beaten)

250 ml (1 cup) flour

50 ml (1/4 cup) oats

250 ml (1 cup) bran

175 ml (3/4 cup) coconut

5 ml (1 tsp) baking powder

5 ml (1 tsp) baking soda

250 ml (1 cup) raisins (optional)

Cream butter or margarine, sugar, and egg together. Combine all dry ingredients and stir in gradually to the butter/sugar/egg mixture. Mix until all ingredients are well incorporated. Drop by teaspoonful onto greased cookie sheet. Bake at 180° C (350° F) for 12–15 minutes. Makes approximately 4 dozen cookies.

   Process writing doesn't get much simpler than this. In fact recipes or instructions in general are about the most basic type of process writing one can find. Notice how the next example of process writing takes the recipe format and uses it as parody:

Recipe for a Canadian Novel

Ingredients: one Indian,
one Mountie, one Eskimo,
one Doukhobor.

Add: one small-town whore,
two thousand miles of wheat,
one farmer impotent and bent.

His fair-haired daughter too,
then a Laurentian mountain
and a Montreal Jew.

Include also, a young boy
with a dying pet
and a mortgage unmet.

Should this sour, sweeten
with maple syrup—
French-Canadian even,

but dilute, if foreign
to the taste.
Stir, until beaten.

Drop in exotic and tangy
place names—Toronto,
Saskatoon, Hudson Bay.

For distinctive flavour:
garnish with maple leaves.
Mix, then leave.

Dice in one Confederation poet
complete with verse
(remove mould first).

To prepare the sauce:
paragraphs of bad prose
that never seem to stop.

Bring to a simmer,

but avoid a boil.

Pour, place in oven, bake.

Slice or leave whole.

Serves twenty million all told—

when cold.

John Robert Columbo, "Recipe for a Canadian Novel," *Abracadabra,*
Toronto: McClelland & Stewart, 1967. 28–29.

Clearly the author is using the familiar and somewhat hackneyed recipe process to satirize Canadian writing. He does not expect us to take seriously the "recipe" he gives us, for there is no possibility that anything edible could come from it. Rather, he's perhaps suggesting that all too often Canadian novels lack imagination, so much so that they can be written by simply inserting the ingredients he mentions in his poem.

The final example of process writing is based upon a writer's response to the question, "How long a day do you put in?"

It's not a matter of a big day. I work, say, till noon and sometimes in the afternoon, but the unconscious is working for you most of the time. I wake up in the middle of the night and do most of my thinking then, and set it up for the next morning. It's not the number of hours. People who actually turn out a great deal of work often seem to spend a very short time at the typewriter. I do a great deal of re-writing. With the beginning of a book, I will often re-write first paragraphs, and the first few pages, thirty and forty times, because another belief I have is that in that moment, in that fix, in those first crucial pages, all the reader's decisions are made. To trust or not to trust? And all stylistic decisions are really made at that point, especially nowadays.

Brian Moore, in [Silver] Donald Cameron, *Conversations with Canadian Novelists, 2,*
Toronto: Macmillan, 1973. 77.

Notice in his response how the writer begins in a fairly conventional way by moving from one time period to the next ("I work, say, till noon and sometimes in the afternoon"). We soon realize that the chronological catalogue does not capture the essence of his method of writing. As a result we move into a description of process that is entirely personal and idiosyncratic, a method that works for the author but might not work for us. We've moved a long way in this process piece from the recipe format which, if religiously followed, will have the same results for all.

Cause and Effect

Cause and effect is that writing strategy that makes use of the relationships that actually *exist* between things or that can be *created* between things. Also, in one of its manifestations it studies the consequences of actions, events, or various phenomena. In this first excerpt of cause-and-effect writing we see a largely irrefutable relationship established between two things. And it is irrefutable because it is personal. In other words we have no right to question the effect that the author describes because it is solely *hers:*

Always, when approaching London, a surge of sinking awfulness swept over me as we came to its outskirts, and the train began slithering through suburban manufacturing districts. Open country turned to human congestion, brick and mortar pressed close both sides of our way—ache of overcrowded space, murk, dullness stared from behind the glazed fronts and backs of brick houses. No matter how hard I tried, I could not take interest in manufacturing districts—they wilted me. Love of everything, that swamped me in the country, was congealed here, stuffed away like rotten lettuce. Nothing within me responded to the hum of machinery.

Emily Carr, *Growing Pains: The Autobiography of Emily Carr*, Toronto: Clarke, Irwin, 1946. 182.

Although the author's attitude toward industrial cities may not be ours—although the *effects* she feels may or may not represent what we feel—we are prepared to respect her views since they are completely hers. She is not trying to suggest that her views should be anyone else's, nor is she trying to convince us that hers are the only proper views of industrial life. Compare the following expository passage on the effects of television on politics:

The enormity of television's impact upon the institutions of society is immeasurable, if only because there is not yet an end to it, only a continuing, deepening process of cause and effect. How can one measure the impact of the medium which has made the afternoon, for example, a killing ground for newspapers? To say that television has made all politics presidential, or driven general magazines and afternoon papers to the wall, is so commonly accepted a fact as to have become trite. But television has done considerably more and is still doing so.

Because it demanded increasingly heavy dollops of money, television "reformed" political financing to give the parties significantly greater resources to purchase not only television time but people and techniques, including computerized direct mail and public opinion research. As a result, while present-day party cadres are very well paid and highly professionalized, voluntarism is all but dead.

The rank-and-file of the parties, once considered to represent an omnibus of interests, have become competing factions acting on behalf of special or regional interests. Their usefulness in the political process is rapidly decreasing. They too perceive the system as presidential; they too think of politics in the same simple or detached terms as do non-partisans. Politics, which once inspired group loyalty and avid commitment, now arouses a consuming interest in techniques and in endless critical evaluations of leadership suitability as deduced from television performance. Were it not for private ambition or patronage interests, anarchy would be certain.

Dalton Camp, *An Eclectic Eel*, Ottawa: Deneau, 1981. xvi.

Since this is a complex cause-and-effect passage, it might be valuable to test your understanding of this strategy by identifying all of the effects that Camp mentions in these paragraphs. Like the first passage, this one shows or informs us of certain effects, but unlike the first one it *assumes* a position about television which we might like to doubt or at least question. It is up to the author of this second passage to *prove* the validity of what he shows us. In other words, in order to win our support for his statements he must, sooner or later, move from the expository mode to the argumentative or persuasive one.

The final example of the cause and effect strategy is taken from a novel. It brings cause and effect together; the speaker begins to contemplate the past as a result of a scene he sees from his car window:

> I am on my way to Union Terrace in the Dart when I am strongly affected by a sense of the past: the early nineteen-forties, the war years in old Middlesburgh. It happens at the corner of Britannia Road and Prospect where I am stopped for a red light. Through my windshield I watch five teen-aged girls running. They have come down Prospect Street from Union Place Secondary School and now run across in front of me, stiff-hipped and pigeon-toed, holding their books to their chests. They are making for the restaurant next to the Pix Theatre. Watching them, I am overcome by haunted feelings, touched by fragments of the past. It is *déja vu* for certain, but also something else, something deeper and stronger. Within me thrives the keenest sense of time and place. I seem able to reach out and feel the texture of those days: the high-school girls in their plaid skirts and bulky white sweaters, their ankle socks and brown and white saddle shoes. I have half a mind to abandon the Dart and follow them into the restaurant, ask if their mothers didn't once grow up in Middlesburgh, Ontario. It's all here at the corner of Britannia Road and Prospect at a quarter to five on a winter afternoon—this lost time, figured forth now in an *ambience* as resonant and palpable as an old sepia retrogravure. The sadness of it is suffocating.
>
> Richard B. Wright, *The Weekend Man*, New York: Farrar, Straus, and Giroux, 1970. 196–197.

In this passage, the sight of some young girls *causes* the speaker to think about the early 1940s, the period of his own youth. The *effects* of this are numerous for him: he is "haunted" by certain "feelings"; he thinks of similar scenes during his own adolescence; he is tempted to abandon his car and follow the girls; he is overwhelmed by sadness. This passage forces the reader to ask why the speaker feels this way; in other words, the effects of this scene on the speaker force us as readers to ask what *caused* those effects; the answer might be that the speaker in this scene realizes his own mortality.

Comparison and Contrast

The comparison and contrast strategy looks at similarities and/or differences between various phenomena. When using this strategy care must be taken to ensure that there is some central and genuine comparative core shared by the items you choose to look at. The first example of this strategy stresses differences rather than similarities:

> I cannot, in other words, divorce questions about progress and technology from questions about the essence of America and Europe. The European character is as essentially bound up with eschatology and the messianic idea of progress as is the American character with the structure of technology, hedonism, pragmatism and so

on. But I cannot honestly find any connection between Canada and such phenomena as progress, technology, hedonism, cynicism or anything else for that matter. Not even with "mediocrity" (a frequently-discussed issue in Canada). If Europeans and Americans are progress-oriented and hedonistic it has (as I understand it) everything to do with the fact of their being Europeans and Americans. If we Canadians are infected with any particular pathology, however, it does not strike me as having anything to do with our being Canadian. It suggests rather the influence of European and American culture on our lives. If anything, Canadianism would seem to be the absence rather than the presence of foreign influence, the suspension rather than the affirmation of ideological commitments to destiny, progress, mission and so on.

Lionel Rubinoff, "National Purpose and Ideology," *Notes for a Native Land,* Ed. Andy Wainwright, Ottawa: Oberon, 1969. 45.

Although you might argue that this passage is about similarities as well as differences because the author compares American and European life, in fact what the author is trying to stress are the differences between Canadian life and American and European life. Therefore the accent in this passage is on the ways in which Canadian life is unlike the other cultures he mentions. It is extremely important to recognize this fact; to ignore it is to miss the important emphasis in the passage on Canadian distinctiveness.

The second example of comparison and contrast writing is a fine instance of the way in which an author can combine and structure differences and similarities to highlight particular aspects of each:

In Canada, neither circumstances nor tradition permitted the evolution of so ebullient and all-embracing a figure. Nevertheless, both English- and French-Canadian poetries in this period had been hard at work attempting to create myths—which may account for the fact that neither resulted in a useful "record of Canadian life." French Canadians, intent on creating a national consciousness that would survive British domination, had paid scant heed to "recording the facts," at least in poetry. English-Canadian poets, struggling to sustain the exaggerated ideals of "the Loyalist response," misrepresented the "facts" not only in the mother country, but to themselves. Both were handicapped by growing up as conservative societies in the shadow of a liberal and expanding United States. But French Canadians held an important advantage. A common religious and agrarian tradition, the cohesion of a folk culture and the presence of foreign overlords all acted as a continuing centripetal force, drawing them together and maintaining unity. In English Canada, circumstances were the exact opposite. The inhabitants, originating from England, Ireland, Scotland and the United States, differing in religion, cultural background and point of view, were dispersed in a strange, frequently harsh environment and disturbed by the proximity of "greener fields" to the south. These factors acted as a centrifugal force, separating English Canadians and preventing the fusion of a much-needed "national ideal."

T.E. Farley, *Exiles and Pioneers: Two Visions of Canada's Future, 1825–1975,* Ottawa: Borealis, 1976. 49.

Farley's passage is such a nicely balanced comparison and contrast paragraph that a brief analysis of its structure seems in order. In sentence two the author introduces a similarity between the two Canadian cultures that are the subjects of this paragraph. This similarity is signalled by the use of the word "both" in the second sentence. Quickly, however, sentences three and four introduce the first difference, nicely captured by the balanced phrases that open each sentence ("French Canadians, intent on creating" and "English-Canadian poets, struggling to sustain"). Sentence five suggests the basic similarity lying behind the differences outlined in sentences three and four. Once again the key signalling word here is "both." Sentences six to ten introduce the second major difference between the two cultures, emphasized by the use of the antonyms "centripetal" (sentence seven) and "centrifugal" (sentence ten).

The final comparison/contrast example is interesting because of the number of items it includes in its sweep. Normally, when we think of comparison/contrast we think of comparison and contrast between two terms. In the following passage the two major terms are Anglophone and Francophone. But notice how categories within these two general terms are also compared and contrasted:

> A surprisingly high 86 per cent of all respondents agreed with the statement, "It would be a good thing if all Canadians could speak both English and French." Francophones were somewhat more likely to agree (97 per cent) than Anglophones (81 per cent); and university education and some fluency in speaking the second language also correlated highly to agreement with that statement. Years of second-language study and relative fluency in the second official language corresponded proportionally to disagreement with the notion that English should be Canada's only official language. In general, there were marked differences between the responses of Anglophones and Francophones and between those of young people and their elders. More Francophones of all ages gave answers we can categorize as "positive" towards the official languages. For most questions, there was also a clear pattern by age, with the 15 to 24 age group being the most positive. The older people were, the less likely they were to have a positive view on the matter. This age correlation showed up most strongly among Anglophones. Young Anglophones generally held much more positive views than older Anglophones. Young Francophones tended to share the positive views of their elders. Furthermore, when asked how useful a knowledge of the second official language was to them now and would be in 10 years, Francophones were much more likely to respond "very" or "quite" useful.

> Commissioner of Official Languages, *Annual Report, 1985,* Minister of Supply and Services
> Canada, 1986. 166–167.

Definition

Using the definition strategy requires in the first instance that you be aware of what makes one thing different from another. Definitions must be precise and clear enough to convey exactly what you are trying to elucidate. For example, to define a dog as an animal is only the first step in what could be quite a long process of discrimination. Definitions may be very conventional or wildly impressionistic, but they must provide enough information to make clear the essence of what they are trying to define. The first example of definition is quite a conventional one that makes use of the strategy of process to define the technique of silk-screening:

> The silk screen is a stencil process, but instead of using cut-out stencils the design is out-lined on a silk screen stretched tight in a steel frame; the colour is squeezed through the silk on stiff cards. After the first colour is applied every trace of it is printed over on the screen with a stop-out varnish; each successive colour is then pushed through the screen and stopped out. When the last colour is applied, it goes through the only part of the screen not stopped out. By this process up to a thousand impressions can be made.
>
> A.Y. Jackson, *A Painter's Country,* Toronto, Vancouver: Clarke, Irwin, 1958; reprinted, 1964. 168.

Although I have described this as a relatively conventional definition, it is also clear that this definition through process is far more detailed than the definition of the term "silk screen" that you might find in an ordinary dictionary. And this is because the person defining the term—A.Y. Jackson—is an artist who has an intimate knowledge of the technique he is describing.

The second example of definition is made up of "fact" and "interpretation." As such, it is an interesting example of the way in which definition can sometimes escape the confines of the cold, uninvolved, and objective dictionary definition:

> The French Canadians (they number about a third of the population) are descended from 60,000 original *habitants* whose roots in France were cut off by the Conquest of 1759. Their involvement with English-speaking Canadians has been less a matter of choice than of necessity. Though French communities may be found scattered from the Atlantic to the Pacific, the St. Lawrence river valley is in the fullest sense the heartland of French Canada. The feeling of inwardness, of a shared and (tragic) history, of loyalty to a common faith and a geographical *patrie* or homeland is very strong among French Canadians. It has enabled them to maintain their unique identity in the face of the most formidable social and economic challenges.
>
> Neil Compton, "Broadcasting and Canadian Culture," *Commentary,* 38 (November 1964): 75.

Try to determine which of the above statements are objective and which are interpretive.

The next example of definition writing gives a good indication of how difficult it is to define the complexities of the human personality. This definition paragraph is interesting as well because it makes use of comparison and contrast to suggest the oftentimes conflicting definitions that various people will arrive at when they are looking at the same person:

> It is possible, on any given day, to hear him described by two equally reasonable persons as a ruthless, cold-blooded autocrat and as a man so soft-hearted that he cannot bring himself to get tough with inept ministers; as a dabbler in issues and as a man who insists with excessive tenacity on finishing anything he starts; as an arrogant, remote patrician and as a person of exceptional charm and sensitivity; as the only leader who can put

Quebec in its place, and as a Quebecer who values the welfare of his own province above all else. As a Liberal insider once put it: "Somebody is going to say some day, 'Will the real Mr. Trudeau please stand up,' and about fifty-eight people will rise."

George Radwanski, *Trudeau,* Toronto: Macmillan, 1978. 25–26.

Classification and Division

Classifying and dividing are ways of sorting human experience or phenomena into orderly systems or categories. When we classify, we group things into particular categories; when we divide we examine the components of the categories we have created. In this first example, the author classifies trees into two types and then spends time examining one type in particular in order to divide it into various sorts of trees:

> To the traveller driving by them on the highway, most trees look fairly much alike, except in winter, when some remain green (the softwoods) and others lose their leaves (the hardwoods). To those who have lived in and by and with the forests, this distinction is only the beginning. For many reasons softwoods have been regarded as much more valuable than hardwoods in North America, and the Northern Ontario forests contain many important softwoods.
>
> In the southeast, between Sudbury and Sault Ste. Marie, and in the far west, between the head of Lake Superior and the Lake of the Woods, the majestic white and red pines were the first softwoods to be cut in great numbers. In the rest of the region, north as far as James Bay (where the forests become less dense because of poorer soils and a colder climate) the most important softwoods have been white and black spruce. Others such as jack pine, balsam, and hemlock, and even some hardwoods such as white birch and poplar, have been of some importance, but the real prizes have been the white pine and white spruce.

Victor C. Smith, "Lumbering, Pulp and Paper, and Forestry," *A Vast and Magnificent Land,* Eds. Matt Bray and Ernie Epp, Thunder Bay: Lakehead University; Sudbury: Laurentian University, 1984. 75.

In the next example the author looks back at his fellow high school graduates and classifies them according to their present occupations:

> Among us, at FFHS, were future leaders of the community. Progressive parents. Reform-minded aldermen. Anti-fallout enthusiasts. Collectors of early French-Canadian furniture. Boys who would actually grow up to be doctors and lecture on early cancer warnings to ladies' clubs. Girls who would appear in the social pages of the *Montreal Star,* sponsoring concerts in aid of retarded children (regardless of race, color, or creed) and luncheon hour fashion shows, proceeds to the Hebrew University. Lawyers. Notaries. Professors and marvellously with-it rabbis, who could not only quote Rabbi Akiba but could also get a kick out of a hockey game.

Mordecai Richler, "Going Home," *Notes on an Endangered Species,* New York:
Alfred A. Knopf, 1974. 182.

Had Richler in this passage stopped to examine the types of lawyers who graduated from his high school, he would have been engaged in the *division* process.

In the final example, the author examines estuaries and divides them into three types:

> Estuaries, even of streams that are approximately the same size, differ enormously, and I think that common sense and personal preference, as well as those two fallibles, experience and local knowledge, should be allowed to enter into the choice of a fishing tide. Most of the small-stream estuaries I know fall into three main types. There are those which run over shallow gravel bars, often dividing into several small channels; those which enter cleanly at high tide over a fall or a rocky bed and cut a long channel through sand or mud flats covered by salt-water except at the lowest tides; and those that enter through salt-water meadows, cutting a long channel between high mudbanks.

> Roderick Haig-Brown, "The Nature of Estuaries," *Fisherman's Fall,* Don Mills:
> William Collins Sons, 1964.

Example or Illustration

All essays worth their salt must provide a sufficient number of detailed statements to elucidate general assertions. One of the most prevalent and effective types of detailed statement is the one based on example or illustration. Sometimes one example is enough to illustrate the general point; more often, however, writers clarify their claims or general statements by providing a number of illustrations.

In this first passage the author gives examples of the way in which Canada can affect the poetic temperament:

> It is a country for poets in other ways too. When first I arrived in Victoria I was taken to a house on Ten-Mile Point, and I wept at the sheer beauty of the country to which I had come. Happiness flooded me like a wave. Travelling through the Rockies, and even riding that long straight road from Calgary to Edmonton, I am awed and dazed at the grandeur of the imagination which is Canada. I have found space here, the freedom to move and, moving, breathe deep. The mountains preserve their solitude. The rivers are copious with life, the shores generous with oysters, mussels, clams and the sinewy symbolism of driftwood.

> Robin Skelton, "O Canada!" *Notes for a Native Land,* Ed. Andy Wainwright, Ottawa:
> Oberon, 1969. 81–82.

In the following examples, the author tries to capture the elusiveness of a particular character by giving examples of how he defied precise categorization:

> But John Hornby eluded all the categories. He had no commercial or scientific ambitions, no will-o'-the-wisp dream of gold or fur. His past was not notably disreputable even though his own account of it had some intriguing gaps in it. He was said to be wealthy—and that at times was about half-true. He was well-educated, a Harrovian, spoke in a soft scholarly voice, was not much given to profane language, and was even by some suspected of being a learned man because he knew a few colloquial phrases

of French, German, and Italian. Professionally, during the ten years before the Fort Norman photograph, he was not an explorer, a trapper, a prospector; he was something of all these, but a caricature of them all. By instinct and habit he was most like a trapper, and could have been a good trapper but for his love of animals and his hatred of steel traps. Unlike many Indians, he never killed except for food; and like many Indians, he was often in the matter of food notoriously improvident. He was not a particularly good shot with a rifle, and was even rather careless in looking after his weapons; yet he managed to keep himself alive.

George Whalley, *The Legend of John Hornby,* London: John Murray, 1962. 6.

HANDS ON: READING INTO WRITING

1. Using our subject and mode classifications (p. 111–114), choose three or four anthology essays that have an *expository* component, and share a *common subject.* Actively read these essays.

2. Answer the questions appended to each essay. Your careful responses to these questions should act as a spur to your thoughts and assist you when you complete the reading workbook entry.

3. Complete a reading workbook entry for each essay.

    (a) Comment on subject, audience, and purpose.

    (b) Identify thesis statement, topic sentence, or controlling idea.

    (c) Comment on developmental strategies.

    (d) Write a summary.

    (e) Write a response of at least 100 words.

4. Once you have finished dealing with the readings on an individual basis, you will have at least 300 to 400 words of informed response on the subject shared by the chosen essays. This body of material will serve as the basis for your own primarily *expository* essay on the *same* subject, which should consist of three or four double-spaced, typewritten pages. Remember what has been mentioned time and again in this book: the techniques that you learn as you actively read will be the ones that you put to good use when you write your own essay. Consequently, you need to follow the various steps we've outlined for the writing occasion:

    (a) Examine your responses.

    (b) Develop a workable topic and thesis in view of your subject, audience, and purpose.

    (c) Determine effective developmental strategies.

    (d) Plan and write a first draft.

    (e) Revise.

ARGUMENTATION

After narration, description, and exposition, we come to the fourth of the writing modes: argumentation and persuasion. Rather than telling a story, describing something, or explaining and informing, argumentation's primary aim is to convince. Of all the modes of writing, argumentation is perhaps the most prevalent, and the one that students will make most use of in their own writing. The prevalence and popularity of this mode can be explained in part by the very nature of the world in which we live: a strongly polemicized one. If we read or think at all, we are regularly asked—or must ask ourselves—about the various merits and demerits of positions, causes, and possible courses of action. Are we in favour of or opposed to nuclear disarmament? In large measure our answer will be based on arguments that we have heard or read, for or against the question. Are the Toronto Blue Jays a better or worse baseball team than the Montreal Expos? The answer to this question will be determined in part by an objective set of statistics. But statistics do not solve all contentious issues, and skillful writers might even use the same figures as their opponents to try to prove the opposite. Should I buy a new car? You may be helped in your answer to this question by reading an article that states the positive points in favour of buying a new car instead of a used one, but ultimately the decision you take in this very personal matter will also be based on the pros and cons you generate as you try to *convince* or *persuade* yourself of the rightness or wrongness of such an action. As long as there is more than one side to an issue, argumentation or persuasion will continue to be an important mode of writing, not only at this stage of your career, but throughout your life. A clear understanding of what is involved in this mode will help you determine the cogency of not only complex polemical matters, but also of shabby and shallow argumentation that is so much a part of the world of advertising and consumerism.

One way of looking at argumentation is to differentiate it from the expository mode. The main difference between exposition (explaining and informing) and argumentation and persuasion (convincing) involves the degree of acceptance the author's comments will have. If you were writing a newspaper article entitled "The Distinctiveness of Sudbury," its content and presentation would change depending on whether you were publishing it in the *Sudbury Star* or the *Toronto Star*. In the first case you could probably assume that the inhabitants of Sudbury accepted your basic views and would read your article mainly for additional information. In the second case, however, you might be up against long-entrenched conceptions of Sudbury as moonscape, and you might have to convince a largely sceptical audience of your views.

A second attribute that has to be considered is the distinction between argumentation and persuasion. The main point here is that you should not, finally, distinguish between them. Although argumentation is often considered to be a mental appeal while persuasion is seen as emotional, an argument that is purely cerebral makes only a fraction of the appeal it could. Similarly, a persuasive piece which studiously avoids any appeal to the reader's mind is little more than a con job. Normally, then, argumentative writing is made up of a judicious combination of both emotion and intellect.

Clearly the essence of argumentation is authorial opinion. In large measure it is the taking of a side or position that differentiates argumentation from all other modes of writing. Notice how the wording of the general subjects in the following two lists can help separate one mode of writing from another:

1. Canadian Fashion in Clothing
2. A History of the Montréal Canadiens
3. Canadian Fiction Writers of the 1980s

As best we can tell, each of these three subject areas is non-controversial. Number 1 could be written primarily in the expository and descriptive modes. Number 2 could probably best be handled in an expository and narrative fashion, while number 3 could clearly be expository. Now notice how the following three related subjects suggest argumentation or persuasion:

1. Canadian Dependence on American Styles
2. The Montréal Canadiens: Canada's Only True Hockey Team
3. Contemporary Canadian Fiction: World Class

The wording of these subjects suggests that argumentation will be the most appropriate mode for demonstrating the validity of the various positions taken. Argumentation, then, is the mode of writing which expresses a contentious or debatable opinion with a view to convincing the reader.

The following opening paragraph of an essay leaves little doubt about the mode of writing:

> Our health care system, while supposed to remedy some of the human ills produced by industrial capitalism, is itself beset with difficulties. We no longer expect that more of the same in health care will produce healthier Canadians. Increasing the number of doctors, nurses, hospital beds and advanced medical technologies has not brought either better cures or better care. Indeed we have discovered that the side effects of many medical techniques are worse than the diseases they are supposed to cure, that the excessive use of prescription and non-prescription drugs constitutes a public hazard, that our system of providing health services encourages the increasing proliferation of unnecessary procedures and an application of technology regardless of its efficacy and of the needs of the patient. Patient care is a forgotten word, lost in the new health technologies of CAT scanners, countless routine blood tests, and endless varieties of drugs.
>
> David Coburn, "Patients' Rights: A New Deal in Health Care,"*Canadian Forum,* 60:699 (May 1980): 14.

It would be naive to think that the claims made in this paragraph would be universally acknowledged as valid and indisputable. Obviously the author of this passage wants to argue the point that "Patient care is a forgotten word." Although many patients who have had a disagreeable experience with the medical profession might agree with the opinion expressed in the opening paragraph, doubtless many others, including a large segment of the medical profession itself, would not. Having made his side of the issue clear in the opening paragraph, the author must now go on to win reader support by convincing or persuading. Certainly, one of the ways to do this is to marshal statistics, facts, and reasonable and verifiable data to his side. It is all very well to make general accusations against an established system; it is quite another thing to demonstrate the validity of the charges with specific facts and clear reasoning. Like all good opening paragraphs, this one makes a series of general claims and indicates the general shape of the essay to follow.

It is particularly important when using the argumentative mode to make clear from the beginning of the piece exactly what the limits of your position will be. Otherwise the reader may be expecting more from the argument than you are prepared or able to provide. In the above paragraph the author has set himself a formidable task: his job is to demonstrate the weaknesses in a highly traditional and generally highly regarded profession. In the process he challenges many of the things we have taken for granted about medicine in this country (see sentence two ff.). Although he uses the pronoun "we" when he criticizes medical practices, he has not necessarily earned our support. Only at the end of the essay will we know whether the use of the word "we" is truly justified. For only then will we really know whether we agree with the author's opinion.

As we argued in the opening chapter of this book, subject, audience, and purpose are central concerns of all good reading and writing. Using only the above opening paragraph, let's try to determine whether the author has provided us with any meaningful clues about these three important areas.

SUBJECT In broad terms it is quite clear from only a cursory reading of this paragraph that the general subject under discussion is medicine and medical care as it affects the patient. Initially we might feel that the author plans to write an expository essay on the difficulties that beset our health care system. Certainly one can see an expository posture being taken in the first sentence. However, when we arrive at the last sentence of the paragraph we encounter the paragraph's true topic sentence and presumably the essay's thesis statement. Clearly the one major difficulty that the author wants to focus on is the problem of patient care, which somehow got lost in the ever-increasing technological wonders that the world of medicine has at its disposal. This particular thesis statement is an interesting one because it uses a structure that is regularly found in argumentative writing and that can, in fact, serve as an important clue to whether a piece is written in the argumentative mode or not. Very often argumentative essays use a thesis statement with a stated or implied "although" clause within them. The "although" clause normally introduces and contains the position that the author wishes to attack; the principal clause of the thesis statement, on the other hand, expresses the position that the author wants to support. In the last sentence of the paragraph, the main clause is "Patient care is a forgotten word," and this represents the opinion that the author plans to support. The implied "although" clause is the rest of the sentence and represents the view that the author is opposed to or wishes to question. To paraphrase this thesis statement, the author is stating that *although* medicine now makes use of many new technologies, blood tests, and many varieties of drugs, true patient care is lacking in the profession. One also might read into this final sentence, on the strength of what has come before it, that the author is seeing a cause-effect relationship between new technologies and the decline in patient care.

AUDIENCE The author refers to "our" in the first sentence and to "we" at other points in the paragraph. Presumably he has all Canadians in mind in these designations, but would it be too much to suggest that he has in mind, in particular, all Canadians who avail themselves of medical services and who are not part of the medical profession itself? Although there is no good reason for it, we do not usually think of doctors and nurses as patients themselves. The author, perhaps taking advantage of this particular way of seeing things, sets up an adversarial situation in his opening paragraph to the point where the "we" and "our" refer to all Canadians who at one time or another have had to put up with the fact that "Patient care is a forgotten word."

PURPOSE Trying to convince or persuade the reader that "Patient care is a forgotten word" is the clear purpose of this essay, but in order to attain his main purpose, the author must also work to persuade the reader of other things. For instance, he must show the validity of the charges he brings against the profession. We must be convinced that "increasing the number of doctors, nurses, hospital beds, and advanced medical technologies has not brought either better cures or better care" (sentence three). Similarly, we must be shown the validity of the claim that he makes in sentence four. In other words, the main aim depends very much on the author convincing us of a number of other bold statements that he makes prior to arriving at his thesis statement. From one point of view, we might say that the author has written the easiest part of his argumentative essay in composing his first paragraph. What now remains is the winning of audience support through cogent and clearly organized argumentation.

Inductive and Deductive Argumentation

Once you have determined your subject, audience, and purpose you can begin to organize your paper. Argumentative organization is usually a combination of induction and deduction. Induction reasons from examples to a conclusion. The writer first surveys a certain number of examples and then makes an "inductive leap" to the conclusion. It is as if everything falls into place all at once. You must, however, be sure to give your reader fair and representative examples to *induce* the desired leap to the conclusion. Otherwise you will simply appear to be "jumping to conclusions" from flimsy evidence. Notice the way in which the following passage builds toward the general conclusion:

> Lingering concerns about Nicaragua's future must be balanced by a realization of where our righteousness about the definition of a democratic government leads. Our own mistakes vis-à-vis the blots in our history of violence, injustice, and discrimination should never allow us to expect either perfection from others or the imitation of our goals born from eighteenth and nineteenth century experience. Nicaraguans and others struggle valiantly to overcome harsh twentieth century oppression. We must allow and sometimes celebrate the birth of new applications of classic democratic principles to redress modern circumstances. This is part of the essential meaning of national liberation to millions of people in the world today. And Canadians should certainly be familiar by now with the complexities involved in such efforts and with the need for consistent domestic and external policies. Foreign policy that does not abide by the same internal principles of freedom and right to self-determination will undermine the real and widespread practice of these doctrines at home.
>
> Marcia Kircher, "Nicaragua: Revolution Plus One," *Canadian Forum,* 60:703 (October 1980): 8.

A reader might be forgiven for thinking that the first sentence in the paragraph is the topic sentence. After all, it is a general assertion that certainly requires proof before we can accept it as valid. But what follows are a number of sentences which exemplify the reasons why Canadians should react tolerantly to the attempts on the part of the Nicaraguans to free themselves from oppression. The final sentence of the paragraph is the one that makes the inductive leap from the examples cited before it. Finally, Canadians are exhorted to show some consistency between our domestic and foreign policies in order to safeguard the very freedoms that others outside our borders are fighting for. Seen in this way, the entire paragraph, including the rather general assertion made in the opening sentence, builds toward the conclusion.

Unlike induction, deduction reasons from premises to a conclusion. The backbone of deductive reasoning is the syllogism—a basic logical structure for verifying the truth of assertions. Aristotle offers a famous example:

> Major premise: All men are mortal.
>
> Minor premise: Socrates is a man.
>
> Conclusion: Therefore Socrates is mortal.

Normally our deductive reasoning does not follow such a schematized pattern. Still, if we take time we can discern the syllogistic structures in much of our thought. We might, for example, come across the following headline in a national newspaper: "Prolonged chemical emissions from factories in Vancouver will cause birth defects." Hidden in this assertion is the following syllogism:

> Major premise: Long term chemical emissions can cause birth defects in nearby populations.
>
> Minor premise: Factories in Vancouver have been emitting chemicals for decades.
>
> Conclusion: Vancouver residents will see an increase in birth defects.

Just as inductive reasoning must have good examples, deductive reasoning needs sound premises. For the syllogism to work, its major premise must be accepted as true. Notice the organizational pattern in the following paragraph:

> Nature dreadful and infinite has inhibited the growth of the higher amenities in Canada. The living has never been easy. The need to wrestle a livelihood from a cruel land has put a premium on some of the sterner virtues—frugality and caution, discipline and endurance. Geography even more than religion has made us puritans, although ours is a puritanism tempered by orgy. Outnumbered by the trees and unable to lick them, a lot of Canadians look as though they had joined them—having gone all faceless or a bit pulp-and-papery, and mournful as the evening jack-pine round the edges of the voice, as if (in Priestly's phrase) something long lost and dear were being endlessly regretted. Or there are those who run—by car, train or plane (flying more air miles per capita than any other people), lickety-split as if the spirit of the northern woods, the *Wendigo,* himself, were on their trails. Nature has not always been an enemy, but she has rarely been something to be tamed either. At best we have exploited her quickly and moved on. No wonder the atmosphere of our towns still often suggests that of a mining camp or the logging drive, the trading post or the sleeping compound. If transportation has been crucial for Canada, and our main-street towns attest to the worship of train and motor car, then communications (more telephone calls than anybody else), particularly radio and television (the world's longest networks), have been vital. It is no surprise when some of old Rawhide's Canadian characters become so addicted to the telegraph key that they can only talk in the dah-dah-dits of Morse code.

> William Kilbourn, *Canada: A Guide to the Peaceable Kingdom,* Toronto: Macmillan, 1970. xiv.

The opening general assertion of the paragraph calls for corroboration and demonstration. The rest of the paragraph provides the details and examples that support the opening sentence. If, however, you do not accept the assertion that "nature dreadful and infinite has inhibited the growth of the higher amenities in Canada," the rest of the argument is of little point. What would have to be done in order to provide proof is to give examples of the validity of the major premise. In other words the author of the syllogism would have to argue inductively until he or she felt confident that the major premise was strong enough to introduce the deductive argument. This mixed pattern is quite common.

Developmental Strategies

Another major organizational decision that you must make when you contemplate writing your argumentation paper is the developmental strategy or strategies that you will employ. For instance, if you want to write a paper arguing that the Toronto Blue Jays are a better baseball team than the Montreal Expos, your best developmental strategy might be *comparison*. If, however, you decide to write on the need for more creative uses of computers in Canadian society, you will probably have to spend a good deal of your argumentative essay *defining* what you mean by the term "creative uses." Clearly, the decision to use one developmental strategy in an argumentative essay does not preclude the use of others; for instance, in the largely comparative Toronto Blue Jays/Montreal Expos paper you might want to use *cause and effect* to explain why the Blue Jays are a better team, *definition* to clarify the type of statistics you are using, and *example* to give specific details in order to gain reader support. Any number of possible developmental strategies can find their way into argumentative essays. Normally, however, one predominates and helps to give your essay a particular shape. What follows is a series of examples of developmental strategies used in various portions of argumentative essays. Notice in these examples how the use of a particular strategy acts as a structural guide for the author in introducing or developing the argument.

Comparison

> As monuments the parliament buildings in Ottawa and the Toronto City Hall have in common the need not just to house government, but to represent it, to create a distinctive presence marked by memorable forms. How this should be done was easily answered when the parliament buildings were rebuilt after the fire of 1916, not so easily by the 1950's when the new Toronto and Ottawa City Halls were built and "modern" architecture was well established in Canada. The greater success of the Toronto building as presence and symbol has everything to do with its distance from the idea of modern architecture which the Ottawa City Hall represents.
>
> Michael McCordie, "Modern Monuments," *Canadian Forum,* 58:681 (May 1978): 26.

The last sentence of this paragraph seems to indicate that in order to convey his position that one thing (in this case, the Toronto City Hall), is better than something else (the Ottawa City Hall) the author is going to use *comparison*.

Analogy

> At present I am developing what I call a "universal" feeling about being a woman. I am what I am because of what I say, how I act, and most importantly, how I think. I feel that a female, whether she is a housewife, mother, or career woman, must do the best she can at whatever she tries.
>
> It's something like Jackie Robinson breaking the colour barrier in baseball. As the first black playing in the major leagues, he had to be "better than the rest" not only for himself, but for all other black sportsmen who would follow him.
>
> Liz McKee, "A Woman's View of Liberation," *Canada and the World*, 40 (December 1974): 23.

In this passage McKee makes a comparison between a woman's plight and a traditionally well-known example of prejudice overcome, namely, the case of Jackie Robinson. Analogy works because it makes graphic through comparison a particular intuition which, by itself, may lack the impact to move people to recognize its significance or importance. In the passage, for example, a well-known instance of oppression is used to exemplify the plight of the oppressed contemporary women who must work as hard in their own way as Robinson did in his.

Cause and Effect

> Modern civilization makes all local cultures anachronistic. Where modern science has achieved its mastery, there is no place for local cultures. It has often been argued that geography and language caused Canada's defeat. But behind these is a necessity that is incomparably more powerful. Our culture floundered on the aspirations of the age of progress.
>
> George Grant, *Lament for a Nation*, Toronto: McClelland & Stewart, 1965. 54.

In this brief passage the author relies heavily on *cause and effect*. Notice how the first sentence boldly expresses a cause-effect relationship: modern civilization, the author argues, results in the displacement of local cultures. A similar cause-effect position is expressed in sentence two. Sentences three, four, and five are rather interesting since they cast doubt on a traditional cause-effect relationship and introduce another to replace or supplement it.

Definition

> Then, you may ask, if my book does not survey, evaluate, provide histories or biographies or offer original and brilliant insights, what does it do? It attempts one simple thing. It outlines a number of key patterns which I hope will function like the field markings in bird-books: they will help you distinguish this species from all others, Canadian literature

from the other literatures with which it is often compared or confused. Each key pattern
must occur often enough in Canadian literature as a whole to make it significant. These
key patterns, taken together, constitute the shape of Canadian literature insofar as it is
Canadian literature, and that shape is also a reflection of a national habit of mind.

Margaret Atwood, *Survival: A Thematic Guide to Canadian Literature,* Toronto: Anansi, 1972. 13.

In this passage the author provides a precise *definition* of her book so as to arrive at an
argumentative thesis statement, namely that Canadian literature is made up of certain "key
patterns" that reflect "a national habit of mind." This thesis statement will, of course, be
proven in the book that she has written.

Example

The best of novels are only scenarios, to be completed by the reader's own experience.
They do not give us feeling: they draw out such feeling as we have. If fiction is going out
of fashion (which is said from time to time but which I do not believe), it is not because
fiction is any worse than it was: apart from the pepper and curry fiction already referred
to, the general level of it is probably better. But great numbers of people find fault with fiction because they do not give themselves a chance to respond to it. It is the way they read
which is at fault. The great success of Emlyn Williams in reading Dickens and Dylan
Thomas to large audiences shows us where the trouble lies. I have seen Mr. Williams hold
a large audience spellbound as he read, in two and a half hours, an abridgment of
Dickens' *Bleak House*. He had their undivided attention, and he read with all the resources of a consummate actor....

Sir John Gielgud moves audiences similarly by reading Shakespeare. Thomas's *Under
Milk Wood* and Fry's *The Lady's Not for Burning* come to life on phonograph records, and
the catalogues of large recording companies contain many examples of recorded plays
and excerpts from books. Ah, you may say, but those are performances by actors. Yes,
and if you want the best from reading, you must learn to give the best performances of
which you are capable, sitting soundless in your chair, with your book before you.

Robertson Davies, *A Voice From the Attic,* Toronto: McClelland & Stewart, 1960;
reissued, 1972. 13–14.

Here the author uses *examples* to demonstrate the point that he wants to argue, namely
that those who find fault with fiction do so because they have not cultivated the habit of
careful reading.

To reiterate: whether your argument is primarily inductive, deductive, or a combination
of the two, you will be able to develop it by employing any or all of the developmental
strategies from narration through to classification and division. Although mention was
made earlier of the mental and emotional appeals being used together in good arguments,
it is clear that certain of the strategies lend themselves more easily to logical appeals while

others favour emotional ones. If your argument is heavily concerned with detailing the consequences of an action, then the cause-and-effect pattern will be appropriate for development. You may find that an analogy is helpful in clarifying a point; comparison and contrast would then be your choice. And of course example and illustration will come into play whenever you are presenting examples, referring to authorities, quoting testimony, or giving statistics. On the other hand, narration and description will be your prime resources when you want to make emotional, ethical, or imaginative appeals. However, since a good writer will want to make *all* these appeals to some extent, most of the strategies of development will come into play in a well-constructed argument.

Argumentative Pitfalls

If the main purpose of argumentative writing is to win reader support for your position, you should do everything in your power to avoid anything that will detract from this goal. Many potentially good arguments have been lost because of sloppy argumentative practices and logical fallacies.

Begging the Question

This often misused term actually refers to the practice of assuming the validity of what you want to demonstrate before you prove it. For example, if you were asked to write an essay arguing that there is violence in the game of hockey, you would be begging the question if you began your essay with a sentence such as the following: "It is high time that the government of Canada took steps to reduce the amount of violence in the game of hockey." It is your job to *prove* that hockey violence exists.

The Post Hoc, Ergo Propter Hoc *Fallacy*

This error in thinking is based on the assumption that because something happened after something else, the first event was the cause of the second. In other words this fallacy confuses sequence with consequence. Many superstitions are based on the *post hoc, ergo propter hoc* fallacy. The young man who believes that his sudden success with women is due to the new sweater he bought last week has fallen prey to the post hoc fallacy. Much television advertising uses this fallacy to convince us, for example, that our lives will change for the better if we buy a certain product.

False Analogy

Using analogies and comparisons are effective ways of arguing only if there is a valid connection between the two items being compared. The hospital chief administrator who insists that his hospital should be run on the same basis as a commercial hotel may soon find himself in trouble with the Canadian government and the Ministry of Health. It is indeed true that hotels and hospitals both have rooms and beds to house people, but the differences between the two institutions are far greater than their apparent similarities.

Generalizations

Perhaps of all errors in argumentation, hasty generalizations are the ones most frequently made by students in their writing. Because students are taught that they must argue their positions strongly, they sometimes feel that using the most inclusive statements will help them attain this goal. In fact, nothing is further from the truth. Overstatements and generalizations encourage readers to question your fair-mindedness and temperance. Imprudent and sweeping accusations or claims put your credibility as an author in doubt. In your writing, be cautious about using words like "all," "everyone," "always," "only," "never," "nobody," and "most." Notice how the following statement makes use of wildly unsubstantiated generalizations:

> Almost all university students in Canada support the New Democratic Party. This is so because students in general are free-thinkers and lean towards the left politically. However, when they leave school, most of these students will end up supporting the Conservative or Liberal parties.

The Either-Or Fallacy

Most issues in our complex world are neither black nor white; rather they are often a middling grey, less extreme than an "either-or" position suggests. In your writing, avoid this fallacy. Sentences such as the following do little to win reader sympathy:

> Canadians should either support free trade with the United States or openly admit their communist sympathies.

The Ad Hominem *Fallacy*

An author who attacks a person, rather than a position, is often engaging in the *ad hominem* fallacy. For instance, if you were accused of stealing money from your company, your main job would be to disprove the charge rather than to attack those who brought the charge against you.

Further Comments on Organization

Sequencing

In writing your basic argument essay, organizing in ascending or climactic order is essential. Avoid at all costs the argument that throws its hardest punch first and then has nothing left. Psychology discusses a phenomenon called the "recency effect," in which people are most strongly influenced by the item in a series that they have seen most recently. The same applies to arguments. Certainly it is good to start forcefully, but then move to establish defining points and gradually develop to your climax. If you have five points in five paragraphs, a possible structure would number them thus: 4, 1, 2, 3, 5 (with 1 being the weakest and 5 the strongest).

Dealing with the Opposition

Any argument worthy of the name faces its opposition squarely. To not do so, to divert your audience's attention away from opposing views rather than to answer those views, is to cheat your audience and certainly not to convince it. If a writer is not prepared to meet the opposition, then the writer's argument cannot carry much weight. A sign of a writer's credibility is a willingness either to acknowledge the rightness of other viewpoints as well as their limitations (a concessive pattern), or to display their weaknesses in a thorough manner (a refutation pattern). In your arguments you will, of course, want to devote more time to your own view than to those of your opponents, and this is natural. Decide what the main opposing points are and counter those—preferably leaving the final quarter or third of your paper for your own points alone. A warning: don't chase down trivial points; doing so makes you trivial in your reader's eyes.

Common Transitional Signals for Argumentation

One of the signs that an essay is written in the argumentative mode is the transitional signals found within it. As has been stated, argumentative essays regularly contain your own opinion plus attempts on your part to counter the opposition. These two elements are often signalled by some or all of the following terms. What follows is the plan of an imaginary argumentative essay consisting of five paragraphs: one opening paragraph, a closing paragraph, and three middle paragraphs which make up the body of the essay. Notice how the transitional signals work.

Paragraph 1: Your opening paragraph introducing the subject and leading to the thesis statement: "Although many studies show, ... it is my view that ..."

Paragraph 2: "Despite the claims made by many people that ..."; your point: "nevertheless ..."; a further point: "furthermore ..."

Paragraph 3: A transitional link with paragraph 2: "Besides ..."; concession to opposition: "Granted ..."; your rebuttal: "However ..."

Paragraph 4: Where you make three strong points: your first point: "Not only ... but also ..."; your second point: "Moreover ..."; your third point: "Indeed ..."

Concluding paragraph: "Therefore," or "As a result," or "We can see ..."

Obviously the above scheme is merely one example of a whole range of possible organizational patterns and transitional signals. The important point to realize is that these signals can help keep your reader on track.

HANDS ON: READING INTO WRITING

1. Using our subject and mode classifications (p. 111–114), choose three or four anthology essays that have an *argumentative* component and share a *common subject*. Actively read these essays.

2. Answer the questions appended to each essay. Your careful responses to these questions should act as a spur to your thoughts and assist you when you complete the reading workbook entry.

3. Complete a reading workbook entry for each essay.

    (a) Comment on subject, audience, and purpose.

    (b) Identify thesis statement, topic sentence, or controlling idea.

    (c) Comment on developmental strategies.

    (d) Write a summary.

    (e) Write a response of at least 100 words.

4. Once you have finished dealing with the readings on an individual basis, you will have at least 300 to 400 words of informed response on the subject shared by the chosen essays. This body of material will serve as the basis for your own primarily *argumentative* essay on the *same* subject, which should consist of three or four double-spaced, typewritten pages. Remember what has been mentioned time and again in this book: the techniques that you learn as you actively read will be the ones that you put to good use when you write your own essay. Consequently, you need to follow the various steps we've outlined for the writing occasion:

    (a) Examine your responses.

    (b) Develop a workable topic and thesis in view of your subject, audience, and purpose.

    (c) Determine effective developmental strategies.

    (d) Plan and write a first draft.

    (e) Revise.

Chapter

5

AN
ANTHOLOGY
OF READINGS

ALPHABETICAL LIST OF READINGS, WITH SUBJECT AND MODE CLASSIFICATIONS

Anonymous, J.H. "Pinocchio Street," *The Literary Review of Canada,* December 1996.
Subjects Popular culture, social behaviour, media
Modes Exposition, argumentation

Blount, Jeb. "O Dirty Canada," *The Idler,* May/June 1989.
Subjects Nature/environment, safety
Modes Argumentation, exposition

Bruce, Harry. "The Alchemy of Sailing," *Maclean's,* July 1973.
Subjects Sport, nature
Modes Exposition, narration, description

Camp, Dalton. "The Decline in Public Morality," *Saturday Night,* January 1981.
Subjects Ethics/morality, social behaviour, changing attitudes
Modes Argumentation, exposition, narration

Charney, Ann. "The Monument," *Saturday Night,* January 1987.
Subjects Social behaviour, heroes, sport, Quebec culture/sovereignty
Modes Exposition, argumentation

111

Cohen, Matt. "Hanukkah," *Canadian Geographic,* November/December 1995.
Subjects Ethnic groups, cultural encounters, family, aging
Modes Narrative, exposition, description

Findley, Timothy. "Better Dead Than Read? An Opposing View," *Books in Canada,*
December 1978.
Subjects Censorship, changing attitudes, social behaviour, ethics/morality, media, art
Modes Argumentation, exposition

Fotheringham, Allan. "Dan George's Last Stand," *Maclean's,* July 1971.
Subjects Ethnic groups, media, heroes, native culture/sovereignty, aging
Modes Exposition, narration

Freeman, Barbara. "'Every Stroke Upward': Women Journalists in Canada, 1880–1906,"
Canadian Women Studies, Fall 1986.
Subjects Canadian culture, heroes, gender awareness, media
Modes Narration, exposition

Frum, David. "Why She Needs the Bomb," *The Idler,* May/June 1989.
Subjects Politics, Canadian sovereignty
Modes Argumentation, exposition

Fulford, Robert. "Charter of Wrongs," *Saturday Night,* December 1986.
Subjects Canadian sovereignty, law, politics
Modes Argumentation, exposition

Gabriel, Ellen. "Kanesatake: The Summer of 1990," in *Nation to Nation: Aboriginal
Sovereignty and the Future of Canada*, Eds. Diane Engelstad and John Bird (Concord:
Anansi, 1992).
Subjects Native culture/sovereignty, heroes, Canadian sovereignty, social behaviour,
politics, law, survival, cultural encounters
Modes Narration, exposition, argumentation, description

Gentles, Ian. "Rethinking Death with Dignity," *The Idler,* Summer 1993.
Subjects Ethics/morality, aging, changing attitudes, social behaviour, law
Modes Argumentation, narration, exposition

Gzowski, Peter. From *The Morningside Papers*. (Toronto: McClelland & Stewart, 1985).
Subjects Popular culture, nostalgia, social behaviour, changing attitudes, self-awareness
Modes Narration, description, exposition

Harris-Adler, Rosa. "Pictures of an Exhibitionist," *Saturday Night,* July/August 1996.
Subjects Social behaviour, censorship, art, aging, changing attitudes, gender awareness,
family, media, ethics/morality, self-awareness
Modes Exposition, argumentation, description

Heintzman, Ralph. "Liberalism and Censorship," *The Journal of Canadian Studies,* Winter 1978–9.
Subjects Censorship, ethics/morality, law
Modes Argumentation, exposition

Keyes, John T.D. "These 22 Minutes Take Hours," *Canadian Living,* October 1995.
Subjects Popular culture, media, art
Modes Exposition, narration

King, Paul, and Barbara Fulton. "Charlevoix, Naturally Quebec," *Leisureways,* June 1996.
Subjects Nature, cultural encounters, Quebec culture/sovereignty
Modes Exposition, description

Kingwell, Mark. "Not Available in Stores," *Saturday Night,* July/August 1996.
Subjects Popular culture, media
Modes Exposition, argumentation

Laurence, Margaret. "The Greater Evil," *Toronto Life,* September 1984.
Subjects Censorship, ethics/morality, law
Modes Argumentation, exposition, narration

Laurence, Margaret. "Where the World Began," *Maclean's,* December 1972. Excerpt from *Heart of a Stranger* (Toronto: McClelland & Stewart, 1976).
Subjects Nostalgia, Canadian sovereignty, social behaviour, family
Modes Description, narration, exposition

Lévesque, René. "Heartbreak," *Memoirs,* Trans. Philip Stratford (Toronto: McClelland & Stewart 1986).
Subjects Canadian sovereignty, Quebec culture/sovereignty, ethnic groups, politics
Modes Narration, exposition, description, argumentation

Milstone, Carol. "Sound and Fury," *Saturday Night,* March 1996.
Subjects Changing attitudes, social behaviour, ethics/morality
Modes Exposition, narration

Onley, Toni. "The Longest Night," *Saturday Night,* February 1985.
Subjects Adventure, nature, survival, art
Modes Narration, exposition, description

Pittaway, Kim. "Sex Offenders: What You Need to Know," *Chatelaine,* March 1995.
Subjects Gender awareness, changing attitudes, social behaviour, ethics/morality, safety
Modes Exposition, narration

Purdy, Al. "Boozy Saddles," *Maclean's,* May 1975.
Subjects Adventure, sport, nature, popular culture, social behaviour
Modes Narration, description, exposition

Richler, Mordecai. "A Clear and Present Danger," *Saturday Night,* February 1996.
Subjects Quebec culture/sovereignty, Canadian culture
Modes Argumentation, narration

Ross, Colin. "The Story of Grey Owl," *The Compass,* Winter 1979.
Subjects Nature, Canadian culture, heroes, ethnic groups, Canadian sovereignty, self-awareness, cultural encounters, family, native culture/sovereignty, adventure
Modes Argumentation, exposition, narration

Schafer, R. Murray. "Canadian Culture: Colonial Culture," *Canadian Forum,* March 1984.
Subjects Canadian culture, Canadian sovereignty, art, media
Modes Argumentation, exposition

Stirling, Jim. "Saving the Marbles," *Beautiful British Columbia,* Fall 1994.
Subjects Nature/environment, changing attitudes, survival
Modes Exposition, description

Stuewe, Paul. "Better Dead Than Read?" *Books in Canada,* October 1978.
Subjects Censorship, social behaviour, ethics/morality, changing attitudes, media, cultural encounters, art
Modes Argumentation, narration, exposition, description

Suzuki, David T. "A Planet for the Taking," *Canadian Forum*, February 1985.
Subjects Nature/environment, ethics/morality, social behaviour, changing attitudes, survival
Modes Argumentation, exposition

Zeppa, Jamie. "Jungle Fever," *Saturday Night,* May 1996.
Subjects Self-awareness, cultural encounters, adventure
Modes Exposition, narration, description

SUBJECT GROUPINGS

Adventure Onley; Purdy; Ross; Zeppa

Aging Cohen; Fotheringham; Gentles; Harris-Adler

Art Findley; Harris-Adler; Keyes; Onley; Schafer; Stuewe

Canadian Culture Freeman; Richler; Ross; Schafer

Canadian Sovereignty Frum; Fulford; Gabriel; Laurence 2; Lévesque; Ross; Schafer

Censorship Findley; Harris-Adler; Heintzman; Laurence 1; Stuewe

Changing Attitudes Camp; Findley; Gentles; Gzowski; Harris-Adler; Milstone; Pittaway; Stirling; Suzuki

Cultural Encounters Cohen; Gabriel; King/Fulton; Ross; Stuewe; Zeppa

Ethics/Morality Camp; Findley; Gentles; Harris-Adler; Heintzman; Laurence 1; Milstone; Pittaway; Stuewe; Suzuki

Ethnic Groups Cohen; Fotheringham; Lévesque; Ross

Family Cohen; Harris-Adler; Laurence 2; Ross

Gender Awareness Freeman; Harris-Adler; Pittaway

Heroes Charney; Fotheringham; Freeman; Gabriel; Ross

Law Fulford; Gabriel; Gentles; Heintzman; Laurence 1

Media Anonymous; Findley; Freeman; Harris-Adler; Keyes; Kingwell; Schafer; Stuewe

Native Culture/Sovereignty Fotheringham; Gabriel; Ross

Nature Bruce; King/Fulton; Onley; Purdy; Ross

Nature/Environment Blount; Stirling; Suzuki

Nostalgia Gzowski; Laurence 2

Politics Frum; Fulford; Gabriel; Lévesque

Popular Culture Anonymous; Gzowski; Keyes; Kingwell; Purdy

Quebec Culture/Sovereignty Charney; King/Fulton; Lévesque; Richler

Safety Blount; Pittaway

Self-awareness Gzowski; Harris-Adler; Ross; Zeppa

Social Behaviour Anonymous; Camp; Charney; Findley; Gabriel; Gentles; Gzowski; Harris-Adler; Laurence 2; Milstone; Pittaway; Purdy; Stuewe; Suzuki

Sport Bruce; Charney; Purdy

Survival Gabriel; Onley; Stirling; Suzuki

Pinocchio Street

J.H. Anonymous

1   History enthusiasts might take some comfort in all the attention bestowed on Yonge Street during its bicentennial this year if only it were dominated less by civic boosterism and public-relations hype. An ahistorical tone was set early on by a bicentennial organizing committee newsletter which breathlessly announced that "On February 20, 1796, Governor Simcoe officially opened Yonge Street." The image conveyed was that of a latter-day politician, scissors in hand, cutting the ribbon to open a new highway as cameras whirred and polite applause rippled from onlookers. Perhaps in the murky shallows of the communications professional's historical consciousness, politicians have always been thus. Just substitute Simcoe's redcoat for the modern politico's suit, and you've got the picture.

2   Of course, there was no official opening for Yonge Street in 1796. Upper Canada was then only a fledgling colony in the backwoods. Sources tell us that on February 20th Lieutenant-Governor Simcoe learned that four days earlier a workcrew of Queen's Rangers had fulfilled his instructions by hacking a trail through the bush from York (now Toronto) to the Holland River leading into Lake Simcoe.

3   This initial misrepresentation was minor in comparison with the whopper used to promote the Yonge Street celebrations throughout the year: the much ballyhooed claim that Yonge is "the world's longest street," extending 1,896 kilometres from Toronto to Rainy River in northwestern Ontario. This "fact" was cited regularly by journalists in their bicentennial articles, but not one of them stopped to explain how it is possible that a very long highway is actually an improbably long street.

4   The claim is patently wrong. Is not a street, by definition, a road through a town or city? That is how most people understand the word. Saying that a highway that extends the length of Ontario is the world's longest street is like promoting an anaconda as the world's longest garter snake.

5   There is no question that Highway 11, of which Yonge Street forms the most southerly portion, runs from Toronto to Rainy River. But it is not a street, by any definition of the term, nor is it the same thing as Yonge Street. One need only look at a map to confirm this point. North of Lake Simcoe, no part of Highway 11 is known as Yonge Street. There are other Yonge Streets in Ontario, including some in Northern Ontario, but none are part of Highway 11.

6   Since only the southernmost part of Highway 11 has ever been known as Yonge Street, the case for Yonge being the world's longest street seems to rest on the assumption that Highway 11 is simply an extension of Yonge Street. But historical evidence clearly refutes this notion.

7   If we examine Simcoe's plans for Yonge Street, we discover that he intended it to be the overland portion of a land and water route between two naval bases: York on Lake Ontario and Penetanguishene on Georgian Bay. By this measure the true continuation of Yonge Street is the Penetanguishene Road, constructed during the War of 1812 to replace the water route from Lake Simcoe to Penetanguishene. In the 1820s, the original Yonge Street was extended northwest around Lake Simcoe to Barrie, allowing overland travel along the entire route.

8   Highway 11, on the other hand, was a twentieth-century creation. The province incorporated Yonge Street into the provincial highways system it created in 1920. It became part of a highway that included its extension to Barrie and a short stretch of the Penetanguishene Road, but then veered off to points east and north, linking up with the Muskoka Road, a colonization road from the 1850s. By the time it was designated as Highway 11 in 1936, it also incorporated the Ferguson Highway, built in the 1920s to provide road access to the resources of northeastern Ontario. West of Thunder Bay, Highway 11 eventually included the Dawson Road, originally a wagon trail that improved a fur trade route from the lakehead to the prairies. In short, Highway 11 simply did not go where Yonge Street was originally intended to go.

9   Like other twentieth-century provincial highways, Highway 11 was cobbled together from a number of roads which were built to serve different purposes at different times. The fact that they are all now part of the same highway is due to the nomenclature of the provincial highways bureaucracy rather than any common origin. To be sure, Highway 11 transcends its component parts by providing a route from one end of the province to the other. In this sense it is more a successor to the Dawson Road and its antecedent canoe route than to Yonge Street. East-west trade that once went by canoe is now transported by tractor-trailer along Highway 11.

10   None of these considerations have restrained Torontonians from promoting their main street as the world's longest on its 200th birthday. The mayor of Rainy River was invited to join Toronto's mayor to launch the bicentennial in Toronto on New Year's Eve. There he was presented with a proclamation which was to be passed from one community to the next along Highway 11 from Rainy River to Toronto. Civic leaders along the way were encouraged to celebrate their connection with the metropolis by signing it. In July, Toronto's mayor paid a return visit to Rainy River. Meanwhile, Toronto's city council wrote to the province to ask that all the street names given to Highway 11 in communities it passed through be changed to Yonge Street.

11   The Toronto *Star,* headquartered at the foot of Yonge Street in Toronto, eagerly promoted the Toronto to Rainy River connection. A *Star* reporter drove the length of Highway 11, taking with him a street sign from Yonge Street in Toronto and asking residents of communities along Highway 11 to pose with it for photographs. He reported that north of Richmond Hill, "most people don't see it [Highway 11] as Yonge Street." But this evidence did not prompt him to question the Yonge Street myth. A resident of Rainy River tried gentle parody to get the point across:

12   Some years ago, there was a move to ask Toronto to change the name of Yonge St. to Atwood Avenue [Highway 11 in Rainy River] but I don't know if we ever heard back from them so I don't suppose they've done it.

13   Still the penny didn't drop. Evidently nothing shakes the confidence of the journalist who comes equipped with knowledge from the big city.

14   The *Star* reporter was certain that Yonge Street extended to Rainy River because he had looked it up in the *Guinness Book of World Records*. It is interesting to examine the origins of this "world record" and consider how it attained legitimacy. Published references to the Yonge Street myth, though sporadic and cryptic, suggest that it is a long-standing oral tradition of Torontonians, a bit of local culture passed on from one generation to the next.

15   The root of the myth can be traced back to an archaic meaning of the word "street." Yonge Street was certainly not an urban street when it was named in 1796. Indeed, it was

little more than a bush trail. However, two hundred years ago, "street" could also denote a straight military road. That was exactly what Simcoe had in mind when he named the route after his patron, British Secretary of War Sir George Yonge, a man known for his interest in Roman roads.

16   Earlier nineteenth-century sources showed an awareness of this etymological distinction. One of the first published references to Yonge Street as the world's longest street was the *Canadian Handbook and Tourist's Guide* (1867) which referred to it as "probably the longest *street* in the world." "Street" was italicized, however, and the sentence concluded "with the exception of the old Roman roads in Britain." The author was taking pains to point out the misunderstanding at the root of a popular belief. A few years later, Henry Scadding would remark on "the peculiar renown which it [Yonge Street] popularly has for extraordinary length" [*Toronto of Old* (1873)].

17   As years passed assertions about the length of Yonge Street shed their provisional character. In the 1890s, Charles G.D. Roberts' *Canadian Guide-book* declared "If we can accept the authority of George Augustus Sala, this is the longest street in the world." Sala was an English journalist who had made extended visits to the United States. As for his "authority," he probably picked up the longest street idea during a side trip to Canada. Although Sala's work was criticized at home as turgid and bombastic, Roberts evidently thought the word of this prominent British journalist was worth repeating.

18   *Encyclopedia Canadiana*, a standard Canadian reference work at mid-century, perpetuated the confusion. After 1965, when a new stretch of Highway 11 opened west of Atikokan, the claim could be made that Yonge Street extended to the Minnesota border at Rainy River. It took a few years for this final stage of highway building to be incorporated into the Yonge Street myth. The catalyst was the 180th anniversary of Yonge Street in 1975. It was celebrated a few months too early, but organizers were probably over-compensating after realizing that they had missed the 175th anniversary. The 180th celebrations attracted attention to Yonge Street at a time when Torontonians were increasingly proud of their city and conscious of its history. William Kilbourn, an historian, heritage activist and alderman, was then in the vanguard of a grassroots movement to preserve Toronto's historic landmarks and traditional neighbourhoods. The local cultural history he helped preserve included the Yonge Street myth. In *Toronto In Words and Pictures* (1977) Kilbourn wrote that "After leaving the city, it [Yonge Street] becomes the main street of several dozen Ontario towns and villages, ending up west of Lake Superior more than 1,200 miles from Toronto Bay." Toronto's claim to having the world's longest street lived on, updated in a popular book by an influential figure.

19   The same year saw the publication of a book devoted entirely to Yonge Street. *The Great Canadian Road* by Jay Myers was an amateurish history which did not bother to make any coherent case for Yonge Street being Highway 11. Myers simply took it as a given that the highway was the organic northern outgrowth of the street. His confidence in the claim may have been bolstered by Kilbourn's writings, but like Kilbourn, he was a native Torontonian who probably first absorbed the longest street story through immersion in local history circles. Myers made international acknowledgement of this community myth his personal crusade. In a concluding chapter, he derided the *Guinness Book of World Records* for anointing Figuero Street in California as the world's longest. He then approached the Guinness publishers directly, lobbying successfully for the inclusion of Yonge Street as the "longest street in the world" in the 1977 edition of the record book.

Since Figuero Street was 48 kilometres long, the uninflated Yonge Street would have qualified for the designation. However, the Myers-inspired Guinness record listed its exaggerated length of 1,896 kms.

20   The major published references to Yonge Street's length over the last quarter century show how the printed word can be distorted through repetition like gossip passed over the backyard fence. In his *Canadian Quotations* (1974), John Robert Colombo printed three early references to the original Yonge Street as the world's longest street. Myers selected the quotations from Colombo that qualified the "longest street" claim the least and reprinted it in the fronticepiece of his book. A decade later, in *1001 Questions About Canada* (1986), Colombo noted the new length accepted by the *Guinness Book of World Records*. To be fair, he did not make the assertion himself, and he took care to distinguish between Highway 11 and Yonge Street. Still, the 1,896 kilometres claim now appeared, whereas it had not in his 1974 publication. And what was the authority for this addition? Colombo cited Guinness, which was convinced by Myers, who had first quoted selectively from Colombo. Thus do one's chickens come home to roost as turkeys.

21   The *Guinness Book of World Records* has continued to confuse Yonge Street with Highway 11 in all subsequent editions. Bicentennial promoters relied on its assurance that Yonge Street was the longest street in the world. Their willingness to accept the authority of a popular reference work published overseas over the evidence that lay before them in their home province was reminiscent of Charles G.D. Roberts' deference to a British journalist on the same subject. Colonial habits die hard.

22   It is tempting to use the Yonge Street myth as a springboard for a homily on the deplorable lack of historical consciousness in our society. The world's "longest" claim is typical of the way in which our popular culture deals with history. Topics are selected and celebrated because they are the best, the first, the oldest or the biggest.

23   The political campaign manager's quest for sound bites is perhaps the best-known illustration of it today. No doubt the information overload of the information age has accentuated such practices in recent decades, but they are fundamentally rooted in human nature. People have always had to simplify and generalize to cope with a complex world. The general public usually gets along just fine with its simplified general knowledge, trusting that experts in various fields will correct any distortions that are dangerously misleading.

24   To an extent, the Yonge Street bicentennial celebrations unfolded in this manner. The "longest street" claim worked inasmuch as it increased awareness of Yonge Street's bicentennial among the population at large. While the city spun slogans and threw street parties, historical groups sponsored publications and symposia which examined questions such as Yonge Street's origin in eighteenth-century military strategy, its influence on settlement in the region, or its cultural role as a centre of consumerism, celebrations, and riots. The only problem was that when the popular simplification process strayed from tolerable distortion into fiction, there was no corrective comment from the historical community.

25   One can only speculate why expert knowledge did not inform the city's promotion of the bicentennial. Academic historians fulfilled the ivory tower stereotype by seeming not to notice or care. Government agencies and voluntary organizations in the field undoubtedly noticed, but probably chose not to kick out the underpinnings of a stage on which they hoped to share the limelight. After all, why stir up trouble over a harmless fabrication?

26   At the municipal level, where direct responsibility lay, there is circumstantial evidence of a behind-the-scenes gulf between the experts and the publicists. In the Yonge Street materials

issued independently by the Toronto Historical Board, the longest street claim is conspicuous by its absence. This suggests that the bicentennial organizing committee did not initially consult experts at the board. Once the city had publicized the myth, it would have been prudent for knowledgeable city employees to avoid embarrassing their employer by refuting it publicly. It may not be wholly irrelevant that the historical board was being downsized and restructured at the time. In a shrinking organization in which jobs are threatened, muteness on such matters has an added allure.

27   The political cost of setting the record straight was all the higher because private-sector partners were involved. Chief among them was the Toronto *Star,* which helped sponsor the city's New Year's Eve festivities. With its location at 1 Yonge Street, the *Star* saw the promotion of Yonge Street as a way to promote itself. Sponsorships of this sort are becoming increasingly common nowadays as corporate dollars are eagerly sought to compensate for shrinking public funds. The cost to the public, of course, is that the sponsor's interests must be taken into account. If nothing else, the lack of a public challenge to the Yonge Street myth suggests that sponsor chill promises to become an increasingly prominent feature of our cultural landscape.

28   Still, factual flaccidity alone cannot entirely account for the way in which the extended version of Yonge Street captures the public imagination. A myth is not perpetuated simply because its veracity is unchallenged; it grows and thrives because it conveys a message which people want to believe. There must be something about the Yonge Street myth that has a special appeal for Torontonians.

29   Naturally, people take pride in being associated with something that is the biggest or the best. This aspect of the Yonge Street myth seems to play to a particular weakness in Toronto's civic psyche—its fabled yearning to be a "world class" city. A place in the *Guinness Book of World Records,* however trivial, reassures Torontonians of their importance.

30   Perhaps the most significant dimension of the Yonge Street myth, however, is what it says about Toronto's relationship with its hinterland. "Hogtown" was once more closely linked to outlying agricultural areas. Now that it thrives as a centre for global financial services and head offices of international corporations, the surrounding countryside functions primarily as a bucolic backdrop for bedroom communities and escapist leisure. Toronto has become an inward-looking city-state without much contact with the rest of Ontario.

31   Ignorance does not prevent it from believing in its superiority to and influence over outlying areas. A charitable observer might conclude that Torontonians' wishful extension of Yonge Street was their way of reaching out to the rest of the province. Yet like U.S. Marines landing on a Caribbean beach, Torontonians with good intentions are not always appreciated by the natives. They are justifiably wary of *Star* reporters bearing Toronto street signs.

32   At its core the Yonge Street myth reflects the imperial centre's presumption of dominance over its hinterland. Of course Yonge Street, Toronto's main street, extends throughout the province! The idea of something from elsewhere penetrating Toronto is unthinkable. Celebrations of Yonge Street's 200th birthday included a limerick contest sponsored by a community newspaper. The final word belongs to the following submission, a rare example of psychohistory in doggerel:

33   Projecting to places far flung
      Toronto's main drag is well-hung

The city's libido

Gave rise to the street so

It should be called Freud and not Jung

J.H. Anonymous, "Pinocchio Street," *The Literary Review of Canada,* December 1996: 2–3.

QUESTIONS

Subject
How does the title of the essay act as an effective shorthand to an understanding of its subject?

Audience
How does a careful, "active" reading of the first four paragraphs reveal a character sketch of the proper reader of this essay?

Purpose
The author's purpose is to respond to the "deplorable lack of historical consciousness in our society." How does he characterize this lack, and what are the main resources he draws on in his response to it?

Structure and Style
(a) How does paragraph 13 signal that a significant transition is occurring between what precedes and what follows it? Briefly explain the shift in content.

(b) Paragraphs 20 and 21 are distinctly more general and theoretical than the rest of the essay. What is their function at this point in the piece?

(c) Paragraphs 22 to the end share a common role in the essay. Explain what it is.

O Dirty Canada

Jeb Blount

1   I used to swim in Lake Michigan almost every summer evening, when I was growing up in Chicago. When I tell this to Torontonians, I get a look that mixes disgust and disbelief. They are amazed that I survived these trips to the street-end beaches of Chicago's north shore. But Lake Michigan at Chicago is remarkably clean. The beaches rarely close, and when they do it is as likely for fear of an approaching sieche—a form of lake "tidal wave"—as from an increase in bacteria from human sewage.

2   The astonishment of my Toronto friends is understandable. Toronto has few beaches, and bacteria levels in Lake Ontario are high enough to cause ear, eye, skin, and intestinal infections. Through the last two summers, almost every beach was closed.

3   When I came to Toronto seven years ago, I hardly gave the polluted waters of Lake Ontario a thought. I was at university, and went back to Chicago each summer. Things

like universal medicare, handgun control, and the lack of random, gang-related street crime, made Toronto seem better than the Windy City. Indeed, for a frustrated, expatriate Democrat in the age of Reagan, dirty beaches and all, Toronto was a paradise. Whenever I got cabin fever, I could go to the Niagara escarpment for a quick dose of fresh, pine-scented air. From Chicago, the largest city on the Great Lakes, it is harder to escape; the inner city blight opens upon mile after mile of suburban sprawl, which merges with flat, dusty, endless cornfields (to be fair: crossed by lazy rivers). By contrast, Canada seems a green and pleasant land.

4   My indifference ended during last summer's heat wave. Although I live downtown near Kensington Market, closer to the lake than I was in Chicago, I did not swim: except in the Atlantic during a vacation. Toronto is now my home, and I begin to realize how cramped and dirty it is. The salty, eye-stinging Atlantic is no substitute for cool, clear lake water.

5   If you ask a Canadian how his country's environmental record compares to that of the United States, he will probably express smug superiority. In the past few years, the Canadian media have stressed acid rain, the pollution of the Niagara River, the prospect of oil drilling on the border of Alaska and the Yukon, and other Canadian problems that can be blamed on the United States. In last fall's federal election, and throughout the free trade debate, the spectre of American pollution was raised. Opponents of the Free Trade Agreement attack provisions for the "harmonization" of environmental regulations and standards. It is taken for granted that the American standards are appalling.

6   It has been in the interest of Canadian politicians to reinforce this sense of smug superiority. While Torontonians endured a beachless summer in 1988, Brian Mulroney attended international environmental conferences in Toronto and Montreal. There, he praised his own government's commitment to the environment, and badgered the Americans about acid rain. In public addresses he congratulated himself for introducing an *Environmental Protection Act,* and setting new limits on the emission of lead. Mulroney's self-praise was largely gratuitous: Canadian lead standards, for instance, remain lower than those in the United States. Still, the sense of Canadian superiority, combined with confusion of responsibility among the levels of government, has made it easy for federal, provincial, and municipal authorities to ignore, obscure, and even abet serious pollution problems.

7   The filth of Toronto's beaches may seem trivial when compared to the depletion of the ozone layer, or the greenhouse effect, but it is a good place to start demolishing this Canadian sense of being holier-than-thou. Torontonians have a high opinion of themselves; their crime rate is low, corruption is limited, and the Mayor likes to call the place "world-class." True, the lake is cut off from the city, and the water is polluted. But my friends are unable to believe that another city might have managed something better.

8   In Chicago, the majestic sweep of Lake Michigan laps at the feet of a powerful skyline. The lakeshore is free of billboards and industry, and it has an expressway that doesn't cut the city off from the lake. Running at ground level through twenty-five miles of waterfront parkland, Lake Shore Drive moves eight lanes of traffic in and out of downtown without disrupting the view. Main streets move under it, and pedestrian subways and bridges link large parks on either side. Trucks are prohibited. The parks contain museums, beaches, a zoo, six large boating harbours, an aquarium, a football stadium, and a convention centre.

9   People can swim along this lakeshore for two reasons: an enlightened city plan and the existence of the Metropolitan Sanitary District of Greater Chicago. The city plan—developed

in the years after the Chicago Fire of 1871 to foster orderly rebuilding and, later, to prepare for the 1893 World's Fair—removed industry from all but the extreme southern end of the city's lakefront and created huge greenbelts along the riverbanks. Chicago was then the world's most advanced industrial city, and was rapidly expanding. Toronto, a city of almost exactly the same age, allowed factories to set up next to the lake, and a high-rise expressway to be built near the shore. Some of the older industry has recently moved, because they are outmoded; but contamination is often left behind. The city's largest industrial area remains along the waterfront, forcing an unpleasant choice between the creation of more parkland, and the preservation of Toronto's economic base.

10   True, Chicago failed to prevent the heavier and dirtier industries from locating by the lake in adjacent areas of northern Indiana; but today, the five million people of Greater Chicago may be envied for their parks and forests. The forty miles of urban waterfront between the Indiana border and North Chicago (roughly the distance between Hamilton Harbour and the Scarborough Bluffs) is comprised of parks, beaches, and residential neighbourhoods. According to the International Joint Commission (the Canada-U.S. body established under the Boundary Waters Treaty of 1909 to manage the Great Lakes), Chicago's waterfront is not a "Great Lakes Toxic Hotspot"; Toronto's is.

11   Toronto's sewage treatment facilities are also inferior. Chicago's Metropolitan Sanitary District was established in 1889 in the wake of a typhoid epidemic in 1885, caused when huge summer rains flushed human waste from the Chicago River (then an open sewer) out beyond water intake pipes in Lake Michigan. Eighty thousand people died. Solutions were, in part, aided by geography. The city sits on the edge of two major watersheds. The voyageurs used the site as a portage between the Great Lakes and Mississippi River systems, and ever since, Chicago has been a major hub of transportation. The "M.S.D." was able to build canals and other works to reverse the flow of the Chicago and Calumet Rivers, and prevent sewage from flowing into the city's source of drinking water. The system was an engineering marvel. In the days before sewage treatment, inflowing lake water was used to dilute sewage in the rivers. When complaints surfaced in the next few decades over reduced lake-water levels and downstream pollution, locks were built to control the flow from the lake, and sewage treatment facilities were installed. Outbreaks of typhoid, cholera, and dysentery were eliminated, and the canal-and-river system improved regional flood control and navigation between the Great Lakes and the Gulf of Mexico.

12   Lake Michigan is now cleaner than it was when I left Chicago. A new system of tunnels and pumping stations, to prevent the overflow of raw sewage during heavy rains, was opened in 1984. Older sewers carry both storm runoffs and human waste, and while the former is relatively clean, the latter must be treated. Most of Chicago's sewer systems are now separate, so that rain water is directed away from the treatment system; but during heavy storms, the older sections of the network disgorge far more water into the treatment facilities than they can handle. Before the tunnel system was built, overflows sometimes forced raw sewage directly into rivers. If the storms were torrential, it was necessary to open locks at the lake mouth to prevent the flooding of basements and low-lying ground. This final emergency measure released sewage-rich backwash into the lake. Now, the overflow is dumped into the thirty-mile "deep tunnel" system, a reservoir four to ten yards wide, three hundred feet underground. When the storm is over, the water is pumped back to the treatment plants. Eventually, the network will contain 130 miles of tunnels. While it continues to be a very expensive project, it was necessary, and it works.

13   Toronto's facilities for sewage and runoff are far less able to cope with storms. Raw sewage is frequently released into Lake Ontario close to drinking water intakes. To compensate for the pollution, filtration plants put more chlorine into the drinking water. New research, cited in last year's municipal report, *Toronto: The State of the Environment,* says the chlorine easily combines with other chemicals to form chloroform and trihalomethanes which are known to cause cancer in animals.

14   Despite long-term programmes to separate storm and sanitary sewers, large combined sewer networks still exist around Toronto. Overflow retention schemes much less grand than Chicago's have been resisted by Metropolitan Toronto Works officials, who argue that the proposals are too expensive, while allowing that the expanded treatment plant that is planned may be inadequate. In effect they dismiss the problem as insoluble.

15   It wasn't always this way. In the twenties, Toronto's water pollution control system was one of the best in the world. Epidemics had forced a clean-up in Toronto, too, but as the city grew, and drugs were developed to treat diseases such as typhoid, less effort was made to treat sewage. Huge new treatment plants were built, but not so huge as the demand. Nor has the technology changed much since the twenties.

16   On the other hand, Toronto has the most sophisticated sewage treatment facilities in the country. More than half of Montreal's raw, untreated human waste flows directly into the Saint Lawrence River. The proposed clean-up of Halifax Harbour would do little more than move the discharge of human waste to a less populated section of the Atlantic shore.

17   While many American cities do no better than Toronto, the standards of the United States *Clean Water Act* are forcing all municipalities to improve sewage treatment facilities. Ontario is the only Canadian province that has taken such action, through the Municipal and Industrial Strategy for Abatement. But the Ontario standards will not be in effect until 1991, and little money is likely to be available from either federal or provincial governments to help pay the cost.

18   A more disturbing problem for Canada is lead pollution. Environmentalists were outraged by the federal government's new lead policy, for which Mulroney expected praise last summer. Implemented years after the United States set strict controls, it is a remarkable example of Canadian complacency.

19   Lead is an ubiquitous toxin that enters the environment chiefly through auto emissions and industrial processes. It is an important paint additive, a solder for metal food containers, and a cheap octane booster for gasoline. A heavy, stable, elementary metal, it is not easily diluted in water or the atmosphere. It does not break down into benign components, and it does not easily bond with other matter to form less toxic compounds. There is no doubt that it is toxic to humans. Unlike some chemicals whose effects are debated, lead poisoning clearly causes brain damage, birth defects, and, in larger doses, coma or death. Several long-term studies in the United States, Australia, Scotland, and Greece, have shown that lead is very dangerous to children and pregnant mothers at levels less than half those Canada now considers safe. Some of the data suggest there is no safe level of lead exposure.

20   When inner-city kids started dying and suffering brain damage from lead poisoning in the fifties and sixties, the United States took action. Lead levels in paint, which in some preparations could reach fifty per cent (enough to kill a child who eats a small paint chip), were reduced. The American *Clean Air Act* also limited emissions from industrial operations, such as lead smelters. The act allows the public to participate in setting standards, and requires strict compliance before operating licences are renewed.

21   Next to paint, lead particles from auto emissions were the leading immediate source of poisoning. Much of this lead enters the food chain by contaminating soil, air, and water. With the implementation of new auto emission standards in 1974, the United States began phasing lead out of gasoline. Unleaded gas was made mandatory for new automobiles, because lead interferes with the operation of catalytic converters, a required air pollution control device. Within six months of the implementation of each new set of lead controls, average blood-lead levels in American children were found to have dropped significantly.

22   The Canadian government was not so swift. Although most cars built in Canada had catalytic converters as standard equipment (so that they could enter the United States), these devices were not required in Canada until January 1988, and many chose to run their cars on cheaper leaded gas. It was not until March 1986, three months after the United States had eliminated lead from gasoline, that Canada announced its programme. The Canadian target for 1993 was the American target for 1986. Last summer, after pressure from environment groups, the deadline was moved up to January 1990. Even after the new lead studies were published, and stricter standards were adopted by the U.S. Environmental Protection Agency, officials of the Canadian Department of Health, and Environment Canada, were reluctant to lower the "level of concern" for lead in blood. (Until late 1988, twenty-five micrograms of lead per decilitre of blood was the level at which the government of Canada would act. Yet the studies suggested that levels as low as seven cause harmful effects.)

23   The Canadian hesitation makes little sense. Most Canadian cars are made to U.S. standards, and most run well on unleaded gas; and much of the Canadian petroleum industry is owned by, or linked to, the much larger United States petroleum industry—which completely retooled for unleaded gas in eighteen months.

24   As for lead in paint, the Canadian standard, set in 1970, is eight times higher than the level allowed in the United States. Paint is less a problem here, because a much higher proportion of older housing in Canada is brick, and many new wood-frame houses have maintenance-free exteriors. But flaking exterior paint contaminates the soil, and interior paint decays into household dust. Home renovation can kick up lots of lead particles. The eventual decline of inner-city housing, and the renovation fad, could cause a serious lead poisoning threat to children.

25   Canada has a funny way of drafting environmental legislation. Most of it is weak, and much is unenforceable. Ministerial discretion is often indicated. Cathy Cooper, a researcher with the Canadian Environmental Law Association, suggests that the Canadian government should simply do a "search-and-replace" through all its environmental laws, substituting "the minister *shall*" for "the minister *may*." In the new *Environmental Protection Act,* much of the power is still discretionary. The same is true for most provincial legislation.

26   American legislation tends to be explicit. Since Congress does not implement the regulations it passes, bills state specifically what the Executive Branch *must* do. The role of the judiciary is similarly defined. If the regulations are not enforced to the letter, citizens may sue; and they often do sue, successfully. Although Canadians may also sue their government if they wish, ministerial discretion makes winning difficult, and prosecutors are subject to the often impossible and always expensive task of proving an offence beyond reasonable doubt. In much of the newer United States legislation, the right to take polluters or enforcement agencies to court is written into the bill. As a result, class action lawsuits have become powerful weapons against polluters of all kinds. The people who are

hurt by pollution—employees of a pulp and paper mill, for instance—need not fear reprisals for speaking out, since the action is taken on their behalf without their direct involvement. Canadian courts are very hostile to class actions.

27   Wide-ranging statutes like the *Clean Air Act* and *Clean Water Act* allow American citizens to have a say in the drafting of standards, and in many administrative decisions. Evidence many be reviewed by citizens in formal judicial proceedings. As a result, large, well-funded private organizations, such as the Sierra Club and the Environmental Defence Fund, have been able to enforce legislation that Republican administrations and the Environmental Protection Agency have been inclined to neglect.

28   Larry Solomon, the executive director of Energy Probe, points out that, "Canadians have more environmental rights in the United States than they do in Canada." His organization monitors Canadian power-generating companies and the nuclear industry. Solomon does not like the way Canadian governments shield industry, particularly the nuclear industry, from legal liability; or the way public priorities such as job creation are used to excuse the invocation of ministerial discretion to bypass environmental laws. Unlike most other environmentalists, Solomon supported the Free Trade Agreement. He hopes the harmonization provisions will force more stringent American environmental standards on Canadian governments.

29   If Canada had legislation like the American *Clean Air Act*, the lead smelter that belonged to Toronto Refiners and Smelters in the Niagara Street neighbourhood might have been closed much sooner. Despite lead emissions that exceeded provincial standards, despite lead levels in nearby soil that required a clean-up, despite blood-lead levels in local school-children more than four times the amount now considered dangerous, and despite the admission of several neighbourhood children to hospital for lead poisoning (one of them in a coma) the plant remained open. Environmental agitators and neighbourhood residents tried for more than twenty years to pin blame on the owner in court, but were unsuccessful; the Province would not intervene. Last fall, the City of Toronto expropriated the land for a road extension: it was the only way to shut the place down.

30   The controversy provided a good example of how the courts view the public's right to know about potential health hazards. In 1974, the plant's owner got a last-minute injunction against a C.B.C. radio documentary that said his plant was responsible for lead problems in the area. The broadcast was interrupted as it ran in prime time. American legislation would have allowed neighbours to present evidence supporting stronger standards during licence renewal proceedings. They would not have had to prove, beyond a reasonable doubt, that a lead smelter was the source of the lead in the neighbourhood, and that this lead was the cause of lead poisoning; probable cause would do.

31   In Canada, environmental licensing is essentially a negotiation between the company and the Province. If the licence agreement is broken, the Ontario government can order the polluter to do something. In theory, the plant can be closed if the order is disobeyed, but this rarely happens. In the past, despite being served control orders, companies such as Inco in Sudbury have been known to continue polluting. The Province, scared by the threat of layoffs, would do nothing, and citizens had little recourse. There is no specific provision for the public to review the enforcement of control orders, and again, ministerial discretion allows the minister to do just about anything he wants.

32   Consider the way the Province of Ontario dealt with another Toronto polluter. Engineered Hotformed Products, a cleaner of industrial fittings, set up in the Riverdale district. The plant heated used nuts and bolts in a furnace to clean them of grit and grime, then dumped the parts in an oil-based quenching agent. The process created clouds of greasy, acrid smoke that

spilled out of the windows and doors of the company's rented warehouse into the surrounding community. There was no smoke stack, and the company had no environmental certificate, a document required for all Ontario industrial operations.

33   Six months after the business opened, and after the Province had determined that the plant was exceeding air quality standards and work-place safety rules, the Province announced that it was negotiating with the owner of Engineered Hotformed Products to make changes. Again, the City of Toronto, which has little if any authority to regulate the environment, ended the problem. Residents begged their local councillor to act; the operation was investigated, declared a heavy industry, and forced to close because it contravened zoning by-laws.

34   Remember: Ontario has the strictest environmental statutes in Canada.

35   Part of the reason the United States has strong environmental legislation is that its federal government has wider constitutional authority than Canada's. Much of the Canadian government's environmental role is to create "guidelines" that the provinces are not obliged to enforce. Pollution was not an issue at the time of Confederation. Federal attempts to write environmental legislation clash with the provincial authority over property, civil rights, "local works and undertakings," and "matters of a merely local or private nature" granted in the *British North America Act*. The 1982 Constitution increased provincial power by adding authority over "the exploration, development, conservation, and management of non-renewable natural resources, forestry resources, and electric energy production." Even where the federal government has clear responsibilities—fisheries, transport, international treaties—its powers often overlap with provincial powers.

36   The Toronto waterfront, for instance, is managed by more than thirty federal, provincial, and municipal departments, committees, and commissions. The federal government controls the port and airport, and enforces agreements with the United States over the quality of lake water. The Province of Ontario is in charge of the day-to-day quality of the water, controls the lake-bed and resources under it, and delegates responsibility to the municipality to build, control, and maintain water pollution control systems. The municipality decides what sort of land use will be allowed on the lakeshore. Indeed, the Prime Minister needs an acid rain treaty with the United States if, under the federal treaty power, he is to legislate effective, comprehensive, national, air pollution standards.

37   Most federal environmental statutes operate under residual authority in the *British North America Act* to make laws for the "peace, order, and good government" of Canada. "POGG" applies in only three circumstances: under a national emergency; where a problem arises that did not exist in 1867 and is neither local nor private in nature; and when a problem that concerns the whole country cannot be resolved by cooperative provincial action. Attempts to interpret this power in such a way to force provincial action could start the type of federal-provincial squabbling Mulroney has tried hard to avoid. It's hard to imagine British Columbia or Quebec quietly accepting federal regulations that would interfere with their right to manage and promote big polluters in the forestry, pulp and paper, or aluminum industries.

38   When United States environmental law clashes with States' rights, Congress still sets the standards it wants and imposes economic penalties on States that don't comply. Under the *Clean Air Act*, for instance, the U.S. government is required to withhold certain grants to them, including some unrelated to the regulation of the environment.

39   The case of the Sydney Steel coke ovens shows how the Canadian government avoids a problem that a province refuses to address. In the seventies, a federal government report

determined that it was dangerous to work near these ovens. The report was seen by both the Province of Nova Scotia and the company, but the federal government did not release it to the public, and did not try to compel the Province or the company to act. Although 64 of the 103 coke oven employees who had died in the last twenty-five years had died of cancer-related illnesses suggestive of the working conditions, attempts to get provincial compensation have been futile. In the United States, lawsuits to make the plant comply with air quality regulations, and to collect damages, would have had a far better chance of succeeding. But large regional development subsidies were being poured into Sydney Steel and Cape Breton generally; neither level of government wanted political pain.

40   It would help if the public had better access to reports like the one on Sydney Steel. Even with improvements in Canadian legislation, governments have little motive to include the public in the process of assessing risk, setting standards, and enforcing law. In many cases, America statutes insist that the public be consulted. The American Constitution and the *Freedom of Information Act* makes government records and documents more available to public scrutiny than they are in Canada.

41   The United States is not an environmental paradise. Wrongheaded Canadian opinions about the quality of American environmental law are based, in part, on an accurate view of the severe problems the laws attempt to solve. Canadian efforts over pesticides, and acid rain, are greater than those of the United States. But even in these categories, Canadians have no reason to be smug—the Inco nickel smelter in Sudbury is still the world's largest source of the emissions that make acid rain. The United States may have larger environmental problems than Canada; but the Americans are in the habit of doing more about it.

Jeb Blount, "O Dirty Canada," *The Idler*, May/June 1989: 16–20.

QUESTIONS

Subject
The initial part of this comparison-contrast essay seems to be a comparison between Toronto and Chicago which would render the title a misnomer. Does the author broaden the focus of comparison and where does this occur?

Audience
Characterize both a reader who would be sympathetic to Blount's argument, and one who would oppose it. How do you know which one he is appealing to?

Purpose
How does the one sentence of paragraph 34 through both its form and content starkly serve to advance the author's purpose?

Structure and Style
  (a) Explain how the final sentence is, in fact, the thesis statement for the essay as a whole.
  (b) Explain the relationship between exposition and argumentation in the essay.

The Alchemy of Sailing

Harry Bruce

1   By March, the bay that lies for miles below our eastern windows begins to break up and turn from white to blue, and move again, and the days lengthen and the sun comes at us from a better height, and I remember that she's not really as dead as a boulder, she's no more dead than the sleeping trees, or a winter bear. She's waiting, and so am I.

2   I begin to fiddle in the basement. I dust off her two small masts, touch things up with Pratt and Lambert Spar Varnish (Quick Drying), take her rusty brown mainsail downtown to get a tiny hole patched. I blow $1.50 on *Yachting* magazine, I go out to the driveway and run my hands along her teak gunwales, inspect her eager bow. I love her plump conformation for the seven hundredth time and I know that, one sweet day soon, she'll be back on the bay where she lives and, together, we'll storm the glittering ocean, and I'll be *alive* again in a way I've not known at any time since winter laid her low.

3   I'll not be alone in this resurrection. In Canada, the sailboat industry is booming now as it has never boomed before. Manufacturers' sales of sailboats have almost doubled in four years, sailboat imports more than tripled between 1966 and 1971, and God alone knows exactly how many amateur sailboat builders were at work this past winter in the garages, basements and backyards of the country.

4   City people are increasingly desperate for evidence that they can be alive in a natural world, and there's a connection in yearnings between the back-to-the-land movement we hear so much about these days and a back-to-the-water movement in sailing craft. Back to Nature. Back to something clean and simple. Back to a life in which the main worries are not other people and what they do to themselves and to us but, rather, the right time to sow and the right time to reap, the proper construction of a root cellar, rounding up a lost animal, how to sink a well....

5   Or the shape of the thunderheads over an empty horizon, how soon to run for harbor, whether you can lay the marker buoy on the tack you're on now, whether or not to reef the main, the fog off the starboard bow, the mysterious breakers off the port bow, the biting flies under the hot sky of a sweaty calm, finding a safe anchorage, what the wind does as the sun dies, and the weather the morning may bring. Sailing reminds millions of men and women that they are alive and, during our moments afloat, a small part of each one of us becomes a Captain Joshua Slocum.

6   Lovers of literature about seafarers will know that on November 14, 1909, the great Joshua Slocum, Nova Scotia-born, aged 65, left the New England port of Vineyard Haven in his famous and beloved little sloop the Spray, outward bound for what he'd told a friend were "some faraway places," and that no one ever again saw either the captain or a trace of his vessel. Eleven sad years had passed since he and the Spray, all by themselves, had made their immortal voyage around the world, and by 1909 they were both in tatters. No one will ever know exactly what was on his mind that morning.

7   Perhaps, somewhere in the williwaws of this strange man's head, there was an obsession blowing and it said the time had come for him to die at sea in the vessel he had come to know as well as any man had ever known anything. Perhaps not. But the thing that is clear— from his classic *Sailing Alone Around The World*—is that, throughout his middle age and maybe his whole life, he never experienced such fear and glory, such peace and high ecstasy,

such visions and grace, such communion with the wild creatures of the seas of the spinning world or so deep and mystical an awareness of the fact of his *being,* as he did during the days and nights of his time alone with the Spray.

8   He loved her, and the meaning of his love is that sailing is not merely a sport; Slocum was not comparable to a Sunday golfer or a lunchtime handball nut; and sailing craft are never just sports paraphernalia. They do not belong to the family of baseball bats, lacrosse sticks, skates, shuttlecocks, Olympic pools and jockstraps.

9   Sailing is as old as riding horses. Men have been going down to the sea in ships to do business in great waters for as long as they've been building roads, raising cattle or writing words; but, despite thousands of years of accumulated sailing lore, no one will ever know all that we need to know about the relationships among sails and seas and winds and the powers of the sun and moon above. No, sailing is not a sport. It's a life....

10   Sailing is active worship, a sacrifice of what we usually are to the children of God we might once have been, a reunion with blowing forces and unknowable chemistries and whirling planetary laws that must surely have something to do with the beginning of everything. Asleep in the black heart of February nights, I have dreams in which I am aboard gargantuan sailboats of unearthly grace and unspeakable power, and they rush me over massive cushions of green ocean toward destinations I never discover.

11   Slocum, says his biographer Walter Teller, was "a kind of prophet of the value of insecurity" and, though yachting experts have described the Spray as an unseaworthy old tub, Slocum himself knew she was beautiful beyond words and on the day he launched her he wrote simply, "She sat on the water like a swan." We can't all sail around the world. We can't all own Sprays.

12   On the days we choose to sail, however, we can smell for a while just a breath of the value of insecurity. We can see the cat's-paw of change move toward us over the water and we can discover for ourselves, again and again, that no well-designed and usefully loved sailboat, no matter how small she may be, ever fails to sit on the water like a swan. (Except when the things none of us can control conspire against her.)

13   An eight-year-old girl, at the helm of a sawed-off seven-foot plywood pram with a pink sail that's smaller than her bedsheet, glides over a brown pond under city trees, through the shimmering reflections of skyscrapers, and across the park and down a long hot summer afternoon of her life. She is messing about with the same principles of propulsion that, each winter, drives tens of millions of dollars' worth of impossibly gleaming yachts crashing and sliding their way through hundreds of miles of tumbling southern seas in the month-long Southern Ocean Racing Conference.

14   The yachts have dazzling equipment, towering grace, great white cloud after cloud of winging, billowing, thundering sails. But they are all sisters to the little girl's pram, and the little girl is sister to the hard-drinking rich men who battle one another in the SORC because all winds are variations of an eternal wind, and those men would have to sail the pram pretty much the way she sails it.

15   It's this wind that brings to life hundreds of thousands of other sailboats, out of thousands of ports and clubs, sailing in hundreds of racing classes, in more regattas than any yachting magazine has ever been able to list, over putrid canals, lifeless reservoirs, greasy harbors, a world of lakes, and among utterly trustworthy tides, currents of treachery, icebergs moving south, buoys, bells, lightships, horns, whistles, flags, markers, hail, warm

REGATTA = COMPETITION.

plopping rain, and out, too, among the strange birds, flying fish, hallucinations and the long swells of the Pacific Ocean at the equator's line.

16   When the little girl hoists her sail, cleats her halyard, drops her centreboard, takes the mainsheet in one hand and the tiller in the other and starts across the park, she is not only joining a fraternity of experience that included Captain Slocum and everyone else who ever sailed a boat, she is not only offering herself to an infinity of possible adventures, she is also accepting the power of whatever laws govern the relationships between people, sails and hulls on the one hand and, on the other, moving water, the location of the stars, and the sun-driven wind. She will watch what she's doing this afternoon. She will consider the influences on the pond because, at the moment, the pond is exactly where she is alive.

17   Sailing restores your ability to hear things one at a time. The city may have wrecked for a while your ear's readiness to discriminate. There is a sound I'll know in my head even when I've lost all true hearing, and it is the gentle, ringing clap-clang of steel halyards slapping aluminum masts aboard boats at their moorings. If you're trying to sleep on one of those boats it can be maddening, but this sound of insomnia is also the sound of evening peace in a perfect world, like cowbells in the pastures of your childhood; and it is the sound, too, of a dew-wet sunny dawn in the fragrance of a port you've just awakened to see by daylight for the first time. It summons you to coffee you can count on tasting better than coffee has ever tasted before.

18   The halyards are a sound of port, like the clunk of ice cubes in plastic tumblers, the creak of rowlocks, or a greeting called across quiet water under the voluminous trees of a friendly shore. The seagoing sounds are more violent: the explosive *thwack* of a balloon spinnaker catching all the wind it can hold in a fantastic split second; the fluttering thunder of a luffing mainsail; the metallic rattle, the smooth, hard, ratcheting click of a jib-sheet winch. There is the sound, in our own boat, of the heavy centreboard vibrating in its trunk— a kind of dull, chattering, humming complaint against the pressures of the sea.

19   Every boat has her unique creaks, groans, rattles and noisemaking partnerships of things; and always, in addition to the wind's whistling affair with the standing rigging, there is the sound of the water rushing against the thin, curvaceous skin in the hull that separates you from the depths. (When our four-year-old was only two and three weeks out of his mother's womb he was a bilious cranky babe, and the one place where he'd sleep for hours on end was down among the gurgling, slapping, bubbling harmonies in the bows of our 24-footer.) If I were to go blind, I'd want people to take me sailing.

20   The sounds are a part of being at the very centre of something important, and aboard a powerboat you do not hear them. Not the ones I mean. You do not glide. You *shake* your way through the water and things that are alive would rather not have much to do with you. "Porpoises," Slocum observed, "always prefer sailing ships." And today, whale researchers out of Halifax track the great beasts of the sea by schooner.

21   Then there are the things you see. There is, of course, no end to them, which is another reason why I say sailing is not a sport but a life. You can't record all the visual experiences of a life, even when they're as moving, as astounding, as significant, as frightening and tranquillizing as they're bound to be aboard a moving sailboat. The things you see are part of a great distance, and all of them swing with the motion of your craft, which obeys the motion of the water, and you can see all of the sky a *complete* horizon, the dome above, the moving ceaseless plain below. Slocum knew.

22   Slocum was well off Nova Scotia, on the first leg of his circumnavigation of the globe, when he discovered the Spray's amazing ability to hold a course on her own and, on the night of July 5, 1895, she was making eight knots, and he was feeling just fine: "The fog lifting before night, I was afforded a look at the sun just as it was touching the sea. I watched it go down and out of sight. Then I turned my face eastward, and there, apparently at the very end of the bowsprit, was the smiling full moon rising out of the sea. Neptune himself coming over the bows could not have startled me more. 'Good morning, sir,' I cried, 'I'm glad to see you.'"

23   It pleases me to live in the province where Slocum was born, to share with the odd fishing boat (there are situations in which marine engines are forgivable) a stretch of the strange cruel shoreline and seagoing heritage of Nova Scotia. We live about four miles from the open ocean on a fjord near Halifax. Our current boat—the one in the driveway—is a chunky, open 18-footer with three loose-footed sails, lots of freeboard and, for her size, marvelous abilities in heavy weather. She must be one of the world's smallest yawls and, though she looks like a converted fishing dory, she sails as an antelope runs.

24   We moor her a few hundred yards from our house and, since the wind usually comes up the bay, she tugs at her float with her nose raised toward the open sea and, all day, she mutely begs us to let her set us free. We buck out to the ocean, tacking between the slowly widening shores of scrubby spruce and bright, bald, salt-scoured rock, and we're still close-hauled as we pass the ever barer islands and the midstream rocks that are deathtraps for vessels and heaven for cormorants ... and then, beyond the farthest islands on the long wave-corrugated skyline, we can see it all, blazing and gleaming under the summer sun, the whole, great, bouncing, marching, magnificent mess—the Atlantic Ocean—and just about then, the boat seems to skip up over one of the more gentle slopes on a roller coaster and we can feel the ride in our stomachs. Then she does it again. She slips up and over the ocean swell and moves on to the open sea, and the feeling is not quite like anything we ever knew in all the hours of happy sailing we spent during the years on Lake Ontario.

25   We reach back and forth along the coast, shuddering at the awful weight of ocean water on rocks, watching it blam skyward like the cold bursts of white firecrackers, and considering uneasily the terrible suck of it as it slides home again.

26   We find secret islands, sweet anchorages in calm backwaters of such Caribbean clarity we can see the fish moving 10 to 12 feet below, and we unpack mountains of impossibly delicious sandwiches, grapes, oranges, soft cheese, and drinks that are exquisite under our own sun. Hawks sail, seagulls wheel and squawk, the ocean roars on the windward shore of the island, and we lie down on the hot sand here on the lee side, and watch our little vessel as she rides at anchor and sits on the water like a swan. Before dark, we run up the bay and home to supper.

27   Usually, we take our three kids on these southbound dashes to the ocean and, once, we all saw two slick black porpoises gamboling and arching and dancing through the cold rollers as though they were lovers in a field of grass, and the sight of them—the big, precious, utterly wild creatures out there exactly where they belonged—shocked us so that the memory is with us now, and for a long time.

28   There was a day, too, my wife and I left the kids at home because the wind was gusting beyond 40, and we got out there a few hundred yards off the real shore, the outer shore, and we saw a sumptuous 40-foot cruising sloop reaching inshore through the long beams of

the late sun, heading for quieter water, and the whole ocean sparkled crazily and threw up such a commotion that this big, prudent deep-sea racer flew only her jib.

29   All three of our little sails were drawing beautifully and our boat charged up one side of the waves and shot down the other with a zest and courage that I was sure could not help but astound the sloop's skipper. (How could he know we were too scared to lose way long enough to reef our main or, indeed, that for a while we were too scared even to try going about so we could go on home?)

30   But enough. You get a sailboat-lover reminiscing, and he'll go on all night. The point is only this: you learn from sailing that, although you must forever deal with forces of wind and weather that predate all memory and still defy our understanding, no two days of sailing are ever the same. If we were capable of measuring the changes, we'd find that no two *seconds* of sailing are ever the same either. Sailing is as infinitely various as the changing face of the sky, and once you begin to feel this you will be able to say with Captain Slocum, "The days passed happily with me wherever my ship sailed."

Harry Bruce, "The Alchemy of Sailing," *Maclean's,* July 1973: 24–25, 42–43.

QUESTIONS

Subject
In the final paragraph of the essay the author introduces a long concluding passage with the phrase: "The point is only this." How does the "point" that follows act as a summary of the subject of the essay?

Audience
The author makes use of a number of particular terms associated with sailing that an audience unknowledgeable about this world might not understand. Identify one of these. Does the use of these terms turn the reader off the essay? Why or why not?

Purpose
It is not enough to say that in this expository essay the author is defining sailing. He is, in fact, doing rather more than this. Of what does this "rather more" consist? Locate areas in the essay where the author makes use of narrative, argument, and the developmental strategies of analogy and comparison. Are these devices used to good effect?

Structure and Style
(a) In what sense is the word "alchemy" in the title of this essay appropriate to the author's purpose?

(b) Comment on the appropriateness of the opening two paragraphs.

(c) How is the final reference to Captain Slocum a fitting conclusion to this essay?

The Decline in Public Morality

Dalton Camp

1   The Canadian Tire outlet in a shopping mall in Fredericton, New Brunswick, is the closest place I can find a good selection of battery-powered lamps. It is also a place where certain lessons may be learned. Living in the country, I am not always aware of the prevalence of shoplifters in the city, but apparently they are everywhere. The stores, and the mall itself, were plastered with warnings to potential thieves. As I entered Canadian Tire I sensed I was among the criminal element.

2   The lamp of my choice was foreign-made, compact, and powered by dry-cell batteries, priced at $19.89, plus tax, batteries additional. Like the Queen—although for different reasons—I do not carry money. I deal in personal cheques and corporate plastic. Gathering up my lamp and batteries, I proceeded to the check-out counter, innocent of the ordeal that awaited.

3   Canadian Tire does not accept out-of-town cheques. Furthermore, among the array of credit cards I offered as a substitute, none was acceptable. Canadian Tire accepts only Canadian Tire credit cards.

4   Not to worry: you can qualify almost instantly for a Canadian Tire credit card by going to another counter and filling out a form. But what appeared to be a ready and congenial solution to the impasse was not. The second question asked on the form was the name of my present employer—difficult to answer, since I have none. The third question—how long employed with present employer?—was impossible. Further questions were outrageous: what was my wife's name, that of *her* employer, and for how long had she been employed by him? I asked to see the manager.

5   The youth appearing before me in the guise of the manager plainly was not: evidence of acne, a stock-room coat beneath an inscrutable smirk. Detecting trouble, he asked what mine was.

6   "What possible business is it of Canadian Tire where my wife works?"

7   By way of reply, a shrug. Then: "If you don't wanna fill out the form, don't fill it out. Sup to you." But, obviously, no form, no plastic; no lamp either.

8   I departed the premises. Any hardware store would do as well. Indeed, the hardware store, an old family firm, had the same lamp, the same batteries, at a comparable price. No inhibitions about credit cards either—all were welcome. The transaction was swiftly completed—almost.

9   "What's your telephone number?" asked the salesperson.

10   "I don't give it out."

11   Though I have seldom been more serious, this produced only a distracted smile.

12   "That's okay," she said, brightly. "Could I see your driver's licence for identification?"

13   "I don't have a driver's licence," I told her. "I travel on horseback. Would you like to know the name of my horse?"

14   "C'mon," she pleaded, "just your telephone number will do."

15   So I lied. "The number is 488"—that much was true—"9992." That much wasn't. But it satisfied her. And I got my lamp.

16   The moral of the story is, of course, never leave home without your identity, the minimal proof of it being your licence, telephone, and SIN numbers. Veterans of the last war will remember their catechism: if captured by the enemy, give only your name, rank, and number. In the jungle warfare of the plazas, who needs a name?

17   A journalist I know, assigned to write a story on the operations of the credit bureau in his community, telephoned to arrange an interview with the manager. He was immediately asked for his social insurance number, which he declined to give. Arriving for the interview, he asked the manager the reason for his request.

18   "So I could look up your credit rating," the man said, laughing, "and see what kind of guy you are."

19   I suspect some correlation between the burgeoning traffic in numbers, files and data banks, and the collapse of public morality. Such is not, of course, endemic to the marketplace, but it is where the corruption of interpersonal relations has become common to the most ordinary of transactions. Testimony to the state of public morality is evidenced daily on the pedestrian rounds of the shopping public. There isn't any.

20   When the subject of morality comes up—which is not often these days—people tend to invert the word to immorality, leading to thoughts of sexual promiscuity. Since it is impossible to quantify promiscuity in an age of avid permissiveness, there is really not much to think about, other than to marvel that celibacy and virginity were once considered importantly virtuous.

21   But there *was* a public morality, one that governed our conduct at least as much as did the law of the land. The wonder of it was that we largely subscribed to it, as did everyone else we knew or would want to know. It allowed us to live in a state resembling harmony by accepting a set of assumptions about one another that were mutually reassuring: that a man's word was his bond, that another's property and privacy were inviolate, that there existed a vast majority of fellow citizens who prized their reputations as highly as we valued our own. There were concomitant norms for social conduct, speech, dress, and general decorum which, taken together, made the behaviour of most of us comfortably predictable.

22   Perhaps the essential ingredient of that public morality was a compelling need for respectability. It now seems quaint, and somehow touching. Still, it encouraged a society, in which trust was pervasive, to function with a certitude that can only be regarded as admirable. Anyway, it is lost. A man's word is no longer enough; disregard for property varies from indifference to wantonness, while the intrusion upon privacy has become relentless. Public morality, as some of us knew it, has gone the way of iambic pentameter and the Ten Commandments.

23   The problem of contemporary society is not that it is so relentlessly impersonal (in a peculiar way, it isn't), but that all members of it are suspect. Day after day, in uncounted, numbing, trivial incidents, we are confronted by the presumption of guilt—as potential forger, bankrupt, thief, counterfeiter, spendthrift, or credit risk—and, day after day, we are obliged to produce evidence of our innocence. To be dealt with routinely as untrustworthy or unreliable is immediately insulting and inevitably demeaning. It would be more tolerable if we were programmed to produce dossier material at the push of a button, like bloodless robots.

24   What has been lost is considerably greater than anything gained, which cannot be much more than the peace of mind of American Express or Visa. The common view that governed society for so long—the presumption that most people were reliable, honest, trustworthy, sharing a common moral earnest of right and wrong—has been succeeded by the

revised presumption that there are simply too many untrustworthy people about to trust anyone. Of all the values we have lost, perhaps the greatest has been face value.

25   Face value is still enjoyed by celebrities; and yet, recollection persists of life in a community in which everyone must either have been a celebrity of sorts—unlikely—or possessed face value sufficient to obtain credit and to negotiate countless other transactions supported only by one's persona and one's word. I once attended a social function at which a woman friend of mine arrived on the arm of a man who had recently been paroled after serving a sentence for murder. She and I discussed at some length the considerable difficulties encountered by her friend in finding suitable employment, a predicament as regrettable to me as it was comprehensible. What remains incomprehensible are the enormous numbers of blameless, law-abiding people whose personal integrity and honesty are routinely discounted for the lack of prima facie evidence of both.

26   If one is not to be recognized on sight as being worthy of trust—or even given the benefit of doubt—how is it possible that most of us could ever become deserving? The truth is that a reputation for responsibility, which was formerly publicly acknowledged, is now a matter of secrecy, something stapled to one's social insurance number in a credit bureau. As a consequence, many of us truly do not give a damn about how we are regarded, leaving such personal credentials as reliability and responsibility to the mysteries of unseen computers. A generation ago, people considered such intangibles vital.

27   Perhaps the recognition of a public morality existed merely as part of a simpler, smaller universe. Perhaps the absence of it is part of our world's gathering size and complexity. We could, then, concede any possibility of a revised public morality, and yield to the prospect of living in a darkening world of infinite scepticism devoid of conscience.

28   The grounds for suspicion and caution are confirmed in the grim discrepancies between sales and inventory; in those long tables, resembling logarithms, recording credit cards stolen, strayed, or withdrawn; in the burgeoning business of collection agencies; in the rising numbers of repossessions, and in the accumulation of cheques marked n.s.f. Unquestionably, one's view of human nature, and of such niceties as public morality, are not impervious to the influence of direct experience.

29   Money, having lost its value, may no longer be the root of all evil: credit has taken its place. The impulse to buy now and pay later admits to a belief that whatever we deny ourselves today will surely cost more tomorrow. Those who still believe in the homely wisdom of living within measurable means can only be regarded as eccentrics. It is not greed or rampant materialism that motivates so many of irresponsibility; it is the realization that money is now the least durable of life's possessions.

30   Many years ago, as a young Liberal, I led the fight against a resolution, moved at a party conference, advocating legalized lotteries. My strongest debating point was to cite in parts of the world where lotteries were legal—Italy, France, South America, Cuba—a certain manifestation of economic injustice, an unstable currency, and a hopelessly depressed lower class. The motion was defeated, though not nearly so overwhelmingly as it would carry were it moved today. The argument against is no longer valid: in a recent essay on neoconservatism Lewis Lapham, the editor of *Harper's,* put it very well: America (like Canada) is changing from an investor society to a speculator society. The only good buck is the fast one, free of tax.

31   Carl Beigie, president of the C.D. Howe Institute, has pleaded for reduced consumption: "The main reason we have to decrease consumption," he says, "is that it's necessary to increase investment, which determines tomorrow's output." Fat chance. As Lapham pointed

out, when inflation reaches a rate of fifteen per cent—a prospect not far distant—you will need to double your income in four years to remain as solvent as you were in the first year—an achievement, for most, that is scarcely realistic. Instead, for the average consumer-taxpayer-citizen, a lottery ticket looks to be ultimately the best hope against terminal overdraft.

32   Public morality may be impossible to sustain in a world that has lost its sense of posterity. Since so many of us live as though there were no tomorrow, the notion of posterity becomes too painful to contemplate—even though, without it, we are left simply in hock, and without plan or purpose. The cruellest deprivation created by inflation has been the loss of posterity as a fundamental consideration in public policy and private life.

33   In the past, the generally accepted relationship between citizen and government was based on the rule-of-thumb objective of the greater good for the greatest number. In the gravity flow between taxes paid and benefits received, there was for many years the illusion of a perfect symbiosis. But with the government now spending some forty per cent of the nation's productivity, and much of that outlay invisible, the relationship seems to have become outrageously parasitic. To add injury to insult, any who manage to save, or who invest in government paper, end up losers, their principal withered by inflation, the yield nicked by the tax-collector.

34   The traditional allegiance of citizen to government has vanished; trust and confidence have been replaced by a brooding suspicion and growing hostility. And as between government and governed, the feeling appears mutual: the mistrust that is the ethos of the marketplace flourishes nowhere more than at Revenue Canada.

35   In 1967–68, Revenue Canada investigated 289 cases of suspected tax evasion, recovering $13-million in unpaid tax as the result of its exertions. In 1979–80, Revenue Canada investigated 949 suspected cases of tax evasion; the yield in tax recovery, fines, and penalties amounted to about $37-million. Along the way, the department's investigative staff has grown from 200 to more than 500—further evidence to sustain the widespread belief that crime increases in direct proportion to the numbers employed to detect it.

36   These figures may not seem remarkable, bearing in mind that there are 12.5-million Canadian taxpayers whose voluntary tax payments total $26-billion a year. But, as a genial spokesman for Revenue Canada told an enquirer, the department's investigative branch "is only scratching the surface."

37   Last year, scratching the surface produced a total of $488-million for all tax recoveries, including those resulting from fraud, evasion, and human error. A tax investigator for the department reckons that it loses $2-billion each year in revenues from those either smart and lucky enough to cheat the system successfully, or from those blissfully unaware they are doing so.

38   At Revenue Canada, the difference between fraud and human error is blurred. The majority of tax evasion investigators don't go to court because there isn't enough evidence to prove fraud. Or enough courts, either. Where discovered, the tax due gets paid, along with the appropriate penalty. The emboldened cheater and the merely confused usually enjoy the same summary justice. In the eyes of the beholder, there is no difference.

39   The perception of government as adversary, familiar enough to tyrannies, is novel to democracy, just as an unspoken, casual anarchy is peculiar to a society supposedly governed by the rule of law. But when the currency is debased and mistrust is made a way of life, what is left of public morality must be enforced in law, by statute, ordinance, and regulation—so many of them that no citizen could be aware of them all.

40   This helps explain why law-abiding people are wary of the police and terrified of the courts. For most, acquaintance with law enforcement extends only to the Motor Vehicle Safety Act and not much beyond. But it is enough: one need only blunder into a speed trap, be ambushed by a ghost car, or pulled over at a check-point, to comprehend the real limits to such illusory rights as protection against entrapment, self-incrimination, search, seizure, and arbitrary judgement. (My God, one wonders, what must it be like for some wretch apprehended for a serious offence?)

41   We are being nudged toward a greater compliance with the law by the strategy of encouraging the stark fear of it. We have become accustomed to living in the shadow of surveillance: routinely interrogated, monitored, detained, searched. Considerations of personal integrity, public morality, right and wrong, become ephemeral. Importantly, we need no longer think for ourselves: a sense of what is right or wrong is no longer a matter of private conscience or broadly accepted public covenant, but the endless business of legislators, magistrates, attorneys, censors, and the police. What is right is whatever is lawful; what is lawful is whatever goes unnoticed.

42   The citizen who won my vote as 1980 man of the year was a fellow in Telkwa, B.C., who refused to accept a piece of certified mail at the post office because his name had been spelled wrong. He then failed to respond to an order to appear in court, being otherwise occupied owing to the pressure of business. He was subsequently waited upon by six officers of the RCMP, each dressed in riot gear, plus two sheriffs, a conservation officer, and a police dog. They removed him from his home in handcuffs and jailed him for two hours, after which a judge fined him $400.

43   The registered letter had been a call for jury duty. He said he told the sheriff he would be happy to serve if they'd only spell his name right. The judge said he was making a mockery of the law by using a technicality. It provides an example of our condition: we are all only approximately who we think we are; the distinction between someone named Camp and one named Cmpr is a technicality, and ought to be as trifling to both of them as to the sheriff.

44   It could be said that we are not as moral as we used to be, but then we never were. More than a hundred years ago, George Eliot's tormented hero of *Middlemarch* discovered the ambiguities of morality:

45   Our deeds still travel with us from afar,
And what we have been makes us what we are.

46   Homily, it is, but now not exactly true—no one who has known this country for what it was would easily recognize it for what it has become. We have not become the sum of our history; we resemble something like the denial of it. Compassion, the willingness to share, tolerance and trust, respect for people and their property, the belief that ends and means are ethically compatible—none of these remembered parts of our public morality has survived.

47   Once, one of the strongest words in the language was "liar." To cover the human capacity for dissembling, we recognized the social necessity of "white" lies. But lying, like cheating, was anathema to the public morality, and perhaps the most conclusive evidence of morality's decline is that lying has become global, epic, persistent, pervasive. A charge that would have been a fighting word a generation ago—that of liar—has been defused of meaning by the generally accepted view that truth has become debatable, subjective, multi-sided, a matter of opinion, unnecessary, and more often than not dangerous. The Gulf of Tonkin resolution, which gave Lindon Johnson a free hand in Vietnam, was inspired by a lie; Richard

Nixon's covert invasion of Cambodia was covered by lies; the chances are good that Canadians will never know the truth about the "apprehended insurrection" in 1970, an event surrounded by lies.

48   The shock of one's value system by the legitimizing of untruths depends on one's age; preference for the truth may be a generational phenomenon. Those raised by television come to know early in life how far removed its illusion is from truth. No one who has reached the primary grades believes "Mean Joe" Greene would give his shirt for a bottle of pop, any more than they would expect to meet Joe Namath and find him reeking of Brut. But it doesn't matter whether they believe it or not; we are not dealing any longer with home truths but with palatable ones. Viewers may watch *the fifth estate*, Oral Roberts, or the prime minister of this country and decide for themselves how much, if anything, they see or hear they need accept as gospel.

49   Some of us, raised by the makers of Camel cigarettes in the belief there was "not a cough in a carload," continue to resist the earnest if awkward blandishment of revisionist opinion that "danger to health increases with amount smoked." We remain ruefully chagrined even though the possibility exists that what would now be irresponsibly dishonest was, in its day, nothing more than puffery.

50   The youthful television generation has acquired a scepticism beyond its years. And while it can be manipulated even as its elders, it is truly not deceived. What our children know, which we happily did not, is that they live in a world of deception and illusion. For them, the TV pitchman's crafts are a part of life. With the added inheritance of our disillusionment, they will not be a generation easily given to trust or moved to revive a public morality.

51   Our public morality declined with the change of both perspective and perception. As to perspective, we no longer look up to anyone; as to perception, we no longer value the role and function of so many who once warranted our respect because of what they did. A generation ago, there *were* those we considered pillars of society, a term in present disuse. They included teachers, physicians, clergymen, politicians, members of the military, the police—even the postman!—and others whose responsibilities bore upon our needs. It now seems so long ago as to be Dickensian, but there were many who evoked a respect not untinged with gratitude. At the root of it, I suppose, was the recognition of selflessness and sacrifice. We trusted teachers to train our children; we knew that doctors not only made house calls but also frequently went unpaid; we felt reassured seeing the cop on his beat, and we were convinced that all of them were motivated by an altruism fundamental to the existence of a public morality.

52   In that altruism there was more than a little injustice, and many were as exploited as they were venerated. Recently, I looked out from an office window at Queen's Park, Toronto, upon a crowd of striking teachers, howling down the minister of education while the police stood by awaiting contingency. It struck me that each of those forces gathered below in the obligatory acting out of their respective roles had improved their lot in everything but public esteem. Presumably, if the price of such esteem is insecurity and a reduced income, then a great majority would say to hell with it. And yet, the understood presence of human pillars in the structure of society once truly held it together: they were a presence beyond price, beyond anything any of us could afford.

53   I have left the politician to the last, as would anyone. Unlike that of their constituents, the lot of politicians has steadily improved over the past decade. They have continued to earn more, accrue more, and gather more perquisites unto themselves than any other class or

kind of Canadian, save professional hockey players. Elected politicians have established themselves as a brahmin caste. It cost today's taxpayers almost $100-million a year merely to attend to the administrative needs of 282 members of the House of Commons. Politics, which used to be considered a form of public service with recognized uncertainties and slight material benefits, is now a full-time job, and its rewards are being scaled to the premise that it's a life's work.

54   Years ago, after the war and the election of a Labour government in Britain, I listened to Beverley Baxter lamenting the fact that members' indemnities had just been increased to £1,000 a year. A Canadian expatriate and professional journalist, himself a member of parliament in Westminster, Baxter expressed the fear that people would inevitably be drawn to politics "because there was money in it." Bloated with idealism, I expressed vigorous disagreement.

55   Years later, however, during a leadership struggle in the Progressive Conservative Party, a Tory MP came to me in tears, saying that if John Diefenbaker were deposed as the party's leader, he himself would lose his seat—his premise being that only Diefenbaker had elected him. "And then what are you going to do for me?" he asked. "Can you find me another job paying $12,000 a year?" He is still in the House.

56   Among the considerations a prime minister or premier must now give to the exercise of his prerogative of dissolution is its possible effect on the morale of his caucus. He will know that foremost in the minds of many of his supporters is the impact an election might have on their pensions. More than one quiet election campaign has been waged for an incumbent based on an appeal for support because, if defeated, he would not qualify for pension benefits.

57   Perhaps the ultimate wisdom was that of Robert Manion, who advised "no man should go into politics unless independently rich or independently poor." But it remains surely one of the anomalies of the welfare state that none have benefitted so much from its generous impulses as the architects of it. Behind the public spectacle of ritual partisan controversy, notably in the federal parliament, there has developed a broad and agreeable consensus to strengthen and improve upon the prospects of incumbency of all honourable members. There cannot be much left for them to achieve in that respect, other than tenure.

58   None of this matters much these days to a citizenry drained of its capacity for righteous indignation. There are other distractions than politics—which have become, anyway, an abstraction. While the world shrinks, the distance from Ottawa grows more distant. Alienation is not quite the word for the prevailing public mood—incredulity might be better. Paradoxically, Ottawa was close to us when it seemed more remote. When it was a mystery, we believed in its ameliorating powers. Our allegiance required our trust, and at the heart of our trust was our need for order, stability, justice, and security. For these, really, there is still nowhere else to turn.

59   Canadians long enjoyed the politics of great adventures and grand designs. Our early politicians were nation-builders, the later ones ambitious to create a new liberal society; even Diefenbaker proclaimed a vision. Canadians went to the polls to reconfirm a moral obligation as their brother's keeper in elections that were celebrations of yet another harvest of shared abundance.

60   Now that it's over, and the politics of scarcity has begun, few know or remember how much has been lost. Without trust, allegiance is gone: there are neither followers nor leaders, but government and governed. Present-day politics lack the once-familiar dimension

of either adventure or grand design, bearing merely the imprint of the stratagems of underlings in a coarse struggle for purposeless power. (We are currently led by a man who became the first leader to be muzzled in a national campaign by his retainers—"We low-bridged him," as one of his key advisers put it. Imagine Jack Pickersgill saying that of Mackenzie King. Or Allister Grosart of John Diefenbaker.)

61   During 1979–80, in less than a year, our political parties spent $21.5-million in two election campaigns, about seventy per cent of that for advertising, mostly television. Seventeen years earlier, the expenditure of $600,000 for campaign advertising would have been considered adequate and, in my experience, all there was to be had anyway. In each of the two most recent elections, the party that spent the most lost: there is no substantive evidence that any of this lavish outlay had any influence upon the result. Indeed, the common public reaction was one of disbelief, since the bulk of the advertising was negative, destructive, and degrading.

62   A public morality presumed self-imposed limits to public behaviour, acknowledging the requirement of restraint as a moderating influence in partisan politics. We have learned from experience—or thought we had—that the risk of excess increases with the scale of the enterprise and size of the stake. In the increasing frenzy that marks the present wars among Canada's political parties, in which incivility and insult are packaged by professionals for home delivery, a bemused citizen must wonder what the struggle has come to be about and what the prize could be.

63   The citizen will not see in the struggle any reflection of his own interests and concerns. If he is aware that all this artful manipulation and tugging at his fears and apprehensions is meant to influence his opinion (perhaps to reinforce it), he will be right, but no wiser. Like government itself, the business of politics is beyond him or, if not that, beneath him.

64   We no longer vote for what we get, but for whom; it has been more than twenty years since a major political party produced a serious statement of its policy intentions and, being elected, acted upon it. I am not so naïve as to believe that politics ever was or will be the activity of solely virtuous people, that promises made must be promises kept. But what sustained our confidence in political parties and in public men was the belief that the contest was not merely between them, but about us.

65   What has been will likely never be again; anyway, nostalgia may well exaggerate the past, as it concedes the present and resigns the future. Alvin Toffler, the futurist, pleads for recognition of "new realities," urging that we redesign our political institutions. Seeing what remains of them, we might as well.

66   "I really believe," Toffler has said, "that unless each of us now begins thinking about and imagining alternatives to present political structures, we will land in something far worse than runaway inflation or an economic depression." The "something far worse" could be to continue to live in a society in which there is neither mutual trust nor shared values, and no public morality to maintain them.

67   Much of our present troubles are of our own doing: a despairing passivity; an insensitivity to insult and arrogance, almost as though we had been immunized against them; and a growing capacity for cynicism to fill the void of a lapsed capacity for indignation.

68   "In the meantime," as Albert Camus wrote of France in its post-war moral depression, "we must live, we must create in the storm ... we must now stop commenting on our time in order to give it form."

69   Our own history indicates that we as a society have been at our best when so much else seemed at its worst. For a brief while, during the anxious suspense of the Québec referendum, one sensed the disciplined restraint and tempered resolve of which we are capable. That it swiftly passed is less important than its rediscovery: we can respond to challenge.

70   It is possible to say, without recrimination, that the failure of our political institutions to inspire either trust or respect has been in large measure induced by the inadequacy of our leadership. If we have left too much to the politicians—and to journalism—and assumed nothing of the burden ourselves, it is fair to say that so long as our leaders appeal to our opinions, rather than to our values, we will have little to say, and less to do. But it is ironic that while politics has been practised in an echo-chamber—politicians repeating majority opinion as their own—the public opinion of politics has plummeted.

71   Toffler proposes we rethink our position, which might be, for us, a first act of creation in our storm. The evidence is ample that the nation cannot be led unless it is inspired to follow, and it will not be inspired to follow until trust and confidence have been resumed in its leadership. Our leadership is exhausted of its moral credit. Only new leadership is sufficient to the task of restoring a sense of moral authority to government, without which there can be no public morality. In the meantime, our society will remain bereft.

Dalton Camp, "The Decline in Public Morality," *Saturday Night,* January 1981: 26, 28–31.

QUESTIONS

Subject
Decide what the author means by public morality and list several examples he gives to demonstrate its decline.

Audience
Explain how Camp's sentence, "Public morality, as some of us knew it, has gone the way of iambic pentameter and the Ten Commandments," gives clues as to the type of audience for whom this essay is written.

Purpose
The author's purpose is to argue a position in order to convince his audience of the vitality of his claim that public morality is in decline. How does illustration serve to support his argumentative strategy?

Structure and Style
(a) How does the Canadian Tire anecdote serve as a good introduction to Camp's essay?

(b) Does the fact that the author deliberately gives a wrong telephone number to a clerk subvert his strong moral stance in the essay?

(c) Is Camp's the only voice of authority in this essay? If not, whom does he call upon to support his view and why does he not invoke them until the last section of his essay?

The Monument

Ann Charney

1   The world's most expensive stadium—a diamond bigger than the Ritz—is located at the modest end of Sherbrooke Street, some five kilometres from downtown Montreal and the elegant Ritz-Carlton itself. The unfinished stadium may be the world's most expensive structure, except that no-one has yet priced the Pyramids. On clear nights, its unmistakable futuristic profile is clearly visible from the lookout points on Mount Royal, sailing through the darkness like a brightly lit spaceship. At close range, its vast, empty hulk, dwarfed by giant construction cranes that loom over the ledge of the open dome, suggests some herculean task that has defeated the Titans themselves. Most of the time, however, you can't really see the place for the numbers. And no wonder. The fantasy, the excess, the extravagance, the pure wondrous waste of it, are dazzling. So far, the cost of the Olympic Stadium runs to something like a billion dollars, and it keeps rising.

2   To put this astronomic sum in perspective, a Montreal newspaper asked an accounting firm to translate the price of North America's eight other domed stadiums into 1984 Canadian dollars. The results showed that together these eight stadiums—the Houston Astrodome ($124.9-million), the New Orleans Superdome ($357-million), the Pontiac Silverdome ($118.9-million), the Seattle Kingdome ($132.4-million), the Syracuse Carrier Dome ($44.2-million), the Minneapolis Metrodome ($78.6-million), B.C. Place ($132.2-million), and the Indianapolis Hoosier Dome ($101.2-million)—cost in total just $97.3-million more than Montreal's one stadium. Quebec has every chance in the world, however, of bridging this gap and surpassing the combined total as it proceeds with plans to complete the original design.

3   One detail alone will suffice to illustrate how the spirit of grandeur flourishes undiminished by time and changing political administrations: specially designed sewing machines, weighing two tons, have been imported from Japan for the purpose of assembling the immense rolls of canvas destined to become the roof. The canvas itself has been preserved in climatically controlled conditions beneath the stadium, with all the care appropriate to maintaining a piece of the Holy Shroud in some sacred crypt.

4   How did Montrealers achieve this singular distinction? Credit must be given to the city's indomitable mayor for a quarter of a century, Jean Drapeau, whose small physical stature belies the breadth of his visions. As Flaubert said of his masterpiece, "Mme Bovary, c'est moi," so Drapeau can truthfully say of "le stade olympique."

5   According to people close to him, the dream of creating a monument graced with a tower from which one could see the entire city was with him back when he was first elected mayor, in 1954. It surfaced during Expo '67, when he manoeuvred to have the Eiffel Tower dismantled and reassembled in Montreal for the duration of the world's fair. As negotiations stalled, the mayor commissioned a French architect, J. Robert Dalb, to design a new tower that would combine the most notable features of the Eiffel Tower and the Leaning Tower of Pisa. It was not built, owing to lack of funds, but the dream survived to appear again in 1970 when the mayor, in a spectacular feat of diplomacy, secured the Olympic Summer Games of 1976 for Montreal. He assured Olympic officials that the games would be "modest" and self-financing, and that their cost would not exceed $125-million.

6   The mayor's visionary schemes, however, were not to be hampered by such practical concessions. With supreme confidence he selected the French architect, Roger Taillibert, known for his complex and extravagant creations, to design the Olympic facilities. "We [French Canadians] can only survive if we accept the challenge of quality. That is why I chose Roger Taillibert ... He is one of the five greatest architects in the world—and I don't know the other four, if they exist." Undisturbed by the fact that Canada thus became the only country in the history of the modern Olympics to have chosen a foreign architect, Drapeau explained with serenity, "Art transcends nationalism." When the Quebec association of architects accused the mayor of planning the Olympics in an atmosphere of "lies and secrecy," he responded that he was the only person competent to decide when and to what extent citizens would be informed. The man was rising to the scale of the monument he envisioned.

7   On April 6, 1972, in a lavish "son et lumière" presentation, the mayor introduced a model of Taillibert's scheme to a select audience of invited guests and foreign journalists. At the heart of the sports complex was the spectacular stadium flanked by a massive, inclined tower which would rise to the height of a fifty-story building and which would support a suspended, retractable roof. The mayor's eloquent performance stressed the magnificence of Taillibert's design and avoided all crass considerations of dollars and cents.

8   A handful of demonstrators representing anti-poverty groups slightly marred the occasion, but they were easily contained. During a question-and-answer period following the presentation, the mayor assured his audience that the whole enterprise would not cost taxpayers anything since revenues would be derived from "extraordinary sources" such as an Olympic lottery, the sale of special commemorative stamps, coins, and so on. Later, the mayor went further in his assurances when he promised, in his usual vivid style, "The Olympics can no more have a deficit than a man can have a baby."

9   In the weeks following the press conference, the few figures obtained by persistent journalists from close-mouthed city and Olympic officials seemed to confirm the mayor's seductive optimism. For the following year, a kind of self-satisfied lull of anticipation settled over the entire issue. The city basked in the expectant glory of the celebration to come. Actual construction of the stadium was not to begin until 1974 for the simple reason, it was later revealed, that detailed plans were not available. Taillibert, who saw himself primarily as an artist, was in no hurry, apparently, to provide the construction drawings and specifications necessary for the realization of his grand design. Meanwhile, the mayor supported his architect with a fervour any artist might well envy.

10   When work finally began on the stadium, less than two years before its official opening, it went less than smoothly. There was the problem of time—the Superdome in New Orleans, then under construction, took five years to build—and the difficulties posed by the complexity of the design which, to make matters worse, continued to evolve according to the creator's whim. Instead of rising upwards, the stadium seemed to be sinking into a financial and technological morass.

11   The mayor, however, never lost faith. While his critics spoke of a lunatic obsession, he evoked the Pyramids, the Sphinx, the Eiffel Tower, and wondered if *they* had been appreciated in their time. He extolled the pride of creating a monument that would last through the ages and draw people from around the world. Speaking to the Montreal Board of Trade, he recalled that Pericles had been rebuked for building the Acropolis instead of warships. "I prefer," said the mayor, "to be chastised now, and understood later."

12   During these hard times, only Roger Taillibert seemed to defend the vision that had united the two men: "That's all Canadians and North Americans think about, money, money, money. It doesn't interest me at all. When you look at the Eiffel Tower, what remains...? The honorarium Eiffel received or the structure?" Taillibert's indifference to money seemed to vanish rapidly in the following years. In 1978, he sued the Olympic Installation Board and the city of Montreal for $32.6-million, above and beyond the $6.8-million settlement offered by the Quebec government. The Quebec Superior Court awarded him another $3.4-million.

13   While the importance of the mayor's role in the creation of the stadium is paramount, credit must also be given to his loyal electorate. Not only did the voters remain faithful to the man and his dream during the years of toil and sacrifice exacted by the elliptical maw of the headless idol, they stuck by him in the unpleasant aftermath of the Olympics.

14   The whole extent of the Olympic folly was detailed by the Malouf Commission, set up in 1977 by the Quebec government and headed by Mr. Justice Albert Malouf of the Quebec Superior Court, which tried to determine how the cost of the games had rocketed from an estimated $120-million to well over $1-billion. The inquiry revealed a sordid tale of graft and incompetence, and concluded that "the choice [of the stadium] was dictated by considerations of esthetics and grandeur without any serious study of costs and feasibility beforehand."

15   The inquiry came and went and the people of Montreal continued to elect Jean Drapeau. More than that, a survey in 1984 indicated that three-quarters of the city's French-speaking voters were in favour of completing the tower and the stadium according to the original design, thus proving the wisdom of a pensée from the writer Antoine de Saint-Exupéry which the mayor is said to be fond of quoting: "Force men to build a tower together and they will become brothers; throw them some grain and they will be at one another's throats."

16   In 1985, the Quebec government agreed to complete the stadium, citing among other reasons the fact that, unfinished, the stadium remained "an embarrassing monument to incompetence." The cost of finishing it is expected to run around $120-million, but a certain understandable scepticism has already been expressed about the firmness of that sum. The government's decision ignored serious doubts about the feasibility of the original design—in 1979, part of a roof of a similar stadium in Paris designed by Taillibert collapsed, crushing thirty then unoccupied seats—as well as less expensive and more proven solutions for covering the stadium.

17   With a roof or without, the stadium leaves something to be desired as a place to watch sports. Designed for track and field, it supposedly had the much-vaunted advantage of being a multi-purpose facility. The stadium does boast a hydraulic pitcher's mound (which rises and descends discreetly) and rolls of astroturf (which can be unzipped as easily as a stripper's costume), but spectators remain so far from the field that, as one sports writer put it, you need a detective to find the ball.

18   Banal common sense and an affinity for the utilitarian have never been characteristic of Quebec society. Quebeckers have usually left such considerations to their thriftier and duller English-speaking neighbours, preferring to affirm their existence in grandiose dreams that exalt the collective spirit.

19   The Olympic stadium is not the first extravagant Quebec monument dedicated to this spirit. Jean-Claude Marsan, an architectural historian, cites several other telling examples.

At the beginning of the nineteenth century, while the English were busy developing the economy, French Canadians were building Notre Dame, the largest church north of Mexico at the time. A century later, in the midst of the Depression, Marsan points out, they built Saint Joseph's Oratory, the fourth-largest sanctuary in the world. During the same period, the University of Montreal, while lacking funds to pay its professors' salaries, was nevertheless creating a lavish campus which Marsan calls "the monument that most resembles Versailles."

20   More recently, there was the celebrated case of Mirabel International Airport. One of the largest airports in the world, Mirabel is used to only thirteen per cent of its capacity, and handles less traffic than the airport at Moose Jaw.

21   Seen in this context, the stadium fits neatly into the psychic landscape of Montreal. Even its billion-dollar aura falls into place. The fabulous figure becomes the essential element of sacrifice that replaces the live offering and renders the place sacred, distinct from the ordinary and the commonplace. As befits a monument created in the image of man, this modern Pharaonic dream has shown that it is not immune to the ravages of time. For all the solidity of this concrete and steel, it seems strangely perishable. Already, after only a decade of exposure to the elements, it bears unmistakable signs of decay.

22   In the not-too-distant future, in its stripped and ruined state, the Olympic Stadium will finally achieve the grandeur of its original conception. Long after Jean Drapeau has gone to his final reward, the Big O—like the Parthenon, or the Colosseum, or the Mayan temples—will draw the curious of the world whom he so presciently awaited.

Ann Charney, "The Monument," *Saturday Night*, January 1987: 122–124, 126.

QUESTIONS

Subject
How does the title of the essay reflect the author's attitude toward her subject?

Audience
Explain how the author creates a divide between her readership and the hero/villain of the essay.

Purpose
What is the author's purpose and how does the literary device of irony help her achieve it?

Structure and Style

(a) Explain why the author alludes at strategic points in the essay to the Pyramids, the Holy Shroud, the Acropolis, and the Parthenon.

(b) Explain how the examples cited in paragraph two and the irony in the concluding sentence provide a powerful argument for calling Drapeau's plan "the Olympic folly."

(c) Comment on the effectiveness of direct question in this essay to support the author's position.

Hanukkah

Matt Cohen

1   One winter, when I was a child, we travelled from Ottawa to Toronto to be with my father's parents for Hanukkah. As we drove slowly through the wintry twilight, the snow crunched and squeaked beneath the tires of our old snout-nosed Dodge. When we arrived, it was almost dark.

2   My grandmother opened the door before we could knock. As always, she was wearing a black dress that made her look even thinner than she was, and square-heeled shoes that emphasized the fragility of her legs and ankles. Although my grandmother lived into her 90s, she had been on the verge of death since she was 35. We children went in first, apparently out of politeness but in fact because my parents were even more terrified of my grandparents than we were.

3   The table was set. The silver gleamed and the ritual candelabra—the *menorah*—was in place along with the patterned white dinner service—big plates with wide soup bowls on top. From the kitchen came the familiar smells of chicken soup, *kasha* (buckwheat), and roast beef that had probably been in the oven since the Pleistocene Epoch.

4   We had been delayed on the road and sunset, which marked the beginning of the holiday, was upon us. As soon as our coats were off, *Zada* (grandfather) led me to the menorah and asked me if I knew the blessing for the Hanukkah candles. He lowered his head so his face was almost level with mine. He wore his invariable dark suit pants, black belt, black shoes, white shirt with expansive bracelets on the arms, suspenders, a tie held in place by a golden tiepin, and of course his *yarmulkah* (skull cap). He had lost his hair following a bout of scarlet fever, but his moustache and beard, trimmed to a squarish spade a few inches below his chin, gave him—to my eyes—a wild and hairy look that was emphasized by the contrasting pinkness of his lips and tongue. Bearded, candid, utterly foreign, his face was an outburst from a past I couldn't begin to imagine. A devout believer, his passionate Jewishness made it completely natural to talk about biblical figures as though they were neighbours we had just met on the street.

5   Soon I was holding the match and reciting, in Hebrew, the blessing I'd learned in the car. My grandfather, knowing full well this was a surface acquisition, nodded and hummed along.

6   Zada Cohen was a short and stocky man, renowned for feats of strength we grandchildren never saw but were told about—the most amazing being that during a fire he had carried two pigs, one under each arm, from a neighbour's barn. This was notable not only because carrying pigs would be so difficult, but because my grandfather had demonstrated an unsuspected ecumenical streak. When the fire happened, I have no doubt he was wearing his usual costume, down to the tiepin, the suspenders and the yarmulkah.

7   The first time I remember meeting him was when I was six years old. He took me by the hand and walked me to an empty synagogue. We stood in the middle of what was—to me— a cavernous dusty room filled with the smell of old books and rotting cloth. My grandfather pointed out the ark where the Torah was kept, the gallery reserved for women, and the Bimah where the rabbi delivered his sermon and the cantor sang the sacred texts. Then he crouched down so his eyes were directly opposite mine.

8   "*You* will be a rabbi," my grandfather announced to me. Fortunately, even at the time, we both knew this was extremely unlikely.

9   Over the years, he maintained this special way of fixing his eyes on mine. At such moments I knew that as the eldest (although religiously unworthy) grandson, I was being singled out to receive, absorb, and somehow shoulder the responsibility for some piece of Jewish lore he felt it essential for me to know.

10   "Mordecai," he always called me by my Hebrew name, "do you know—"

11   Of course, I never did.

12   Hanukkah, the Feast of Lights, is celebrated each year for eight days beginning on the 25th day of the Hebrew month Kislev. Since the Jewish calendar is based on the lunar month, Hanukkah's date in the modern calendar varies from late November to late December. For Jews, the year's most important holidays are Yom Kippur and Rosh Hashanah. Although these holidays often allow Jewish children to miss school during the World Series, they feature fasting, repentance and promises to be good.

13   Hanukkah, a relatively minor holiday in the Jewish religious pantheon, has not only presents, but a terrific story. "Do you know?" Zada would ask me, "that we celebrate Hanukkah because a certain man with a name like yours, a Mattathias, had the courage to say no?" Or: "Do you know that to join his army, a young man had to be strong enough to rip a tree from the ground with his bare hands while galloping past on horseback? At full speed?" At first I viewed the story merely as about wild battles won by out-numbered Jewish soldiers. But the real story of Hanukkah is broader, because it is also the story of the Jewish rejection—after a period of great temptation—of the Greek Empire and Greek culture.

14   In the 5th century BC, the Jewish people, after a brief exile in Babylon, returned to Judea and restored the Temple in Jerusalem. Then began a period of consolidation in which the scribes and the written word gained a predominant influence. Meanwhile, in the Greek city of Athens, another intellectual revolution was taking place. This was the era of Socrates, Plato and Aristotle.

15   In 334 BC, Alexander of Macedon began his conquests, which included Palestine. The Greeks allowed the Jews a prominent role in the founding of Alexandria, and it was in conjunction with the Greek Empire that the Jews began to establish themselves as a mercantile force in the Mediterranean basin. The Jews found themselves tremendously attracted to—and seduced by—Hellenic culture, customs and language. The translation of the Hebrew scriptures into Greek became a major event in Jewish intellectual life. During this period, the Jews, although Hellenized in many respects, were still free to follow their own religious practices.

16   But in 175 BC, Antiochus, an Athens-born Greek warrior, ascended the throne. He soon established domination over Judea and in the process, Jerusalem was converted into a Greek city. A proclamation was issued that forced all citizens to follow the Greek religion. Even the Temple in Jerusalem would be used for pagan religious rituals, including the slaughter of pigs on its altar.

17   At this time, through the influence of the scribes, Judaism favoured piety and tolerance over fighting. As a result, thousands of religious Jews martyred themselves. Even the less devout refused to fight on the Sabbath, and opposing armies soon learned that was the day on which the Jews were most easily attacked.

18   In 168 BC, in the marketplace of a small town called Modein to the northwest of Jerusalem, the Syrian soldiers erected an altar. The men of Modein were assembled there and the soldiers' captain ordered Mattathias, a Jewish priest and elder, to sacrifice a pig to Jupiter in honour of Antiochus. Mattathias did not budge. Another stepped forward, offering

to perform the sacrifice. The plan was that those Jews who refused to eat the meat of the pig would be executed. Suddenly, the aged Mattathias snatched the sword from the captain, killed the traitor who had offered to perform the sacrifice, then killed the captain. Mattathias's sons then surrounded him, and they and their followers fled to the hills.

19   So began the Maccabee uprising. The rebels—not the first Jewish guerilla group in history—had made the singular decision to temporarily suspend the ordinance against fighting on the Sabbath, giving them a tremendous military advantage over their unsuspecting enemies. In a matter of four years, the Maccabees' victories brought them to Jerusalem itself, where their first task was to clean and reconsecrate the Temple. Removing the stones that had been used for pagan sacrifices, they built a new altar.

20   On the 25th day of Kislev, 165 BC, they lit the sacred lamp—only to discover there was enough oil for just one day. Horsemen were sent in every direction to find more oil. Eight days later, someone finally returned—but remarkably, the lamp had continued to burn. Hanukkah commemorates the reconsecration of the temple and the miracle of the lasting oil.

21   Because my wife is not Jewish, Hanukkah in our family doesn't compete with Christmas or replace it. It has its own special status and everyone enjoys it for what we have made it. Hanukkah is also familiar to my children from their classrooms and day-care. For them, this holiday is a normal part of their public and private lives.

22   The situation was entirely different in the late 1940s when I grew up. Then, Jews were still trying to come to terms with the enormity of their losses during World War II. If the word "holocaust" existed then, I never heard it. There was no single word to describe what had happened. Nor was Hanukkah celebrated and discussed in school on an equal footing with Christmas. Such a possibility was unthinkable because Judaism and Hanukkah had no public place. On the contrary, being Jewish was something best kept to oneself: when I was in Grade 5, my refusal to say the Lord's Prayer led to my spending each morning in the corridor while the teacher, a Sunday School organist in his spare time, led the rest of the class through their religious exercises. For me, Jewish holidays were not only religious events, but also another way of being singled out, set aside, sent to the corridor until secular life resumed and I was returned to the main room.

23   Hanukkah's gift-giving aspects are constantly growing, but when I was a child it seemed a weak and almost pitiful counterpoint to the public splendour that made Christmas the emotional and commercial centrepiece of winter. For this extravaganza, people put up trees in their houses and store windows, chains of lights festooned downtown and residential areas, Santa Claus and his reindeer dashed through skies and shopping centres. On the day itself, I knew, Christian children would receive armloads of presents, then, after a huge lunch, settle down to watching television specials that celebrated the triumph of their virtues and their happiness.

24   For whatever reason, the Jews in Ottawa did not compete by putting electric Stars of David on their roofs or erecting Hanukkah bushes in their living rooms. It's true that Jewish children got presents, but they weren't the sort of thing you'd brag about at school if you wanted to survive recess. Nonetheless, though it took a long time, I came to value Hanukkah for its own virtues and—mostly because of my grandfather—to realize how complex and full of contemporary resonance its story was.

25   Now that I am an adult and a parent, I look forward to Hanukkah as a warm family celebration that over the years has become a mid-winter opportunity to explore with my children a little of the meaning and history of Judaism. It is also an occasion for gift-giving and family visiting which—aside from the potato pancakes and the candles—are the main attraction for the children.

26   When potato pancakes—*latkas*—were served at that long-ago Hanukkah at my grandparents' house, Zada explained the traditional holiday food had originated during the battles
of the Maccabees: passing through a village one time, the Jewish guerillas were served the
pancakes because that was the only food there was time to make.

27   After tea, presents were distributed. As they did every single Hanukkah for decades,
my grandparents gave my brother and me white shirts. These were always "Eatonia" shirts,
with starched collars and holes for cufflinks, and they were for wearing to synagogue—a place
we didn't go very often. Then my grandfather recounted the battle when the Jews defeated
the Syrians, who rode powerful elephants instead of horses. He asked us if we thought we
would be strong enough to tear trees out of the ground. Of course we would.

28   When the evening was finished—not before we'd all had several desserts and numerous
helpings of chocolates and cookies—we went out to the car. Despite the cold, my grandparents
stood in the open door, framed by the yellow light, and watched us drive off. They were, I
suddenly realized, like survivors on some magical ark that had arrived from thousands of years
ago. To them, Hanukkah had nothing to do with Christmas or being sent to the hallway or
television specials—it was a magic ritual mysteriously connected to their mysterious past.
One I could participate in and grow into until I, too, appeared to my children or grandchildren as a friendly but bizarre relic out of a past they will never otherwise touch.

Matt Cohen, "Hanukkah," Canadian Geographic, November/December 1995: 86–90.

QUESTIONS

Subject
In what way does the rather complex subject of the essay move beyond simple narrative?

Audience
Give evidence to show that this story is directed to a largely non-Jewish audience or to a
Jewish audience unaware of its mythology.

Purpose
When this essay was first published, its title was "Zada's Hanukkah Legacy." Look up the
word "legacy" in your dictionary and decide whether it's an appropriate word to convey
the essay's purpose.

Structure and Style
   (a) Explain how the essay moves from narrative to exposition to narrative and comment
       on how this movement contributes to the author's purpose.

   (b) Give one example to suggest that Zada's image in the boyish eyes of the author mir-
       rors that of the warriors of Mattathias who ripped trees from the ground with their bare
       hands "while galloping past on horseback."

   (c) Explain how the author's view of the foreignness of his grandfather reflects the au-
       dience's sense of foreignness about much that is related in the essay.

Better Dead Than Read? An Opposing View

Timothy Findley

1   Paul Stuewe's report ("Better Dead Than Read?") in the October issue of *Books in Canada*, though admirable in its concluding passages, is nonetheless sufficiently peppered with cant and inaccuracies to warrant a reply. Most of the inaccuracies and pretty well all of the cant appear in quotation marks. So far as the cant is concerned, that's entirely appropriate. But when it comes to facts, Stuewe has failed to probe the integrity of what he is quoting and, therefore, leaves his readers with a false impression of where matters stand with regard to the banning of books in this country. Throughout the course of his report he relies, for the most part, on the statements and opinions of two men. Only two. Based on what they have to say, however, he draws definitive conclusions that do not reflect the facts about what is happening. One of Stuewe's conclusions, for instance, is that the censorship problem is not at all widespread and that wherever it does appear it is not to be taken seriously. He confines his report to recent events in Huron County, Ont., where the local Board of Education has voted to remove Margaret Laurence's *The Diviners* from the list of books approved for study in high schools. Stuewe's conclusion? "If a large number of such communities acted in concert, then the alarm might well have to be raised. But that isn't happening and it isn't likely to happen...." Wrong. It has happened before. It is still happening. And the more we slough it off as being of no consequence, the more it is going to happen in the future.

2   Mister Stuewe himself points out that book banners are currently hard at work in Nova Scotia and New Brunswick, although he dismisses them as living "mostly in rural areas." As if that didn't matter. He also says that those of us who are concerned about this problem arc looking for "rcd-nccks in thc woodpilc" and that wc aren't going to find them. I agree. The woodpile is deserted. Whatever you want to call whoever was in there, they've come out. Some people come out of closets. Some come out of woodpiles. I wouldn't call them "red-neck." I wouldn't call them anything. I only know that Huron County has set a precedent. So did Dade County, Florida, and the results of that single county precedent have been disastrous for human rights all across the U.S. I don't want the same kind of disaster to happen here—either to people or books. And if you look at the books that keep coming under fire in this campaign (and don't fool yourselves for one minute that it isn't a campaign), you will find they all have something in common: concern for people and compassion for the human condition. I find that very odd.

3   Stuewe's report is based, as I've said, on the statements and opinions of two men. Both are residents of Huron County and both represent a group that calls itself Concerned Citizens. The report states that "the strength of groups such as Concerned Citizens lies only in their shared perception of a threat to the values of their community," and that "there are no large funds, no outside agitators, no Canada Council grants inflating a minority gripe into a public issue." Every word of this is inaccurate. To begin with, the opinions reflected in the report are those of the leading spokesman for an evangelical association that calls itself Renaissance International. I refer to the Reverend Kenneth Campbell, a man who has mounted a major campaign against books and the education system of this country. He voiced these opinions almost word for word over CBC-Radio only a few months ago.

Yet, though his words are parroted again and again by those directly quoted in Stuewe's report, his name is not even mentioned. Here, perhaps, is why:

4   While protesting that there are no large funds at their disposal, Renaissance International and its sister citizens' groups have been able to support their campaign in very high style indeed. Renaissance was established with a budget of $100,000. It is registered as a non-profit, charitable organization and publishes a magazine called *Encounter.* You can become a member for $10, $100, or $1,000. Membership fees and subscription fees to the magazine are all tax-deductible. Whenever Renaissance goes on the road it hires large and expensive arenas and public halls in which to sell its rhetoric. Posters and media advertising announce its presence.

5   For several months now Campbell has had a persistent American guest on his platform. But, of course, who would dare call Anita Bryant an "outside agitator?" And how many readers are aware that the Reverend Kenneth Campbell, using Ms. Bryant as his come-on, only this past summer set up his platform in London, Ont., from which place you can spit into Huron County? And Campbell's target on the literary front? You guessed it: *The Diviners.* Funny isn't it, that everywhere that Kenny goes, Margaret Laurence gets in trouble. Of course, it's the local citizens' groups who do the shooting.

6   Lastly, with regard to the phrase about "Canada Council grants inflating a minority gripe," I assume this refers to the fact that The Writers' Union of Canada, a recipient of such grants, has had the audacity to mouth off in opposition to the damage being done to books and writers by the pro-banning campaign. If my assumption is correct, then I can only say that an inflated minority soon becomes a majority. And more power to it. Financial and otherwise. Thornton Wilder wrote a marvellous thing about money in his play, *The Matchmaker:* "Money, you should pardon the expression, is like manure. It should be spread around encouraging young things to grow!" However, the way Reverend Campbell is spreading money on this current campaign against books and the education system makes me think that what *he* has in mind is more like encouraging young things to *ossify*.

7   I come now to an insinuation in the report that has been repeated once too often: namely that in *The Diviners* Margaret Laurence advocates immoral behaviour. Kenneth Campbell has been on about this for long enough. That he has now spread his garbage into the mouths of his disciples is really very tiresome and childish. This time, the source of the insinuation is a pharmacist in Huron County by the name of Elmer Umbach, who states that "young people get venereal disease because they practise free love the way Margaret Laurence and such writers advocate."

8   To begin with, if I were Margaret Laurence I'd sue Elmer Umbach for that statement: flat out, no holds barred. Once and for all, let it be said that the only kind of "free love" advocated by Margaret Laurence is compassion. And that is not an opinion. That is a fact. Accusations of the kind levelled by Pharmacist Umbach and Evangelist Campbell are nothing less than tragic blunders of the intellect. In damning this book they have slandered and damaged a rare and moving document of human aspirations and a work of art, the sole aim of which is to express the spiritual reconciliation between human beings and life.

9   As for Pharmacist Umbach, if he were to read the whole of Margaret Laurence's work instead of excerpting only those passages that suit his needs he might find it in himself to stock a little of the compassion she advocates on his shelves. He might even discover that it averts more human ills than the whole amplitude of pharmaceutical prophylactics he now dispenses. When reading this man's blindly obtuse statements ("What I'm saying is a declaration of truth and I am not interested in discussing or dialoguing with you") I wondered if he had

not perhaps misunderstood the terms of his profession. As a pharmacist, he is only required to sell prophylactics: he is not required to become one.

10   The report states that "Concerned Citizens was formed [in Huron County] as a direct result of what was interpreted as an invasion of alien elements with no stake in the community and an obvious vested interest in promoting such books as *The Diviners*." This harks back to an earlier reference in the report to a time when "the Writers' Union sent a delegation to Huron County ... to defend the books under attack." To begin with, the Writers' Union did not, willy-nilly, send a delegation. One of that union's members, Alice Munro, is a citizen of Huron County and consequently the Writers' Union was already a presence in that area. The truth is that a group of concerned teachers and students invited two other members of the union to bolster their fight against the book banning. And if Alice Munro cannot stand up in her own community (with or without fellow writers by her side) and defend Canadian books—including her own—against discrimination, then the final paragraphs of the report, in which Stuewe points out the dangers of censorship and people's innate responsibility to fight it, are meaningless. Furthermore, the whole accusatory stance that writers only go to bat for books because they have a "vested interest" is just as tiresomely innocent of intelligence as Reverend Campbell's other quotes dotted about the Huronian canon of stock phrases. The only vested interest one writer has in another's work is his investment *as a reader* in its integrity. Alice Munro doesn't make a cent out of Margaret Laurence's books. And do I really have to point out that Margaret Laurence did not set foot in Huron County during any of this debate? But Alice Munro did, and *she* had a vested interest in her own endangered books. Strange, aren't they, these writers: how they will want it both ways? Wanting both to write and to be read. And to eat and live in houses and pay bills and stuff like that. Really strange. Stranger still that they believe in the value of their own work.

11   The whole of this current movement concerned with the censorship and banning of books—whether in schools or libraries or courts of law—is riddled with false moral indignation and fake concern for the hearts and minds of our children. It stems, in my opinion, from a truly evil manipulation of people's genuine fear and uncertainty about the world we live in. And the society we've created. And the children we've borne. The voices that inform the report and give it its tone speak often of their children and of hopes for their moral and spiritual character. Well, those are the same concerns of the books these people want to ban and of the men and women who wrote them. Why are we so afraid of our own children that we want to close their hearts and minds to the fund of compassion they would find in these books? *Who Has Seen the Wind?*, *Lives of Girls and Women*, *The Diviners*, *One Day in the Life of Ivan Denisovitch*, *The Diary of Anne Frank*, *Huckleberry Finn*. The list goes on and on, and it grows and grows every year. It scares the hell out of me. The Reverend Campbell even speaks of bowdlerizing Shakespeare.

12   Do we really have to go through all this again? Has nothing been learned? Of course, it has been argued that these books have "only been banned in the high schools. Anyone can read them after that." Wrong. Once banned in schools books will always be read without respect for their true qualities. Even now children riffle the pages of these books—wherever they may find them—looking for "the dirty bits." This is not the book's fault. Nor the fault of its writer. It is the fault of those who have condemned the book as "obscene" or "pornographic" or "filled with profane language." Literature is being locked away with the truly obscene, as much as to imply that Margaret Laurence is an advocate of "child abuse." And this, of course, is nothing less than intellectual blasphemy.

13   It is an artist's privilege to see what others cannot see. Sometimes this is not a happy privilege. Sometimes what is seen is very hard to bear, and equally difficult to voice. But if it is the artist's privilege to see, it is also his job to tell what he sees. As W.H. Auden did, looking over his shoulder into Europe in 1939 and writing: "Intellectual disgrace stares from every human face, and the seas of pity lie locked and frozen in each eye."

14   These days, he wouldn't even have to look over his shoulder. But I don't want to close on that note, any more than Auden did. His poem, from which those lines are taken, was about the death of a poet—W.B. Yeats. Its last verse makes a far better epigraph for the idea I have tried to express here, which is the idea that a false issue is being raised by people who, for motives of their own, want to prevent certain books from reaching the minds that most require them, minds that can make the future better than the present and infinitely better than the past. What Auden wrote is as fine a definition of the desired effect of an artist's work as anyone will ever give. And, like it or not Huron County, it applies to Margaret Laurence's *The Diviners*.

15   In the deserts of the heart,
        Let the healing fountain start,
        In the prison of his days
        Teach the free man how to praise.

16   Of course, Auden understood these things. He was censured, too. And banned. But he's still in print.

Timothy Findley, "Better Dead Than Read? An Opposing View," *Books in Canada,* December
1978: 3–5.

QUESTIONS

Subject
Findley's essay is a response to Stuewe's (found in this anthology, pp. 270–274). Outline the major point of Stuewe's essay that Findley tries to answer. How successful is he?

Audience
How is the reader meant to feel the dangers of groups who advocate book censorship? Much of Stuewe's point about their innocence is based on a quantitative argument. How does Findley counter this view?

Purpose
Is Findley's response a purely objective rebuttal of Stuewe's position or does he allow emotion to enter his discussion? If he does, does it work for or against his argument?

Structure and Style
(a) Locate two sentence fragments in Findley's essay and comment on their use.
(b) Why might Findley find it necessary to quote W.H. Auden, an important British poet of the twentieth century?

Dan George's Last Stand

Allan Fotheringham

1   The flame from the refinery stack on the south bluff of Burrard Inlet casts a moving reflection across the waters of the fjord that reaches into the innards of Vancouver. Day and night, that wavering flame from the Standard Oil refinery reflects all the way over the mile of water to the north shore of the inlet, where the faded wooden houses of the Burrard Reserve are scattered. Thirty yards up the slope there is a small white cottage, a front door awaiting unbuilt steps. As you struggle up the incline with puppy dogs at foot, past the Coke bottles and abandoned car, there appears in the window above a face like a copper moon. The face is the face of a man paying obeisance to *his* section of earth, *his* view, the portion of the realm that belongs to *his* eyes. Dan George has lived 71 years on this slope, 100 yards covering the distance between the house where he was born, the house he built, and in which he raised his family, and the house where he now lives. Two cultures face each other across the mile of water—linked by the constancy of the flame. There is a similar consistency to the life of Dan George. He is a portage across time.

2   Burrard Reserve No. 3 forms a tattered buffer between the boxes of a North Vancouver subdivision and the summer homes and cabin cruisers of Deep Cove farther up the inlet. It is just along the shore here, some six miles from downtown Vancouver, that the tormented novelist Malcolm Lowry lived in a squatter's shack and fueled his genius with fatal quantities of alcohol. The feel of Dan George can best be appreciated by imagining him on this slope for 71 years, looking across the water and watching his world change. "The government came through Canada and measured out a piece of land for us and called it our 'reserve.' We did not have the freedom to roam as we were used to do," he says. He could see the housing march out from the city, decade by decade, reducing the thick timber to subdivision squares. Now, peeking from the tip of Burnaby Mountain at left are the stark towers of Simon Fraser University, which will serve this summer as the site for the eight-million-dollar filming of Aldous Huxley's novel *Brave New World*.

3   In the house a dark-eyed grandchild in diapers paws at Dan's knee. His pretty daughter, Marie George, lives with him in the house with her three children. Dan George is a short man, just five-foot-six. But it is as if his body had come from two separate men. All the weight of those 165 pounds is in massive shoulders and chest, the product of 27 years as a longshoreman. The powerful arms hang to tiny hips, the flat belly of a teen-ager and to short, bowed legs. His triangular form is that of a trapeze artist. And from that thick chest is rationed out, in spaced intervals, the soft fog of his voice. It is impossible to translate into print the husky whisper of Dan George's voice, or the measured cadence of his speech. And there is that face, like a bronzed catcher's mitt. It is full of canyons and gullies and arroyos, the soft folds of hills—erosions of time and spirit that in fact have made it more beautiful. When he begins to smile, there is a slow-motion telegraphing. The seams begin to soften. The face unfolds like a wrinkled brown shopping bag, the lines and creases taking new shapes and directions. It is both timeless and one of the magnificent faces of our time. He points out the window and across the river to the oil refineries which have come to defile the bluff. "They wanted to build them on this shore. My father stopped them."

4   It is unnerving to talk to a man with such a face and voice who muses over the possibility of touching three different centuries. He was born in 1899 and conceivably could reach the

year 2000, since his uncle lived until 110 and his mother to 95. He takes quiet satisfaction in the idea. There is a personal object lesson in history to sit down with a man, still active, who loaded lumber by hand onto full-rigged sailing ships from foreign ports. European stock came to this country to put down roots. With Dan George it is the other way; he seems to flow from the earth. He is a fixed position in a world of impermanence.

5   His mother was a full-blooded descendant of the warrior Wautsauk, who walked with a wolf. Wautsauk kept a wolf as a constant companion and went aboard Captain George Vancouver's ship when it explored Burrard Inlet in 1792. He can remember a great-great-uncle who could tell stories of the dark-colored men who came even before Captain Vancouver—the Spanish explorers with their Moorish slaves.

6   Just below where Dan's little house sits there was once an enormous fort which the tribe built for protection from raiding parties of war canoes. Not far away is the spot where the first Mass in that part of Canada was conducted over a century ago. Queen Victoria gave the tribe three apple trees to commemorate the event. Two perished and the third died when Dan's mother did.

7   Today the Dollarton Highway cuts through, speeding motorists to the new housing beyond on streets named Beachview and Baycrest and Seashell Lane. Burrard Reserve No. 3 and the George family remain, some of the 32,000 of BC's 48,000 Indians who still live on reserves. In the old house Dan built is son Bob, his wife and their 14 children. Beside it is the $12,000 aluminum house trailer of son Lenny, the moody, talented youngster who seems to have a promising acting future if he wants it.

8   For Dan, the only time away from the reserve were the 12 years at the residential school run by the Oblate Fathers in a clearing of timber in North Vancouver. At 19 he married Amy Jack, a beautiful and strong-willed woman. "I made up my mind to try to get her when I was 16," Dan remembers. Amy, from another reserve, was 15 when her mother told her she was to marry a young man from the Burrard Reserve. She cried all night and her parents let her wait a year before the marriage. Amy died a lingering death of cancer just weeks before Dan had to undergo his Academy Award ordeal.

9   When a bit player in the Los Angeles Music Centre called out the name of veteran British actor John Mills as the Best Supporting Actor for his role as the village idiot in *Ryan's Daughter,* Dan, nominated for his role in *Little Big Man,* turned and said, "I feel as if someone's just pulled a wet blanket off me."

10   "I'm glad in a way that he didn't get it," broadcaster Hilda Mortimer said later. She was one of the friends who accompanied him to Hollywood and who broke into tears when the result was announced. "You could just feel the trapdoor closing on all those people down there who wanted to *use* him. We sat in a room together the next day and waited for all those promised people who never came. The magazines. The agents. The studio people. The trapdoor simply closed."

11   The makers of *Little Big Man* first sought Sir Laurence Olivier for the role of Old Lodge Skins. Then they sought the brilliant Paul Scofield. Richard Boone was offered $300,000 for the part. Dan George received $16,000 for the same role. There is little of it left.

12   "The only thing Dan has ever bought for himself," says a friend, "was a secondhand 1964 Acadian with the money from his first movie. He'd never even had a car. That's gone. Someone smashed it up." Another part of the money went to natives in Peru and to Father Joseph Kane, who helped Dan before leaving BC for South America as a missionary.

13   Dan has never had much money. Mostly Indians and half-breeds were used in lumber handling when he went to work on the docks in 1920. Forty cents an hour, 10 hours a day.

Four men packing 40-foot lengths of four-by-12s. ("I liked to sit and listen to him talk," remembers Sam Engler, a retired longshoreman who worked the same ships. "He seemed so cultured.")

14   Dan stayed at it for 27 years until a swinging timber, 24 inches square, crashed into him and tossed him 30 feet. It smashed all the muscles in his hip ("my bones were too strong to break") and brought on complications that caused one leg to shrink. He failed to get compensation and has never received any pension benefits from the now powerful International Longshoremen's and Warehousemen's Union.

15   "I could have fought the compensation people," he now says, "but it is the nature of our ancestors. We don't have the staying power of the white man. If we get a bad deal, we don't go back."

16   At a banquet not long ago, Dan told the story of the drunk staggering home late at night to find a sardonic wife who gently removed his shoes, slipped a pillow under his shaky head on the sofa and asked if he wanted to make love. "Oh we might as well," mumbled the drunk. "I'm going to get hell when I get home anyway."

17   The old man with the long white hair waited for the laughter to subside, then said, "That story's true, 'cause I was the man." They laughed at that, too, but while the story may have been apocryphal the message wasn't. There was a younger time on the docks when drink was a problem.

18   "We were Gang 44," remembers Dan, fondling the child at his knee. "I can remember when our number went up on the board at the hiring hall. Eleven men—you learn to know each other. We quit at three so there was always the beer parlor. We had pride in Gang 44. They called us the Wolf Pack." The interviewer recalls Wautsauk.

19   There were also those longshoring accidents that happened when a cargo of rum or whiskey arrived. A case dropped was a case that must be disposed of. "One of the reasons I quit the docks. Drink was getting into a habit. We raise our children by example. Not a good example coming home every night half-cut."

20   It was during these times that the problems of the succession to band leadership arose. Dan and the eldest brother Henry were enjoying life, perhaps too much so for the liking of old Chief Slaholte George. He surprised everyone by bypassing them and reaching 20 years down the family scale, naming 15-year-old son John as the next chief.

21   The responsibilities of the role were obviously heavy on a teen-age boy and eventually John George left to live in the United States. Dan was elected to succeed him and by the time he was voted out of office in 1963, after serving 12 years, he had begun his television appearance in the Cariboo series scripted by Vancouver journalist Paul St. Pierre, now the Liberal MP for Coast Chilcotin. The title "chief" naturally adhered to his publicity, but by this time his younger brother was back from the U.S. and affirmed by band vote as their leader.

22   "He thinks I don't like him," Dan says softly, gazing out the window toward the house where Chief John George lives. He turns away sadly. "How can you hate someone who's your brother?"

23   Dan has since been named "honorary chief" of both the Shuswap and Squamish tribes but the resentment from his brother runs deep. "Chief John L. George" is defiantly emblazoned on his mailbox down the road and from that position he must watch the steady procession of TV crews and reporters climbing the slope to Dan's house. It is not a pleasant situation. "You've got to understand," says someone close to the George family, "that there is internecine warfare on every reserve. You have people cooped up within a restricted

space. It's bound to happen. It's just that there is practically no one but Georges on this reserve so they have to fight with one another." The apparent anger led to a vote which barred one of Dan's own daughters from reserve status. The vote was a product of the alienation between the brothers. Many of the band resent the hip world of Dan's son Lenny, who has brought some of the temptations of the young to the reserve and has married a white girl. Through all this contempt, the old man has been a bridge over troubled waters.

24   Slumped under a tree in front of his house is an old blue cart with "Dan George and his Indian Entertainers" printed on the side. The time is past when, with his children, he hauled that around to small rodeos, when his rickety-tick band played legion hall dances, Dan solemnly slapping the double bass and twirling it around as comic relief during the two-bar breaks.

25   Earlier this year 800 guests packed a Hotel Vancouver ballroom to see him accept the Canadian Council of Christians and Jews' prestigious Human Relations Award. As the TV cameras edged in, Dan slipped off his glasses and told of how his father, Chief Slaholte George, took him hunting as a boy for the first and last time. "He taught me to love animals," said Dan. "And for the next 19 years he taught me to love human beings. It is a proud feeling to be a man. We Indians have been luckier than most."

26   "A proud feeling to be a man." The words sat there and hung above that banquet room of dinner jackets, inhabited by businessmen who would go to office towers next morning to dispatch bits of paper to other office towers. "Luckier than most." It is a remarkable statement to come from an Indian and it comes from a man who has been acclaimed for adding dignity to his people while leveling bitter accusations at the white man.

27   "We used to talk of the 'noble red man,'" says Father Bert Dunlop, an Oblate who is a close adviser. "It became a cliché. But really, that's what Dan is. Noble."

28   A buoyant birthday crowd of 32,000 in Vancouver's Empire Stadium on July 1, 1967, was silenced by Dan George's speech, a noble figure on the field reciting his bitter soliloquy of how his people had been treated. A "Lament for Confederation" Dan called it:

29   "How long have I known you, O Canada? A hundred years. And many many *seelanum* more. And today, when you celebrate your hundred years, O Canada, I am sad for all the Indian people throughout the land.

30   "For I have known you when your forests were mine; when they gave me my meat and my clothing. I have known you in your streams and rivers where your fish flashed and danced in the sun, where the waters said come, come and eat of my abundance. I have known you in the freedom of your winds. And my spirit, like the winds, once roamed your good lands.

31   "But in the long hundred years since the white man came, I have seen my freedom disappear like the salmon going mysteriously out to sea. The white man's strange customs which I could not understand pressed down upon me until I could no longer breathe.

32   "When I fought to protect my land and my home, I was called a savage. When I neither understood nor welcomed this way of life, I was called lazy. When I tried to rule my people, I was stripped of my authority....

33   "O Canada, how can I celebrate with you this Centenary, this hundred years? Shall I thank you for the reserves that are left me of my beautiful forests? For the canned fish of my rivers? For the loss of my pride and authority, even among my own people? For the lack of my will to fight back?"

34   His moving performance in George Ryga's play *The Ecstasy of Rita Joe* was not so much a role as a personal statement on the skid-road treatment of Indian women. It was

not acting, but an acting out of himself, his own experience. I remember when the Playhouse Theatre took *Rita Joe* to the National Arts Centre and, the word of his performance seeping over to Parliament Hill, Prime Minister Trudeau and Justice Minister John Turner sought him out one night backstage, shaking his hand and peering into his eyes as if expecting to find therein the answers to a new government's guilt for past treatment of the native people. Afterward we went to a party at the home of an Ottawa millionaire, and, while the actresses frolicked in the pool and squealed in the sauna, Dan sat there, an island in a sea of theatrical kisses and celebrations. He wanted his slope.

35   It is Father Dunlop who helps him work out his speeches and soliloquies, the two of them working rather as a composer and a lyricist, sensing each other's moods and developing a theme.

36   He has become conscious of his power as a celebrity and often uses it to help his people. He is now a culture hero soliciting applause on entering any room. Aware of the power his presence has given him, he recently appeared as an expert witness at an inquest into the skid-road death of another Indian woman. A charge of discrimination involved daughter Marie, who trained as a hairdresser but couldn't get a job because "some of the white ladies didn't like an Indian touching them."

37   Then there was the fine moment in television when Dick Cavett asked him, "Is it any different being an Indian in Canada?"

38   "No," said Dan George.

39   Dan George's sense of being an Indian is a great distance from that of Red Power advocate Harold Cardinal, who takes fact-finding tours of New York's Bedford-Stuyvesant poor people's corporation and who talks of touring Israel's kibbutzim.

40   Dan George transcends Red Power, equaling its advocates in bitterness (they quote his speeches, while dropping the positive endings) but going beyond to the Indian roots of natural harmony and communion with the land and the living things on it.

41   It has been explained that *our* sense of time can be expressed in a series of tight circles—the boundaries of weekend to weekend, month to month, or year to year that govern our activities. The Indian has no such concept. Time for him is expressed as one long straight line, stretching off into the distance. It is why, Dan explains, the Indian has such trouble adapting to the white man's rigorous concern for fixed hours of work. "It is hard for others to understand. We keep things inside. Our sense of humor, everything. It's all inside."

42   "What Dan has taught me is the language of silence," says Kay Cronin, a gentle woman who is director of the Oblate Fathers communications centre. "Indian boys come into my office and may not speak for the first 10 minutes. You have to learn to empty your heart so that it can be a receptacle. Indians concentrate on perfecting human relationships. That's what Dan is so good at. *We* concentrate on acquiring material things."

43   She tells of conferences at the University of British Columbia, with all the experts delivering their papers on solutions to the Indian problem, "when suddenly they'll remember that perhaps they might ask the Indians. They turn to Dan and say, 'Now what do you think?' There is about 12 seconds of dead air. When he finally *does* speak, they're ready to listen.

44   "He's the only man I've seen who uses timing as well as Jack Benny. He uses the silence to communicate."

45   Phil Keatley, a Vancouver CBC producer, has guided his career and tried to protect him against those who would use him. It was Keatley who first recognized the acting potential inherent in the old man's natural dignity and soft expressiveness. It is Keatley who

advises him on movie roles and it is Keatley who would like to see Dan cast in the role of a cardinal. On reflection, an interesting idea, not inappropriate.

46   Dan George's skill is not overly exploiting his role as a "chief" but in the meantime using the prestige it gives him to work for his people. It's a narrow trail to tread. He picks his spots and occasions, and with that remarkable timing and those electric spaces of silence leads us to a few insights into a man "luckier than most."

47   "I think we need to listen to him," says Kay Cronin, "not for what he can tell us about Indians but what he can tell us about ourselves." He's the portage over time.

48   Behind Dan's little house is the scraggly second growth that will no longer support game. As we walk down the hill away from the house, an ungainly freighter slides over the water, headed for the loading dock at the end of the inlet that will fill it with coal. A clothes-line sags under the weight of the laundry of Bob George's 14 children. Across on the opposite bluff the Standard Oil refinery plans an expansion that would double its output.

49   "Eight years ago I dedicated myself to try to do something that would give a name to the Indian people," says Dan in his whisper. He pauses. "I feel I've attained my goal. Moving off the reserve is for another generation."

50   The puppy dogs yelp playfully around the aluminum trailer of Lenny George. We shake hands and I leave him on the slope—*his* slope—the copper moon of his face watching the water.

Allan Fotheringham, "Dan George's Last Stand," *Maclean's,* July 1971: 28–29, 50–52.

QUESTIONS

Subject
Explain how the title captures the author's attitude toward the subject and comment, if you can, on the title's irony.

Audience
Fotheringham's portrait of Dan George is clearly sympathetic. Explain how the author tries to win sympathy from a reading audience which might not be of George's race or share his culture.

Purpose
Part of the purpose of this essay is to document exploitation. Find instances of the way in which exploitation is expressed in the essay.

Structure and Style
   (a) Explain how and why the essay comes full circle, that is, how it seems to end where it began.

   (b) Locate three different ways the author describes Dan George's face and comment on their effectiveness.

   (c) Examine and comment on the significance of the environments depicted in the essay.

"Every Stroke Upward": Women Journalists in Canada, 1880–1906

Barbara Freeman

1 One morning, in the spring of 1904, Margaret Graham, a nineteen-year-old newspaper writer, marched into the Canadian Pacific Railways office in Montreal looking for publicity director George Ham. Her goal was to persuade him to take a group of newspaper women to the St. Louis World Exposition. He had earlier escorted a party of male journalists there, but had never offered the same trip to women writers. The angry Graham, Ham later wrote, felt that "women had altogether been ignobly ignored and she demonstratively demanded to know why poor downtrodden females should thus be so shabbily treated." He promised her that, if she could find a dozen press women, he would be happy to oblige her. She came up with fourteen and, true to his promise, Ham took them to St. Louis in two private railway cars, free of charge.

2 Women who were working as journalists in Canada at the time were used to being disregarded by the men in the profession. Like women entering other fields, such as medicine and law, they found that they had to struggle to make their presence felt.

3 Some of the women on the St. Louis excursion were new to the newspaper world; others had been writing for years. Some wrote only for their home-town newspapers, while others moved all over Canada during their journalism careers. There were francophones as well as anglophones, Easterners as well as women from the West.

4 Together, they were representative of those who had been entering a new profession for women—journalism—since the late 1800s. Their ranks included the "dean" of female literary journalists in Canada, Agnes Maule Machar of Kingston, Ontario; journalist-turned-novelist, Sara Jeannette Duncan; the popular women's page writer, "Kit" Coleman of the Toronto *Mail and Empire;* the Agriculture editor of the *Manitoba Free Press,* E. Cora Hind, who was one of the very few women in a senior editorial position; and the unconventional Maritimer, Kate Simpson Hayes, who eventually brought them all together as members of the Canadian Women's Press Club.

5 Their reasons for becoming journalists varied. Some had always wanted to write; others entered the field because they suddenly found themselves without financial support and needed to make a living. They were single, married, separated and widowed, with and without children. All were, however, educated, middle-class women who were doing something quite untypical for many women of their generation—pursuing a career.

6 Like many pioneers, these women often found the going rough. Before the mid-1880s, women were not allowed into newspaper offices at all, with their gruff male inhabitants banging away at typewriters beneath clouds of tobacco smoke. Newsrooms were dirty, noisy places and considered quite unsuitable for respectable middle-class women. According to newspaperman Hector Charlesworth, men wrote the scattered bits of "women's news" until the 1880s when newspapers became more compartmentalized—partly to appeal to advertisers—and the women's pages were created. The few women who were already working for newspapers as short story writers, literary journalists or society editors, did so at home and sent their items in by messenger.

7   In the nineteenth century, there was no firm division between creative writing and journalism. Newspapers often published short stories, poetry, book reviews, opinion columns and
editorials, all written by the same people.

8   One of the most prolific was Agnes Maule Machar (1837–1927); she wrote novels, poetry and opinion pieces on issues close to her heart (such as temperance, education for
women, and improvements to the squalid living conditions endured by working-class people). Her work appeared mainly in periodicals such as *Rose-Bedford's Canadian Monthly and
National Review* and *The Week,* during the 1870s, '80s and '90s. She also contributed to
the Toronto *Globe* and other daily newspapers, and continued to write well into the 1920s.

9   Machar was a rarity among women of her generation. She was well educated by her father, who was the second principal of Queen's College in Kingston, decades before girls
in Canada were given equal education with boys. It was a time when women writers often
disguised their presence on the literary scene by using male *nom-de-plumes* or by remaining anonymous—ploys that allowed them some success while upholding the Victorian code
of female modesty. It was considered unseemly for a middle-class woman to "go public" about
anything.

10   Machar was an early "social gospel" advocate in Canada who felt that practical application
of the lessons from the Sermon on the Mount did more good in this world than piety without action. Much of her writing dealt with this theme.

11   For a long time, apparently to please her conservative mother, Machar did not sign her
name to her articles. Upon reaching middle age, she finally began to use a pen-name,
"Fidelis," a reflection of her strong Christian faith. The use of pen-names such as hers was
a common practice among journalists of both sexes, but particularly for women, who often
took on a male persona. For example, Sara Jeannette Duncan (1861–1922) enjoyed a meteoric
early career as "Garth Grafton" before she finally began to sign her own name to her work.

12   Duncan was a young career woman of the 1880s—a member of the generation that succeeded Agnes Maule Machar's. She started at the Brantford *Expositor,* her Ontario home-
town newspaper, moved to Washington where she wrote editorials for the *Post,* and later
returned to Canada as women's page editor for the *Globe* and then as Ottawa correspondent
for the *Montreal Star* and *The Week.*

13   This was an amazing record of journalistic accomplishment for a woman who was still
in her twenties. But despite this success, she was still cautious about her vulnerability as a
woman writer. One way to circumvent unfair criticism, she once explained, was to use a
male *nom-de-plume:*

14   ... in the case of a distinctively masculine pen-name as George Eliot or Charles Egbert
         Craddock, I believe the selection is due to a dread of that instinctive bias in criticism which
         a woman's acknowledged literary effort invariably suffers (Toronto *Globe,* May 27, 1885).

15   Duncan had her own biases about what women could accomplish in journalism. She
believed women could write literary criticism, political and social commentary, advice
columns and travel features. But she drew the line at day-to-day news reporting with its
strict deadlines: she did not believe that women could think and work fast enough for that
kind of assignment. Her bias was consistent with her middle-of-the-road approach (for the
time) on other issues: she believed, for example, that women should have the vote but that
they did not know enough about the law to be Members of Parliament.

16   Duncan herself had been the victim of some prejudice in the journalism field. As a
rookie, she once approached a Toronto newspaper editor, E.E. Sheppard, and asked him

for a job. He turned her down, explaining that the last woman he had hired had not done a good job. Years later, he rued that day in print, devoting much of his column to praise of Duncan's writing ability and literary success. Certainly, Duncan can be given much credit for opening the eyes of male editors to the potential of female journalists. She represents a transition point between the somewhat elite intellectual journalist and the everyday women's page editor: she was both in her time.

17   The women's page offered the most opportunity for ambitious female writers because it was the only editorial department of a newspaper in which women were generally welcome. Of course, they were not treated the same as the men. Their male editors often refused to take them seriously because they wrote "women's" news—and indeed, whatever their ambitions, they were relegated to the women's pages from the start. Very few managed to slip over the gender border into the "male" reporting areas of politics, business and crime. Those who did—like Duncan, Cora Hind and occasionally "Kit" Coleman—received greater recognition than most of their female colleagues.

18   Kathleen Blake Coleman, "Kit" of the Toronto *Mail,* was the most popular woman's page writer of late nineteenth century Canada. Her Saturday page, "Women's Kingdom," appealed to both sexes, thereby helping to boost the *Mail's* circulation. Coleman (1864–1915) was a tall, spirited red-head, of aristocratic Irish connections, with a bright, lively and sometimes irreverent style. She did not confine her writing to fashion notes and recipes, but commented on most of the political and social events of her day.

19   In fact, it is a mistake to assume that the women's pages were less than serious journalistic efforts. Coleman, like Duncan and other female colleagues, was very much interested in federal politics; Canada's relations with Britain; international events and many social concerns (such as the movement of women into the workforce, female suffrage, street urchins, poverty, prostitution, and temperance).

20   "Kit," a small-l liberal with conservative leanings, had her opinions on all of these issues, as did the other writers. Her politics were not always consistent, but they did reflect the experiences of a woman brought up in a genteel environment who never expected to have to earn her own living.

21   Kathleen Blake was born near Galway in western Ireland and had a privileged upbringing, during which she received a good education. At sixteen, her parents persuaded her to marry a local squire who was forty years her senior—apparently their attempt to keep the family finances in order. But when her husband died four years later, he left her destitute.

22   The young widow emigrated to Canada, worked as a secretary in Toronto, married her boss, E.J. Watkins, and moved to Winnipeg, where she had two children, a girl and a boy. When her second husband died suddenly, she moved back to Toronto where she did freelance writing to support herself and her children. When she was hired by the *Mail* in 1889, she became an immediate success and was a leading figure in journalism for the next twenty-five years. She was, in fact, a self-made woman and proud of it.

23   This is not to say that she became a rich woman. The pay for both sexes in journalism was poor and it was usually worse for women, because their work was not considered as important as the men's. There were no paid holidays, or unions, or other advantages for the newspaper writer of either sex. When Coleman first started in the business, she made $20 a month—not much more than a domestic servant—and had to do light housekeeping overtime to make ends meet. Even after she became a successful writer, she complained of long hours, few holidays and inadequate pay. One source has it that she received $35 a

week from the day she was hired—a generous sum for the time. It is more likely that she was earning that much by the time she quit the *Mail* in 1911 and began syndicating her columns at $5 each.

24   Her popularity did mean that her editors gave her certain privileges. Unlike most women's page writers, "Kit" was occasionally allowed to escape in order to cover events in other parts of the world.

25   In 1898, after much wrangling with the United States Army, she managed to make her way to Cuba to write about the grim conditions being suffered by young soldiers fighting in the Spanish-American war. On another occasion, in Cleveland, she smuggled herself into the cell of a notorious female fraud artist, Cassie Chadwick, and got an exclusive story.

26   It cannot be said that "Kit" was typical of women's page writers. Few were as sophisticated, as bright or wrote as well as she did. But she was the acknowledged leader in her field at the time and, by all accounts, well-loved by most of her sister-journalists, especially the young "cubs," who looked to her for encouragement and advice.

27   "Kit" would tell them that a woman must serve her apprenticeship, as hard and discouraging as rejection letters from editors could be, if she expected to be successful. But an awareness of one's image as a woman was also important in journalism:

28   ... and if she would try to infuse a little of her charming femininity into her writing—then, indeed, she will be a great success. Her individuality will shine out strongly, and she will charm, intoxicate and allure you in dull, cold type just as much, perhaps more, than if you were sitting beside her, looking into the depths of her soft eyes (Toronto *Mail,* November 16, 1889).

29   It is clear that writing was becoming acceptable as a profession for women—as long as the writers in question maintained a certain propriety in print. Female pen-names were now preferred and were commonly used from the time the women's pages were established. There were, of course, exceptions to the rule: there were mavericks among the women journalists in Canada who, for one reason or another, did not conform to social expectations.

30   One was E. Cora Hind, the Agriculture and Commercial Editor of the *Manitoba Free Press*. When she first applied there for a newspaper job in 1882, she was turned down because she was a woman. She set up a typewriting service, got to know the farmers and businessmen who were her clients, and started writing freelance articles about the agricultural market. When newspaper editors urged her to use E.C. Hind as her byline, she refused, insisting on E. Cora Hind because she wanted her readers to know she was a woman.

31   By the time she was finally hired by the *Free Press* in 1902, Hind had established a reputation as an agricultural expert, one she maintained for the next forty years. She became world-renowned for the accuracy of her crop forecasts—and the acidity of her tongue in the face of male disapproval.

32   But maintaining a feminine image was important to her as well. Because Hind brooked no nonsense, did a "man's job" and never married, it was easy for her detractors to question her femininity. Probably the best-known photograph of her shows her standing in a field, dressed in what was considered masculine attire—riding britches, boots and a scout's hat—examining a sheaf of wheat. This particular image of the woman on the job appears to have made some of her more protective women friends uneasy. They were quick to point out that when Hind was not out on her rural rounds, she wore dresses, large feminine hats, and always had her knitting basket by her side. She was, one younger contemporary recalls today, a very "womanly" woman, who loved to crochet lacey underwear for her female friends!

33   There were other women who maintained a proper outward image, but who were not typical of their generation. One of the more interesting women in journalism was Kate Simpson Hayes, who worked in a number of Canadian cities and was well-respected by her peers, despite a very unconventional private life.

34   Hayes started her career in 1873 at the age of sixteen, writing a children's column under the byline "Ivy" for the *St. Croix Courier* in St. Stephen, New Brunswick, for the sum of one dollar a year. As an adult she taught school for a while, and then married a senator. But the marriage failed and, despite her Roman Catholic upbringing, Hayes left her husband and struck out on her own. During her career, she worked as George Ham's assistant in the CPR offices in Montreal and, as "Mary Markwell," first women's page editor of the *Manitoba Free Press*. Eventually she moved to Ottawa to work as a journalist and, not incidentally, to be with her married lover, Nicholas Flood Davin, a journalist-turned-Member of Parliament.

35   Her private life probably did raise eyebrows among her sister-journalists, but Hayes filled a prominent role among them as the organizer of the Canadian Women's Press Club. The club had been "Kit" Coleman's idea, an offspring of George Ham's trip to the St. Louis Exposition, and Coleman was its first president. But it wasn't until 1906, when Hayes organized its first national conference in Winnipeg, that the fifty-member club became firmly established and branches started to spring up across Canada.

36   From its beginning the CWPC deliberately cultivated a professional, patriotic image—but an intriguing clause referring to its members' proper "social and moral connections" was discreetly dropped from its constitution at that first conference. The club's records do not explain what happened, but it appears that the women agreed not to judge each other's private circumstances, but to emphasize professional qualifications. It is likely that Hayes, who took over as president, had something to do with the change.

37   The press club's members were prominent and not-so-prominent women who had been working in various capacities on newspapers and other publications across Canada for years, but who had never before banded together for mutual professional and personal support. The members included Agnes Maule Machar, Sara Jeannette Duncan (married by then and writing novels in India), "Kit" Coleman, E. Cora Hind, and Kate Simpson Hayes. Other names that appeared on the membership list were: Lucy Maud Montgomery, former society editor of the Halifax *Echo* and future novelist; Robertine ("Francoise") Barry, who had her own women's weekly, *Le Journal de Francoise* in Montreal and who led the francophone contingent of the press club; Sara McLagan, the first female newspaper publisher in Canada, who took over the Vancouver *World* from her late husband; Agnes Deans Cameron, who explored the Canadian North and made her living by writing and lecturing about her adventures; and small-town newspaper journalists such as Gertrude Balmer Watt, the cub reporter "Peggy" of the Woodstock, Ontario, *Sentinel Review*.

38   Full of optimism, they adopted a motto for their club—"Every Stroke Upward"—and vowed to work together to advance journalism as a career for women—women who wanted to write in their own names, do whatever job in journalism they wanted to do, and be considered the professional equals of the men with whom they worked. In 1906, after more than twenty years in the profession, they wanted women journalists to be given the recognition they so rightly felt they deserved.

Barbara Freeman, "'Every Stroke Upward': Women Journalists in Canada, 1880–1906,"
Canadian Women Studies, 17:3 (Fall 1986): 43–46.

QUESTIONS

Subject
Explain the significance of the phrase "Every Stroke Upward" for the subject of this essay.

Audience
Although this essay is about women it probably appeals to an audience of both sexes. Explain why this might be so or disagree with this claim.

Purpose
The author's purpose is to provide several portraits of early female Canadian journalists. What are some of the characteristics that these women shared?

Structure and Style

    (a) How does the anecdote in the first paragraph serve as a good introduction to this essay?

    (b) Examine the transition in the first paragraph between each portrait. How does the author achieve smooth transitions?

    (c) Comment on how illustration works as the main device in the essay.

Why She Needs the Bomb

David Frum

1   Whenever a world crisis erupts, it's easy to spot the Canadian foreign minister: he's the man demanding a special session of the United Nations. In matters great and small, from the invasion of Afghanistan to the *Satanic Verses,* Canada seems always to take the prissiest line in the Western world. This doesn't do the Western world much harm—who listens?—but it's not very gratifying to national pride.

2   But then, national pride never seems to have much influenced Canadian foreign and defence policy. Throughout our history, we have relied on others to take care of us: first the British, then the Americans. In renouncing the obligation of self-defence, Canada has refused to discharge for itself the one responsibility that no State can ever fully entrust to another. This must once have seemed like a clever money-saving idea, but over the years the seeping psychic costs of taking shelter behind the warships, troops, and missiles of someone else have gnawed at the country's always fragile self-esteem. Canada has tried to compensate for this military dependency by erecting cultural and economic barriers to foreign influence. It doesn't work, because the trouble with Canada is not that we don't produce our own television shows, but that we don't defend our own borders.

3   This is what has made our forty-five-year-old decision to deny ourselves nuclear weapons so consequential. The bomb is the decisive weapon of our epoch. Without it, we must forever hide behind the strength of others. That hurts. And asserting our national sovereignty

in oil-drilling and publishing and all the areas where it does not belong cannot begin to remedy our failure to assert sovereignty in the one area where it does. Yet we could still correct our mistake.

4   Canada is no nuclear virgin. Canada's contributions to the invention of the atomic bomb are largely forgotten now, but they did not go unnoticed at the time. President Truman, not a man for empty compliments, described Canada and Great Britain as "our associates in this discovery" in his first formal message to Congress on the atomic bomb, on October 3rd, 1945. Canadian scientists at Chalk River in Quebec manufactured the heavy water for the atomic bombs dropped on Hiroshima and Nagasaki. The uranium that formed their explosive cores was mined in Canada. Mackenzie King had been briefed on the Manhattan project on July 15th, 1942—the first world leader, after Churchill, to get the news. While Canada did not know all the secrets of the atomic bomb at the end of the war, it knew almost as much as Great Britain, and more than the Soviet Union. The mission of the spy ring betrayed by Igor Gouzenko was the infiltration of Chalk River.

5   Not only did Canada assist in the development of the American bomb, and supply many of its raw materials, but Canadian troops used to be equipped with nuclear weapons. Until 1972, the Canadian forces in Europe deployed battlefield nuclear artillery, and nuclear-tipped Bomarc missiles guarded Montreal and Toronto against Soviet bombers from 1963 until 1972. American nuclear delivery systems, like the Cruise missile, have been tested here, and nuclear-armed American ships and aircraft dock in our ports and land at our airbases.

6   Still, this history of involvement with nuclear weapons does not really call into question Canada's status as a non-nuclear power. Canada never fielded an *independent* nuclear deterrent. The warheads we deployed were made in the United States and were always subject to American control. In peacetime they were kept under American lock and key; in war, the order to fire them would have had to come from an American officer.

7   After the war, the nuclear technology that Canada had helped invent was rapidly diffused. The Soviet Union tested an atomic bomb on its own in 1949, and Britain followed in 1952. Later in 1952, the Americans upped the ante by detonating a thermonuclear "hydrogen" bomb with many times the destructive power of those used on Hiroshima and Nagasaki. The Soviets caught up in 1953; Great Britain in 1957. China exploded a thermonuclear device in 1965, France in 1968, and India in 1974. Israel seems to have acquired the bomb in the early seventies. Twenty-five years after the end of the Second World War, every one of the world's top economic powers that had not been on the losing side of the War possessed the bomb—except for Canada.

8   This is strange behaviour. Why *wouldn't* a State acquire the most powerful weapons it could afford? Especially a State that is not quite a major power? The bomb is, after all, a great equalizer. In 1939, a middle power like Czechoslovakia or Poland could hope to stand up to a great power like Germany or the Soviet Union for a few weeks at best. Now, a nuclear-armed middle power like France can convincingly threaten to inflict terrible devastation on a superpower—not comparable, certainly, to what the superpower could do to France, but ghastly enough to cause the superpower to hesitate before an act of aggression. Nuclear nations, even quite small ones like Israel, can act with a self-assurance unimaginable to the most powerful of non-nuclear states—Japan, for example, or West Germany. Canada's behaviour is stranger still, because it has not only deprived itself of nuclear arms, but of conventional strength as well. The 2.1 per cent of the gross domestic product we spend on the military has bought us a navy of twenty-three warships, an ill-equipped army, and a tiny, over-extended air force.

9   As with many of the more embarrassing incidents in our diplomatic history, the explanation lies in the peculiarities of the External Affairs mandarins who devised Canada's role in the post-war world. These men have dazzled two generations of high school textbook writers with their adept imitations of English manners, costume, and accent; their subtle manoeuvrings at the United Nations; their artful softening of NATO communiqués; their self-congratulatory idealism; their intricate memoranda on the opportunities for honest-brokerage; and their lingering presence in the background while houseboys served cocktails at surreptitious meetings with American and Chinese diplomats. But despite their innumerable learned degrees, these men—the "smooth Canadians who haunt the corridors of Washington with their confidential ineffective briefs," as James Eayrs called them—never quite figured out how the game was played.

10   Their master, Mackenzie King, piously reproved conservatives in his diary because "they do not rely on international friendships. They rely only on force and power. Force and power bring force and power to oppose them." And so his underlings believed. The celebrated mandarins of External Affairs never relied on force and power. To the suppressed amusement of the Americans and Europeans, Canada insisted on inserting a section on cultural and social affairs in the NATO treaty, lest the Russians get the idea that the new alliance intended to rely on force and power. Norman Robertson, then Canada's top foreign policy official, urged the Americans to share the bomb with the Soviets to enhance peace and international understanding. At the Truman-Atlee-King summit of 1945, Lester Pearson piped up that "we could prevent global catastrophe only by global agreement of an unprecedented character." As far as the written record shows, in all their thousands of hours of anxious meditation about the bomb, never did it occur to any of these highly sophisticated men that Canada might want one for itself. Did they perhaps speculate that Canada's position in the world might be secured by the cleverness of its diplomats and the benevolence of its intentions? Did they fear the bomb so much that they felt safer with it in anybody's hands but their own? Did they feel so little pride in Canada's war effort that they did not feel we were entitled to a permanent place of honour in the post-war world? Or were they so confident of the gratitude of the greater powers for Dieppe and the Battle of the Atlantic they thought no further effort necessary to preserve their place?

11   In any case, the possibility of acquiring nuclear weapons was so alien to them that Canada can hardly be said to have ever made a positive decision *not* to build a bomb. In all the memoirs of the period, the only reference I can find to any consideration of the possibility is an aside in George Ignatieff's *The Making of a Peacemonger:* before the Quebec Conference of 1943, Mackenzie King "had already decided that Canada was only interested in atomic energy for peaceful purposes." King's diaries (as edited by Jack Pickersgill) never discuss this momentous subject. Canada accepted a position in the third tier of nations, below the superpowers and the nuclear middle powers, without question or demur.

12   Why? When Charles de Gaulle assumed the presidency of France in 1959, it was a poorer and less technologically advanced country than Canada. But de Gaulle insisted on strict equality with the superpowers, and his utterly unrealistic determination that France be treated as a nation of the first rank, propelled her from the third into the second. Ever since, France has been strikingly immune to the periodic outbursts of anxiety common in the rest of Europe. In the Great Nuclear Fear of 1982, France was the only country in the West not afflicted by a mass unilateral disarmament movement: not just because the French instinctively know that *anything* that gets a million Germans marching in the streets is a bad idea,

but also because in France, as nowhere else in Europe, the bomb is a symbol of national independence, not of subordination to the United States.

13   The Americans have always objected to the acquisition of nuclear weapons by their allies, in part to preserve their own hegemony, in part because they believe that allies who have defence money to spend should spend them on tanks and aircraft. Although the British had helped immeasurably in the creation of the American bomb, and although Roosevelt had promised Churchill at Quebec that the United States would consult Great Britain before using the bomb, the United States Congress cut off atomic cooperation as soon as the war ended. The British built their first bombs on their own; they got American help for their maintenance of a thermonuclear arsenal only because the supple Harold Macmillan massaged the credulity and anglophilia of Jack Kennedy. The French and Israeli bombs were built in the teeth of unrelenting American hostility. The haughty de Gaulle fearlessly stood up to the Americans; and the Israelis, surrounded by mortal enemies, are not disposed to listen to anybody. But Canada—well, Canada anticipated the American reaction.

14   It would have been especially difficult for Canada to withstand American pressures (had an atomic project ever begun) because it would not have been easy to articulate a strategic doctrine for a Canadian nuclear force. The nuclear arsenal of the United States does a more than adequate job of deterring Soviet attacks on North America, so what precisely would a Canadian bomb do that an American bomb does not already do better and more cheaply? And the answer, of course, is Nothing. The strategic ramifications of a Canadian deterrent would be identical to those of an American deterrent, with a single difference: the ultimate means of our national defence would be in our own hands.

15   Canada has never clearly thought through how much independence in our foreign policy we can reasonably maintain. The Atlanticist school of thought, which was almost universal in Canada until the Vietnam War, and which has continued to predominate, holds our freedom to be quite limited. As a small nation beside a hugely powerful one, Canada had better not cross the United States on anything it really cares about. This way of thinking induced Lester Pearson to flip-flop in 1963, when he suddenly changed his mind about putting American-controlled nuclear warheads atop the Bomarc missiles the Diefenbaker government had purchased. The opposing, nationalist point of view that has spread since the middle sixties, insists that we can safely dissent from the Americans on the Soviet Union and the Third World.

16   Weirdly, the apparently more pro-American school, the Atlanticist one, is more afraid of the United States than the anti-American one. The opinion of the nationalists was articulated in their seminal collection of essays, *An Independent Foreign Policy for Canada?*: "The danger of anything deserving the name retaliation is minimal. 'Pressure,' yes; 'retaliation,' no." Like true children of the sixties, the nationalists knew that the authorities they were defying wouldn't smack them. The older generation wasn't so sure.

17   Yet there was always something unreal about the debate between the Atlanticists and the nationalists. The proposals for an independent foreign policy floated by the nationalists never dwelt very long on Canada's particular needs and circumstances. In fact, they bore a curious resemblance to the previous week's editorial in *The Nation*. If the ideas of the Atlanticists were neo-colonial borrowings from Dean Acheson and Dean Rusk, the ideas of the nationalists were neo-colonial borrowings from Henry Wallace and Gabriel Kolko. Assessing Canada's interests in the world, and then creating the necessary means for securing them, would have entailed, at the very least, an effective intelligence service and

military sufficiency. This never captured their imagination. They believed independence to be a matter of speeches, and taking tea with African guerrilla leaders, and voting at the U.N. They worried as little about laying the material basis for exploring the limits of our independence as the Atlanticists. Intellectually, they mimicked the American Left even more slavishly than the Atlanticists followed the American Centre. Neither faction troubled to peer out from under the American nuclear umbrella at a stormy world beyond.

18   Canada has developed a number of attractive but implausible justifications for not having nuclear weapons. The one most often heard in official circles is that we are setting a good example for the principle of non-proliferation. Admirable, perhaps, but the world is not inclined to follow our lead. When Mackenzie King vetoed a Canadian bomb, there were only two atomic powers on the horizon, the United States and Great Britain. Today there are at least fifteen nuclear or near-nuclear states. Countries acquire or refrain from acquiring weapons out of consideration of their interests, not because they are inspired by superior moral example: States, as de Gaulle observed, are rather inhuman monsters. Anyway, Canada's contribution to nuclear non-proliferation is a touch more—shall we say ambiguous—than official self-congratulators will admit. Canada supplied India with the raw materials and technology to make its bomb, although India had not signed the non-proliferation treaty (and still hasn't). When Israel, in the only successful enforcement of the principle of non-proliferation, bombed the Iraqi nuclear reactor at Osirak, Canada voted with a majority of the United Nations to condemn her.

19   Related to this justification is another, more popular thirty years ago than now. Peace-loving Canada, it was said—most fervently by Diefenbaker's external affairs minister, the gooey Howard Green—was in a unique position to win the respect and admiration of the newly decolonized nations of Africa and Asia. At the time, this was widely considered to be something worth having. But even if it were, it's hard to win the respect of others by failing to do what they themselves would wish to do. Virtually every Third World country with the money and know-how—Brazil, Pakistan, Argentina, Iraq, Egypt, Taiwan, and South Korea, to cite the most prominent—has tried, or is trying now, to build itself a bomb. India and China have succeeded. And yet all of these States have had the benefit of innumerable improving lectures from idealistic Canadians. Psychology, not politics, explains why the people who run our country are so peculiarly prone to attributing supreme moral virtue to the despots and dictators of backward countries.

20   Popular opinion has had a more basic reason for opposing a Canadian bomb: the conviction, or hope, that the Russians will be less likely to bomb us if we cannot bomb them. It is true that nothing on Canadian soil is so urgent a Soviet target as the missile fields of North Dakota, or the submarine pens of Norfolk, Virginia, and Puget Sound, Washington. But what little we know of Soviet nuclear strategy suggests that if North Dakota gets hit first, we get hit two minutes later. Once they make the awful decision to use nuclear weapons, they will not intend to restrict their attack to the enemy's warheads; they will mean to devastate his total warmaking power. Few places contribute more to NATO's warmaking power than the industrial complex that stretches around the western edge of Lake Ontario from Oshawa to Rochester. The Russians will not be inclined to spare the northern two-thirds of the complex because it happens to fly a red and white flag instead of a red, white, and blue one.

21   As the post-war order slowly dissolves, the time for a reconsideration of Canada's defence posture approaches. Mikhail Gorbachev seems to be trying to do two things: to ease the imperial burdens upon the Soviet Union, and to remove some of the ideology from its struggle with the United States. If he succeeds, human beings will not be suddenly cured of aggression.

Nor will our location under the missile paths of the two greatest nuclear powers change. If anything, the dissolution of the big ideological blocs could make the world a more unpleasant place. When democracy confronted totalitarianism across the Elbe, Canada could feel no choice but to enlist as a junior partner in the democratic alliance. In a five-cornered tussle between Western Europe, America, China, Japan, and Russia, it's every State for itself. A world in which nations jockey free-lance for position, in which many Third World States—Brazil, for example, or India—combine modern weapons systems with hot-blooded national ambitions, is not necessarily going to be safer, or kinder, than the world of the Cold War.

22   At the moment, Canada will not correct Mackenzie King's mistake. So long as the basic arrangements of the post-war order linger, we are going to retain the place we chose in 1945. But when that order vanishes, what should we do?

23   The defence strategy of the Mulroney government, which directs Canada's expenditures away from its land forces to the navy, is fine, as far as it goes. The Europeans hardly need us to supply their infantry. And the emphasis on submarines is right too: if the surface warship isn't quite obsolete yet, it will be by the end of the century.

24   But none of this amounts to an independent military capacity. Independence requires the power, on our own, to hurt an aggressor. Until we acquire our own nuclear deterrent, we will be wards of our allies.

25   A Trident submarine, which is the most survivable nuclear launch pad, can carry up to a hundred and twenty small but very accurate nuclear warheads. A Canadian government that took its rhetoric of independence seriously might look into buying three or four: enough to frighten off any international bully without asking for help. In the coming season of détente, it may be possible to buy them second-hand.

David Frum, "Why She Needs the Bomb," The Idler, May/June 1989: 12–15.

QUESTIONS

Subject
List the evidence Frum marshals to support his argument that Canada should become a nuclear country.

Audience
How does Frum try to win audience support? Are his arguments based on reason, emotion, or a combination of both?

Purpose
Explain why Frum might use the word "she" in the title of the essay. Does it have anything to do with his later comment that Canada is "no nuclear virgin"?

Structure and Style
   (a) Comment on the effect of Frum's use of rhetorical questions in paragraph 10.
   (b) Explain what Frum means by the word prissy ("prissiest," paragraph 1). Does Frum give other examples of Canadian prissiness in the essay?

Charter of Wrongs

Robert Fulford

> The Constitution is what the judges say it is.
>
> —U.S. Chief Justice Charles Evans Hughes

1   Nobody ever called Pierre Trudeau a supporter of the American way of life, but it has recently become clear that in a strange and unexpected way he presided over the Americanization of Canada. It has been commonplace for a long time to say that our major political institutions have been growing steadily closer to those of the United States: the concentration of power in the person of the prime minister has often and justly been called "presidential," and our political parties—with their flamboyant and expensive leadership conventions, their opinion polling, and their TV advertising—have slavishly copied the American models, often bringing in hired American experts to tell them how to do it. It might be argued, however, that these are simply modern practices and techniques, made inevitable by the growth of government and mass communications. But the principle that Trudeau brought us with the Canadian Charter of Rights and Freedoms is absolutely and intrinsically American and reaches back to the roots of the U.S. Constitution in the eighteenth century. It is the principle that judges know better than politicians what is good for everyone.

2   Trudeau, of course, is the main author of the Charter, and many a future history book will cite it as his main legacy; but his two predecessors, John Diefenbaker and Lester Pearson, will deserve mention as collaborators. During all his years in opposition Diefenbaker campaigned for a bill of rights, and as prime minister he put one through Parliament. That wasn't "entrenched," however—it was a bill like all others and could be erased by Parliament as easily as it was passed. Diefenbaker wanted a permanent and relatively untouchable bill, but couldn't get it. Pearson, when Trudeau was his justice minister, proposed to follow through on Diefenbaker's earlier idea—a bill that would be agreed on by the provinces, would be written in the constitution, and could not easily be breached by Parliament or a provincial legislature. Pearson failed too, but Trudeau took up the idea and tirelessly pursued it through meeting after meeting with the provincial premiers. In general, they didn't like it—at times they vehemently opposed it—but Trudeau wore them down. His Charter became a crusade, and as he and his ministers pushed the idea it grew popular. After a while entrenched rights seemed necessary, and then they seemed inevitable. Some Canadians must have begun to wonder how in the world we had ever managed so long without them. Voices opposing the idea grew steadily weaker. When Premier Sterling Lyon of Manitoba said in 1980 that an entrenched charter of rights would be inconsistent with democratic theory or even with the principles of parliamentary government, he was easily dismissed as a reactionary Tory standing in the way of national progress. So in 1982, along with patriation, the Charter of Rights and Freedoms became constitutional. All of us, overnight, were freer.

3   Or were we? Did we, before 1982, suffer under some form of tyranny? Our democracy was surely imperfect, our governments made mistakes and infringed our rights—as all governments, even the best, sometimes do. But were we any less free than the citizens of those democracies, such as the United States, with constitutionally entrenched rights? I never heard anyone say we were, except during the autumn of 1970, when the Trudeau government

used the arbitrary powers of the War Measures Act to deal with the October Crisis (whether the Charter would prevent a recurrence of that, we may never know). And yet our governments agreed that we needed *guaranteed* freedoms, not just the (perhaps) temporary freedoms under which we had been living for generations, first as British subjects and then as Canadians with the British tradition of parliamentary supremacy. Parliament, and the people we had sent to it, were till 1982 the main guarantee of our rights. Now we had rights that were written down, and would be enforced by court orders. Parliament and the legislatures might pass laws limiting or threatening our freedom; but we would have recourse to the judges, who would then make certain that our rights were not abridged. In future the politicians could override these rights only with difficulty—and would in the process be publicly perceived as being guilty of breaching the Charter, now a sacred document.

4   When Chief Justice Earl Warren wrote the U.S. Supreme Court's unanimous decision in *Brown v. Board of Education of Topeka, Kansas,* in 1954, he changed the course of American life. This was perhaps the most important single judgment of a court anywhere in the world in modern times. With a stroke the Warren Court made the pernicious practice of segregated public education illegal and started the process of broadening civil rights for blacks. Everywhere, people of liberal views rejoiced. The U.S. Constitution, speaking through Warren and his brethren, had beaten down the racism of state legislatures and local school boards.

5   It would be hard to argue that the Warren Court was wrong that day, but the judicial events that followed were not in all cases so clearly beneficial. The U.S. Supreme Court became "activist," and began handing down rulings on every aspect of American public life. Lower courts swiftly followed in the Supreme Court's wake. The United States became, to a degree it had not been before, a court-driven society. The citizens became more litigious than at any previous time or place in the history of civilization. It came to be assumed that rights of almost every kind were defined in court. Soon it was routine for U.S. city governments, state legislatures, Congress, and even the president to defer to the courts. Should white students from the suburbs of Boston be sent by bus to school in downtown Boston, and black students from the slums in the city core sent to the suburbs? The court would decide. Then how many students should be bused, from exactly where to exactly where? The court would decide that, too.

6   When Chief Justice Hughes said, half a century ago, that the Constitution is what the judges say it is, he was talking about the broad principles of the Constitution. He didn't mean that judges should be expected to dictate every detail of public policy; but that is what eventually came to pass. Not everyone agreed that this was ideal democratic practice, or even an improvement over rule by politicians. Inevitably, many Americans have grown restive under the power of the courts. Certain presidents, most recently Ronald Reagan, have tried to curb that power by appointing judges with more modest views of judicial discretion. So far, these appointments have not made a notable change. In 1967 the great American legal philosopher, Sidney Hook, wrote: "One recent and not uninfluential view maintains that no law can be properly regarded as the law of democratic American society until it has been validated by the United States Supreme Court." At the time Hook meant it almost satirically; he raised the point only to denounce it. Today that quotation would be close to a description of reality. American law is now judge-made law.

7   And so, increasingly, is Canadian law. Before 1982, Canadian law rested on the principle of parliamentary supremacy. Then, the courts could do little more than interpret Parliament's

will; now they can say that Parliament is wrong. As D.D. Carter of the Queen's University law faculty recently put it, "The Charter now allows our courts to overrule legislation.... This shift of authority is nothing less than a fundamental alteration of our constitutional arrangements." Carter admitted that in 1982 he expected nothing of the kind. After all, the Charter said that the guarantees of fundamental freedoms were to be qualified by the limits that could reasonably be justified in a free society. Moreover, Canadian judges had traditionally been cautious about dealing with political and economic issues. As Carter then saw it, the Charter would certainly apply to criminal justice and to language rights; but it would not, surely, affect in any serious way those areas where ground rules were already settled.

8   Carter, like many others, was wrong. Emboldened by their new powers, judges have decided that every arrangement that comes before them can be tested against the Charter. More important, they have apparently determined that anyone who defends established practices must accept the responsibility of demonstrating that these practices are consistent with the Charter. In Carter's specialty, industrial relations, the result may be chaos. Challenges that are now moving through the judicial system threaten labour laws that unions took generations to win. Is the certification process, a key element in orderly labour relations, consistent with the Charter? No-one knows for sure. Is collective bargaining itself protected by the Charter? That's unclear too. For decades Canadian law has tended to favour collective rights over individual rights; the Charter may reverse that preference. Carter's conclusion: "The Charter now creates the potential for virtually every labour relations issue to be outfitted in constitutional clothing, handing over to constitutional lawyers and judges a wide discretion to re-shape the Canadian labour law system."

9   That is not what the Charter's most fervent supporters intended. Tommy Douglas, the first national leader of the New Democrats, was an early advocate of an entrenched bill of rights; David Lewis, the second national leader, was equally enthusiastic. Were they alive today, would they be delighted to see that the Charter is now threatening the future of the labour movement? How would they greet the news that the right of labour unions to donate money to political parties—a right that makes the NDP possible—is now in jeopardy because of a challenge under the Charter sponsored by the National Citizens' Coalition?

10   Many a lawyer, it now seems clear, will be made wealthy by the Charter. A major constitutional challenge, running right up to the Supreme Court, can consume hundreds of thousands of dollars. Only those who can pay exorbitant lawyers' fees will pursue such a challenge; the logical inference is that the Charter will, in the long term, favour the rich. Corporations have happily fastened on the idea that a corporation, in law, can have the same status as a person; a corporation, therefore, can use the Charter as easily as a person can, and with less financial pain. Last spring the *Globe and Mail's* Report on Business told its readers: "The jury is still out on exactly how widely the courts will apply Charter rights to business. But the early trends are favorable to corporate interests." It should be no surprise that judges, most of them drawn from the same class that produces managers and owners, will listen carefully to the complaints of corporations.

11   Almost anything done by Parliament or a legislature can be challenged. The doctors of Ontario, by making their dispute over extra-billing into a Charter case, may defeat the government and win the right to charge whatever their patients can pay. Those of us who happen to support the doctors may be momentarily pleased. But will we be happy that the majority decision of the Ontario legislature, enthusiastically supported by the electorate, has been overturned? Will we be as anxious to defer to judicial review when a government measure we support is under attack?

12 American constitutional theorists have often argued that judicial supremacy is a check on the irrational impulses of the mob, that judges can be relied upon to overturn those laws that are pushed through the democratic process by the passions of the moment. But judges may be as susceptible as anyone else to fashions in ideology; and, unlike politicians, they cannot easily be unseated when their views prove unpalatable to the citizens. Sidney Hook, in *The Paradoxes of Freedom,* asked: "If the Court is to serve as the keeper of the community's conscience, who is to keep the Court's conscience?" Canadians know very little about their judges (far less than Americans know). For all of our history, until now, judges have been distant figures who applied—for the most part uncontroversially—the laws. Now we have asked the same people not only to apply but to reshape and even (when they please) overturn the laws. They are plunged deeply into what we normally think of as the political process—defining who can do what, balancing this need against that right, determining which cause deserves society's sympathetic attention and which does not. And yet they remain above that process. Who dares to picket judges? Who (the contempt-of-court rules being what they are) will dare to scrutinize and criticize the judges as we normally scrutinize and criticise the politicians? Since so many broad business issues will be decided by the courts, will it soon be necessary to examine the financial holdings of judges, as we now examine those of cabinet ministers?

13 Trudeau recognized, rightly, that there are elected politicians who can—out of stupidity or lust for power—turn into dictators. He set out to save us from them. Instead, he created a whole new class of potential dictators. The Charter was the great legal project of Trudeau's generation; undoing it may turn out to be the great legal project of the generation following him.

Robert Fulford, "Charter of Wrongs," Saturday Night, December 1986: 7–9.

QUESTIONS

Subject
How does the title direct us to the thesis statement of the essay in the first paragraph? Without the title, would Fulford's first paragraph be potentially misleading? How so?

Audience
Draw a profile of Fulford's audience, taking into account (a) level of diction; (b) subjects referred to; (c) knowledge assumed; and (d) tone.

Purpose
If Fulford's subject is the problem for democracy of having the courts as final decision makers, how do his pointed references to the US further his argumentative purposes?

Structure and Style
 (a) The essay has three sections. What is the unifying factor for each?

 (b) How are the six paragraphs of the middle section organized in a deliberate fashion?

 (c) Fulford asks numerous questions in this essay. What are at least two functions they fulfill?

Kanesatake: The Summer of 1990

Ellen Gabriel

In the summer of 1990, Mohawks living in Kanesatake, Quebec, erected a blockade to prevent the municipality of Oka from expanding a golf course on traditional Mohawk land. A Quebec police officer was killed when the Sûreté du Québec raided the barricade. The raid and shooting sparked a seventy-eight-day armed stand-off.

1   It is difficult to know where to begin the story of the so-called Oka Crisis, especially since so many who do not even know the true story have claimed to be able to explain why those events took place. I suppose one could write an epic novel on the subject, but I suspect that will not happen: the truth is hard to swallow for most Canadians.

2   History in Canadian schools has been taught from a very biased and racist point of view. Native people have much educating to do, both of the public and of themselves, concerning the true history of our culture and our people.

3   Kanesatake, or Oka, as it is most commonly known, has always been a Kanienkehaka community. Kanienkehaka is our own name for ourselves; it means People of the Flint. To outsiders we are known as Mohawk, one of the five founding nations of the Iroquois Confederacy.

4   Even before any European set foot on this continent, Kanesatake was flourishing in every sense of the word. Located near the confluence of two major waterways, the Ottawa and St. Lawrence rivers, Kanesatake was a central location for many nations besides the Kanienkehaka people. Pottery shards found at Oka Park date back as far as 1000 BC. Agriculture and the exchange of goods amongst different native nations were taking place long before any white man developed the idea of the fur trade.

5   When the businessmen-disguised-as-priests of the Sulpician order first arrived in Kanesatake from France, they did so under a land grant from the king of France. However, in Kanienkehaka culture, as in any other Iroquoian cultures, the women are known as the custodians of the land. If any land is to be sold or given to another nation, the process must be overseen by the women of the Iroquois Confederacy. The Canadian and American governments have never been able to produce any documents showing that the women of the Kanienkehaka nation gave, sold or ceded any of our lands to them, or to the French or English who preceded them.

6   Since the arrival of Europeans in North America, native people have been coerced, killed and maimed to allow non-native culture to prosper. In Kanesatake, my ancestors were jailed for cutting wood to heat their homes and cook their food. If they refused to convert to Roman Catholicism while in jail, they remained there until they died. Many missionaries used Christianity to exploit the native people and to justify their governments' policies of genocide.

7   When Canada was being formed, the British Parliament passed the British North America Act, a racist act that declares sovereignty over every native nation in Canada. This declaration was meant to override all the treaties made with individual native nations who were supposed to be allies, not servants, of the British monarchy or empire.

8   The same racist attitude, based on the non-native belief that their way of life, their religion and their system of government are far superior to those of any native nation, still reigns today in the structure and actions of the Department of Indian Affairs and Northern Development (DIAND). DIAND created the band-council system, in which the Minister of Indian Affairs is the grand chief. It does not matter how intelligent or educated a native chief is in the white man's ways; when it comes to the crunch, it is the Minister of Indian Affairs who has the final say in any program affecting native people's lives.

9   Over the past twenty years, as band-council systems became more predominant and the Indian agent position was phased out, the federal government began working out deals with those people of native descent who had little or no respect for their own traditional forms of government and cultures. These people made deals that helped the government perpetuate the genocide that has been going on against native people for almost five hundred years.

The Blockade

10 When we started our blockade of an access road in the Pines on March 9, 1990, we did so because most of us had lost faith in the system which is called "justice." But we had lost faith even more completely in the band-council system. Closed-door meetings and secret agreements between the Feds and the Six Nations Traditional Hereditary Chiefs (the misleading name for the band council in Kanesatake) had led many of us to the conclusion that the only way to stop the illegal development of our land was to take matters into our own hands.

11   At first, the people who participated in the twenty-four-hour vigil came from different backgrounds. By this I mean those of the Christian faith, atheists, and of course, the Haudonosaunee, or People of the Longhouse, which is truly the traditional political, cultural and religious structure of the Iroquois and includes all the people who still follow the traditional ways.

12   During the period that led up to the police raid on July 11, those of us who watched over our Pines were harassed by a vigilante group known as Les Citoyens d'Oka, and by the Sûreté du Québec. These events usually took place at night, often when the barricade was being guarded mainly by women.

13   For example, one night, several men dressed in black came and tried to take our banner down. When we caught them in the act, they ran away across the golf course, within clear sight of where the SQ patrol cars were parked to keep us under surveillance. Yet the SQ did nothing about the incident.

14   Other times, usually late at night, members of Les Citoyens d'Oka would drive up the highway to the access road where we had our blockade, stop to shout obscenities at us and give us the finger, then gun their motors and squeal their tires as they spun round and raced away.

15   On May 1, 1990, a police raid was called off in the final planning stages after we found out about it. Representatives from the federal government and the province met with the People of the Longhouse. On May 2, 1990, a few of our men reported seeing the police harbouring boxes of guns in one of the sheds in the golf course. The police, of course, denied it, and told the press we were trying to hamper negotiations.

16   The two governments in the meantime offered us nothing new. What we had asked for in order for the blockade to be removed was to have, in writing, a guaranteed moratorium on all development within a 253-square-mile area. No one would give us the guarantee, so the blockade remained.

17   Over the past year and a half, I have heard many community members point accusing fingers at one another over who brought in the weapons. This issue is irrelevant as far as I am concerned, since it was also irrelevant to the Sûreté du Québec. The police did not care whether the men, women and children at the Pines were armed or unarmed when they opened fire. To say we asked to be shot at is like saying the Jews asked for the Holocaust.

18   To condemn the Kanienkehaka people who defended the lives of their families against a police force totally out of control, is to condone the human rights abuses committed by the SQ. The governments of Canada and Quebec allowed these abuses to continue, with resulting damage to their reputation as defenders of human rights in the international community.

19   I realize that the propaganda against the Kanienkehaka people of Kanesatake, Kahnawake, and even Akwesasne, has damaged our credibility in the public eye. However, as far as I am concerned, no one is as immoral as the bureaucrats who wanted to send in the army on July 12, 1990, even at the risk of bloodshed.

20   Jean Ouellette, the mayor, and Gilles Landreville, the deputy-mayor of the Oka town council played pivotal roles in creating an atmosphere of hysteria among the public by telling the press the Kanienkehaka were threatening the lives of the non-native residents of Oka. Nothing could have been further from the truth. On the other hand, the Oka town council stood to lose millions of dollars in revenue if the golf course expansion did not go through.

21   As traditional people, we are obliged under our own law, Kaienerakowah, to stop any encroachment upon our land. In spite of a 1924 resolution passed in the Canadian Parliament outlawing the government of the Iroquois Confederacy, we, the Haudonosaunee, still maintain that we are the only legitimate government who can negotiate concerning the lands of our territory. Band councils are only an extension of the Department of Indian Affairs.

22   Throughout the period that led up to July 11, 1990, the Kanesatake Haudonosaunee reached out to other members of the Confederacy for help and advice about what to do in this situation which has deteriorated continuously over the past two hundred years. All people of every Longhouse were asked to attend a meeting in Kanesatake, and to put their personal differences aside. However, it was only two months earlier that two deaths had occurred in community conflicts at Akwesasne, so we knew that there would be a problem in that direction as far as unity was concerned.

23   I must also stress that the Kanesatake blockade was never a "Warrior" blockade. Everyone was asked to unite, including the members of the Warrior Society and those who opposed them. The Warriors were allowed to fly their flag, however, just as the Micmacs were. The press took off with the notion that we were all members of the Warrior Society. The Longhouse people in Kanesatake established the initial barricade on the access road, and since we are citizens of the Kanienkehaka nation, this was an issue for the people of the nation, not just the Warrior Society.

24   In the meantime, while we were trying to reach all members of the Iroquois Confederacy, the Municipality of Oka continued in its path of destruction. Jean Ouellette held press conferences to assure his investors that their project would go through in spite of our determination not to vacate the Pines.

25   On June 23, 1990, in Ottawa, the Haudonosaunee advised the Minister of Indian Affairs, Tom Siddon, that he could not make any deals with the band council, the Six Nations

Traditional Hereditary Chiefs (since renamed the Mohawk Council of Kanesatake) concerning the land, since the band council is only an extension of the Department of Indian Affairs and not a legal entity in a position to negotiate lands within Kanienkehaka territory. The traditional government of the Haudonosaunee participated in the original treaties, and they, not the makeshift governments of the band-council system, are the legal entities authorized to negotiate land treaties. Besides, the women of the Haudonosaunee have never signed away the future of children the way the band councils have been doing.

26   It was at the June 23 meeting that Mr. Siddon told the Haudonosaunee and the band council under Chief George Martin that there was no money left in DIAND's budget to "buy" land for the Kanesatake Kanienkehakas. This is a ridiculous statement to us; how can we buy back something that is already ours? The federal government should compensate the people to whom they fraudulently sold land in the first place—not take it out of Indian Affairs' budget.

27   We returned to Kanesatake and immediately went back to our vigil in the Pines.

The Police Raid

28   Some community members, including some of the traditional people, were predicting violence and bloodshed. They even made statements like: "It's not worth dying for." Those of us who did not leave the Pines wondered why these people were making such statements. We did not feel our lives were on the line. We felt the police would come in using excessive violence, possibly beating us, but we never imagined they would actually shoot at us.

29   On July 10, Mayor Ouellette made a public statement requesting the Sûreté du Québec assistance in dismantling our barricade. When asked whether he was worried about the possibility of bloodshed, he answered that it was not his concern. He was only asking the SQ to enforce the law against those who were breaking the law.

30   Reporters asked us at the barricade what we would do if the SQ came in to dismantle the barricade. We replied that we would inform them they were trespassing and that they had no jurisdiction on Mohawk Territory. We expected to be arrested for public disobedience. We never thought they would fire concussion grenades, tear gas, and, eventually, aim and fire their M-16s at us.

31   At approximately 2:00 a.m. on July 11, several members of the community, including Allen Gabriel and the band council, were informed of the SQ raid that was to take place in the Pines at 5:15 a.m. These people, however, never informed those of us sleeping overnight at the Pines that there would be a raid.

32   What took place on the morning of July 11, 1990, was the attempted perpetration of murder and genocide against an identifiable group of traditional people of the Kanienkehaka Nation. We were and still are a thorn in the side of the illegal government known as Canada. But through our belief in our Creator and our perseverance in our ceremonies, we were spared and have lived to tell about the morning of July 11 and the summer of 1990 in Kanesatake. Some bureaucrats wanted the Canadian army brought in from the start to finish the stand-off. However, politicians like John Ciaccia, the Quebec minister in charge of Indian Affairs, did try in earnest to peacefully end the siege. People like Mr. Ciaccia were in the minority.

33   I will never forget the summer of 1990, nor will anyone else who lived behind barricades in Kanesatake and Kahnawake, I imagine.

34   We did not initiate the violence of 1990, nor do we feel it was our first and only choice, as the government of Canada has led the public to believe.

35   I believe in survival. My nation, and especially my ancestors, understood the extremes people have to go to in order to protect what is rightfully theirs. We are a peace-loving nation, otherwise hardly any non-natives would have survived the centuries of "European Contact" in North America.

36   The policy of genocide is unacceptable in the name of God. These days, of course, it is carried on in the guise of enforcing the Indian Act and perpetuating the band councils.

37   My nation has been fed lies by Tom Siddon and his bureaucrats. DIAND has never compensated the Municipality of Oka for the parcel of land where we were fired on. They bought an adjacent parcel of land, but not the Pines area that was intended for the golf course itself. In fact, the Pines is still slated for development—condominiums—but that project has been put on hold for now too.

38   Justice in Canada is non-existent at the present time in the story of the "Oka Crisis." The real criminals and terrorists who held guns and canons to Kanienkehaka women, children and men have been rewarded with public accolades from Canadian Prime Minister Brian Mulroney and others. Meanwhile, our people went to trial.

39   What is apparent to us is that the government of Canada has no intention of honouring our treaties. Instead we continue to struggle with tokenism in the new "Reformed Constitution," although our rights have already been, and still are, entrenched in the treaties, in our own laws and in international law. Unfortunately, Canada respects international law only when it does not apply to itself.

40   As a Kanienkehaka woman, I would still like to see peace between native people and ordinary Canadians, for I know that the politicians do not represent the people's voice. Until that day, all of us should continue to seek the truth and justice, for what it's worth, in all our environments.

Ellen Gabriel, "Kanesatake: The Summer of 1990," Nation to Nation: Aboriginal Sovereignty and
the Future of Canada, Eds. Diane Engelstad and John Bird, Concord: Anansi, 1992. 165–172.

QUESTIONS

Subject
Ellen Gabriel begins her essay by saying "It is difficult to know where to begin the story of the so-called Oka Crisis." How does understanding this difficulty help the reader recognize Gabriel's full subject?

Audience
What words, phrases, sentences, and concepts suggest who the primary audience for this essay clearly is? How does "tone" contribute to audience-identification in this piece?

Purpose
If the second paragraph pinpoints Gabriel's purpose, identify three instances of that purpose being carried out.

Structure and Style

    (a) How do the three sections of the essay serve to develop the subject and fulfill the purpose?

    (b) Identify two places where narration and exposition work hand in hand to move the essay forward.

Rethinking Death with Dignity

Ian Gentles

1   The final taboo has been breached. Over the past decade dying has become a subject of intense public debate. Does a patient's family have the right to order the withdrawal of medical treatment if she is in an indefinitely prolonged coma (the issue in the Karen Quinlan case)? Does a doctor have the right to help his patients commit suicide (the claim of the Strangelovian doctor from Michigan, Jack Kevorkian, inventor of the "death machine")? Does a young woman suffering from an incurable and paralyzing disease have the right to order her respirator unplugged, in the near-certain knowledge that death will result (the demand of Nancy B. of Quebec City, victim of the rare Gullian Barré syndrome)? Is there anything objectionable about a writer publishing a long and detailed list of ways by which you may do yourself in (Derek Humphry, author of the 1991 best seller *Final Exit*)?

2   Not only is death now the subject of endless talk shows and journalistic think-pieces; the interested public are invited to watch programmes in which terminal patients die before their very eyes. The dignity or indignity of the witnessed event is then discussed by sober panels of journalists and experts.

3   To anyone who follows the debate, it is clear that the visual and print media in North America are overwhelmingly in favour of "death with dignity," by which they usually mean the legalization of active euthanasia. After all, runs the argument, most behaviour not manifestly dangerous to others—suicide for example—is now permitted in our tolerant society. Why should a doctor or nurse be penalized for assisting people in exercising their recognized right to take their own lives? Public opinion polls show that journalists are merely the vanguard of an apparently growing majority who support legalized euthanasia.

4   Reflecting this steady trend in public opinion, there have been a number of attempts in Parliament in the past year or two to pass private members' bills which embody this objective. Last February, Robert Wenman's bill, which would have lifted legal sanctions against a physician who administered "measures intended to eliminate or relieve the physical suffering of a person for the sole reason that such care or measures will or are likely to shorten the life expectancy of the person," was defeated. Chris Axworthy has introduced a bill which straightforwardly legalizes physician-assisted suicide.

5   This enormous concern with the issues of death and dying has at least something to do with demography. Advances in medicine, nutrition, and public hygiene have transformed life expectancy in the industrialized world. People can now expect to live twice as long as their

ancestors did a century and a half ago. Most of us shudder at the stories we have heard about incurably ill elderly people dragging out a vegetative existence in hospital beds, kept alive only by drugs, intravenous tubes, and respirators. Could anything be more meaningless and undignified? Is it any wonder that a soon to be published survey indicates that a majority of the occupants of two Canadian senior citizens' homes want euthanasia to be legally available? (Significantly though, most of them do not want it for themselves.)

6 But there is more than one fly in the ointment. In the first place, most health care professionals who treat the dying do not support legalized euthanasia. The same study, carried out by the Human Life Research Institute, reveals that medical workers have no trouble with withdrawing treatment at a patient's request. Nor do they oppose the use of drugs to alleviate pain, even if it hastens a patient's death. But by a margin of two to one they think that active euthanasia should remain illegal.

7 Some will interpret this as just another example of doctors presuming to tell patients what they cannot or should not do. However, there is more to it than that. Keep in mind that these health care professionals are with the dying on a day to day basis. Cicely Saunders, the founder of hospice care for the terminally ill in Britain, maintains that when a person asks for death it is usually because someone has failed them. Dr. John Scott, a Canadian authority on the management of pain, insists that the very cry for death may be the contrary— a cry for reassurance that continued life still has value. A patient who is tenderly cared for and whose pain is relieved (which is possible in almost all cases), does not normally ask to die. Moreover, it is in hospices and palliative care units, both in Britain and in North America, that genuine death with dignity takes place. Dignity is manifested in the courage, humour, and grace with which the terminally ill meet death, and also in the respect and tenderness shown by those who care for them.

8 The root difference between the advocates and the opponents of euthanasia lies in their attitude towards life itself. Most of those who work with the dying tend to see each patient as a unique human being to be respected and valued. These people often view life in religious terms, as a gift which evokes a response of wonder and awe. They usually do not think of euthanasia as an attractive option. By contrast, those whose attitude towards human life is utilitarian tend to ask the question, "If you're in intractable pain, or no longer any use to anyone, why go on living?" They are usually euthanasia advocates.

9 I would go farther and assert that the writings of some health care professionals demonstrate a greater ethical sensitivity and concern for the well-being of the terminally ill than the advocates of "death with dignity." Consider the background to the authorship of that strange tract of our times, *Final Exit*. When Derek Humphry's first wife, Jean, was diagnosed with breast cancer in 1974 she requested that he end her suffering. He accordingly supplied barbiturates with her morning coffee. Then he married Ann Wicket, and together they founded the National Hemlock Society in 1980. In 1986 they assisted in the double suicide of Ann's parents. Again barbiturates were used, but Ann also had to smother her mother. Afterwards she reflected: "I walked away from that house thinking we were both killers. Two days later I couldn't live with myself."

10 Then, in September 1989, Ann too was diagnosed with breast cancer. Three weeks after her operation Humphry abandoned her, leaving a message on her answering machine. He insisted that she was mentally deranged and had her removed from the board of the Hemlock Society. Ann launched a suit against him charging that his actions were "timed and calculated to exploit ... the weakened condition of the plaintiff, to induce her despair and her suicide."

In October 1991, shortly after the appearance of *Final Exit,* Ann rode into the wilderness near her Oregon farm and took a fatal overdose. She left a note for Humphry which she photocopied and sent to her friend Rita Market with a handwritten postscript.

11   Derek:

There. You got what you wanted. Ever since I was diagnosed as having cancer, you have done everything conceivable to precipitate my death.

I was not alone in recognizing what you were doing. What you did—desertion and aban-donment and subsequent harassment of a dying woman—is so unspeakable there are not words to describe the horror of it.

Yet you know and others know too. You will have to live with this until you die.

May you never, ever forget.

Ann

Rita: My final words to Derek. He is a killer. I know. Jean actually died of suffocation. I could never say it until now; who would believe me? Do the best you can. Ann

12   According to her friend, Ann Wicket related that she did not realize until she got cancer what subtle and not so subtle pressure can be put on people to die and get out of the way. Many elderly people already feel that pressure acutely. They have been persuaded that they are a burden and a drain on an overstretched health care system. Were euthanasia to be-come legal, this perception would inevitably be reinforced. Dying would turn into an oblig-ation for those no longer capable of contributing to society, rather than a right for those whose lives have become unbearable.

13   There are other ramifications to legalizing euthanasia which reveal the shallowness of the arguments for it. Will an absolute right to die make it illegal, for example, to rescue a would-be suicide? Will the pharmacist be obligated to sell a lethal dose of hemlock to anyone who is temporarily depressed?

14   There will also be enormous potential for corruption. Let us say that I am the principal heir of my aged Aunt Agnes. I happen to know that I stand to inherit a million dollars once she kicks the bucket. Might I not find it tempting to nudge Aunt Agnes in the direction of accepting a lethal injection in order to shorten the waiting time for my inheritance? And will there not be a supporting chorus of praise from those who consider this a fine and public-spirited thing for Aunt Agnes to do?

15   Corruption can take other forms as well. Does not the biography of Derek Humphry suggest that in many hearts there may lurk a less admirable motive for wanting to ease the elderly and chronically ill towards their final exit? Few are so tasteless as to link euthana-sia and health care costs in the same breath. Yet in recent years, the fact that medical care of the elderly is a heavy financial drain on the system has frequently been underlined.

16   Finally, what of the corruption of the relationship between doctors and their patients? If the same physician who heals is the one who administers death, how trustful will the el-derly feel towards their physicians once their health begins to fail? What emotions will they experience when a nurse approaches them with a full syringe? How soundly will they sleep

in hospital? A high proportion of those who care for the terminally ill are worried about an erosion of patient trust, should euthanasia become legal.

17   That such fears are not alarmist is suggested by the example of the Netherlands over the past few years. Active euthanasia is illegal there, but for a decade the Dutch government has tacitly agreed not to prosecute physicians who report having assisted their patients in committing suicide. Last year, a government-sponsored investigation into the practice of euthanasia resulted in the publication of a two volume report. Based on extensive interviewing of health care professionals, the investigators concluded that physicians kill over a thousand patients a year without their explicit request. (Voluntary euthanasia and assisted suicide account for an estimated additional 2,700 deaths per year.) Of the thousand who do not request to be put to death, one-quarter are fully or partly able "to sum up the situation and decide upon it in an adequate way." Besides the one thousand cases of active involuntary euthanasia, there are 8,100 cases in which morphine is given in excessive doses with the intent to terminate life, of which 27 per cent occur without the patient's consent, even though the patient is fully competent at the time the decision is made. There are a further 8,750 cases in which life-prolonging treatment is stopped or withheld with the intent to cause death, without the patient's consent. Almost all the physicians working in nursing homes withhold or withdraw life-prolonging treatment without the patient's consent. In 86 per cent of the cases in hospitals, the "do not resuscitate" decisions are made without the patients' knowledge. These statistics concern mainly the elderly. Not included are the deaths of newborns with disabilities, children with life-threatening diseases, and psychiatric patients.

18   Even more disturbing than the extent of involuntary euthanasia is the discovery that many physicians systematically flout the official guidelines for carrying it out. Over one-fifth do not consult a colleague, while over two-fifths do not consider the requirement of a written report important. Over half omit to record the proceedings in writing, while between two-thirds and three-quarters issue death certificates declaring that the deaths are due to natural causes. In view of the stipulation that euthanasia is regarded as an unnatural cause of death, this represents plain falsification of the returns. It is further revealed that virtually all the physicians who intervene without the patient's explicit request issue certificates stating natural causes.

19   The Netherlands is widely thought to be a civilized country. The main goal of the physicians and nurses practicing euthanasia or withholding treatment would appear to be not to save money, but to relieve suffering. We may wonder what the experience of legalized euthanasia would be to countries that are more economically hard pressed, or have a more impatient attitude towards the elderly.

20   A few months ago the question of euthanasia took on a personal meaning in my life, when I had to confront the death of my own father. For a long time my father had vehemently expressed his determination not to spend the last part of his life in a state of senility, or lying on his back with his mouth gaping open in a hospital ward, unable to recognize anyone, waiting for death to carry him off. After retirement he had worked as a volunteer, repairing TV sets at his local hospital in Scarborough. On his rounds through the hospital he had seen many examples of what he referred to as "human vegetables," and had vowed that he would never allow himself to suffer the degradation of these pathetic, forgotten individuals. A confirmed atheist, he wanted nothing to do with funerals or any of the traditional panoply of mourning, which he regarded as an expensive form of hypocrisy and a waste of time.

21   When in the 1980s the movement for legalized euthanasia gained a higher profile, my father embraced it enthusiastically. He joined the local chapter of Dying with Dignity, and drew up his own "living will." In this document he laid down that nothing was to be done

to prolong his life should he fall prey to a terminal illness, and requested that his attending physician administer a lethal injection to hasten his death, if the law permitted. He gave copies of the document to my brother and me, assuring us there would be no trouble finding a physician to carry out his wishes, since he had heard that doctors did it all the time. Feeling uncomfortable, we none the less swallowed our objections, comforting ourselves with the thought that, since our father was then enjoying robust good health, we would not have to face the quandary of his wish for assisted suicide for a long time to come.

22   In the summer of 1991 my father began to lose weight, and was frequently tired. Sometimes he could not keep food down. He assumed that he had a nasty bout of stomach flu and moderated his diet. With his inveterate suspicion of doctors and his successful avoidance of hospitals all his life, he postponed seeing his physician for several months. Finally, at the urging of a friend, he made an appointment for the end of January 1992. The diagnosis wasn't long in coming: cancer of the bowel, which had spread to the stomach and liver. To me it now became clear why he had talked so much about death during the previous year and a half. Refusing the specialist's offer of surgery, chemotherapy, and radiation, he announced that he would die at home, and would accept nothing beyond elementary nursing care to control pain and help him stay as comfortable as possible. He summoned my brother and me to separate interviews, and, to our distress, reiterated his determination to curtail his suffering by ending his own life.

23   For as long as we could remember, neither my brother nor I had been able to confront my father on major issues, since he did not brook argument. If we disagreed with him once his mind was made up, we had to get out of his way, use subterfuge to frustrate his will, or capitulate. This time the issue was momentous enough, and his request for help explicit enough, that we had to be straightforward. We told him that we respected and supported his decision to refuse all medical treatment; we would back his decision to die at home, even though he was living alone at the time. But assisting suicide was illegal, and we didn't care to be involved.

24   Although my father was an atheist, many of his friends were religious believers, including his closest friend, who did not refrain from telling him that his talk of suicide appalled her. Finding himself thwarted, he became angry. But rather than rail against his friends and relatives, he attacked the legal and medical establishments. Bitterly, he accused them of not caring about the suffering of those who were dying.

25   In a last half-hearted effort to engineer his own death, he sent his friend's daughter out to the shopping mall to buy a copy of *Final Exit*. From that he learned how you could take an overdose of sleeping pills, and tie a plastic bag around your neck. But he realized that by now he was so weak he would need assistance to perform even these simple acts. So he tried once again to enlist our help. We were dismayed. Tying a bag around your head seemed the opposite of dying with dignity. Again, we tried as much as we could to avoid crossing him by changing the subject whenever he talked of suicide. Our stalling achieved the desired effect of putting things off until it was almost too late for him to arrange his own death. Contrary to his expectation, his attending physician, a woman of considerable cheer and compassion, showed no propensity to help him do away with himself. So he had to fall back on his children. Was this deliberate? Had he in reality left it this way because he knew he could count on us to say no? The thought occurred to me only weeks later.

26   By the time he had been taking painkillers for a couple of weeks and was on a regimen of morphine pills, he told his best friend that if he couldn't get the sleeping pills recommended by *Final Exit,* he would take a fistful of morphine pills instead. At this stage his children and close friends were worn out with anxiety and dread. His best friend, who happened

also to be a nurse, had taken leave from her job to spend the better part of every day caring for him and trying to cheer him up. I, who had done some reading on the subject, summoned up my courage to confront him one last time. Have you considered just stopping eating, I asked him. Many people, when they are approaching death, lose interest in eating and refuse all food. You are nearing the end; it will only be a few days. Your children, grandchildren, and your friends will all be terribly upset if you take your own life. Why not just let yourself slip away as others have done before you? Would that not be a dignified way to go? After all, nobody is trying to prolong your life, only to keep you comfortable. He didn't bother to answer my all-too-cogent (cogent to me at least) reasoning, but I did note that from that point on he virtually gave up eating.

27   Eventually his morphine dosage was greatly increased, and was administered in liquid form through a needle and small plastic tube strapped to his arm. This seemed to eliminate most of his discomfort, and put him in a better frame of mind. The nurses who were with him now—both his friend and the professionals supplied through the home care agency, handled him with tenderness and professional competence. He seemed almost pleased at the superb attention he was getting, and still managed to exchange jokes with them. Thanks largely to the high standard of palliative care he received during his final week, he said nothing more about wanting to hasten his own death. In the last three days he took only small quantities of water, mainly to moisten his mouth; his heartbeat accelerated, while his breathing became progressively faster and shallower. Finally, early on a Friday morning, his heart stopped beating. He had achieved the dignified death for which he had yearned.

28   Reflecting on these events a few months later, I am persuaded more than ever that taking one's own life, far from being a dignified way to die, is usually an act of despair, a statement that one feels bereft of comfort. In his last weeks, my father ran into the perplexing opposition of friends and family to his expressed desire for suicide. He was frustrated, too, by the refusal of medical professionals to give him any assistance in realizing this goal. But to his surprise he found himself encircled by the love of people who cared deeply for him, and were competent enough to suppress his pain, make him feel that he was the centre of their attention, and ease his passage out of this life. He died in peace and with dignity.

29   If this fierce atheist, who was bound and determined that no one was going to stop him from enjoying the benefit of active euthanasia, finally abandoned his insistence on pursuing such a course, then I am convinced that the great majority of other individuals who think they would like to end their lives could be rescued by first-rate palliative care and the love of those close to them. The question is, do we want to make the sacrifices called for so that people who want to die at home can, in comfort and dignity, but without demeaning pressure to accept a lethal injection?

Ian Gentles, "Rethinking Death with Dignity," *The Idler,* Summer 1993: 50–53.

QUESTIONS

Subject
Comment on the way the author uses anecdote (paragraphs 1 and 9–12) and statistics (paragraphs 17–18) to support his argument against legalized euthanasia.

Audience

Indicate the various methods the author uses to gain audience support for his position.

Purpose

The latter part of this essay is almost entirely personal anecdote. Does this narrative support or subvert the author's thesis? Feel free to be critical of the author's conclusion found in the last two paragraphs of the essay.

Structure and Style

(a) Explain what the author means by "the final taboo." Would everyone reading this essay agree with this description of euthanasia?

(b) Argumentative essays should at least strike a balance between reason and emotion. Do you find such a balance in this essay?

From **The Morningside Papers**

Peter Gzowski

1   At one time or another during the past few days I have done, at least once, each of the following things:

2   I have had Chinese food delivered to my house. Barbecued chicken wings, honey-and-garlic spare ribs, beef and snow peas and an order of steamed rice, with extra mustard and plum sauce. Not very good, as it turned out, too bready and tasting of rewarmed cardboard—but delivered right to my door.

3   I have played with the converter on my rented cable TV, flicking and jumping between *Hollywood Squares* and a panel discussion on the nuclear holocaust, intercutting a young cable reporter's guide to the traffic courts with a concert of the Boston Pops, simultaneously watching a soccer game and the provincial news, checking up on the prices of stocks I cannot afford, the departure times of airplanes I'll never ride and the fluctuations in the costs of foods I do not care for, and never once, because of the magic control at my fingers, having to watch a commercial.

4   I have lurched to the door in the mornings and found my local paper lying soggy on my doorstep. I have summoned a taxi to the same door. I have shooed away someone who wanted to park his Volvo on the bricks that cover what once was the front lawn of the house I live in, bought a package of cigarettes at two in the morning, gone to a movie within three blocks of where I live, shovelled up the junk mail in my foyer, been wakened by the sound of breaking glass at four AM, worried if the neighbours can see me stride naked to the bathroom, locked my door at night, ridden the subway, bought a morning newspaper the night before, seen a major-league baseball game in a real—well, since it was in Toronto, almost real—major-league park and walked to work. And every day, my list of new adventures grows.

5   I have, you see, recently moved back to the big city. I was born here, and raised nearby, and after all the other places I've lived and worked I've always come back to it. But for the past five years I've really been away. During those years I made new friends and found new pleasures, and yet now I've come back again. This time, the city seems to have changed. Or maybe I have. I see it now through new eyes. In five years the city mouse has become a country mouse and now he sees his old turf differently.

6   In the country, I couldn't get Chinese food delivered, or watch the cable, or get the paper brought to my home. To go to a movie theatre has been a major excursion. What I needed to buy (or read) I bought by travelling, usually by car and always by daylight. Now, I'm having some difficulty adjusting to my new conveniences, and during the next few days I thought I'd ruminate out loud about some of the things I'm learning—as well as some of the things about my life as country mouse I'm already beginning to miss.

II

7   On the morning of the first Saturday I moved back to the city, I went shopping. In itself, this was not a new experience for me, for in the past five years, while I have lived as a country mouse, I have often spent Saturday mornings shopping. I have jumped in my car and driven to the local bakery for a dozen sticky Chelsea buns and a copy of the morning paper, which lacked, because of my distance from its printing presses, the previous evening's sports scores. Later, if I have needed stuff, I have cruised the local merchants, chequebook in hand, and driven twenty kilometres to the nearest bookstore, where I have kept a charge account, or the provincial liquor outlet for another jug or two of the wine I know goes well with fresh sweet corn.

8   In the city, though, I needed no car, and my chequebook would have been only slightly less useful than a walletful of *zlotys* or a necklace of wampum. In the city you need hard, cold cash—or the 1980s equivalent of cash: hard, cold plastic.

9   In the city, I live downtown, on the edge of what my friend Harry Bruce, who has since moved to Halifax, christened the land of the white-painters. There are more BMWs on the street where I walk than there are trees. The houses are closer together than seats on a subway train. As evening falls you can hear the Jacuzzis flush as if in unison, and right around the corner there are more stores than there were in all of Rome. Without crossing the street I could buy, if I had the money, a Cuisinart or the *New York Times,* vitamin B12 or a quiche to go. There are three kinds of orange drink in my neighbourhood convenience store, and twenty-four kinds of doughnuts next door. I could have my suede cleaned, my fuel pump tuned, my walls hung or my aquarium stocked. If I did cross the street I could buy a silken kite or a Stilton cheese, a German knife, a Danish peppermill, a Swedish bar stool, a Hungarian table wine or a Mandarin orange. I could get egg bread or bread rolls, breaded veal or a well-bred parakeet. I could buy a marinated leg of lamb, a chocolate-coated cherry, Kiwi fruit, canned artichoke hearts, fresh lobsters, hot croissants and cold Heineken. I could take home a live Dieffenbachia or ice cubes made of glass, a wicker end table, the latest issue of a magazine I would not like my children to see me reading or a copy of the kind of book I used to carry under my arm at university, title-side out.

10   I could live my life in the neighbourhood I have moved to, I think, and never sample all its wares.

11   And yet, as Mordecai Richler says, and yet.

12   On Saturday morning I went to see if I could buy something that would make me a cup of cappuccino before I came to work. Cappuccino in the morning is one of my fantasies, although the only person I have met yet who can afford to drink it is Peter Pocklington. I went to my neighbourhood kitchenware store. (In the village I have just moved from, the equivalent is one corner of the Home Hardware, just behind the fertilizer.) A lady with a German accent came to help me. First she asked me how many cups I wanted to make, and when I just said one or two she gave me a one-sentence lecture about the need to entertain my friends. Then she showed me a machine that looked as if, were I to pull the right levers in the right order, it would leave in eight minutes for Brandon. When I said that was too complicated she showed me something automatic that, I think, would not only have made me a cappuccino but have served as the centrepiece for next week's exhibition on shapes of the future. When I demurred, my helpful storefrau led me to something that appeared to have been made for filling the gas tanks of model airplanes.

13   Nothing I saw cost less than $198.50.

14   And all I wanted was a cup of coffee.

15   I felt as my first-born son must have felt on the second Christmas of his life when, surrounded by half-opened packages and urged on by his loving parents to open more, more and more again, he burst into tears of sadness and being overwhelmed.

16   I went back to my rented house, past the parked BMWs, past the silent Jacuzzis, past the white-painted bricks, to my white-painted townhouse.

17   I had been gone for an hour and a half, window shopping in the casbah of the trendies, and I had bought … nothing. My plastic was intact.

III

18 On the first turn you take if you drive toward the city from the house I have been living in for the past five years is a pond. I'm not sure why it lies there; on a golf course it would be casual water, and you could move your ball from it, and on the prairies it would be a slough (a word unknown in the east). But beside Highway 7 in rural Ontario it is a pond; no river runs in, no stream out. A willow tree droops over one corner, and in the summer and early fall there are cat tails and bull rushes at its edges. Even when the wind is high, it is quiet and still. On the last morning I drove in from the country, a tall blue heron posed a dozen feet from its shore.

19   I stopped my car to stare; the heron did not move.

20   If I had dared to predict, when I moved to the country five years ago, how much I would become intrigued by birds, my friends would have laughed at me. I was a total city mouse then; I rode taxis and ordered meals in, and for adventure took my kids to the zoo. In the country, blue jays jabber at me outside my kitchen window, and I jabber back, and run out with a handful of Thompson's wild bird food, $1.39 the four-pound bag, to pacify them. I am their servant. My mornings are better when they start with a brilliant male cardinal, tip-toeing in to get food for his lady. In the afternoons, an oriole pipes from the black walnut and I stop work. One summer evening as I sat with the latest P.D. James in the garden a hummingbird hovered over my teacup. I have seen grackles and juncos, bluebirds and warblers, woodpeckers and flickers, jays, buntings, larks and nuthatches, chickadees, thrushes, whippoorwills and enough sparrows to start my own cathedral—all outside my windows, or just over the first rolling hill. I do not always know what they are, for I am not always quick enough

to find the right page in Roger Tory Peterson, my copy of which is now as well-thumbed as a family Bible. One magic morning I watched in wonder as a college of mourning doves waddled up through the early mists.

21 I am a sucker for all of this, and during the years I lived in the country my books, binoculars and birdseed have become as much a part of my life as backgammon once was, or Beefeater gin.

22 And now, I think I'm going to miss it.

23 There are compensations for all this, I know. Better shopping and faster taxis—or, in my case, taxis at all. Strangely, I can walk to work in the city, where I had to drive for anything in the country—or anything except work, most of which I did at home, next to the chattering blue jays. The snow won't shut me in this winter, and I don't have to worry about the well freezing or the door blowing off the barn.

24 The country surprised me when I moved there, and the city is surprising me again. This morning on my way to it I saw four sparrows, a starling and one of the last robins of the fall. But what I thought about was the blue heron, standing still near his private pond.

IV

25 One of the things I have not yet had to do in the first days of living back in the city is fill the gas tank of my car. This is not a part of country living that I miss. In the country, I have had to buy gasoline almost as often—or so it seemed—as I have had to change my socks, and the habit has come close to breaking me.

26 I don't know what gasoline cost when I used to live here. They sold it by the gallon then, and every couple of weeks I'd notice the tank was low and cruise in for a top-up. It cost ten dollars, or thereabouts, if I was empty. A nuisance. Now they sell it by the litre, and I know *exactly* what it costs. The car I drive is fuel-efficient, and I read the prices on the pumps before I buy, but it's twenty bucks minimum when I'm close to empty and I seem to be in gas stations more often than I'm in my kitchen. The nuisance has become a real factor in my fiscal affairs, and I am having no more luck with my budget than Allan MacEachen has had with his.

27 That's only one part of what, I've come to realize, my flight to the country has cost me in dollars. Another part is the phone. I know I talk on the phone a lot, and that phone calls are part of my work, but I never before realized that the rest of the world has lived in a place called long distance. If you had asked me my phone number any time over the past five years I would have begun my answer with my area code, and even my kids, now grown and living in the city, think my number begins with a one. While this has some advantages—one of them is that I know, when someone wants to interrupt my solitude, he has been willing to spend a dollar to do so—it makes my monthly letter from the Bell look like the stock-market columns in the Friday Report on Business.

28 I had not thought of any of this when I left. I thought of the country as a retreat, a quiet place, where life would be simple and pleasant and cheap, and where I could cut down on the need I have felt most of my adult life to make as much money as I could just to stay even. Well, quiet and simple and pleasant it has been, I assure you, but cheap? I might as well have bought a racehorse. I pay rent on my mailbox and a tax on my trees. Fertilizer costs money so the grass will grow long, and the local university student charges me to keep it, occasionally, short. The tomatoes I have tried to grow have been more expensive—if better—than those I could buy in a city supermarket, and I have not been able to put up the capital

to buy equipment to do my own preserves. Even my daily newspaper, which I have to use gasoline to go to buy, costs me more than it would have cost in the city. At times I have looked at my city friends the way the have provinces have looked at the have-nots in a federal conference, as if I were subsidizing them and they didn't realize it.

29   Look, I know I've done lots of things wrong. I ought to have bought a sheep for the lawn and started making my own soap instead of driving four miles to buy it at inflated rural prices. In the winters, I ought to have huddled over an oil stove rather than watching the fireplace cheerfully crackling away with the last of my paperback royalties. I have not, I promise you, lived extravagantly, and the old stone house where I've been hiding out—once the home of a working quarry-master—is more cottage than estate, even though it burns more fuel than Premier Davis's private jet. But one of the strongest lessons I have learned in my time away from the life I grew up with is that being a country mouse is at least as expensive as being a city mouse, and I don't think city mice realize it.

30   Am I wrong about this? I don't think so. I don't think the city slickers know what it costs us hayseeds to stay where we want to stay. You may want to add to what I've discovered. Or argue with my conclusions. Or tell me what you know about saving money in the country that—short of trying to ride my sheep to the store on Saturdays—I didn't think of when I was there. If you do, please drop me a line. I'd ask you to call me, but I know the cost of long distance. Boy, do I know the cost of long distance.

Peter Gzowski, The Morningside Papers, Toronto: McClelland & Stewart, 1985. 16–22.

QUESTIONS

Subject
Explain exactly what Peter Gzowski is attempting to outline in this essay and comment on his attitude toward his narration.

Audience
To whom does Gzowski direct his essay? Does the audience need to experience *exactly* what Gzowski experiences about city and country life to appreciate the point or is there enough general mythological material present about these contrasting sides of existence to help us understand the distinctions he is drawing? The antiquity of the city mouse/country mouse notion might help you in your response to this latter point.

Purpose
Explain how the use of the narrative mode in this essay helps to convey the author's main point.

Structure and Style
(a) By focusing on paragraphs 2, 3, and 4 of this essay, comment on the effectiveness of Gzowski's use of detail. Does this detail and the way in which it is presented convey the author's attitude toward city living? In what sense is the phrase "new adventures" (last sentence, paragraph 4) ironic? Justify the author's use of a sentence fragment in sentence 2, paragraph 2.

(b) In what sense is paragraph 9 an encapsulation of the author's entire attitude toward city life?

(c) Compare the contrasting attitudes found in paragraphs 12 and 20.

(d) Comment on the effectiveness and appropriateness of some single-sentence paragraphs in this essay.

Pictures of an Exhibitionist

Rosa Harris-Adler

1   Sixty-three photographs by Donigan Cumming, most of them nudes, became a minor cause célèbre when they toured Canada a while back in a show called Pretty Ribbons. The Montrealer's work has also been a source of controversy among the usually unflappable arts crowd in Europe, where the pictures are now making gallery rounds. The reason: the often harrowing, raw, and surprisingly erotic photos are of Nettie Harris, eighty. My mom.

2   If Cumming's photographs of Mother have caused much heated bleating within the arts community, it's not surprising. They depict her in a variety of improbable and often blatantly sexual stances. There's one of her bare, beturbaned, toothless, and intense, swinging a golf club in her cluttered apartment, sepia family portraits on the wall behind her. Another shows her with eyes closed in the bath, leathery face turned upwards, palooka nose overwhelming the camera, aged breasts bobbing in the water. In a third she's starkers and cackling, pantyhose around her thighs, in front of the open fridge in her bizarrely painted kitchen. And there's one of her leaning a skeletal arm against the thigh of a prone, naked fat guy. These pictures are weird.

3   When images of Mother appeared in an issue of the Winnipeg-based arts magazine *Border Crossings*—including one as a centrefold—editor Robert Enright characterized them as "the most uncomfortable ... I've ever looked at." Warming to his subject, he described her body as a "topography of loss and misdirection—a breast appears like the ear of an old animal" and went on to say of one particular photo, "It's impossible not to read [it] as a pathetic metaphor for Nettie's life, emptied out and scattered, leaving her naked and vulnerable." He's quite right. The metaphor *is* pathetic. My mother's life had its share of pathos, certainly, but it was just one shade on the palette of her emotions, and not a principal one at that.

4   The photos proved to be a true Rorschach test, revealing the strange psyches of art types. Parisian reviewer Patrick Roegiers wrote of one of my mother's pictures: "The final view of a disintegrating figure, the fetal position of suffering and sacrifice, evokes the nightmare of remembering, the obligation to memory that her Jewish identity brings closer—unbearable visions of death camps, the Holocaust, the crematoria and the gas chambers—endowing this seemingly private epic with undeniable historical dimension."

5   Huh? I don't *think* so, but what do I know?

6   Nicole Gingras, who served as curator of an exhibition Cumming had at the Art Gallery of Windsor, is equally dense about the pictures.

7   "Nettie Harris is an ambivalent figure who is difficult to get a hold on, but she offers her body to our gaze. Detailed, seen in her different facets and poses, she is a body; at the same time, however, she is a character from a novel with an astonishing power to fascinate the viewer." Mom would have loved that last bit, at any rate.

8   Other critics saw her as a defiant feminist, an eighty-year-old Madonna giving aging the finger. A few, meanwhile, were in a foam about the heartless violation of the model. Inevitably, Lise Bissonnette, *Le Devoir*'s pompous doyenne of high culture, weighed in with her comments, describing my mother as a "very old woman, naked, and poor" and Cumming's work as "just as vile a form of exploitation as that of commercial kiddy porn." One voice in the wilderness, *Globe and Mail* arts columnist Morris Wolfe, rightly decried the patronizing tone of the arguments and wondered what my *mother* might have had to say about it all.

9   She would have said—and I can vouch for it—that Lise Bissonnette was wrong on one important count. Certainly my mother was "a very [check!] old [check!] woman [check!], naked [check!] and poor [well, iffy …]." But she definitely wasn't exploited. Cumming's photographs can be cruel and shocking, and when he found an aged model willing to pose nude, I'm sure he thought of Arbus and Mapplethorpe, and the commercial possibilities didn't escape him. He's a guy with an eye for the main chance, all right, but I don't hold that against him. He's an artist, too, and a pretty good one. He spouts a lot of art-school talk about "photographing the space between her poses" and the scary thing is that I think he means it. He also talks quite poignantly about the death of his own mother and how important his model became to him. All along, he may have unconsciously worried that he *was* exploiting her, but the real question was, who was zoomin' whom?

10   The truth? Nettie was a bawdy old dame, with her own eye for the main chance. She was a prima donna with an arch Dorothy Parker wit who lived for publicity, smack dab in the hurricane's eye. She was also a major pain to those of us who loved her and had to bail her out (once or twice quite literally) when she failed to pay her bills or otherwise misbehaved.

11   In the last third of her life, she was an actress and a model—an extra in virtually every movie made in Montreal, from *Bethune* to *A Man Called Intrepid*. It suited her lifelong lust for the limelight to a T. I remember her attending premieres of her less notable flicks (no skin flicks that I'm aware of), carrying herself like a fashion model with her cherished mink stole tossed insouciantly over her shoulder, wearing fingerless, elbow-length gloves of silver mesh. She never had a speaking role, but she was determined to make it big. She probably thought posing nude would be good for her career, especially with the age factor thrown in for notoriety. Cumming paid her the standard model's fee—twenty dollars an hour— and he photographed her over a twelve-year period. For his efforts, he's probably made about $20,000 or $30,000. She may have been underpaid. But, as a professional model, albeit a risk-taking, mischievous one, she was not exploited.

12   Did I mention my mother was eccentric? She ran a gamut of contradictions: she drank too much, for example, but trumpeted convention. She was coy and tough, arrogant and vulnerable, infuriatingly obtuse and a giggle. As a former journalist of no small note, she remained up on all the hot topics until the day she died. When I took her out for supper on her eightieth birthday, she wanted to know whether I thought Dylan's appearance on Letterman was up to his usual standards.

13   Like her spiritual granddaughter, Madonna Ciccione, she was constantly reinventing herself. Growing up in the teens and twenties as the tar-black sheep of a religious middle-class Jewish Sudbury family, my mother, as her nine remaining strait-laced siblings are still fond of saying, marched to her own drummer. In the late 1920s, she landed a job at *The Sudbury Star* where she would eventually cover such events as the birth of the Dionne quintuplets and the mysterious death of the heir to the Dodge family fortune while he was

in the company of his new wife, a former telephone operator. She was an intrepid stringer for the American papers and when she covered a royal tour in 1939, she sent her copy off on a lark to *The New York Times*. The article described how the king and queen's entourage was forced to stop (for water to refuel their train's steam engine) in White River, Ontario. (The village was so small at the time it didn't have a mayor to greet the royal couple—so the community elected one on the spot.) The piece was an exercise in spare, elegant journalism: it was so colourful, the *Times* not only ran it on the front page, they wrote an editorial about my mother as well.

14   She married in 1942 at the age of thirty, forfeiting her career at my father's behest: it was the way things were in those days. I remember well my mother's resulting rather pathetic attempts at domesticity. I have one recollection of her baking chocolate-chip cookies with what I can only describe as a vengeance, slapping them on the cookie sheet as though they had personally offended her. She dearly loved my father, a newspaperman himself, but was never comfortable in the kitchen, and when he died in 1960, she was freed to work again, as a freelance researcher and writer.

15   In her later years, she was at odds with three of the basics of life—food, clothing, and shelter. The healthier the diet, for instance, the more it seemed to lay her low: milk disagreed and lettuce was a killer. And she often complained that elastic waists and the tight hooks of undergarments bound her and made her uncomfortable. She wore clothes for propriety only, a mismatched cacophony of plaids and stripes onto which she'd often attach her own pockets—doilies she'd crocheted of wildly coloured acrylic.

16   What's more, she had fought her apartment long ago—and lost. Everywhere there was the debris and detritus of daily life. "The dishes are done, long live the dishes," she used to proclaim in despair as I was growing up, as a new pile mounted in the sink. But when we were kids, she still did them. When we left home, she stopped. Eighty-five pounds when she died, I calculate she'd smoked about 100,000 cigarettes in her time for each of those pounds. There was evidence of this all over her apartment—brimming ashtrays, empty matchbooks, discarded packages.

17   It was the fourth basic drive of life that she was really in tune with—sex. An inveterate flirt, she never stopped putting the talent to use, refining it with encroaching age. I remember going to a party with her when I was eighteen and she was fifty-six; "Dump your mother," a fortyish charmer said to me, "and we'll go somewhere." Five minutes earlier he had advised my mother to dump *me*.

18   I always thought my mother would beat the odds and live forever, but she died three years ago October. I suppose the time was right: she was a huge baseball fan and the Expos had just ended a most respectable season. More important, she was a star at last. A video entitled *A Session With Nettie* had just debuted to raucous and good-natured cheers in a chic little café on Montreal's terminally trendy Boulevard St-Laurent.

19   She had posed in the raw for the video, as Cumming snapped away and film-maker Bruno Carrière recorded them at work.

20   "At first, I was shy," she confesses demurely on camera about posing naked in embarrassing positions, "but then, once I did it, I felt free, without accoutrements, like I could fly." There is telltale melodrama in her voice, and she is mugging. In one sequence, she balks at Cumming's request that she remove her false teeth. "You're a monster," she chides him coquettishly, but she does it just the same with an actor's stoic professionalism. Her mouth

implodes, her face ages instantly. But her hooded bedroom eyes, barely dulled by blindness, are sassy as hell. And Cumming's camera clicks away.

21   It was an ambitious little film about the working relationship between model and artist, but she was front, centre, controversial, and vivid and she would have loved the crowd reaction. She never saw it: she was too frail to leave her nursing home for the vernissage. In fact, she was gone within a week or two of the event: I should have known it was coming when she missed *that* party. But she died hip and famous, and that would have pleased her.

22   To this day, I suspect my mother was tricked into dying. You know that blinding white light that you're supposed to see as you cross over? I'm sure she thought it was the flash of a camera—and that she walked eagerly towards it, hamming it up shamelessly, as naked and perfect as the day she was born.

Rosa Harris-Adler, "Pictures of an Exhibitionist," *Saturday Night,* July/August 1996: 27–31.

QUESTIONS

Subject
The title of this essay is probably a parody of a piece of music meant to commemorate an art exhibit in Russia. The piece of music, written by Modest Mussorgsky, is called *Pictures at an Exhibition*. To what extent is this essay about pictures, pictures of Nettie Harris, and the author's own picture of Nettie Harris?

Audience
Give some examples to show that the reader of this essay might be shocked by the portrait the daughter paints of her mother. Do these references show disrespect on the daughter's part?

Purpose
The author uses exposition to make clear to the reader the true nature of her mother. But the essay itself is basically argumentative. To whom does the author take exception and whom does she argue with?

Structure and Style
  (a) The essay is divided into two parts. What are they and where does the break between them occur?

  (b) Comment on the appropriateness of the sentence fragment at the end of the first paragraph.

  (c) Explain Robert Enright's comment on the photographs when he calls them "a pathetic metaphor for Nettie's life." What does the author mean when she says that "The metaphor *is* pathetic?"

Liberalism and Censorship

Ralph Heintzman

1   After a period of more than a decade in which it had seemed to fade from view, the issue of censorship has emerged again in the last year as a matter of public debate in Canada. The re-emergence of the issue suggests that certain questions many had thought settled were in fact only temporarily set aside. The assumption of a portion of the community—that the state has no right to restrict public expression—has proven to be less widely accepted than seemed for a time to be the case. The attempted reassertion of the state's right to control certain kinds of public expression—apparently with the support of a wide segment of opinion—has alarmed those who assumed such a right was already extinct, or on the point of becoming so.

2   The reaction of many within the intellectual and artistic community has been commendably energetic. The Book and Periodical Development Council has formed a special task force on censorship chaired by Timothy Findley. A recent broadcast of *Cross-Country Check-Up* was mobilized against censorship. Among many others, the editor of *Saturday Night* and the book columnist of the *Globe & Mail* have strongly deplored the reassertion of a right to censorship, the latter repeatedly and in sensational terms.

3   All of these voices are perfectly correct in diagnosing a problem of censorship, but the real problem is a rather different one than most of them seem to think: it is a failure to think clearly about the issue. The bulk of recent commentary on censorship in Canada has been a crude mixture of knee-jerk reactions, unexamined premises, and the wielding of bogeys. This is as true of those who oppose censorship as of those who favour it, but it is perhaps more surprising and regrettable in the case of the former. The censorship debate has not been characterized by the careful thought and distinctions one would hope to find on such a sensitive and divisive issue, especially from the "intellectuals" whose special care it ought to be to make just such distinctions.

4   The result is a state of high confusion in which a number of separate issues have been mixed together and the real issue has been almost entirely obscured. One is scarcely justified, for example, in mixing up the right of parents and school boards to decide what the children in their care shall be required to read with the issue of censorship properly so-called. The exercise of this right does not interfere with what may be published and sold, or even with what young people may read, but only with what they may be *required* to read, which is a different matter altogether. Like all other rights, this one may be exercised with good judgment or bad—and, more often than not, with the latter—but the existence of the right itself cannot be questioned. Indeed, parents who failed to exercise it would probably be more open to censure than those who did.

5   Similarly, it is an abuse of common sense to confuse the well-meaning efforts of a city council to license and supervise—not ban—the sale of pornographic literature with a limitation, even a potential one, on political expression, as William French has done. The lack of proportion involved in this kind of judgment goes to the heart of the confusion surrounding the discussion of censorship and the refusal of those engaged in it to make the necessary distinctions.

6   It is essential to distinguish, for example, between the maintenance of a minimum level of public decorum and the censorship of political debate. Those who refuse to acknowledge

this distinction and who argue, as Robert Fulford has, that any form of censorship leads inevitably to totalitarianism are just as guilty as if they were to attack liberals as communists or conservatives as fascists: they are indulging in a form of intellectual McCarthyism. It cannot be seriously maintained that insistence on a certain standard of public decorum is a threat to political life, any more than concern for a decent level of manners is a threat to social life. In fact the reverse is more probable in both cases: a high standard of public manners may well be the condition for a high standard of political and social life. In any event, the increasing license of our own time does not seem to have raised the level of political discourse noticeably, to say the least, above the standard achieved in another age by a Burke, a Marx, or a Mill.

7   One ought also to make a more careful distinction than is usually the case today between the practice of censorship and the level of artistic expression. It is by no means self-evident, as many today assume without adequate reflection, that the existence of censorship inevitably entails a loss of artistic power. As everyone knows, nineteenth-century Russia was subject to a high degree of political censorship (though not nearly as high as in the Soviet Union today), yet it also witnessed one of the greatest flowerings of literary creativity in the history of the world, thus perhaps confirming Northrop Frye's suggestion that literature actually flourishes in difficult circumstances. The facts are so striking that one is almost tempted to suggest that a measure of censorship might be a reasonable price to pay for a Pushkin, a Turgenev, or a Chekhov, let alone a Dostoevsky or a Tolstoy! Though utterly facetious, such a thought does underline the fact that those who oppose any form of censorship cannot do so on the ground that it inevitably means a lowering of artistic standards. Once again the reverse could be just as easily maintained. In fact, the celebrated critic George Steiner has done precisely that in his most recent book, *On Difficulty.*

8   That certainly does not mean, of course, that the case against censorship is without merit, but it suggests that those who argue it must give more sustained attention than they have yet done to their premises. All too often these remain unexplored, while the weight of their argument rests on a number of bogeys exploited to intimidate and silence their opponents. Since these bogeys will not withstand serious criticism, the opponents of censorship must strengthen and refine their case. In doing so, they will have to take a harder look at their own presuppositions.

9   One of the curious things is the inconsistency these presuppositions often involve. In my own experience—and it is worth emphasizing that the views expressed here are those of the editor alone and do not necessarily reflect those of any other persons or institutions associated with the *Journal*—virtually all those who oppose censorship on principle are equally strongly in favour of legislation against hate literature and various forms of racial abuse. Yet this too is a form of censorship. Thus the opposition is not really to censorship at all but only to certain forms of it. The right of the state to enact controls on public expression is admitted: only the objects of censorship remain in dispute.

10   This concession alters the nature of the debate fundamentally. It is no longer a question of whether censorship should exist—this being now admitted—but of what should be censored, and how. Answers to these questions presuppose answers to others. Most of the recent controversy about censorship in Canada has been about censorship of pornography or of explicitly sexual material. If, as I have suggested, one cannot successfully argue that censorship in any form is necessarily a threat to political life or to artistic integrity, then in order to decide whether the state ought to exercise its right to censorship in relation to these matters one requires a coherent view of the place of sexuality in the human spirit and of the implications of this view for the development or preservation of a civil society.

11   Supplying answers to *these* questions is enormously complicated in our time by the role of liberalism as the prevailing ideology of the intellectually influential. In fact, the intellectual confusion surrounding the issue of censorship—the *real* problem of censorship defined above—is largely the consequence of both the strengths and weaknesses of the liberal mind.

12   As Lionel Trilling remarked in his suggestive review of the Kinsey report, later reprinted in *The Liberal Imagination,* the good side of liberalism in sexual matters is "its impulse toward acceptance and liberation, its broad and generous desire for others that they be not harshly judged." This generous side of liberalism is greatly to be cherished and admired, but when it has been given due credit "as a sign of something good and enlarging," Trilling wrote,

13   we cannot help observing that it is often associated with an almost intentional intellectual weakness. It goes with a nearly conscious aversion from making intellectual distinctions, almost as if out of the belief that an intellectual distinction must lead to a social discrimination or exclusion. We might say that those who most explicitly assert and wish to practice the democratic virtues have taken it as their assumption that all social facts—with the exception of exclusion and economic hardship—must be *accepted,* not merely in the scientific sense but also in the social sense, in the sense, that is, that no judgment must be passed on them, that any conclusion drawn from them which perceives values and consequences will turn out to be 'undemocratic.'

14   The prevailing liberal view of sexuality is shaped by the behaviourist assumption that human acts can only be judged—if indeed they can be judged at all—according to generalizations drawn from the observation of what people actually do. The liberal mind shrinks, therefore, from judging sexual behaviour

15   except, presumably, in so far as it causes pain to others … the preponderant weight of its argument is that a fact is a physical fact, to be considered only in its physical aspect and apart from any idea or ideal that might make it a social fact, as having no ascertainable personal or cultural meaning and no possible consequences—as being, indeed, not available to social interpretation at all. In short, [liberalism] … by its primitive conception of the nature of fact quite negates the importance and even the existence of sexuality as a social fact.

16   Yet it is precisely the meaning of sexuality as a social fact with which one must grapple before the question of censorship can be satisfactorily resolved. This is a very large matter and no approach to it can be suggested here, but it is obvious that much will depend on one's notion of the human mind or spirit. It is not common nowadays to think of the mind in Platonic terms, that is, as requiring mental "guardians" to keep in order the potentially unruly energies and forces of which it is in large part composed. But since this view of mind has been held even longer than our modern one, perhaps it deserves more attention than it now receives.

17   In this view, the passions are conceived as being a vitally important element of mind, perhaps even its centre, but, by their very power, being also capable of great destruction and therefore in need of careful direction and control. The individual citizen's control over his own passions is, in fact, the foundation of social discipline and social order. The sexual passions in particular have almost always been regarded as forces of tremendous power for good or evil. An intuition of their awesome power explains why so many religions incorporate elements of sexuality into their own mythology and worship, yet also encircle them with a great variety of prohibitions and taboos. The purpose and origin of such prohibitions vary greatly but their fundamental source is the intuition that this power cannot safely be trifled

with, that it should not be taken in hand lightly or frivolously, but reverently, discreetly.... They are warning signs posted around the passions to caution the unwary: "Handle with care." Chastity, as Benedict Domdaniel remarks in *A Mixture of Frailties*, is having the body in the soul's keeping: just that and nothing more.

18   The modern or liberal frame of mind regards the passions in a very different light. For one thing, it approaches them with far less awe. In its classical mood, it is more sanguine about the power of naked rationality to control and direct them for good. In its romantic mood, it is inclined to look on every impulse of the human spirit as potentially creative and therefore not to be checked or disciplined without loss: the romantic hero is often one who by giving in to his passions and violating the taboos achieves a level of knowledge or experience denied to others. The view that almost every impulse is potentially creative is not wrong, of course. But it overlooks the complementary Platonic or Augustinian insight that there is a hierarchy in the realm of the good and that evil enters the world not through the triumph of bad over good, but through our own preference for a lesser good to the exclusion of a greater. Thus it gravely minimizes the potential for evil implicit in acts or impulses which may be, in their own terms, good.

19   For another thing, the liberal mind interprets sexuality in terms of certain analogies drawn from modern technology. The Freudian or twentieth-century notion of sexuality was shaped by the analogy of the steam engine. As pressure builds up within the steam boiler or the human psyche, it must be let off in some form if an explosion is to be avoided. Thus the liberal mind concludes that the basic sexual "drives" demand "release" if damage is not to be done to the personality. However, as Tom Wolfe has pointed out, the usefulness of this analogy appears increasingly doubtful. As both electronic technology and neurological research advance, we have learned that the mind is far more comparable to a computer than to a steam engine. If so, the conclusion to be drawn about human behaviour is exactly reversed. Far from providing a healthful "release," each successive act or thought actually "programmes" the mind for continued activity of the same kind, until, if the programming is sufficiently complete, the mind can dwell on little else. Obviously a theory of mind which took this contemporary analogy seriously would adopt a very different attitude to censorship than the prevailing one, especially censorship of material which might become available to children and so "programme" their imaginations.

20   If the assumptions of the liberal mind about human nature and sexuality are shown to be flawed or incomplete, then it may be wise to give correspondingly greater attention to that other tradition of thought which approaches the powers of the spirit with greater awe, which conceives the mind as requiring "guardians" and as having to be kept in order, with no little difficulty. If the need is admitted, then influences which increase the difficulty can be rightfully considered anti-social, since tending to break down that inner self-control on which social order depends. In this view, the process of civilization, the process of establishing an ever-increasing degree of civility in social and political life, depends upon each member of the community establishing greater dominion over his or her own psyche and emotions. To the degree that self-control is inhibited by the deliberate arousal of passion or desire, to that degree a civil society becomes a more distant and elusive goal and society moves closer to a state of barbarism.

21   If so, the recent reassertion of the public's right to establish minimum standards of decorum may not be necessarily unwelcome. Now that we have enjoyed the fruits of forty years or so of liberalism in sexual matters as in political, there is perhaps room for the reassertion of another range of values and for a reexamination of the claims of excellence, in human

behaviour and social conduct as in other things. The liberal impulse to tolerance and acceptance is wholly admirable, but it needs to be balanced and complemented by something else. If it leads to a paralysis of the faculty of judgment, it becomes one of those good things by which so much evil can be done. We need to transcend what Trilling called liberalism's "primitive conception of the nature of fact" and to learn again to make balanced judgments about the ultimate meaning and consequence of human behaviour.

22   If the apparent public concern with censorship expresses a confused groping toward a revival of critical judgment in sexual and social matters, then it may deserve more than contempt, however misguided or badly motivated some of the noisiest advocates of censorship may be. The role of the intellectual community should not be to thwart or deny the right to censorship—a denial which would not be sincere in any case—but rather to guide it and help it avoid the crude and harmful purposes to which it might be put. If certain works, films, or publications do not undermine civility as alleged but contribute instead to the process of civilization, then it should not be beyond the power of the intellectual community to say why. But it will have to do so with greater intellectual and moral rigour than in the recent past. The public is not as foolish as the *cognoscenti* often believe. It may sometimes fall into the error of thinking that a truly moral work of art cannot contain what it considers to be "immoral" scenes or characters, but it rarely makes the opposite mistake, to which so many artists and intellectuals are vulnerable, of thinking that art is beyond good and evil, and should not be judged, in the final analysis, by moral standards as well as aesthetic ones.

23   The intellectual, artistic, and journalistic communities would perhaps do well to embrace the claims of civility and excellence and to work out their implications for the public depiction of sexuality in more satisfying terms than they have yet done, rather than fighting the principle of censorship itself. Above all, they should avoid basing opposition to censorship on the defence of civil liberties. For one thing, there is no opposition between them. In fact, the first may be a prerequisite for the second, since it is improbable that civil liberty would long survive in a society threatened by social decadence and disorder. For another thing, there can be little doubt which of the two the public would ultimately choose if forced to do so. That is why the choice should not be forced upon it. To suggest that civil liberties and censorship are not compatible is to call into question, in the long run, not censorship, as many assume, but liberty itself.

Ralph Heintzman, "Liberalism and Censorship," *The Journal of Canadian Studies,* 13
(1978–79): 1–2, 120–122.

QUESTIONS

Subject
Locate the thesis statement of this essay (hint: search the first three paragraphs) and show how the author argues this position in this essay.

Audience
Do you find any evidence in the essay to suggest that the author is writing for an educated audience? If you do, say how the author takes pains to explain his sometimes arcane references to a less educated audience.

Purpose

Give proof to show that Heintzman's argumentative purpose attempts to point to the values of both the libertarian point of view and the pro-censorship point of view.

Structure and Style

(a) Explain what Heintzman means by the following sentence (paragraph 22): "If the apparent public concern with censorship expresses a confused groping toward a revival of critical judgment in sexual and social matters, then it may deserve more than contempt, however misguided or badly motivated some of the noisiest advocates of censorship may be."

(b) Explain the relationship between general statement and detail in paragraph 7.

(c) How does the final sentence of the essay reiterate the thesis of the entire essay?

These 22 Minutes Take Hours

John T.D. Keyes

1   In a large dingy room in downtown Halifax, red, white and blue crêpe decorations span the ceiling, chairs are stacked near the door, and old newspapers and computer printouts slump along one wall. Except for a man who's sweeping up, the place is abandoned, summoning an image: that here, last night perhaps, some political party went down to an unexpected and crushing defeat.

2   In fact, this is CBC Halifax's Radio Room, the think-tank of Canadian television's hot comedy show "This Hour Has 22 Minutes." For two seasons Mary Walsh, 43, Cathy Jones, 40, Greg Thomey, 33, and Rick Mercer, 25—all from St. John's, Nfld.—have used the space as the launching pad for their mock newscast, lampooning politicians and the week's events, and creating a slew of characters the likes of which we haven't seen since the heyday of "SCTV."

3   It is sometime after 9 on a Monday morning, midseason. By 8 p.m. on Friday, an audience of 100 will be crammed into bleachers at nearby CBC studios, expecting another half-hour blast of brilliantly topical hilarity. As the stars arrive, they join the show's writers—Alan Resnick, Ed MacDonald and Paul Bellini—and begin to read newspapers.

4   Creative producer Gerald Lunz announces that Mary Walsh won't be contributing in person this week. She has had to fly to St. John's to tend to an ailing aunt, although she will be calling in daily to lend support—comic, moral and otherwise. Thanks to a pretaped sketch, featuring Walsh as Prairie correspondent Connie Bloor, she'll still appear in the show that goes to air a week from now. (Extra sketches are taped and put "in the pantry" each week for precisely this sort of eventuality.) Lunz now moves to a large easel. "OK," he commands, "Whadda we got?"

5   As the producer who works most closely with the performers, Lunz is taskmaster, cheerleader, script doctor and troubleshooter, but right now his job is to write down as many ideas as possible. Little prompting is required. Over the next 45 minutes, 50 ideas tumble forth

at a pace that allows Lunz to do little more than write a title: *Steak Makes Humans Smart, Prozac for Kids, RCMP and Tacky Souvenirs.*

6   "Did ya see that Steve Fonyo is in trouble again?" asks Bellini, looking up from a newspaper.

7   "What this time?" asks Jones.

8   "Fraud," says Bellini.

9   "Yeah, turns out he has two legs," cracks Mercer, impromptu, triggering a rare outburst of laughter. (*Fonyo Is Back,* writes Lunz.) Strangely, the mood is generally like a corporate strategy session. And the cast and writers know not to get prematurely excited by responses. Less than half of the 50 ideas will make it to Friday night's performance.

10   "Is it too early to do Babe?" asks Jones late in the meeting, referring to her hugely popular sexual affairs correspondent, a '40s movie dame living in the '90s.

11   "What are you thinking?" asks Lunz.

12   "I wanna do why Prince Charles should be allowed to want Camilla," says Jones. "How men are supposed to want younger women." (*Babe Bennett: New Older Women,* writes Lunz.) Several weeks tend to pass between appearances by major characters like Babe Bennett, partly because the creators rotate them to avoid playing them until they're ready. Without much chat, everyone acknowledges that *Babe Bennett: New Older Women* is a keeper. They've learned that when Jones says she's ready, she'll deliver.

13   There's a last flurry of ideas and then, just as suddenly as it started, the meeting ends. Mercer, Thomey and Jones head for their desks. Mercer will work on the script for his into-the-camera rant that's shot on the streets of Halifax; Thomey, the show's acknowledged master of the short perfect joke, is soon tapping away on his laptop; Jones begins to wrestle with her Babe script. They'll work alone or with one of the writers, and what gets done between now and Tuesday's meeting at 4 p.m. had better be funny.

14   When "This Hour Has 22 Minutes" had its debut in the fall of 1993, CBC management did not know what to expect, but they needed a replacement for "Friday Night with Ralph Benmurgui," and everyone forged ahead. Frequent pre-emptions during the first season, made worse by time-slot changes, resulted in mediocre ratings, but, says Walsh, the troupe stuck to its goal: to make fun of the appalling, greedy and stupid things that real people do, while never letting the facts get in the way of the joke. "The real crowd-pleasers are jokes that stick it to the government," says Bellini. "Silly behavior is good. Hypocrisy is best." But it was never the intention of "22 Minutes" to disguise social-action commentary in the cloak of comedy, Walsh says. "I worry about being on the moral high ground."

15   Renewed for a second season, then given the coveted time-slot immediately preceding "CBC Prime Time News" (which allowed Mercer to sign off one night by encouraging viewers to stay tuned for the second half of the news), the show more than doubled its ratings. Its stars hosted the "Junos" in March, just weeks after their show won three Gemini Awards.

16   The meeting at 4 p.m. on Tuesday brings out a crowd. It's still way too early for a script, but editorial producer Geoff D'Eon wants to know what news footage to chase; line producer Jenipher Ritchie wants to know which sketches need to be pretaped around town; and Patti Baines-Parsons needs wardrobe instructions. Another 18 ideas get onto the easel, including one Thomey has written about O.J. Simpson's book; he delivers the setup but refuses to divulge the punch line.

17   "I don't think it's a stretch to call this journalism," says D'Eon when the meeting breaks up. "When I open *The Chronicle-Herald,* I know that the most trenchant journalism on the

op-ed page will probably be the editorial cartoon." D'Eon uses his connections from a decade as a news producer to cajole far-flung CBC colleagues into giving him satellite footage. Right now he is chasing five seconds of video of the Pope and an uncooperative dove. "The show is truthful without being factual," he says. "At the beginning of a piece, the facts are editorially sound. By the time we give the punch line, we assume our audience knows where we made the turn from real to funny."

18   Back at her desk, Jones is working on the Babe skit as Lunz passes by. "How would you describe Prince Charles?" she asks.

19   "Jughead," he says.

20   "Jughead," types Jones. "Jughead … uh, Lunkhead!" She types furiously.

21   Another sure hit this week will be Mercer's streeter, about the pathetic student protest over tuition increases, shot on Wednesday afternoon on the campus of Dalhousie University. The director, cameraman and sound man move smoothly alongside Mercer as he paces through the words. He nails it in four rehearsals and three takes, then everyone races back to the Radio Room for the most important meeting of the week.

22   The "humilitorium" takes place every Wednesday at 5 p.m. Here, every idea is discussed. If it's written, the performer reads it aloud, as hilariously as possible, which is why Thomey wanted to be fresh with his O.J. joke. For Walsh, the humilitorium can be "particularly humiliating. I often show up with an awful lot of stuff unfinished. It's hard for anybody to say whether it's going to be any good or not. So there I am saying, 'I have this really good idea—believe me, it'll be funny.'"

23   As the writers and performers head for dinner or their computers again, the producers, including executive producer Michael Donovan, decide which two dozen of the 68 ideas will make the best show—affordably, creatively, and with the best attention paid to the egos of its talented stars and crew. Donovan regards "22 Minutes" as "an antidote to the news, which is so universally oppressive" yet he's not beyond paraphrasing Shakespeare to suggest that the show serves a social purpose: "The play's the thing to prick the conscience of the king."

24   Thomey waits on this Wednesday evening in a pub a few blocks away. "You're trying to push for your stuff," he says, "but there has to be balance. Maybe we're wrong. Maybe they're wrong. Nobody's infallible about what's funny." At 9 p.m. Lunz tracks his stars down by telephone to give them the verdict. Thomey returns from the conversation, grimly resigned to losing an idea he has been pitching for the past two weeks, correlating the ups and downs of the Canadian dollar and the ups and downs of the Amanda character on "Melrose Place." "It didn't fly," he says glumly. But other ideas have. On with the show.

25   On Thursday the entire "22 Minutes" team moves to trailers in the parking lot of CBC's Bell Road studios. After a noon read-through of the script—now 70 per cent complete—Mercer and Thomey head to a frozen pond to pretape a segment of *Hockey Notebook,* starring the buffoonish coaches Peter (Boom Boom) MacCormick and Bob (Nobby) Spurrell. Later, Mercer and Jones commandeer the real Newsworld studio to tape a spoof of the network's coverage of the O.J. Simpson trial. Later in the day Jones steels herself for the arduous task of taping her Babe Bennett sketch.

26   After 90 minutes in hair, makeup and wardrobe, Jones is driven to the posh Halifax Club. Wearing a tight black suit, hat, veil and fox stole, she could have stepped straight out of *Mr. Deeds Goes to Town,* the movie that inspired her to create the character. It's 10 p.m. and the scene is complicated, calling for Jones to stroll, butt out a cigarette, pour a glass of sherry and deliver an ode to the sexiness of older women.

27   "You know what roasts my corn?" she says, instantly becoming Babe, as if a button has been pushed. "Every day, guys old enough to be your father go waltzing Matilda with gals young enough to be your baby sister, and nobody says boo. But when a curly-haired lunkhead like Charles turns his back on a bulimic bimbo like Di for the passion of a horse-ridin', self-made older woman like Camilla, out come the claws, and she's shredded faster than a head of cabbage on Oktoberfest!" With rehearsals, false starts, technical hitches and Jones's perfectionism, the scene isn't in the can until 1:15 Friday morning. Including wardrobe time, it has taken more than five hours to capture what will be two minutes on screen.

28   If the week has been a marathon, Friday is the sprint to the finish line. The noon read-through of the script, complete except for a few jokes, is a raucous affair. The cast and crew are both their own harshest critics and their most appreciative audience. The afternoon is spent rehearsing on the "22 Minutes" set, which could pass for a real newsroom were it not for a few details: 20 identical clocks, all of them set to different times but none of them explained; six television screens, supposedly providing live footage from Edmundston, N.B., Victoria, Rio de Janeiro, Toronto, New York, Hong Kong and St. John's, Nfld.; and, in the background, a map of the world on which Newfoundland is approximately the same size as continental North America. The 6 p.m. rehearsal is taped as a backup, and finally, at 8 p.m., the studio audience is seated. Lunz comes out to warm up the crowd, but given that there's an eight-month waiting list for tickets, he need hardly worry about a bad reception.

29   The show proceeds with no sketch longer than two minutes lest a viewer become bored. The desk items are read, and the pretaped skits are shown on monitors. After a break, Jones, Mercer and Thomey return in new costumes to perform as three rookie MPs back after two months off for Christmas. Jones wraps up the show as Sandy Campbell, sister of the former prime minister. Sporting a brassy blond wig and enough pearls to stock a jewelry store, she has the audience in stitches with a report that ranges from Cher's fashion catalogue to Vladimir Zhirinovsky.

30   Shortly after 10 p.m., cast, crew and friends unwind in one of the trailers, where the fridge is full of refreshments. On Monday they'll start again. "Once it's over, you can't dwell on it," says Mercer. "Sometimes, the show comes out no sweat. Some weeks are a lot harder than others. It's like any job, basically. Except your mom is watching."

John T.D. Keyes, "These 22 Minutes Take Hours," *Canadian Living,* October 1995: 99–104.

QUESTIONS

Subject
Explain how the first paragraph of the essay serves as an appropriate introduction to the subject.

Audience
What words, phrases, and ideas are there in this essay to indicate that this piece would better appeal to an audience who has already seen, or at least heard about, "This Hour Has 22 Minutes"? Are there technical terms in the essay which might disqualify some portion of the reading public from fully understanding Keyes' exposition?

Purpose

In your opinion, what is the author's purpose in writing this essay? Highlight aspects of the essay in which the author tries to capture the "flavour" of the programme. How does the title serve to encapsulate the essay's purpose and what does it suggest about the nature of comedy?

Structure and Style

(a) Comment on the time sequence and chronology of the essay as a structural device. Does each time period mentioned receive equal expository treatment by the author?

(b) How does the sentence "If the week has been a marathon, Friday is the sprint to the finish line" work in support of the essay's title?

(c) Comment on the tone of the final two sentences. How is this tone consistent with the image of the comedy troupe that the author conveys in the rest of the essay?

Charlevoix, Naturally Quebec

Paul King and Barbara Fulton

1   Charlevoix! It's the world's oldest land formation and Canada's oldest tourist destination.

2   Embracing 16,000 square kilometres of the mighty Laurentians, Charlevoix stretches for 200 km along the St. Lawrence's north shore to the majestic Saguenay fjord. With only 30,000 inhabitants, and two-thirds of its area thriving with forest and wildlife, it remains Quebec's premiere region for tourism and cuisine.

3   Driving east from Quebec City, two famous sites on Route 138 are worth a visit before hitting Charlevoix's roller-coaster highway. The spectacle of Montmorency Falls, cascading 83 metres down a cliffside, was recorded by explorers in 1542, a century before Champlain named it. Though not as awesome as the sweeping Niagara, Montmorency is actually 30 metres higher—and far more historic.

4   On the falls' eastern bluff in 1759, British General Wolfe made his first (if rash) attack on General Montcalm's troops, losing both the battle and 443 men. Two decades later, Britain's governor built an opulent summer house above the falls. Then in 1791, Prince Edward—George III's detested 24-year-old son—moved into the villa with his mistress for three summers of non-stop soirées. Alas, Edward was forced to forsake her 27 years later, marry a princess and sire Queen Victoria.

5   In 1885, for the first time in history, electricity was transported long distance—11.7 km from Montmorency's power plant—to light Quebec City's Dufferin Terrace. Within a decade it was also powering the city's electric trams, plus a tramway to the falls.

6   Today, 40-passenger cable cars whisk one million visitors a year from the base station up to the terraced, beautifully renovated Manoir Montmorency (with dining for 300). Besides the shops and summer theatre, visitors can cross the footbridge atop the falls to various look-outs on Wolfe's eastern bluff, and trudge the 487 steps down.

7   Just down the road are the towering twin spires of the famous Sainte-Anne-de Beaupré shrine, where more than 1.5 million pilgrims flock each year, many seeking miracle cures from the Virgin Mary's mother. Early settlers, believing Sainte-Anne saved various shipwreck victims, built the first church (of four) on the site in 1658. The present neo-Roman stone basilica is renowned for its vast size, superb stained-glass windows and artistic treasures.

8   Charlevoix (named after Quebec's first Jesuit historian) begins atop the mountain where Le Massif's ski slopes plunge. On then to Baie-Saint-Paul nestled deep in an alpine valley. One of Quebec's oldest towns (since 1678), it still boasts numerous 200-year-old houses with traditional mansard roofs, many now converted into quaint boutiques and a dozen art galleries.

9   Baie-Saint-Paul's stunning backdrop has been luring famous artists (from Clarence Gagnon to the Group of Seven) for more than a century. The two main galleries are the Centre d'Art, with a weaving workshop and works by local painters, and the new three-story Centre d'Exposition with its rotating international shows.

10   Switch onto Route 362, which climbs nearly 400 metres to Domaine Charlevoix. It's a family hiking centre in a 240-hectare forest with winding foot-paths, five waterfalls, a tea-house on a tiny lake, summer concerts at the terraced restaurant overlooking Ile-aux-Coudres, and far below (if you've got the legs) a beach.

11   Further on, after a spectacular snaking descent, Saint-Joseph-de-la-Rive stretches along the shoreline. The village boasts five inns, an ancient church and the unique Papelerie Saint-Gilles, famed for its "Grand Luxe" stationery with inlaid local wildflowers. The only Canadian paper maker of its kind, its craftsmen use almost three tonnes of cotton pulp mixed with paste to produce 90,000 pieces of stationery a year.

12   But it's these tiny embedded petals of Purple Loosestrife or Indian Paintbrush that create the $3.50 price per sheet—it takes two girls two weeks to pick a pound of petals worth $600. Then, using a 17th century technique, they're mixed with the pulp and pressed by hand. Amazingly, the remote Papelerie attracts 30,000 visitors annually.

13   From Saint-Joseph's wharf, a free 50-car ferry crosses to L'Ile-aux-Coudres (Hazel Island), named by Jacques Cartier who anchored there in 1535. In 1720, its islanders started trapping beluga whales by setting nets on the tidal flats; they also became famous for their home-made canoes, towboats and rough-water schooners. There's still a shipyard near the pier, as well as Cartier's monument.

14   Leaving the ferry, turn right on the road that circles the island for 26 km, and you'll come to Musée les Voitures d'Eau. This unique shrine to river navigation, crammed with nautical gear and photos, was built from boat beams by its owner, Captain Eloi Perron, in 1973. An eighth-generation islander, he's a merry soul who sailed the St. Lawrence for 43 years. And he'll proudly guide you through one of the three 18-metre schooners he built by hand. "Took just a year to make," he grins, "but two years to cut the trees."

15   Right beside it is Le Musée de l'Ilse-aux-Coudres that describes the local folkways, and boasts a remarkable collection of insects, flowers and animals in natural settings.

16   And just down the road is Les Moulins, a site unique in Canada. On a single location there's a large working watermill built in 1875, and windmill (1836), as well as a forge store and a miller's home. You can watch the millers grind buckwheat on genuine millstones—you can even buy the resulting flour. Guide interpreters gladly explain the mill's operations to its 35,000 annual visitors, imparting amusing bits of information like, "To grease the windmill's axles, they used squashed river frogs."

17   Along the southern shore you pass two km of peat bogs harvested in layers to a depth of six metres. Then you come to the cozy Hotel Cap-aux-Pierres, owned by Quebec's famed Dufour hotelier family who settled there in the 1700s. One Dufour built the 46-room hotel in 1932 as his home, in fact. Why so big? He had 16 children.

18   Back on the mainland, drive on to Points-au-Pic, the scenic birthplace of Canadian tourism. Rich Yankees started coming here in 1776 after the American Revolution, and another wave hit when the elegant Manoir Richelieu opened in 1899. Luxury steamships brought the Vanderbilts, Charlie Chaplin, the King of Siam and President Taft, who built his summer home there because, he said, "The air is heady as champagne, without the hangover." Today, besides the stately homes, inns, museums and galleries, the new casino at the Manoir lures the crowds.

19   If you've time, switch back onto 138 north to Saint-Aime-des-lacs. Then follow the narrow, twisting dirt road into spectacular Hautes-Gorges park for a ride up the Malbaie River canyon between towering cliffs on a 48-passenger Bateau-Mouche.

20   Then back to town, and on to visit nearby Domaine le pic-bois, a forested, five-lake fishing camp ($55 daily for cabin and boat), where owner Gilles Quintin guarantees "at least five, 15-inch speckled trout." But he also offers something even better: bear watching. Trekking through the woods to a tree house and up a ladder, you silently sit and wait. And sure enough, minutes later, out ambles massive mama bear and three cavorting cubs, attracted by the bait that Gilles has hung below. A sight you won't forget.

21   The nearby l'Auberge le Relais des Hautes-Gorge, a cozy family-run guest house, offers inexpensive rooms and superb home-cooked dinners. Then back on 138 to Port-au-Persil, a bucolic village with whooping kids sluicing down a waterspill on polished rocks. There's also the tiny white church (open to visitors) on the craggy shore, built in 1897 by the area's only Protestant.

22   Then back on the rolling highway, and across the Saguenay River by free ferry to Tadoussac. Beside the grand old Hotel Tadoussac (also owned by the Dufours) sits a replica of Canada's first trading post built in 1600, and near it a 250-year-old Jesuit chapel, Canada's oldest wooden church. There's also a marine museum and impressive Interpretation Centre, which focuses mainly on whales, because the teeming pods of local whales—beluga, sperm, minke, humpback, blue—are the attraction for tourists who come on various water tours.

23   We took the four-hour cruise up the Saguenay on the large Cavalier Royal, and within 10 minutes spotted a dozen white belugas near the shore. They come for the abundance of tiny fish (that they gulp by the tonne) and warm, fresh surface-water. Sadly, pollution and over-hunting have reduced their numbers by 90 per cent in a century. Interpreters aboard relate wondrous tales of the whales and early rivermen who cruised the truly spectacular fjord.

24   You can stay on the boat for another three-hour cruise in the river's mouth, where blue whales and humpbacks (who swim up from Haiti) surface, splash and blow their spumes. Ten miles out, once whales are spotted, the captain swerves and zeros in. The thrill of seeing "Moby Dick" plunge just yards off the bow is as keen as watching those bear cubs tumble.

25   For over two centuries Charlevoix has been luring tourists. Just cruise its rivers or mountain passes. You'll see why.

Paul King and Barbara Fulton, "Charlevoix, Naturally Quebec," *Leisureways,* June 1996: 31–32, 34–36.

QUESTIONS

Subject
Decide to what extent the brief history of the Charlevoix region that the author provides at the beginning of the essay is central to its subject.

Audience
Show how the author's description of the Charlevoix area would appeal to both nature lovers and those who seek creature comforts when they travel.

Purpose
Discuss the effect of the author's use of the first person plural personal pronoun and the second person personal pronoun; i.e., the "we" and the "you" of the essay.

Structure and Style
(a) Comment on the way in which the authors organize their travelogue. To what extent does the essay rely on both process and illustration developmental strategies?

(b) Explain the pun in the title of the essay.

Not Available in Stores

Mark Kingwell

1   It begins like one of those cosy Women's Television Network chat shows, complete with bad lighting, fuzzy lenses, and warm looks. The host is an attractive, soft-spoken woman of a certain age. She purrs at the camera. She and her guests are here to tell you about what she chucklingly calls "Hollywood's breast-kept secret." Yes, it's true: Accents, the Plasticine bust enhancers favoured by movie stars and models alike, are now available to you, the lowly viewer. No surgery. No hideous contraptions. You don't even have to leave home to get them.

2   And what a difference they make! Soon a line-up of gorgeous but slightly flat-chested women are being transformed before your eyes into jiggly supermodels or "Baywatch" lifeguards. These flesh-coloured slabs of silicone gel that "fit into any underwire bra" and "within minutes warm to your natural body temperature" can actually be used in the swimming pool! At the end of the half-hour, the ever-smiling host and her guests admit that *they are all wearing Accents themselves!* Well, shut my mouth.

3   "Accents" is only the most outrageous of the current crop of television infomercials: those over-the-top attempts to hawk make-up, cleaning products, and ab-flexers under the guise of a genial talk show ("Kathie Lee Talks") or breathless science programme ("Amazing Discoveries!"). Turn on your television late at night or on a weekend afternoon—even, these days, at midmorning—and the good-natured hosts, a has-been actress (Ali McGraw) or never-was celeb (Ed McMahon), are touting cosmetics or miracle car wax as if they are

doing us a public service. Information + commercial = infomercial. Line up the word, and the phenomenon, next to those long advertising features in newspapers and magazines, often slyly imitating the publication's actual typeface and design, known as "advertorials."

4   Patently absurd, maybe, but if emerging trends continue, infomercials will not remain what they have been so far: a marginal and benign, if irritating, television presence. With the loosening of CRTC regulations, the explosion of cable channels, and the crude economics that can make them more lucrative than regular programming for network affiliates, infomercials are showing up in more and more places on the TV schedule, elbowing aside such popular quality fare as Sunday-afternoon sports, syndicated comedies, and old movies. They are also getting more and more sophisticated, as big-name companies with mainstream products—Ford Motor Co., Procter & Gamble, Apple Canada—enter the infomercial market.

5   And if, as enthusiasts in the business press insist, this is the future of TV advertising, then that is very bad news indeed for television and its viewers. But not because there is anything inherently wrong with infomercials, at least not as they have existed until now. The delicate pact between ads and shows that makes television possible has always been able to withstand the amateurish, ad-becomes-show genre they represent. But when infomercials are everywhere, and especially when they go high market, that pact is in danger of being overturned, and the thin line between entertainment and pitch may be erased for good.

6   Blame Ron Popeil. Blame him a lot, and at length. Blame him until his smiling, trout-like face is imprinted on your mind as the fount of all evil. Because Popeil is the one who started the sort of television hard sell that reaches its tacky terminus in today's infomercials. Founder of Ronco, restless inventor of the Popeil Pocket Fisherman, the Patti-Stacker, and other cheesy "labour-saving" devices too numerous to mention, Popeil is the guy who all but invented television shopping. In the late 1970s he discovered that people got very excited, and very willing to spend, at the thought that you need never leave your couch to have the entire Ronco or K-Tel product line delivered to your home. His favourite author was the guy who came up with *Call this toll-free number now.*

7   Popeil has recently come out from behind the camera to appear in his own convection-oven and pasta-machine infomercials. Looking like an also-ran from a professional tanning competition, he slops flour and water into slowly spinning machines that disgorge brightly coloured goo for thirty minutes. Your own fresh pasta every night! Operators are standing by!

8   It isn't hard to decipher what makes these and other low-end infomercials so successful. Potential buyers are never made to feel bad, even as their baser desires are being pandered to. For example, we are told at least four times that Accents "are shipped confidentially" and arrive at your door in (get this) "a beautiful designer chest that will look great on your vanity." The Accents people even muster expert opinion, the *sine qua non* of the TV hard sell. In this case, it's a panel of Hollywood make-up artists and photographers. "I tried everything," says one. "Foam pads, wires, push-up bras, duct tape. Nothing works like Accents." (Duct tape?)

9   The same forms of reassurance are visible on all the successful infomercials now airing, from The Stimulator to the Ab-Roller Plus. The Stimulator—a small syringe-like device that is supposed to kill pain by means of mild electric shock, a sort of mini stun gun—also produces what has to be the funniest infomercial moment of all time. Evel Knievel, the all-but-forgotten daredevil of the 1970s, shares, over footage of his famous Caesars Palace motorcycle crash, his belief in the pain-relieving properties of The Stimulator. "If it hepped me," Knievel twangs, "it can hep you." Now that's expert opinion.

10   This is so silly that it is easy to imagine a kind of self-parody operating, of the sort in the hilarious "Money Show" spots on CBC's "This Hour Has 22 Minutes": "Gus, I want to pay less in taxes, but I'm not sure how." "Marsha, it couldn't be easier; stop filing your returns!" But that would misread the intentions of the makers—and the attitudes of the audience, whose response to infomercials has been wholehearted. Canadians spent $100-million on infomercial products in 1995, up thirty-four per cent from 1994. One Ontario company, Iona Appliances Inc., quadrupled annual sales of its "dual-cyclonic" vacuum cleaner when it started marketing via infomercial.

11   In fact, the point of infomercials has so far been their lack of sophistication. The niche is still dominated by the charmingly inept likes of Quality Special Products, the Canadian company responsible for such thoroughly trailer-park items as the Sweepa ("The last broom you'll ever have to buy!") and the Sophist-O-Twist hair accessory ("French braids made easy!")

12   Most current efforts eschew the cleverness and quality visible on more traditional commercial spots in favour of the low-ball aesthetic of public-access cable. Instead of competing with shows for our attention—and therefore being pushed to find better writing, multimillion-dollar budgets, and gilt-edged directorial talent—infomercials become the shows. Yet they do so in ways so obviously half-hearted that nobody, not even the quintessential couch-potato viewer, could actually be fooled. The talk-show cover story is really nothing more than a tacit agreement between marketer and viewer that they're going to spend half an hour in each other's company, working over a deal.

13   And this is what many critics miss: most infomercials, as they now appear, aren't really trying to dupe the viewer. They are instead the bottom-feeding equivalent of the irony observable in many regular commercials. Bargain-basement infomercials offer a simpler form of customer complicity than the crafty self-mockery and self-reference that appeals to young, kitsch-hungry viewers. Infomercials are a pure game of "let's pretend," taken straight from the carnival midway.

14   That's why the entry of high-end marketers into the field is so alarming. Big-money companies are not content to maintain the artless façade that now surrounds infomercials. They break the carny-style spell of cheap infomercials, where we know what we see is fake, but we go along anyway, and offer instead the high production quality, narrative structure, and decent acting of actual shows.

15   A recent Apple Canada effort, for example, which aired last year in Toronto, Calgary, and Vancouver, is set up as a saccharine half-hour sitcom about a white-bread family deciding to buy a home computer ("The Marinettis Bring Home a Computer"). It is reminiscent of "Leave It To Beaver" or "The Wonder Years," complete with Mom, Pop, Gramps, the family dog, and an annoying pre-teen narrator named TJ. Gramps buys the computer, then bets grumpy Pop that the family will use it enough to justify the expense. Soon TJ is bringing up his slumping math grades, Mom is designing greeting cards for profit, and Gramps is e-mailing fellow opera buffs. It's nauseating, but effective. Heather Hutchison, marketing communications manager for Apple Canada, explains the company's decision to enter the infomercial universe this way: "Having produced something of higher quality," she says, "there's a recognition at—I hesitate to use the word 'subconscious,' but at a lower level— that it says something about the quality of the product. The Canadian market responds well to this kind of softer sell."

16   We all know that television, as it now operates, is primarily a vehicle for the delivery of advertising. That is, we know that if it weren't for ads, nobody would get to spend a million dollars on a single episode of an hour-long drama or employ some of the best dramatic writers and directors now working. True, this symbiosis is uneasy at best, with good shows all but free-riding on the masses of dreck that keep the advertisers happily reaching their targets. That's fine—or at least not apocalyptic. We can accept that advertising is the price we have to pay (every seven minutes) for good television.

17   But slick infomercials, unlike their cheapo forebears, threaten to destroy this shaky covenant. Only a moron could mistake a low-end infomercial for a real show. (And only a condescending jerk could think that all people who buy Sweepas and Abdomenizers are, in fact, morons.) Up-market infomercials have a much greater potential to muddy the waters between advertising and programming. It may be that, without the cheesy aesthetics and side-show barker style, these new infomercials won't find an audience. But it's more likely that big companies with big budgets and top advertising talent will be able to suck even non-morons into these narrative ads that masquerade as entertainment. The new corporate offerings, in other words, may actually do what Ron Popeil couldn't: strip TV of extraneous effects like quality programming so that it finally reveals its essential nature—selling things, selling things, and selling things.

18   When that's true, maybe it's time to turn the damn thing off for good.

Mark Kingwell, "Not Available in Stores," *Saturday Night,* July/August 1996: 57–58.

QUESTIONS

Subject
Comment on how the irony/parody in the first two paragraphs establishes the author's attitude toward his subject.

Audience
Who is the intended audience for this essay and how accurate is the author's comment "that nobody, not even the quintessential couch-potato viewer, could actually be fooled" by infomercials?

Purpose
Indicate where the essay uses illustration, definition, and comparison and contrast to achieve its purpose.

Structure and Style
   (a) Look up "portmanteau word" in your dictionary and find two examples of such a word in this essay.
   (b) Explain why the author might use the slang expression "Well, shut my mouth" at the end of the second paragraph.

The Greater Evil

Margaret Laurence

1   I have a troubled feeling that I may be capable of doublethink, the ability to hold two opposing beliefs simultaneously. In the matter of censorship, doublethink seems, alas, appropriate. As a writer, my response to censorship of any kind is that I am totally opposed to it. But when I consider some of the vile material that is being peddled freely, I want to see some kind of control. I don't think I am being hypocritical. I have a sense of honest bewilderment. I have struggled with this inner problem for years, and now, with the spate of really bad video films and porn magazines flooding the market, my sense of ambiguity grows. I am certain of one thing, though. I cannot be alone in my uncertainty.

2   I have good reason to mistrust and fear censorship. I have been burned by the would-be book censors. Not burned in effigy, nor suffered my books being burned, not yet anyhow. But burned nonetheless, scorched mentally and emotionally. This has happened in more than one part of Canada, but the worst experience for me was in my own county of Peterborough a few years ago, when a group of people, sincere within their limited scope, no doubt, sought to have my novel, *The Diviners*, banned from the Grade 13 course and the school libraries. The book was attacked as obscene, pornographic, immoral and blasphemous. It is, I need hardly say, none of these things. Open meetings of the school board were held. Letters, pro and con, appeared in the local newspaper. Some awful things were said about the book and about me personally, mostly by people who had not read the book or met me. In retrospect, some of the comments seem pretty funny, but at the time I was hurt and furious. One person confidently stated that "Margaret Laurence's aim in life is to destroy the home and the family." In an interview, another person claimed that the novel contained a detailed account, calculated to titillate, of the sex life of the housefly. I couldn't recollect any such scene. Then I remembered that when Morag, as a child, is embarrassed by the sad, self-deprecating talk of her stepmother, the gentle, obese Prin, the girl seeks anything at all to focus on, so she need not listen. "She looked at two flies fucking, buzzing as they did it." Beginning and end of sensational scene. The reporter asked if the fundamentalist minister himself had found the scene sexually stimulating. "Oh no," was the reply. "I'm a happily married man." At one open meeting, a man rose to condemn the novel and said that he spoke for a delegation of seven: himself, his wife, their four children—and God. In another county, a bachelor pharmacist accused me of adding to the rate of venereal disease in Canada by writing my books. He claimed that young people should not be given any information about sex until they are physically mature—"at about the age of 21." I hoped his knowledge of pharmacy was greater than his knowledge of biology.

3   Many readers, teachers and students did speak out for the novel, which was ultimately restored to the Grade 13 course. But the entire episode was enough to make me come down heavily against censorship, and especially against self-appointed groups of vigilantes. At the time I made a statement, which said, in part: "Surely it cannot do other than help in the growing toward a responsible maturity, for our young people to read novels in which many aspects of human life are dealt with, by writers whose basic faith is in the unique and irreplaceable value of the human individual."

4   I hold to that position. Artists of all kinds have been persecuted, imprisoned, tortured and killed, in many countries and at many times throughout history, for portraying life as they

honestly saw it. Artistic suppression and political suppression go hand in hand, and always have. I would not advocate the banning of even such an evil and obscene book as Hitler's *Mein Kampf.* I think we must learn to recognize our enemies, to counter inhuman ranting with human and humane beliefs and practices. With censorship, the really bad stuff would tend to go underground and flourish covertly, while works of genuine artistic merit might get the axe (and yes, I know that "genuine artistic merit" is very difficult to define). I worry that censorship of any kind might lead to the suppression of anyone who speaks out against anything in our society, the suppression of artists, and the eventual clamping down on ideas, human perceptions, questionings. I think of our distinguished constitutional lawyer and poet F.R. Scott. In an essay written in 1933, he said: "'The time, it is to be hoped, has gone by,' wrote John Stuart Mill, 'when any defence would be necessary of the principle of freedom of speech.' His hope was vain. The time for defending freedom never goes by. Freedom is a habit that must be kept alive by use."

5   And yet—my ambiguity remains. The pornography industry is now enormous, and includes so-called "kiddie porn." Most of us do not look at this stuff, nor do we have any notion how widespread it is, nor how degrading and brutal toward women and children, for it is they who are the chief victims in such magazines and films. Let me make one thing clear. I do not object to books or films or anything else that deals with sex, if those scenes are between two adults who are entering into this relationship of their own free will. (You may well say—what about *Lolita*? I hated the book, as a matter of fact, and no, I wouldn't advocate banning Nabokov. Ambiguity.) I do not object to the portrayal of social injustice, of terrible things done to one human by another or by governments or groups of whatever kind, as long as this is shown for what it is. But when we see films and photographs, *making use of real live women and children,* that portray horrifying violence, whether associated with sex or simply violence on its own, as being acceptable, on-turning, a thrill a minute, then I object.

6   The distinction must be made between erotic and pornographic. Eroticism is the portrayal of sexual expression between two people who desire each other and who have entered this relationship with mutual agreement. Pornography, on the other hand, is the portrayal of coercion and violence, usually with sexual connotations, and, like rape in real life, it has less to do with sex than with subjugation and cruelty. Pornography is not in any sense life-affirming. It is a denial of life. It is a repudiation of any feelings of love and tenderness and mutual passion. It is about hurting people, mainly women, and having that brutality seen as socially acceptable, even desirable.

7   As a woman, a mother, a writer, I cannot express adequately my feelings of fear, anger and outrage at this material. I have to say that I consider visual material to be more dangerous than any printed verbal material. Possibly I will be accused of being elitist and of favoring my own medium, the printed word, and possibly such a charge could be true. I just don't know. The reason I feel this way, however, is that these films and photographs make use of living women and children—not only a degradation of them, but also a strong suggestion to the viewer that violence against women and children, real persons, is acceptable. One of the most sinister aspects of these films and photographs is that they frequently communicate the idea that not only is violence against women OK—women actually *enjoy* being the subject of insanely brutal treatment, actually enjoy being chained, beaten, mutilated and even killed. This aspect of pornography, of course, reinforces and purports to excuse the behaviour of some men who do indeed hate women. I could weep in grief and rage when I think of this attitude. As for the use of children in pornography, this is unspeakable and should be

forbidden by law. The effect of this material is a matter of some dispute, and nothing can be proved either way, but many people believe that such scenes have been frighteningly re-enacted in real life in one way or another.

8   But is censorship, in any of the media involved, the answer? I think of John Milton's *Areopagitica; A Speech for the Liberty of Unlicensed Printing, to the Parliament of England,* in 1644, in which these words appear: "He that can apprehend and consider vice with all her baits and seeming pleasures, and yet abstain, and yet distinguish, and yet prefer that which is truly better, he is the true wayfaring Christian. I cannot praise a fugitive and cloistered virtue, unexercised and unbreathed, that never sallies out and sees her adversary, but slinks out of the race, where that immortal garland is to be run for, not without dust and heat." Obviously, Milton was not thinking of the sort of video films that anyone can now show at home, where any passing boy child can perhaps get the message that cruelty is OK and fun, and any pass-ing girl child may wonder if that is what will be expected of her, to be a victim. All the same, we forget Milton's words at our peril.

9   The situation is not without its ironies. It has created some very strange comrades-in-arms. We find a number of feminists taking a strong stand *for* censorship, and being praised and applauded by people whose own stance is light-years away from feminism, the same people who would like my books, Alice Munro's books, W.O. Mitchell's books, banned from our high schools. We see civil libertarians who are *against* censorship and for free expression ar-guing that "anything goes," a view that must rejoice the hearts of purveyors of this inhumane material, but certainly distresses mine.

10   I consider myself to be both a feminist and a strong supporter of civil liberties and free speech, but there is no way I want to be on the same team as the would-be book-banning groups who claim that no contemporary novels should be taught or read in our schools. There is no way, either, that I want to be on the same team as the pornographers.

11   What position can a person like myself honestly take? The whole subject is enormously complex, but I must finally come down against a censorship board, whether for the visual media or for the printed word. I think that such boards tend to operate by vague and ill-defined standards. What can "acceptable community standards" possibly mean? It depends on which community you're talking about, and within any one community, even the small-est village, there are always going to be wide differences. Censorship boards tend to be in-sufficiently accountable. I believe that in cases of obscenity, test cases have to be brought before the courts and tried openly in accordance with our federal obscenity laws. The long-term solution, of course, is to educate our children of both sexes to realize that violence against women and children, against anyone, is not acceptable, and to equalize the status of women in our society.

12   What about Section 159 of the Criminal Code, "Offences Tending to Corrupt Morals"? My impression of federal law in this area is that its intentions are certainly right, its aims are toward justice, and it is indeed in some ways woefully outdated and in need of clari-fication. Clarification and amendment have not been and will not be easy. The clause that is most widely known to the general public is Section 159(8): "For the purpose of this Act, any publication a dominant characteristic of which is the undue exploitation of sex, or of sex and any one or more of the following subjects, namely, crime, horror, cruelty and violence, shall be deemed to be obscene." I think the first use of the words "of sex" could be deleted. How much sex between consenting adults is too much? Are three scenes OK but ten excessive? Frankly, among the many things I worry about in my life, as a citizen and as a writer, this is not one of them. But how are we to enshrine in our laws the idea that

the degradation and coercion of women and children, of anyone, is dreadful, without putting into jeopardy the portrayal of social injustice seen as injustice? How are we to formulate a law that says the use of real women and children in situations of demeanment and violence, shown as desirable fun stuff, is not acceptable, while at the same time not making it possible for people who don't like artists questioning the status quo to bring charges against those who must continue to speak out against the violation of the human person and spirit?

13   In one case cited in the Criminal Code, the judge declares: "The onus of proof upon the Crown may be discharged by simply producing the publication without expert opinion evidence. Furthermore, where, although the book has certain literary merit particularly for the more sophisticated reader, it was available for the general public to whom the book was neither symbolism nor a psychological study the accused cannot rely on the defence of public good." "Public good" is later defined as "necessary or advantageous to religion or morality, to the administration of justice, the pursuit of science, literature or art, or other objects of general interest." If this precedent means what it appears to say, it alarms me. It appears to put works of "literary merit" into some jeopardy, especially as expert opinion evidence need not be heard. If a book of mine were on trial, I would certainly want expert opinion evidence. I do not always agree with the views of the literary critics, or of teachers, but at least, and reassuringly, many of them know how to read with informed skill.

14   Realizing the difficulty of accurate definitions, I think that violence itself, shown as desirable, must be dealt with in some way in this law. It is *not* all right for men to beat and torture women. *It is wrong.* I also think that the exploitation of real live children for "kiddie porn" should be dealt with as a separate issue in law and should not be allowed, ever.

15   The more I think about it, the more the whole question becomes disturbingly complicated. Yet I believe it is a question that citizens, Parliament and the legal profession must continue to grapple with. It is not enough for citizens to dismiss our obscenity laws as inadequate and outdated, and then turn the whole matter over to censorship boards. Our laws are not engraved on stone. They have been formulated carefully, although sometimes not well, but with a regard to a general justice. The law is not perfect, but it *is* public. It can be changed, but not upon the whim of a few. An informed and alert public is a necessary component of democracy. When laws need revision, we must seek to have them revised, not toward any narrowing down but toward a greater justice for all people, children, women and men, so that our lives may be lived without our being victimized, terrorized or exploited. Freedom is more fragile than any of us in Canada would like to believe. I think again of F.R. Scott's words: "Freedom is a habit that must be kept alive by use." Freedom, however, means responsibility and concern toward others. It does not mean that unscrupulous persons are permitted to exploit, demean and coerce others. It is said, correctly, that there is a demand for pornography. But should this demand be used to justify its unchallenged existence and distribution? Some men are said to "need" pornography. To me this is like saying some men "need" to beat up their wives or commit murder. Must women and children be victims in order to assuage the fears and insecurities of those men who want to feel they are totally powerful in a quite unreal way? I don't think so. If some men "need" pornography, then I as a woman will never be a party to it, not even by the tacit agreement of silence. We and they had better try together to control and redirect those needs. I think that citizens can and should protest in any nonviolent way possible against the brutalities and callousness of pornography, including one area I haven't even been able to deal with here, the demeanment of women in many advertisements.

16 In the long run, it is all-important to raise our children to know the reality of others; to let them know that sex can and should be an expression of love and tenderness and mutual caring, not hatred and domination of the victor/victim kind; to communicate to our daughters and sons that to be truly human is to try to be loving and responsible, strong not because of power but because of self-respect and respect for others.

17 In *Areopagitica,* Milton said: "That which purifies us is trial, and trial is by what is contrary." In the final analysis, we and our society will not stand or fall by what we are "permitted" to see or hear or read, but by what we ourselves choose. We must, however, have some societal agreement as to what is acceptable in the widest frame of reference possible, but still within the basic concept that *damaging people is wrong.* Murder is not acceptable, and neither is the abasement, demeanment and exploitation of human persons, whatever their race, religion, age or gender. Not all of this can be enshrined in law. Laws can never make people more understanding and compassionate toward one another. That is what individual people try to do, in our imperfect and familial ways. What the law *can* do is attempt to curb, by open process in public courts, the worst excesses of humankind's always-in-some-way-present inhumanity to humankind.

18 This is as close as I can get to formulating my own beliefs. It is an incomplete and in many ways a contradictory formulation, and I am well aware of that. Perhaps this isn't such a bad thing. I don't think we can or should ever get to a point where we feel we know, probably in a simplistic way, what all the answers are or that we ourselves hold them and no one else does. The struggle will probably always go on, as it always has in one way or another. The new technology has brought its own intricacies. I doubt that the human heart and conscience will ever be relieved of their burdens, and I certainly hope they are not. This particular struggle, *for* human freedom and *against* the awfulness that seeks to masquerade as freedom but is really slavery, will not ever be easy or simple, but it is a struggle that those of us who are concerned must never cease to enter into, even though it will continue to be, in Milton's words, "not without dust and heat."

Margaret Laurence, "The Greater Evil," Toronto Life, September 1984: 58–59, 92, 94, 96.

QUESTIONS

Subject

(a) How does the title "The Greater Evil" reflect the subject of this essay? Focusing on the irony in the essay may help you with your answer to the question.

(b) Explain the difference Laurence draws between eroticism and pornography.

Audience

Indicate how the author tries to gain audience support through her example in paragraph 2.

Purpose

Explain how the argumentative purpose of this essay not only makes a point, but also gives voice to difficult questions in the author's mind.

Structure and Style

(a) Comment on how the final paragraph of the essay serves as an appropriate summary of Margaret Laurence's position.

(b) Make clear how the "And yet—" phrase of the opening of paragraph 5 indicates a major change in thought in the essay.

(c) Explain how the author's ambivalence helps determine the structure of this essay.

Where the World Began

Margaret Laurence

1   A strange place it was, that place where the world began. A place of incredible happenings, splendors and revelations, despairs like multitudinous pits of isolated hells. A place of shadow-spookiness, inhabited by the unknowable dead. A place of jubilation and of mourning, horrible and beautiful.

2   It was, in fact, a small prairie town.

3   Because that settlement and that land were my first and for many years my only real knowledge of this planet, in some profound way they remain my world, my way of viewing. My eyes were formed there. Towns like ours, set in a sea of land, have been described thousands of times as dull, bleak, flat, uninteresting. I have had it said to me that the railway trip across Canada is spectacular, except for the prairies, when it would be desirable to go to sleep for several days, until the ordeal is over. I am always unable to argue this point effectively. All I can say is—well, you really have to live there to know that country. The town of my childhood could be called bizarre, agonizingly repressive or cruel at times, and the land in which it grew could be called harsh in the violence of its seasonal changes. But never merely flat or uninteresting. Never dull.

4   In winter, we used to hitch rides on the back of the milk sleigh, our moccasins squeaking and slithering on the hard rutted snow of the roads, our hands in ice-bubbled mitts hanging onto the box edge of the sleigh for dear life, while Bert grinned at us through his great frosted moustache and shouted the horse into speed, daring us to stay put. Those mornings, rising, there would be the perpetual fascination of the frost feathers on windows, the ferns and flowers and eerie faces traced there during the night by unseen artists of the wind. Evenings, coming back from skating, the sky would be black but not dark, for you could see a cold glitter of stars from one side of the earth's rim to the other. And then the sometime astonishment when you saw the Northern Lights flaring in swift ice flames across the sky, like the scrawled signature of God. After a blizzard, when the snow-ploughs hadn't yet got through, school would be closed for the day, the assumption being that the town's young could not possibly flounder through five feet of snow in the pursuit of education. We would then gaily don snowshoes and flounder for miles out into the white dazzling deserts, in pursuit of a different kind of knowing. If you came back too close to night, through the woods at the foot of the town hill, the thin black branches of poplar and chokecherry now meringued with frost, sometimes you heard coyotes. Or maybe the banshee wolf-voices were really only inside your head.

5   Summers were scorching, and when no rain came and the wheat became bleached and dried before it headed, the faces of farmers and townspeople would not smile much, and you took for granted, because it never seemed to have been any different, the frequent knocking at the back door and the young men standing there, mumbling or thrusting defiantly their requests for a drink of water and a sandwich if you could spare it. They were riding the freights, and you never knew where they had come from, or where they might end up, if anywhere. The Drought and Depression were like evil deities which had been there always. You understood and did not understand.

6   Yet the outside world had its continuing marvels. The poplar bluffs and the small river were filled and surrounded with a zillion different grasses, stones and weed flowers. The meadowlarks sang undaunted from the twanging telephone wires along the gravel highway. Once we found an old flat-bottomed scow, and launched her, poling along the shallow brown waters, mending her with wodges of hastily chewed Spearmint, grounding her among the tangles of yellow marsh marigolds that grew succulently along the banks of the shrunken river, while the sun made our skins smell dusty-warm.

7   My best friend lived in an apartment above some stores on Main Street, an elegant apartment with royal-blue velvet curtains. The back roof, scarcely sloping at all, was corrugated tin, of a furnace-like warmth on a July afternoon, and we would sit there drinking lemonade and looking across the back lane at the Fire Hall. Sometimes our vigil would be rewarded. Oh joy! Somebody's house burning down! We had an almost-perfect callousness in some ways. Then the wooden tower's bronze bell would clonk and toll like a thousand speeded funerals in a time of plague, and in a few minutes the team of giant black horses would cannon forth, pulling the fire wagon like some scarlet chariot of the Goths, while the firemen clung with one hand, adjusting their helmets as they went.

8   The oddities of the place were endless. An elderly lady used to serve, as her afternoon tea offering to other ladies, soda biscuits spread with peanut butter and topped with a whole marshmallow. Some considered this slightly eccentric, when compared with chopped egg sandwiches, and admittedly talked about her behind her back, but no one ever refused these delicacies or indicated to her that they thought she had slipped a cog. Another lady dyed her hair a bright and cheery orange, by strangers often mistaken at 20 paces for a feather hat. My own beloved stepmother wore a silver fox neckpiece, a whole pelt, *with the embalmed(?) head still on.* My Ontario Irish grandfather said *sparrow grass,* a more interesting term for asparagus. The town dump was known as the *nuisance grounds,* a phrase fraught with weird connotations, as though the effluvia of our lives was beneath contempt but at the same time was subtly threatening to the determined and sometimes hysterical propriety of our ways.

9   Some oddities were, as idiom had it, "funny ha ha"; others were "funny peculiar." Some were not so very funny at all. An old man lived, deranged, in a shack in the valley. Perhaps he wasn't even all that old, but to us he seemed a wild Methuselah figure, shambling among the underbrush and the tall couch grass, muttering indecipherable curses or blessings, a prophet who had forgotten his prophecies. Everyone in town knew him, but no one knew him. He lived among us as though only occasionally and momentarily visible. The kids called him Andy Gump, and feared him. Some sought to prove their bravery by tormenting him. They were the medieval bear baiters, and he the lumbering bewildered bear, half blind, only rarely turning to snarl. Everything is to be found in a town like mine. Belsen, writ small but with the same ink.

10   All of us cast stones in one shape or another. In grade school, among the vulnerable and violet girls we were, the feared and despised were those few older girls from what was charmingly called "the wrong side of the tracks." Tough in talk and tougher in muscle, they were said to be whores already. And probably were, that being about the only profession readily accessible to them, there.

11   The dead lived in that place, too. Not only the grandparents who had, in local parlance, "passed on" and who gloomed, bearded or bonneted, from the sepia photographs in old albums, but also the uncles, forever 18 or 19, whose names were carved on the granite family stones in the cemetery, but whose bones lay in France. My own young mother lay in that graveyard, beside other dead of our kin, and when I was 10, my father too, only 40, left the living town for the dead dwelling on the hill.

12   When I was 18, I couldn't wait to get out of that town, away from the prairies. I did not know then that I would carry the land and town all my life within my skull, that they would form the mainspring and source of the writing I was to do, wherever and however far away I might live.

13   This was my territory in the time of my youth, and in a sense my life since then has been an attempt to look at it, to come to terms with it. Stultifying to the mind it could certainly be, and sometimes was, but not to the imagination. It was many things, but it was never dull.

14   The same, I now see, could be said for Canada in general. Why on earth did generations of Canadians pretend to believe this country dull? We knew perfectly well it wasn't. Yet for so long we did not proclaim what we knew. If our upsurge of so-called nationalism seems odd or irrelevant now to outsiders, and even to some of our own people *(what's all the fuss about?),* they might try to understand that for many years we valued ourselves insufficiently, living as we did under the huge shadows of those two dominating figures, Uncle Sam and Britannia. We have only just begun to value ourselves, our land, our abilities. We have only just begun to recognize our legends and to give shape to our myths.

15   There are, God knows, enough aspects to deplore about this country. When I see the killing of our lakes and rivers with industrial wastes, I feel rage and despair. When I see our industries and natural resources increasingly taken over by America, I feel an overwhelming discouragement, especially as I cannot simply say, "damn Yankees." It should never be forgotten that it is we ourselves who have sold such a large amount of our birthright for a mess of plastic Progress. When I saw the War Measures Act being invoked, I lost forever the vestigial remains of the naïve wish-belief that repression could not happen here, or would not. And yet of course I had known all along in the deepest and often hidden cave of the heart that anything can happen anywhere, for the seeds both of man's freedom and of his captivity are found everywhere, even in the microcosm of a prairie town. But in raging against our injustices, our stupidities, I do so *as family,* as I did, and still do in writing, about those aspects of my town which I hated and which are always in some ways aspects of myself.

16   The land still draws me more than other lands. I have lived in Africa and in England, but splendid as both can be they do not have the power to move me in the same way as, for example, that part of southern Ontario where I spent four months last summer in a cedar cabin beside a river. "Scratch a Canadian and you will find a phony pioneer," I used to say to myself, in warning. But all the same it is true, I think, that we are not yet totally alienated from physical earth, and let us only pray we do not become so. I once thought that my lifelong fear and mistrust of cities made me a kind of old-fashioned freak; now I see it differently.

17   The cabin has a long window across its front western wall, and sitting at the oak table there, in the mornings, I used to look out at the river and at the tall trees beyond, green-gold in the early light. The river was bronze; the sun caught it strangely, reflecting upon its surface the near-shore sand ripples underneath, making it seem momentarily as though a whole flotilla of gold flickerings sailed there. Suddenly, the silver crescenting of a fish, gone before the eye could clearly give image to it. The old man next door said these leaping fish were carp. Himself, he preferred muskie, for he was a real fisherman and the muskie gave him a fight. The wind most often blew from the south, and the river flowed toward the south, so when the water was wind-riffled and the current was strong, the river seemed to be flowing both ways. I liked this, and interpreted it as an omen, a natural symbol.

18   A few years ago, when I was back in Winnipeg, I gave a talk at my old college. It was open to the public, and afterward a very old man came up to me and asked me if my maiden name had been Wemyss. I said yes, thinking that he might have known my father or my grandfather. But no. "When I was a young lad," he said, "I once worked for your great-grandfather, Robert Wemyss, when he had the sheep ranch." I think that was the moment when I realized something of great importance to me. My long-ago families came from Scotland and Ireland, but in a sense that no longer mattered so much. My true roots were here and would remain so, whatever happened.

19   I am not very patriotic, in the usual meaning of that word. I cannot say, "My country right or wrong" in any political, social or literary context. But one thing is inalterable, for better or worse.

20   This is not only where my world began. It is also the land of my ancestors.

Margaret Laurence, "Where the World Began," *Maclean's,* December 1972: 23, 80. Excerpt from
Heart of a Stranger, Toronto: McClelland & Stewart, 1976.

QUESTIONS

Subject
Looking back over the essay after reading it once, we can see how the opening paragraph moves beyond the particular reference of the prairie town. How do the descriptions of the subject in paragraph 1 also apply to the author's comments on the country?

Audience
The author moves from a particular description in this essay to a general commentary on the nature of the country Canada. How might an audience feel at being pulled into the essay when the pronoun shifts from "I" to "we"?

Purpose
This essay is divided into two sections. In what sense can the first be seen as an extended metaphor for the second? How do narration and description work together to create a unified impression for the reader?

Structure and Style

   (a) Comment on the relationship between the topic sentence and illustrative detail in paragraph 8.

   (b) Explain what the author means by the final sentence of paragraph 9. How does it relate to the paragraph of which it is a part?

   (c) Speculate on why the second paragraph of the essay is a single-line sentence.

   (d) What exactly does Margaret Laurence mean by "world," a word which is found both in the title of the essay and in its first sentence?

Heartbreak

René Lévesque

1 *The government of Quebec has made public its proposal to negotiate a new agreement with the rest of Canada, based on the equality of nations;*

   this agreement would enable Quebec to acquire the exclusive power to make its laws, levy its taxes and establish relations abroad—in other words, sovereignty—and at the same time to maintain with Canada an economic association including a common currency;

   no change in political status resulting from these negotiations will be effected without approval by the people through another referendum: on these terms do you give the Government of Quebec the mandate to negotiate the proposed agreement between Quebec and Canada?

2 It was rather long and heavy but, to use a word that is fashionable today, it was perfectly "transparent." In three short paragraphs and some hundred words the essence was there for anyone who knew how to read.

3   The holiday season [Christmas, 1979] gave all a chance to talk it over in their families, and seeing that on the whole the question was pretty well received, we began to look forward confidently to the debate that would mark the real opening of the campaign in February.

4   A first leitmotif would naturally be a critical analysis of the federal regime. But the most important theme, one that everyone would have to explore according to his or her own feelings and experience, was the promise sovereignty-association held for the future. On this score what was required of our elected members was nothing short of the best performance

of their careers. I never saw such discipline in our ranks nor such willingness to work. With the help of a battalion of research assistants we had mobilized, even the least articulate MNAs strove like slaves, absolutely determined to surpass themselves. And they succeeded. We had really thought of everything, right down to crash courses for those who didn't "come across" on TV. From delivery to dress, everything was impeccable, for everyone knew how crucial the issue was, and for once there was no absenteeism.

5   Nor was there the least false note. Day after day on our side one could witness the most extraordinary performances. An unprecedented flood of tight arguments backed by stunning examples soon began to flow from this marvellous teamwork, contributing to an atmosphere that was emotional and almost euphoric. Claude Charron, who had replaced Robert Burns as parliamentary chief, patrolled the ranks handing out advice and encouragement, an administrative task that did not prevent him from turning in one of his most unforgettable speeches. Emulation constantly improved our output.

6   What a contrast to the disarray in the opposite camp. Elected party leader in 1978, and just recently MNA for Argenteuil, Claude Ryan was as awkward as a debutante and, worse still, showed sure signs of inebriation at being close to the goal of political power. Since his party had been winning by-elections handily, he was beginning to see himself as head of government already. But although he was sure of himself, he was skimpily and poorly prepared for the debate. Content to harp away that the referendum question was dishonest and must surely hide sinister intentions, from the start he took the path of pure and simple demagoguery. There is nothing old veterans of the House like better, accustomed as they are to playing with clichés rather than ideas, so his Liberal cohorts followed his example with relish. In reply to dense and passionate statements on our side, they sat back and croaked "séparatisses, séparatisses." Our determination to situate ourselves on a level worthy of the subject was met by mean-minded, repetitive, and most often childish refrains. The merciless eye of the camera revealed a Claude Ryan staring about vacantly while the rest of the herd, floored by the steady broadside we directed at them, no longer managed to conceal their confusion.

7   The public could see very well what was going on. Rarely has a political debate been anticipated so impatiently and then followed so closely by so many Québécois, and they got our message all the better because our adversaries could only conjure up the most trivial contradictions.

8   The polls were not slow to confirm that we had won this first round hands down....

9   Keyed up by the clear victory we had won in the National Assembly, "Committees for the Oui" spread throughout the country like wildfire. There was at least one in every riding. In many businesses employees had their own groups, too. One after another we saw "Economists for the Oui," "Lawyers for the Oui," "Scientists for the Oui." Crowning the pyramid, the "Regroupement National" could boast spectacular members: senior civil servants like Thérèse Baron, military heroes like General Allard, writers and artists like Marie-Claire Blais and Fabienne Thibault, an important collection of former ministers and members of both the federal and provincial parliaments, front-line combatants like the Association des Gens de l'Air, well-known university figures like the Rector of Sherbrooke, Yves Martin, and the Vice-Dean of Laval, Christine Piette, and a good number of the most respected spokesmen for rural Quebec. Painting a moving picture of the future he hoped to assure his children by his option, the leader of the Union Nationale, Rodrigue Biron, also joined our ranks.

10   The eminent businessman and veteran indépendantiste Fernand Paré was in charge of the "Foundation for the Oui" that was to collect more than three and a half million dollars.

Its vice-president was Madeleine Ferron, wife of the late Robert Cliche, who shortly before his death had written these prophetic words: "In my view, one of the gravest dangers would be a Non in the referendum. English Canada would believe that the crisis was over and would slip back into its lethargy."

11   And what precisely was happening in English Canada? Forget for the time being the Quebec branch of the Anglo establishment where the halt, the sick, the lame, and the dead were being conscripted for the "Non" and where the exceptionally rare dissidents, huddled together in their CASA (Comité Anglophone pour la Souveraineté-Association), risked the same fate as that meted out to former Liberal minister Kevin Drummond, whose "Oui" had cost him the loss of friends and a rift in his family.

12   Outside Quebec, on the contrary, opinion was less entrenched. The situation appeared to be still quite fluid. Bill Davis and his Ontario government might refuse in advance to negotiate as much as they liked, but they were far from reflecting the opinion of people most directly concerned. Since they had always been the principal beneficiaries of the federal regime, the leaders of Ontario society obviously preferred to retain the status quo, but if Quebec said "Oui," wouldn't they come to terms to maintain a hold on the common market of association? This, at any rate, was the conclusion a team of researchers from York University came to when a solid majority of decision-makers chosen from every sector of society admitted that in the event of a victory for the "Oui" they would opt for accommodation. In the Atlantic Provinces there wasn't the least hesitation. Quoting a study made for the Task Force on Canadian Unity, the *Globe and Mail* noted that they "would be favourable to economic union between their region and an independent Quebec. In the same breath 65% of those polled said that if a 'free and democratic' vote went in this direction, Quebec should be authorized to quit the Canadian federation."

13   Economist Abraham Rotstein provided figures that eloquently describe the economic interdependence that binds a great number of Canadians: "In Ontario no less than 105,800 jobs depend directly on the Quebec market. Ontario enterprises annually export 4.6 billion dollars worth of manufactured goods to Quebec.... [Rotstein] estimates that there are 9,000 workers in the Maritimes whose salaries depend on sales to Quebec. The Prairies sell $432,000,000 in consumer goods to Quebec (particularly beef they are unable to sell elsewhere in America) which supports some 10,000 jobs. Finally, 3,000 persons in B.C. have jobs related to exports to Quebec. In the reverse direction the number of jobs is approximately identical."[1]

14   Could Québécois have been right, then, when at the end of March they replied 71 per cent "Oui" and only 16 per cent "Non" to the question: Will Canada negotiate? Perhaps they were, as long as one kept in mind, applying it to the present context, the judgement Mazzini passed on the British in the last century, a view that has been constantly confirmed by history since: "From time immemorial it has been English policy [read Anglo-Canadian] to put obstacles in the path of any factor that might seem to introduce a new element into the European [Canadian] picture, and then to accept it as soon as it has been solemnly accomplished...."

15   As could be expected, we, too, were to be presented with every kind of obstacle imaginable. But just the same, we felt that a great many of our people, perhaps even that small majority the polls indicated, expected to see the "Oui" succeed and, though they did not always show it openly, had actually come to hope it would.

---

[1] *Le Devoir,* December 19, 1979

16   This was all the more so because in Ottawa, as among provincial federalists, the situation remained fluid. When the multi-billion-dollar decision came up whether to build the F-16 fighter plane, the economic benefits of which would go principally to Quebec, or the F-18, with 80 or 90 per cent of contracts going to Ontario, Trudeau's government was faced with turbulence in its Quebec caucus. Claude Ryan's cohorts, meanwhile, continued in the depression caused by their parliamentary discomfiture. The "Non" were feverishly seeking a strike force but, failing to discover a trigger mechanism, seemed incapable of inventing one.

17   It was we, alas, who were going to give them the booster they needed. One day in March in a modest meeting that would normally have sunk quietly beneath the sands of time, Lise Payette got caught up in one of those feminist declarations prompted by her job as Minister of the Status of Women. In the most logical way imaginable she had set about exposing a school text presenting two great incarnations of traditional sexism—little Guy, future champion and perfect macho, and little Yvette, model miniature housewife, broken in to be perfectly submissive. So far so good. But carried away by her subject and "pushed by some devil," our colleague dropped a remark to the effect that Quebec women would have to learn to sit up and sit still if ever Claude Ryan took power because he was married to a protracted "Yvette." This was not only in poor taste but untrue and Lise Payette soon heard about it, for several journalists made a point of enumerating Madame Ryan's exceptional accomplishments and made it a duty to execute the guilty party in the public square.

18   This deplorable slip was a small enough cause, but it was destined to have resounding effects. Toward the end of March, well supported by Liberals, several hundred "Yvettes" met in Quebec City. And when, on April 7, thousands more filled the Montreal Forum waving the Canadian flag in one hand and the fleur-de-lys in the other, having quickly forgotten the incident that had served as a pretext to launch their reinvigorated "Non," we understood that the opposition machine had finally got off the ground.

19   The next forty days that took us up to May 20 deserve to be described in detail, hour by hour, for the edification of future generations, if not for those who were steamrolled by them.

20   It was an unqualifiable deluge of lies, threats, and blackmail. The federal Minister of Energy, Marc Lalonde, promised a sovereign Quebec an energy deficit of exactly $16.6 billion. His colleague in social affairs, Monique Bégin, predicted a phenomenally high level of taxation just to be able to maintain old age pensions and family allowances. Taking what could be called the "low road" and hitting shamelessly below the belt, unscrupulous terrorists infiltrated the weakest sectors of society, for example, an old folks home where one of them, seeing some oranges in a bowl, had the gall to tell the senior citizens sitting around: "Watch out now, if the separatists win, you'll never see any more oranges in Quebec." No one knew how to evoke this pitiful, down-at-heel Quebec with more verve than Jean Chrétien, belching out in conclusion his caricature of Claude Morin, promoted ambassador of some equally under-developed country driving around in a Cadillac "avec le flag su'l'hood."

21   Despite rules that we had legitimately established but that had been rapidly trampled underfoot, the "Non" camp had no scruples about floating their campaign on floods of money, the exact total of which, unless I am mistaken, will never be known. The tribunals we addressed prudently sidestepped the issue with a few remarks that amounted to placing federal public funds beyond the reach of any Quebec law. How many millions were swallowed up in Ottawa back offices where all the "Non" propaganda was prepared, including

material used by the provincial Liberals? How much more to paper the media and every corner of the country with "Me? I'm staying in … for my own good," and that "NON merci" that even cropped up in anti-alcoholic advertising from Honourable Madame Bégin's Ministry of Health and Welfare?

22   Nerves and stomach pinched and pummelled by such savage blows, public resolution began to falter. In the most fragile strata, among seniors and "floaters," who are always like a feather in the wind, the hurricane of "Non" propaganda wreaked havoc. It seemed to be irresistible and dealt in fear. From West to East, from Blakeney in Saskatchewan to Hatfield in New Brunswick, came the heralds of the Anglo-Canadian refusal. Sniffing their victory to be, they felt free now to write us off in the most callous tones. By the end of April everyone knew, in Ottawa as in Quebec, that we would not reach our 62 per cent and that even a straight majority was no longer a sure thing in French Quebec.

23   It was at this point that Trudeau, who had become prime minister again the month before, decided to step on stage and participate without risk in the last act. First on May 2, 1980, presenting himself before the receptive audience of the Chamber of Commerce, he began by indulging in heavy irony, citing our cowardice, saying we hadn't dared to go straight to the goal, machine gun in hand … like Zimbabwe or Algeria. Seeing that he was on the wrong track he fell back on another analogy, less explosive though just as misplaced. "Suppose," he said, "that Cuba or Haiti came proposing to associate with us, because down there they like Canadian prosperity, the Canadian countryside, Canadian women … So they vote on it and agree, massively, yes, we want association with Canada. Would we, in the name of democracy, be obliged to accept them? Would our only choice, in the name of fair play, be to consent: 'Well, yes, they voted for it, so we don't have anything to say in the matter'? *(Much laughter and sustained applause.)*" Finally, betraying both his peevishness and his relief, our improviser imagined the care with which a Castro or a Duvalier would have felt out the ground in order to avoid simply being told "Go and get lost!"

24   To my mind such remarks deserve a choice place in a little manual entitled "The Way to Insult People Without Risk Who Don't Think the Way You Do." It would be a very thin volume, for history doesn't record many who have treated their fellows so grossly. As for the anthology of political duplicity that would fill several fat volumes, the historic encounter of the following week certainly deserves to be enshrined there.

25   On May 14, one week before the vote, here, in résumé, is how Trudeau, before thousands of Montrealers and addressing the whole of Quebec, proclaimed that he and his were ready to put their heads on the block: "We, MPs from Quebec, ask Québécois to vote Non, and at the same time we warn Canadians in other provinces that this Non should not be interpreted as proof that all is well here, or that there are not changes to be made. On the contrary, it is with the aim of getting things changed that we are putting our seats on the line."

26   Change, okay. But what change? That remained a mystery. Considering the past and so many claims so often reiterated, any right-minded person couldn't help thinking that nothing less than greater autonomy and better guarantees for Quebec were in question. If not, it was just an airy promise, or else something no democratic politician could permit himself at this moment—sheer deceit.

27   Every chance we had to speak in public over the next days we demanded specifics. In vain. The sphinx kept his secret, knowing full well that if he revealed the true nature of his thought, innumerable Québécois would turn away in disgust. He was biding his time while we spent our last strength trying to reach that vital minimum of a strong majority French

vote. Describing the instinctive and perfectly comprehensible solidarity Anglophones showed in throwing their support massively to the other side, I went around begging our people to show the same solidarity for once in our history. But it was too late. Or perhaps it wasn't yet time....

28   To this day no one knows if our two-fifths vote for the "Oui" represented 49 or 51 per cent of French Quebec that night. On the other hand, the three-fifths vote for the "Non" was sadly incontestable. And hard to swallow, I had to add when speaking to some 5,000 partisans who had gathered at the Paul Sauvé Arena just the same. At the back of the platform, side by side, stood Corinne holding back her tears and Lise Payette dressed in black like a penitent; before me swam a sea of faces that no other defeat had thrown into such dejection.

29   "The day will come, however," I said, trying to convince myself, "and we will be here to greet it. But I must admit that tonight I would be hard pressed to tell you when or how. In the meantime we must live together...." To cut words short I struck up the Vigneault song that had practically become our anthem, "Gens du pays," off-key, as usual. Then I took my leave with "À la prochaine!"—a sentiment that was also a bit off-key but might at least help forget the present a little.

30   In Ottawa Trudeau lost no time in transforming himself into the wheedling healer full of solicitude for the downtrodden, pretending to spread balm on our wounds by praising our sense of democracy, a perfect Tartufe as we would soon discover, once again.

René Lévesque, "Heartbreak," *Memoirs,* Trans. Philip Stratford, Toronto: McClelland & Stewart, 1986. 301–309.

QUESTIONS

Subject
Does the title accurately reflect the subject of this essay? Explain.

Audience
Compare paragraphs 4 and 6. How does Lévesque's choice of metaphor direct his audience's sensibilities?

Purpose
Lévesque clearly has a larger purpose than narrating the events leading up to the referendum day in 1980. What is it, and how do you know?

Structure and Style

(a) The essay is structured with an ascending movement followed by a descending movement. Explain the appropriateness of these terms and identify the turning point.

(b) The first half of the essay is divided into two different areas of focus. What are they, and what is the transitional paragraph between them?

(c) How does Lévesque use Trudeau's comparisons of Quebec to a Third World country against him?

Sound and Fury

Carol Milstone

1   In 1989 four-year-old Krista Donaldson of Ottawa became a poster girl for the advancement of handicapped people through modern technology. Krista was born profoundly deaf, with insufficient residual hearing to benefit from a hearing aid. The cause of her impairment is unknown, which is typical with congenital deafness. Because Krista's parents did not want their daughter living in a silent world, they leapt at the opportunity for her to receive a cochlear implant, even though technology wasn't yet available in Canada. Cindy Donaldson reports that her daughter, now ten, can hear well and discriminate sounds for understanding language (although the sounds aren't like regular hearing). She describes her daughter as happy with the implant, and her teachers report that Krista is doing well in her neighbourhood school without special teacher aids.

2   The Donaldsons view deafness as one of life's challenges, an obstacle to be overcome to the best of their abilities and with the latest technologies. The opportunity to "implant" Krista was from their perspective ideal, and an offer from the local Kiwanis to assist with costs (the family had to go to New York for the implant) was one they could not even contemplate refusing.

3   But their decision was not so well received by other members of the deaf community, a community the Donaldsons had assumed would be on their side. Because Krista was among the very first Canadian children to receive an implant, she drew more media attention than Cindy Donaldson had expected, and of a nature that was totally shocking to her. Incredulous to this day, Donaldson vividly recalls a 1994 anti-cochlear-implant rally at the Ottawa area's Children's Hospital of Eastern Ontario. "They had posters with drawings of children strapped to chairs, with their ears covered with blood. I was disturbed to find out how militant they were, and yet the protesters admitted none had actually spoken to a parent who chose to implant their deaf child. It made me so angry. They don't want us to help our children in the hearing world. They just want us to hand them over to their deaf culture…. I've had horrible messages left on my answering machine. Someone called me a 'cruel parent' in her letter to the editor."

4   Unlike Cindy Donaldson, who remains certain she made the right decision, some parents do develop doubts about their children's cochlear implants. A 1990 speech by deaf writer Roger Carver includes this quote from the mother of a deaf child: "At night, sometimes I think about foot-binding in China…. At the speech and hearing clinic, I was trained to bind the mind of my daughter. Like the twisting of feet into lotus hooks, I was encouraged to force her deaf mind into a hearing shape. I must withhold the recognition of her most eloquent gestures [sign language] until she makes a sound, any sound. I must force her to wear hearing aids no matter how she struggles against them. The shape of a hearing mind is so much more attractive."

5   This mother's anti-interventionist sentiments are typical of (and influenced by) a subculture of deaf people who fight vehemently for the protection of deafness. The minority of deaf people who subscribe to this view describe themselves as members of Deaf culture (with a capital D). They approach deafness with reverence, viewing it as a passport to an exclusive culture. The challenge, as they view it, is not to overcome deafness but to preserve it.

6   "When I first heard about the cochlear implant, I felt hurt inside," signed Deaf culturalist Charlene LeBlanc for the *Ottawa Citizen*. "Did that mean people didn't like deaf people?" LeBlanc was one of the protesters at the anti-cochlear rally that Donaldson recalls, and is vice president of the Ontario Association for the Deaf, a lobby group whose members don't consider themselves "hearing-impaired," and for whom deafness is not a pathology.

7   Deaf culture has its roots in the traditional residential schools that many of today's deaf adults attended. In these schools lifelong bonds were formed.

8   While residential schooling has largely been replaced in North America over the last two decades with integration into local schools, these bonds have since been extended to other settings for the deaf. Today, Deaf culture is promulgated largely through sign language in deaf organizations, as well as through the Internet, academic publications, organizational newsletters, and popular books on deafness. The most exhaustive chronicle yet available of Deaf culture in Canada is to be published later this month. Dr. Clifton F. Carbin's encyclopedic *Deaf Heritage in Canada* (McGraw-Hill Ryerson) is a project of the Canadian Cultural Society of the Deaf. (It is perhaps therefore not surprising that the book's brief section on cochlear implants is strongly anti-implants.)

9   Krista Donaldson's story, then, is only a miniature version of a raging, worldwide tempest about how deafness should be viewed. The debate is not over an adult's right to choose the cochlear implant but rather a parent's right to choose the implant for his or her child.

10   In 1993, 800 deaf people protested cochlear implants at the University of Lyon in France, during a national conference on the technology. Mime skits were performed, depicting doctors who perform cochlear implants as "power/money-hungry people." Even renowned neurophysician Oliver Sacks has entered the fray. In a newspaper interview, Sacks said that he feared the insertion of a "crude" object, but mostly he feared the risk of "psychological" damage to the individual who is tuned into the hearing world.

11   At the extreme end of deaf protectionism are sentiments similar to those expressed by American Deaf culture activist Ann Silver: "The Food and Drug Administration's approval for the implants reeks of manipulation and oppression. There is absolutely no question that our government has a hidden agenda for Deaf children much akin to Nazi medical experiments on Holocaust victims."

12   Here in Canada, the Ontario Association of the Deaf demands that the provincial government ban cochlear implants in children, identifying them as "communication/emotional and mental abuse.... a form of genocide prohibited by the United Nations Treaty on Genocide."

13   Come the revolution, say Deaf activists, parents who have "handicapped" their children with cochlear implants will face the consequences of their decision: "When the Chinese revolution came," writes Judith Treesberg in a publication of the National Association of the Deaf, "the cadres unbound the feet of the women and forced them to run through the streets on their putrid stubs. Is that the future that awaits implanted children, for a revolution of consciousness and pride is surely taking place in the Deaf community."

14   The offending (or God-sent) cochlear implant, the instrument Oliver Sacks has referred to as "crude," is actually made up of three separate components: the cochlear implant itself, which is a tiny network of electrodes surgically implanted into the cochlea through a drilled hole in the mastoid bone behind the ear; the speech processor, which looks like a pocket calculator and which can be worn on a belt or in a pocket; and the microphone, which looks like a behind-the-ear hearing aid and carries electrical impulses to the speech processor and transmitter by two cords. The microphone and processor can be removed easily by the recipient, restoring deafness at will.

15   As the technology has advanced, the number of implanted electrodes has increased the range of frequencies that can be received through the auditory nerve. Each nerve fibre in the inner ear is "tuned" to a different pitch depending on its location in the cochlea (like the strings of a piano). The new Mini System 22 has twenty-two electrodes, enabling it to stimulate nerve fibres at twenty-two different locations, thereby providing the implant recipient with a much wider range of pitches than was previously possible. Sometimes dubbed the "bionic ear," the Mini System 22 achieved FDA approval in 1990 for the treatment of profound sensorineural hearing loss in children. There are at present over 1,000 children with these implants worldwide.

16   Cochlear implants differ from hearing aids, which are amplifiers of sound and which can therefore serve only people with residual hearing. Most people with sensorineural hearing loss have destroyed hair cells in the inner ear, and the cochlear implant was devised to take the place of these hair cells. Because the operation destroys the inner ear it is sensible only for those who are completely deaf and cannot benefit from a hearing aid.

17   Among the objections deaf activists have to the cochlear implant are the expectations built up by the cochlear-implant industry. From its academic review of the issue, the Greater Los Angeles Council on Deafness concludes that "implants offer hope beyond what educators of the deaf and audiologists are realistically able to promise. To be fair, [clinical staff] are not promising miracles for their implants, but they are enthusiastically selling hope, and hope is a powerful commodity."

18   Cochlear implants are not a miracle cure for deafness: recipients cannot gain full hearing, and the implants cannot help all profoundly hearing-impaired children. The company manufacturing the Mini System 22 admits in its literature that "even those children who benefit from the implant hear sounds that are different from normal hearing. To obtain optimal benefit from the device the children and their families must be willing to work with the implant team and rehabilitation/educational programs so that the child can learn to interpret and use these new sounds effectively."

19   On the other hand, more than one-third of the children who participated in the FDA clinical trials could identify car horns, doorbells, and birds chirping; they recognized speech in context, showed improvement in speech-reading, and more than half showed improvements in speech production and loudness control. The most recent research claims that under favourable conditions almost all children can develop a useful level of proficiency.

20   On a pragmatic level, the cochlear implant offers not only some qualified hope for improved speech, but increased educational, social, and vocational opportunities as well. Families of deaf children know only too well that the average deaf adult reaches only a grade-four level of reading proficiency. On a more intimate level, the cochlear implant brings children closer to the hearing world of their families and enables a child like Krista to talk on the phone and chat with her sister Melissa after the lights have been turned out.

21   But the Deaf culture's objections to cochlear implants go beyond false hopes. Society's historical treatment of the deaf is an issue members of the deaf community find difficult to put behind them.

22   During the Second World War, deaf people were identified for the gas chambers. Even Alexander Graham Bell, long considered a champion of the deaf for his contribution to lip-reading and the oral approach, began a crusade to put an end to sign language, deaf teachers, and residential schools (so the deaf couldn't mingle). Bell also discouraged marriage between deaf persons, to avoid "a deaf-mute race."

23   Nor has the educational establishment distinguished itself by its treatment of the deaf. The traditional residential schools for the deaf in North America insisted on teaching largely unsuccessful forms of oral habilitation—lip-reading and vocalization. Sign language (the preferred language between friends outside the classroom) was thought to be simplistic and unsophisticated, and was for the most part forbidden. (The movie *Children of a Lesser God* is considered a joyful vindication of sign language in this regard.)

24   According to research done by a University of Ottawa student, Rosemary McCrae, whose own son's hearing was severely damaged during infancy, the history of deaf education is rife with evidence of cruelty: "For years the Deaf [at residential schools] were forced to speak using the crudest of hearing aids. The methods of teaching were inadequate and the children were too old to learn spoken language. The deaf children were physically punished for using sign language, even though it was their language and the best method of communication available to them."

25   In part, then, the Deaf culture's rejection of cochlear implants is based on the historical failure of the oral approach. If sign language works, they argue, why risk the same cycle of failure and rejection many of them experienced before joining Deaf culture? Any attempt to make deaf children speak will only set them up for failure, say the most adamant supporters of Deaf culture, because they could never do as well as hearing children.

26   But most hearing parents of deaf children see this pessimism as flying in the face of recent improvements in training methods for the deaf. The Ontario Ministry of Education's 1990 review of Deaf education noted that in a survey of 689 parents, only eight said they would choose sign language for their children. Rosemary McCrae is among the majority of hearing parents who reject the Deaf culture's anti-oral manifesto for their children, opting for their children's integration into the school system. McCrae's eleven-year-old son John is severely hearing-impaired in both ears and is assisted with hearing aids. John is playing "Sim City" on the computer with his nine-year-old brother Richard and their new friend Steven. When the boys are out of earshot Steven discreetly inquires of his mother, "Mom, which is the one who's deaf again?" In the McCrae household there is no room for special allowances: "When John doesn't respond to me it's either because he doesn't have his 'ears' on or because he is not paying attention. It's not because he can't understand me."

27   John is fortunate to have been a student of auditory-verbal therapist Judy Simser at the Children's Hospital of Eastern Ontario. Simser teaches deaf children how to use their residual hearing (assisted through aids or implants) to enable them to develop oral speech and language. Simser received the Order of Ontario in 1992 for her success in helping hearing-impaired children learn to speak. Because the auditory-verbal approach encourages hearing, children are dissuaded from using sign language and lip-reading. Simser has no objections to signing per se, but feels that it can be picked up later on.

28   Simser's own son Scott was discovered to be deaf at seven months and started auditory-verbal therapy in Montreal at an early age. Scott was one of the first deaf children in the Ottawa area to attend public school, and he went on to receive an MBA. "We wanted Scott to be as much like ourselves as he could," declared Simser unapologetically in an *Ottawa Citizen* interview.

29   It is true, as the Deaf culturalists would argue, that there are many deaf children who cannot enjoy the privileges of linguistic precocity, a well-staffed community, and parents who are dedicated to the laborious programme of oralist training. For these deaf individuals the

prospects of succeeding in the hearing world remain grim, and it is for these individuals that the Deaf culture's sirens should ring.

30   But do these cases justify Deaf culture's unqualified rejection of cochlear implants and oralism for all deaf children? And, a more troublesome question for some parents: would their objections change at all if technology could provide perfect hearing for all such children?

31   Among the most extreme spokesmen for the movement, the answer seems to be an unqualified no. Dr. Harlan Lane, a distinguished university professor of linguistics at Northeastern University, discusses the cochlear implant in his book *The Mask of Benevolence.* "Members of the American deaf community affirm that what characterizes them as a group is their shared language and culture, and not an infirmity.... So medical intervention is inappropriate, even if a perfect 'bionic ear' were available." Along with this bottom-line rejection of implants by these members of the Deaf community go a refusal to lip-read, a rejection of hearing aids (what deaf writer Kathryn Woodcock refers to as "sort of a Deaf-liberation equivalent to bra-burning"), and even objections to new technology that can detect deafness in infancy. "If I had a bulldozer and a gun," signed a student leader at the deaf's Gallaudet University in Washington, D.C., "I would destroy all scientific experiments to cure deafness. If I could hear, I would probably take a pencil and poke myself to be deaf again."

32   The truth about these views of Deaf culture, though, is that only a minority of hearing-impaired people elect to join it. (In Ottawa, for example, twenty-five percent of the severely hearing-impaired identify with Deaf culture.) And Deaf culture's new militancy in attempting to ban cochlear implants may be starting to backfire. Parents of deaf children, those with the most critical role in instilling pride in their children's identity, are becoming short-tempered. Rosemary McCrae feels that Deaf culture is using deaf children as political pawns, rather than viewing them as people with real feelings. Organizations are forming to defend themselves against anti-oral, anti-implant pressure, including Cochlear Implants International, and Voice for Hearing Impaired Children, a Canadian oral-approach support group for hearing parents of deaf children.

33   In his own memoir of deafness, *What's That Pig Outdoors,* Chicago book editor and columnist Henry Kisor refuses to go along with what he sees as the "New Orthodoxy" of his activist deaf colleagues. "As with so many social movements throughout history," he reminds his readers, "the oppressed can become the oppressors."

Carol Milstone, "Sound and Fury," *Saturday Night,* March 1996: 25–26, 28.

QUESTIONS

Subject
Outline the accusations brought by each side against the other in the dispute over cochlear implants.

Audience
To what extent might a reader's positive attitude toward implants change after reading what they are, how they work, and how they are installed?

Purpose

Do those who support Deaf culture lose reader support by employing emotional language and extreme analogies to point out their sense of the cruelty of implants? Or do you disagree that their language is highly emotional and their comparisons extreme?

Structure and Style

(a) Discuss the organization of the essay by focusing on various developmental strategies such as illustration, definition, and cause and effect.

(b) In paragraph 13 the author uses the word "handicapped" to describe those who have had cochlear implants. How is the use of this word ironic in this context?

(c) The final sentence mentions "oppressors" and "the oppressed." How do these terms apply to those who support either side of the argument?

The Longest Night

Toni Onley

1   Nothing is inevitable, they say, but death and taxes. In a recent twelve-month period, however, I have stared both in the face and survived. In September, 1983, I came within hours of burning my inventory of paintings and prints to escape the harassment of Revenue Canada, but I won the dispute. In September, 1984, I came within seconds of losing my life when my skiplane crashed on a glacier in Garibaldi Provincial Park, 120 kilometres north of Vancouver, but I lived to tell the tale.

2   I've been flying for more than eighteen years. In 1966 I was teaching at the University of Victoria and living near the airport. I had done only art-related jobs and I wondered if I could do something that required mechanical finesse. I took flying lessons, got my licence, and in 1967 bought a used Champion Skytrack with the $5,000 I had made from an exhibition in Montreal. I flew it for eight years, across Canada, to Mexico, landing it on beaches on the West Coast, rarely stopping at airports except to fuel. Then I wanted to get to the eastern Arctic. I bought an amphibious Lake Buccaneer, which I still have for exploring mountain lakes. But once on the lakes I would look up at the glaciers and yearn to be in their pristine environment. In 1981 I sold all the watercolours from my book, *Silent Thunder,* for nearly $100,000 and put it into a Polish-built Wilga 80, which I equipped with skis.

3   I couldn't have painted the glaciers unless I had been on them. Above the timber line the painting was often painted for me. Surrounded by sky, rock, and ice, I was able to concentrate on the things that were essential, to spend hours looking for the particular elements that would describe the whole atmosphere. The mind became uncluttered, perception cleared, and I seemed to flow with nature. The painting just rolled off the brush like a song, and there were days when I could do no wrong.

4   Some of the most enjoyable times of my life have been up in the mountains. The silence enveloped me, punctuated occasionally by the sound of a distant waterfall or the rumble of a far-off avalanche. The ringing in my ears was the sound of my own blood circulating. I was where few people, maybe no-one, had ever been, in a private universe far above the

crowded, smoky valleys. All that stood between me and my return to those valleys was a fragile piece of technology, my skiplane, with the call letters C-FLUF—after my mother's nickname, "Fluff."

5   I can remember when I first landed on a glacier, on Powder Mountain on September 17, 1982. I had an animal fear of being out of my environment, in a world I was unprepared for. It was as if I had been thrust into the ice age from the lush green gardens of Vancouver thirty minutes away. I had felt godlike while flying around the mountain peaks, but on the glacier I felt small and powerless. I walked with unsure feet and thoughts of impending avalanches and crevasses ready to swallow me up.

6   John Reeves, the Toronto photographer renowned for his portraits of artists and writers, had been commissioned by CP Air's in-flight magazine to do a photo essay about me— "The Flying Artist" or some such thing. Later, when we were stranded together in the wreckage of my plane, he said, "I suppose you realize this scotches our story. CP Air won't want to publish something that ends in an aircraft disaster."

7   On September 6 we went up to the Bishop Glacier on the shoulder of Mount Garibaldi, but we had got a late start and the weather was poor so we stayed only half an hour. The next day would be better, I promised. Our plan was to go up to the highest glacier in the area, the Cheakamus, at 8,000 feet; to land on it, do some painting and photography; and then go down 1,000 feet to a spectacular glacier on Mamquam Mountain, after which we would return to the Bishop, down at 5,000 feet, so that John could see the peaks of Garibaldi that had been clouded-in the first day.

8   The next morning we got onto the Cheakamus without trouble, but it was not so easy to get off. The winds were gusting—one minute calm, the next up to forty knots, not unusual in the mountains—and the snow was wet and sticky, which slowed the takeoff down the face of the glacier. I waited for the winds to die, then started my first run, but I couldn't get a good speed because of the snow. So halfway down I chopped the power and taxied back up the steep knoll for a second try. My first tracks were packed ice now, so I shouldn't have had another problem with speed. I waited for the winds to drop, then I fired off again, holding in the tracks. When I reached the end of them I had enough speed to take off. I pulled on full flaps, which is usually sufficient to "pop" the plane off the ground by moving the weight from the skis to the wings. But nothing happened. It felt as if I had no flaps, that the wings were flat. I looked out and saw that the flaps were in position. I also saw that the gusting winds had caught up with us. Fine snow was blowing on the surface of the glacier in the direction we were going. That meant my wings had no lift. Essentially, though we were going fifty miles per hour, we were standing still.

9   It was too late to stop or turn. My options were to chop power, slow, and drop into the horizontal crevasse that stretched ahead, fifty feet wide and two hundred feet deep; or maintain power, try to leap the crevasse, and hope we wouldn't smash into the crevasse's ice wall or slide across the other side and drop into the next wide crevasse that loomed ahead. In retrospect, I made the right decision. I held power and we leaped the first crevasse. Then, by the greatest good fortune, the plane nestled into a narrow, perpendicular crevasse. It was the only one on the mile-wide glacier that ran in the direction of our descent; it formed the stubby stem of a T immediately across from where we jumped the broad crevasse; and it was just wide enough to accommodate the body of the plane while supporting the wings. It minimized the impact of the crash yet prevented us from sliding on toward the next fall. Six feet to the right or left and we would have smashed into the ice.

10   I would like to say that this was a magnificent piece of flying, but the truth is that I had lost control. Some other hand had pushed us into the only place that could have stopped our fall and cradled us through the long night. We hung suspended there from two o'clock in the afternoon until our rescue at eight the next morning.

11   I have no memory of the impact, no sight or sound. My first recollection was that my legs were pinned behind the controls and twisted, jagged metal. The engine had been pushed back into the cabin and my seat had been uprooted and pushed sideways. It was a wonder I hadn't been cut in half. Meanwhile my seat had pushed John's almost out of the plane to the right. John was unconscious. His head was hanging down and blood was dripping from his mouth. I had felt no fear before the crash, because I had been too busy, but now I was filled with a raw terror. I was on the edge of panic. For an hour, as I tried to free my trapped legs by working my feet out of my shoes, I kept shouting at him, "John, are you all right?" He flinched at the sound of my voice, but I thought I had lost him, that I would have to live with that for the rest of my life.

12   Metal ripped into my legs as I struggled to unpin them, but the pain was diminished by my adrenaline and my concern for John. I was also afraid that at any moment we would burst into flames, because I could see gasoline pouring onto the hot engine and live wires. That fear subsided after fifteen minutes or so as the engine cooled. Finally I got free. The floor beneath John had been ripped open when the engine had pulled to the left. I remember thinking how lucky John was that his seat belt and shoulder harness hadn't sprung open, as mine had, or he might have followed his cameras out of the plane and dropped 200 feet into the crevasse below. He was still unconscious. I slapped his face and his eyes opened wide immediately. His memory had gone, but the blood running from the corner of his mouth was only from a tooth having gone into his lip.

13   "What kind of place is this?" he asked. "I hope they have a good wine cellar."

14   I unbuckled him and got him into the back seat. It was 3:15. I wondered if my emergency locator transmitter (ELT) had gone off on impact. I turned it on manually. Later I learned that the search-and-rescue unit at Comox had picked up my signal by satellite at that time. My radio was dangling through the hole in the floor. I reached down and pulled up the headset and microphone. I could confirm on the emergency frequency that my ELT was transmitting, but I couldn't call out a Mayday because the cable to the antenna was severed.

15   I crawled back into the luggage compartment to stretch out my broken leg and bind up my left ring finger, which had been opened to the bone. John put on my parka and tried to make himself comfortable in the left back seat. I was lying beside him, and I spread out my one sleeping bag to cover me and cover John's feet and legs. There was nothing to do but wait. At 4:30 we heard the unmistakable drone of an armed forces Buffalo and then it came into view through the six-inch gap where the windshield had been. It circled over the valley, probably 500 feet above us, getting closer but not too close because Mount Davidson and Castle Towers Mountain were near and the weather was worsening. When it flew away we at least knew we had been spotted. It was only a matter of time before help arrived.

16   A half-hour passed, then we heard the sound of a big Chinook Rescue Helicopter working its way up the face of the glacier into what must have been whiteout conditions because of the snow that had started to fall. It was searching for us. I wanted to contact the pilot on the radio and say, "Please go back. We're O.K." We could see its grey outline and yellow searchlights. It was maybe 300 yards away, but between us and it lay many great crevasses. The helicopter put down on a shelf of ice and appeared to be looking for signs of life.

We were down in the crevasse and couldn't wave, and our shouts wouldn't have been heard above the wind and the engines. I was tempted to push out the rear window, climb out, and wave, but that window provided the only shelter we would have for the cold night. After ten minutes, the helicopter backed into the gloom and the drifting snow. All was quiet except for the wind that gusted up to sixty miles per hour, driving snow in through every opening. Soon it was dark.

17   It must have struck me at some point during the night that I was with one of the most entertaining, voluble men in Canada. But John was not talking. He had a fractured cheekbone, which would have made talking painful, and we preferred to be quiet. John was later to describe his looks as "asymmetrical chipmunk." He suggested that in future I should pack a chessboard or at least Trivial Pursuit in my survival kit. He was so nonchalant about things that no-one would have guessed that we were in a desperate situation. "Another fine mess you've got us in, Ollie," he said. But John Reeves on the surface is very different from John Reeves underneath. Later, the doctors discovered that his heart rate was almost off the chart, so there had been an enormous amount of inner turmoil and shock.

18   We were like cavemen, our language reduced to the most basic. I would say, "Cheese? For strength," and he would answer, "No, not hungry." At one point, before the sun had gone, I asked him if he wanted to shoot some photographs for the record with the one camera that had been saved. He said something like, "No, I'm not a crash photographer."

19   Our only difference occurred when he said, "Toni, I think maybe we should get out of this bloody wreck and bivouac out on the snow."

20   "John," I said, "with that wind, we'd freeze to death. We've got the only shelter between here and Vancouver, and we can't walk out of this."

21   Most of the time we were too deep in our own thoughts for conversation. I often thought of my wife, Yukiko. By eight in the evening she would have phoned the number I had given her for the rescue coordination centre in Victoria. They would have told her that my skiplane had been spotted but that there was no sign of life. I felt so helpless being out of contact. I knew she would have phoned our friends, George and Inge Woodcock. I pictured them together. At ten I made an image of them and repeated in my mind, "I am alive, I am alive." Yukiko was to tell me later that she didn't get the message but that Inge had called at that time to say she had a strong feeling that John and I were all right. One never knows how one will behave in an emergency. Yukiko was very calm. She didn't fall apart or phone my family and get everyone tied in knots. She asked the RCMP not to release my name. And she spent much of the long night tidying the house.

22   Meanwhile, John and I tried to sleep. I nodded off and had a strange dream. I dreamed that a Revenue Canada ski patrol had found us. Their leader asked if I intended to declare a loss with the crash of my plane and would I fill out a form. I tried but had difficulty in my cramped position; besides, it was dark. I protested and asked for help, but the leader said, "This is not the responsibility of this department." I asked him to contact search-and-rescue, and he said, "We do not communicate with that department or any other government department." I awoke and there was only the wind and the snow.

23   The gusting wind kept moving the plane, which creaked and groaned like a ship, then settled a little deeper into the crevasse. My fear was that the tail would drop down and the plane would be supported only by the flaps and ailerons of the wings. I would be head down in the luggage compartment; John would fall on me; and we might both be carried out the rear window into the crevasse. Once during the night the plane's tail did fall suddenly.

24   "Oh my God," I thought. "We're going to drop."

25   Despite my broken leg, I leaped into the front as the plane lurched. I grabbed hold of the structure to receive John's weight if he fell back on me. But the tail had dropped only a few feet and the elevator had lodged on the edge of the crevasse. We were safer now, so I crawled back.

26   I was wet to the skin. The snow had melted in the aircraft and soaked me. John was dry but somewhat uncomfortable in his cramped lotus position. I was shaking uncontrollably and said to John, "I might not get through another night like this." I knew from a survival course how dangerous it is to be wet. My main worry was that the ceiling would stay down and we would be in the clouds through the next day so that a helicopter could not get in. John and I intertwined our feet to keep warm, and three or four times in the night he tucked the sleeping bag tightly around our legs.

27   Dawn came slowly, then suddenly I was blinded by a flash of yellow light as the sun rose over the black mountains. The snow melted off the rear window and soon the inside of the plane grew warm. I was impatient for our rescue and kept imagining that I heard helicopters, but it was only the wind. At eight, however, I definitely heard the chop-chop-chop and a Bell Jet Ranger passed overhead. But it went out into the valley again. John described the scene as from a movie: "They're coming, they're coming, they're coming. They're going, they're going, they're gone." Minutes passed before the helicopter came back, heading straight for us. I pushed on the rear window and it popped out, making a slow pirouette before plunging into the crevasse. I stood up on my good leg and frantically waved a yellow stuffbag. The helicopter came in and hovered off our left wing. It couldn't land on the sloping ice, so a paramedic hopped out and crawled along our wing. I held John's legs as the paramedic grabbed his arm and pulled him out, and the two of them inched their way back across the wing. Then I crawled across it, pushing myself with my good leg while the paramedic pulled my arm. I couldn't stand, so he dragged me to the helicopter. John pulled me in, and soon we were off.

28   In Squamish, I was placed on a stretcher and wheeled to a waiting ambulance. A young reporter from the Vancouver *Province* was taking notes on a folded pad and I asked her to phone my wife and tell her we were safe. That's how the reporter found out that I was the infamous artist who had defied Revenue Canada. She stuck to me and eventually had to be ejected by a strong nurse as I was being prepared for an x-ray at the hospital. Her determination seemed an incredible affirmation of life, I thought, even if I was the victim of it.

29   In the aftermath it was hard to get back to ordinary living. I'm not a religious person in the sense that I don't belong to an organized group, but I believe there's a power at work. I don't understand it and I wish I did. There are things I can't put words to but am always thinking about. Was I saved for some reason? Is there a divine plan? Do I have unfinished work?

30   As to whether I'll fly again, I'll have to discuss that with my wife and family. Flying has become such an integral part of my art that I can't imagine painting without the fresh, mysterious images I bring home from the coastal islands, glaciers, and mountain lakes. I'll miss my mountains and snowfields, and I'll not be able to bring myself to paint them until I can wander among them again.

Toni Onley, "The Longest Night," *Saturday Night,* February 1985: 24, 26–27.

QUESTIONS

Subject
In the essay, the author is telling a story about a near brush with death that he and a friend had. But the subject of the essay clearly involves more than this. The subject, in fact, is very much bound up with spiritual notions of both a non-religious and a near-religious nature. Explain.

Audience
The author seems to know that the vast majority of humankind is primarily interested in an adventure story. Discuss the ways in which he builds his story into an exciting adventure.

Purpose
Look up "memoir" in your dictionary. Does the meaning of this word help explain the essay's narrative purpose?

Structure and Style
(a) Although we are regularly warned not to use clichés, the author makes use of one in his opening sentence. Does the cliché help make the opening effective?

(b) Explain why the subject about which the author dreams in paragraph 22 is appropriate and helps contribute to the unity of the essay.

(c) Comment on why you feel the dialogue throughout the essay is appropriate.

Sex Offenders: What You Need to Know

Kim Pittaway

1 On November 18, 1994, Wray Budreo became a free man—and every parent's nightmare. For days, his face had been plastered on newspapers throughout southern Ontario. Budreo had a 30-year history of child molesting. But, because he had served his full six-year term, there would be no parole or probation, no restrictions on his movements, no conditions for mandatory treatment. He was bundled into the trunk of a police car and spirited past the protesters who awaited him outside Kingston Penitentiary.

2 There was a time when the bogeyman's face remained hidden in the shadows of children's dreams. Today, his picture makes the front page, captioned "child molester." As for the children's faces, they're missing, the identities withheld in the name of belated protection. Our imaginations fill that space with the school photos that hang on our own refrigerators—today's bogeyman resides in the restless minds of parents. While fear may make us doubt our abilities to shield our children, the fact is that most parents *can* take

steps to protect their children from sexual abuse—and without becoming paranoid or obsessive. Your first weapon: knowing the facts.

3   Not every child is equally at risk. Offenders target especially vulnerable children: lonely kids, those with disabilities or difficulty communicating, youngsters with absent dads who may be looking for a father figure, and those whose behavioral problems make it unlikely they'll be believed if they do speak up.

4   Of course, the biggest risk factor is contact with a potential abuser. And here the facts contrast with the headlines: the dangerous stranger is the exception rather than the rule. A 1992 Statistics Canada survey found that, in cases of child sexual assault, 48 percent of the abusers were parents or family members. Another 43 percent were friends or acquaintances. Only 5 percent were strangers.

5   Whoever the offender is, the law is clear. It is always illegal for an adult to engage in sexual contact with a child under the age of 14. It is also illegal for an adult who is in a position of trust or authority to engage in sexual contact with a young person under the age of 18. The law recognizes what adults know: children can be manipulated, especially by the people they trust. Whether they say yes doesn't matter, because the adult is the one who is expected to say no.

6   The number of cases is much disputed, but there's nothing comforting in a 1992 Statistics Canada survey of 13 sample police departments. The researchers found that of every 10 reported victims of sexual assault, four were under the age of 12, four were aged 12 to 19—and only two were adults. There are no national statistics on the number of children molested every year, but whatever the figure, it's too high.

7   And it can only be reduced one child at a time. For parents, that means recognizing potential molesters, keeping kids out of risky situations, and trusting your instincts when something just doesn't seem right.

Know Your Enemy

8   "He was my best friend. My kids loved him—he was their Uncle Keith," says a father in small-town British Columbia. He and his wife asked to be called John and Mary Smith, their real names shielded by the court order that hides the identity of their daughter "Jean." Last fall, "Uncle Keith," 39, pleaded guilty to molesting Jean. John Smith says the abuse went on for more than four years, beginning when Jean was 5. The guilty man was sentenced to 18 months in jail. Jean's parents think that's not enough, and have joined Citizens Against Child Exploitation, based in Kelowna, B.C., to lobby for stiffer sentences.

9   John Smith had known "Uncle Keith" for 20 years, and the man had spent long weekends, summer vacations and Christmases with the Smiths and their three daughters. When he lost his job, John and Mary gave him a room in their home and helped him get back on his feet.

10   He thanked them by molesting Jean. The abuser began by showing her pornographic material; later, he fondled her while masturbating. "He made my daughter feel that he had a right to do that, that it was okay," says Jean's dad. "And of course he said, 'This is our little secret.'"

11   The words are tinged with anger and bewilderment, and a hint of guilt because John didn't spot the abuse sooner. But spotting an abuser isn't easy. They come from all socioeconomic backgrounds. Some are charming and appear well-adjusted, although it's true that many more are socially awkward and immature. Though the vast majority are male, a few (less than one in 10) are women.

12   There are some warning signs, though. Laurie LeBlanc, Ontario executive director for Big Brothers of Canada, points to the clues that his agency watches for in screening its volunteers. One of the most significant is overinvolvement with children and children's activities, to the exclusion of adult relationships. "If there are no adults in his life, that's a real red flag," says LeBlanc.

13   Other red flags include controlling behavior, a lack of steady relationships with adults, an unstable work history, immature behavior, and preoccupation with children as "clean" or "pure" or a habit of describing children in inappropriately romantic or intimate terms. While LeBlanc warns that no single factor means a person is a molester, a "cluster of check marks" is cause for concern.

14   In retrospect, John Smith says there was a sign that he wishes he'd paid closer attention to: his buddy Keith's obsession with pornography. At one point, the man plastered the walls of his living room with nude centerfolds. "I thought it was weird, but I figured I didn't have to live there, and you know, different strokes," says Smith. And while John and Mary tried to "streetproof" their children, they realize now that they didn't go far enough. "We said if a stranger ever touches you, you let us know. Keith wasn't a stranger."

Stand on Guard

15   A child's wariness isn't necessarily the answer even when the offender is a stranger. Except in those extremely rare cases where a child is literally snatched off the streets, strangers operate according to the same principles as abusers who know the child: they use tricks or psychological manipulation to win a child's trust, and then they betray that trust.

16   That's what happened with 16-year-old Daryn Rosenfeldt, who disappeared during Easter break in 1981 about two blocks from his Coquitlam, B.C., home. Daryn was walking home from a drugstore; that afternoon, he planned to go looking for a summer job. A car pulled up. The man inside was clean-cut and friendly. A hard hat and construction paraphernalia cluttered the car's interior.

17   "I need some kids to clean windows at my construction site," said the driver. "I pay well—$10 an hour. Know any kids who might be interested?" Daryn jumped at the chance, and the man suggested they visit the site. As they drove past the Rosenfeldt home, the driver asked the boy a question designed to cement the trust that his plausible story and personable approach had inspired. "Are you sure you don't have to check with your mother?" he asked. Daryn said no.

18   Three weeks later, police found Daryn's body. He had been raped, then killed by a blow to the head. That August, police arrested the man who would become known as Canada's most notorious child murderer, Clifford Olson. He provided details of the abduction.

19   "I raised my son to be wary of strangers," says Daryn's mother, Sharon. "But it wasn't good enough." Today, Sharon Rosenfeldt and her husband, Gary, pour their anger and energy into Victims of Violence, an Ottawa-based national organization that provides information about crimes against children and advocates tougher sentences. The group has published a fund-raising children's cookbook called *Kids in the Kitchen*, which features a cartoon section designed to teach children about risky situations. It identifies tricks strangers use, such as asking a child to open a car door because the stranger's hands are full, asking for help in finding a lost puppy, and asking to join in a children's game. "I'd rather have my child a little frightened than to not have my child at all," Sharon says. But she doesn't discount parents' concerns about fearmongering. She advises teaching kids about risky

situations while pointing out that not all strangers are bad. "The clerk at the corner store is a stranger but that doesn't mean a child should be afraid of him," Sharon says. "But, if he asks the child to go into a back room alone, that's a dangerous situation that a child should run away from."

20   In the end, though, we should not expect children to protect themselves. Protection is primarily a parent's job, says Dr. David Wolfe, a professor of psychology and psychiatry at the University of Western Ontario. He's done extensive research into the physical and sexual abuse of children, and he and his wife, lawyer Barbara Legate, have three young children of their own.

21   "In physical abuse, we never say to children 'Don't let anyone hit you,'" says Wolfe. "With sexual abuse, it's as if we're afraid to make adults responsible, and so we put the responsibility for self-protection on the kids. Of course offenders know how to work around that." Children do need to be taught about "good touches" and "bad touches," about privacy and boundaries, says Wolfe. But it's parents who are best equipped to judge character and risk.

22   For example, Wolfe says he tries not to allow his children to be alone with another adult he does not know extremely well, because abuse requires privacy. Overnight visits and out-of-town trips are safer when there are more children and more than one adult involved. In the case of organized activities, like soccer leagues and theatre groups, Wolfe advises parents to ask about the organization's policies around sexual abuse prevention. Are background checks done on employees and volunteers who work with children? Surprisingly, many volunteer and recreational groups don't carry out criminal record checks.

23   Spot checks can be another tool of parental vigilance. Wolfe suggests showing up unexpectedly during a music lesson or skating class. If there's nothing going on, the instructor shouldn't mind. But if there is a risk, the abuser will get the message that he's unlikely to have uninterrupted time with your child. The same tactic works with baby-sitters, day-care centers and schools.

24   "The best protection kids can have is somebody to watch out for them, who is sensitive to any signs of distress," says Wolfe.

Trust Your Instincts

25 Every parent hopes that if something does happen, the child will tell them. But that won't happen unless you explicitly tell your child she won't be in trouble if she speaks up. Jean Smith's parents wish they had done that; she didn't tell anyone of her abuse at "Uncle Keith's" hands until she was 13, four years after the abuse had stopped—and then only because she was afraid her 7-year-old sister was at risk. "Kids tend to think they've done something wrong," says John Smith.

26   But sometimes children speak with actions, not words. For instance, if your child is unusually reluctant to spend time in a particular adult's company, a little gentle questioning isn't out of order. And trust your instincts about adult motivations. It's not unreasonable to be concerned if an adult appears to be overly interested in your child, perhaps by inappropriately lavishing gifts on the youngster. In all of these circumstances, sexual abuse isn't necessarily the cause, but maybe there's something going on that you should know about.

27   At the same time, we need to nurture the protective instincts of the children themselves. So often, those instincts get short-circuited because adults habitually command rather than explain ("Do it because I told you!"). As well, when we inadvertently place our kids in risky situations, we condition them to think the risk is normal. Taking simple unobtrusive steps to avoid risky situations is the sexual-abuse equivalent to locking up the drain cleaner and matches when toddlers come to visit.

28   Wolfe uses the example of a teacher alone with a child after school. "If I were that teacher, I'd ask the vice principal or another teacher to stop by," he says. "And I'd leave the doors open." In fact, some schools have policies that compel teachers to take such steps. The point is that it shouldn't be up to the child to ask that the door be left open. It's up to the adults to ensure there isn't even the appearance of risk. And when open doors are the norm, a child is more likely to speak up if an abuser tries to isolate her behind closed doors.

29   Abusers are to blame for their own actions. But all adults need to take on the responsibility for making thoughtful vigilance—rather than scaremongering—the norm. Because it's always been an adult's job to keep the bogeyman at bay.

Kim Pittaway, "Sex Offenders: What You Need to Know," Chatelaine, March 1995: 57, 59,
105, 107.

QUESTIONS

Subject
How does the title of the essay indicate that it is going to be essentially an expository piece of writing? Look for other linguistic clues that indicate the expository nature of the essay.

Audience
Based on much that is said in the essay it seems self-evident that it is pitched to parents. However, can you find examples that show that the author wants to appeal to people other than parents? How does the author's allusions to Dr. David Wolfe help support her case and win reader trust?

Purpose
Obviously the author wants to inform people, and parents in particular, about sexual offenders. However, in what way(s) does she also try to dislodge some of our prejudices about such offenders and their offences?

Structure and Style
(a) Comment on the part that narration and anecdote play in this essay.

(b) Explain how the author ties the end of the essay to the beginning and decide whether this is an effective device.

Boozy Saddles

Al Purdy

1   My friend Tom Howe and I left Vancouver for Anahim Lake in the Chilcotin in early June, driving his father's nearly-new, three-quarter ton, pickup truck. Tom is a writer and photographer who worked on a Chilcotin ranch two years ago. He was returning there, as I was, to write about the annual three-day rodeo.

2   The 400 miles or so to Williams Lake is good highway despite the loops and twists of Hell's Gate and the Fraser Canyon. Some 200 miles from Vancouver the monster snow-capped mountains become mere giants, almost barren of trees, and brown from lack of rain in the near-desert BC interior. After Cache Creek comes Cariboo country, with cattle ranges reaching all the way north to Prince George. We stop for gas at 100 Mile House; I once wrote a poem about this town which certainly nobody in the community has heard of.

3   We reach Williams Lake on the evening of the first day. Next morning we buy some beer, and then we drive west into the Chilcotin. The first 30 miles are paved as a come-on for tourists; the remainder, a mythical distance to Anahim, varies according to whom you ask for directions. (Reminds me of the Khyber Pass or maybe just a place where road builders moved all rocks into the middle of the road.) Tom drives around 30 mph, then down to 20; even 10 sometimes.

4   "Migawd, Tom, if it's really 200 miles we won't get there till snow falls at this rate."

5   "You wanta drive?"

6   "Tom, you know you wouldn't trust me to drive your dad's truck."

7   "Then shaddup!" So we have a beer, but it's getting a little flat now because the beer bubbles were burst by bumps in the road. "Hold on," Tom says, and hits the truck up to 50. All I can feel at that speed is soothing rhythm, like some six-foot gal was giving my spine a hard rub-down in a Yonge Street massage joint. Since crossing Fraser for the umpteenth and last time, we have entered an empire—cattle country—remote from even the remote Cariboo. No towns, only clusters of six or a dozen houses; the clusters have names but they all look alike. High mountains are returning, shawled with snow; the Coast Range. Blue lakes spring up with every curve in the road; occasional cowboys clop around in the increasing grassland areas. I want to open the window and yell "Hi podner," but refrain because of the dust. Fifty miles ahead is Anahim Lake (named for a Chilcotin Indian chief). A hundred miles farther or through a pass in the Coast Range is the Pacific Ocean, and the town of Bella Coola, and the rock where the explorer Mackenzie scribbled: "Alexander Mackenzie, from Canada by land...."

8   The beer is flat by Anahim—definitely and conclusively. But we can't waste it, being unsure of where to get a further supply. I check into Anahim's one motel, and Tom takes his tent and camping equipment to the rodeo grounds and sets up shop. Then both of us go our separate, exploring ways.

9   Anahim is a village of fewer than 200 people. The stampede grounds and jackpine jungle around it are thronged with jalopies, trucks, campers, pickups and trailers. White tents glimmer in green clearings, campfires crackle at night. More than 1,000 people are encamped. The entire Chilcotin Indian tribe has arrived for its annual birthday party of booze and laughter. Carrier Indians, called "Sticks" derisively by the warlike Chilcotins, are also in attendance. Everyone is being primed or already primed with scotch, vodka, gin, rum, wine

and beer, and/or the local variety of poison called "Itcha Mountain Fog" (said to have occasioned more fatalities than the last Indian war). Carl, the grocer at nearby Nimpo Lake, has 300 cases of beer.

10   The rodeo at Anahim is more than a game. It a honing of necessary, but everyday skills; the players are reenacting the daily events of their lives. Calf- and steer-roping and broncbusting are basic cowboy activities of the big Chilcotin and Cariboo ranches. But beyond that, it's an occasion where old friends (who may not have seen each other for months) gather to gossip, drink and discuss the business of living. And for three days in early June nearly everyone gets gloriously drunk in one big whoop-up, a concentrated and deliberate undoing of sobriety.

11   Sometimes, the Mountie corporal in charge of order tells me, there are knifings and robberies; fights are commonplace. "At the Williams Lake Stampede five people died this year." But, he hastens to add, "Three of the deaths were from natural causes."

12   The stampede ground roughly resembles a football field; it's a kind of oblong arena floored with floury grey dust, 150 yards long but not quite that wide, fenced with lodgepole pine. Spectators—tourists, Indians and local people—perch atop the fence or peer through railings. Mounties prowl the perimeter, deterrents, hopefully, to any trouble.

13   In a high tower above the cattle chutes, Slim Recknock, six feet and 200 pounds of 30-year-old cowboy, is the PA announcer. He sounds like a caller at a barn dance. When a calf is reluctant to leave the chute, Slim bellows: "Crank his tail a little."

14   A brown calf bursts from Chute No. 2, maybe 300 pounds of veal on the hoof. George Palmatier bursts after him. Grey dust explodes in a moving cloud. The big calf is ahead of him. The cowboy disappears entirely, then reemerges, his rope snaking out to snag the twisting terrified head. Rapidly securing one end of the rope to the saddle, he dismounts and follows the rope hand-over-hand to the brown calf.

15   Then it's a swift wrestling match. The idea is to get that calf down quickly, one arm around his neck, the other encircling his front leg. But the calf is reluctant. "That there's a strong calf," Slim says dryly. But George manages. Front and hind legs are roped together and Palmatier stands like an actor, arms thrown wide to take a bow from the first-day audience. The drama consumes only 18 seconds.

16   A fine grey dust begins to settle over everything. And everybody: Indians, whites, tourists, Mounties. The hot Chilcotin sun urges sweat under armpits and over foreheads, and the sweat streaks patterns in the dust. After a while you can taste dust.

17   Bareback riding looks most dangerous to me. Broncs are chosen on the basis of being the most cantankerous of the most cantankerous. The convulsing animal is supposed to be ridden for eight seconds. William Billy Boy doesn't last that long; he flies upward and downward at such speed that when he lands, the dust bomb obscures him for a period longer than the ride itself. I think: no wonder these broncs are slightly irritable, the way they're mounted in the chutes; they stand in this passageway narrow enough to keep them from turning to kick, or sink those strong yellow teeth into a rider. I did see one try to turn around in that passageway. He got stuck.

18   Dave Lewis comes from the launching pad of Chute No. 3 on a horse called Drifter, who doesn't drift much. He keeps trying to kick the sand with both hind legs; almost manages too. In a space of eight seconds Drifter scrapes his rider against the fence, rocks forward and backward, damn near stands on his head, bucks, fishtails, and does some upside-down spins for good measure. (I'm not sure what fishtailing means, but the horse knew.)

19   Lewis gets taken off by another mounted cowboy in full flight. He's done his eight long seconds. Drifter remains in orbit until he gets chased into the corral, where he stands trembling, and blessedly alone.

20   Cow milking is next: now there's something ridiculous about grown men trying to make a range cow stand still long enough to squeeze a few flying drops of milk into a beer bottle.

21   Calf-roping again: Wes Jasper misses lassoing the flying critter with his first cast, but produces a reserve rope and scores a ringer. His time is lousy, but there's some satisfaction in not failing completely, especially with your girl watching.

22   Chilcotins and whites, and maybe a few of the Sticks, drink beer in the Stockmen's Hall. The Indians tend to be in little groups off by themselves, but not entirely so. Some mix with the ranchers and cowboys: old friendships exclude racial prejudice. I drink beer with Tom Howe, some Kamloops tourists, a rancher and his wife, and an Indian named Marvin Paul. Marvin is an artist: he's just spent three weeks carving a small totem pole, for which he accepted four dollars. He is slightly drunk, and he shows me a pencil sketch of himself and I give him five bucks for it. I feel virtuous.

23   Returning from the privy, I notice an old Indian sleeping beside the steps. His face is carved black walnut and he might have posed for some of Paul Kane's 19th-century paintings. There's a western bluebird nesting in the roof's overhang, unbothered by all the noise, doing routine bluebird things. Inside the hall I say Hi Again to Marvin Paul (who is pretty far gone by now), chat with the riding's Social Credit MLA, and buy beer for Ben Belanger, one of the rodeo judges.

24   Only cowboys, sailors and a few others have a ready-made mythology with which to identify. They love the movies of John Wayne and Gary Cooper; they listen to country and western music, practically standing to attention when Wilf Carter sings *Oh, That Strawberry Roan*. But they are real-life cowboys and real-life cowboys work hard and long.

25   And the Indian cowboys have the additional picturesquity of being Indians. With a name like William Billy Boy or Sundayman Lashaway, you have a right. If it weren't for the take-home pay, I'd much rather be Sundayman Lashaway than Al Purdy.

26   Panhandle Phillips, a local old-timer with bowed legs and beak nose, is something more than a colorful hometown boy. He figures prominently in all of Rich Hobson's three books, but mainly in *Grass Beyond The Mountains*. He's 67, came here from the U.S. with Hobson in the mid-Thirties. The two men went out with packhorses in search of grasslands. Sixty miles north of Anahim, peering through binoculars at a small opening in the Algak Mountains, they saw the beginnings of grazing country that funneled out into an eventual ranch of four million acres. Those high grasslands belonged to the crown, and were then available at a dollar or so an acre. Four million dollars. But you didn't need to lay all that cash on the barrelhead. Anyway, the two men discovered the grass beyond the mountains, in high alpine country unknown to white men, surrounded by a dull-green jackpine world stretching more than 1,000 miles from the 52nd parallel to the Arctic tundra.

27   Talking with Panhandle Phillips is experiencing an echo from the Hobson book. I mention there are only three graves in the Anahim cemetery. Panhandle says: "People don't die up here very often." Then he looks at me out of his eye's corner to see how I'm reacting.

28   We have some trouble in finding the 10-foot-by-eight-foot cabin Panhandle and his partner built in the Thirties, then abandoned quickly when the stove smoke nearly asphyxiated them. It sits roofless and rotting in the altered landscape, and must have given him an odd feeling, this being the first time he's returned to the site. He says: "You don't get lost

in this country, you just get kinda confused for two weeks." I am a bit wary at this point, anticipating another picturesque remark. He knows I'm waiting. He keeps me waiting.

29   On Saturday night Slim Recknock, the rodeo announcer, got something stuck in his throat while eating supper. His good friend, Ben Belanger, found him choking for his life near their camp. Ben whomped his friend on the back so hard Slim got mad and wanted to fight. But instead he went to the hospital, fuming a little but unable to express proper indignation. Ben took over the rodeo announcing job Sunday: the day 10-, 12- and 14-year-old cowboys replaced the adults. There was this little black dog that kept yapping after the arena livestock. After enduring the dog a few minutes, Ben announced coldly: "That dog ain't helping the cowboys at all. If he doesn't leave, I'm gonna cut his tail off—right behind the ears!"

30   Ben came to the Chilcotin from Barrie, Ontario, when he was 18, and worked as cowboy and lumberjack; he's a strapping, slim-hipped, wide-shouldered man. Several years ago Ben decided he wanted to be a writer, taught himself to string words together, then wrote for the Kamloops *Daily Sentinel*.

31   But writing's only one of his ambitions: the other is to find a green spread of high grasslands, the same way Panhandle Phillips and Rich Hobson did 40 years ago. But there isn't much good ranch country left now, what with the influx of people from outside. Ben has often taken a packtrain into the mountains over the past 12 years; he's lived on fish and bannock for up to three years. He wants to own a ranch: "You know, start small with a milk cow so she can look after her calves, and gradually build up a beef herd."

32   Despite Ben Belanger's capabilities, it seems doubtful he'll ever attain ownership of his dream ranch. In Victoria, the government has frozen sales of all crown land, reasoning that only 5% of BC's total area is arable land. It wants to take a good look even at cattle raising land, before it's sold cheaply. Several years ago on one of his packtrain expeditions Ben located 1,280 acres of promising land, and stayed two summers to investigate water and grass potential. When he applied to Victoria for the right to purchase, he was turned down. And this was long before the land freeze. Every time he has applied during the past 12 years, exactly the same thing has happened: not always a flat no, but no, nonetheless.

33   "I'm not the only one," he says grimly. "A friend of mine, Ken Karrens, leased 320 acres of crown land some time back. The government told him to go ahead with improvements, so he drained some meadows, built a cabin, bought a Cat, spent quite a chunk of money. Then they raised his lease fee 800%, and finally took the land away from him altogether. Ken went to Victoria raving mad, and got thrown out of the Parliament Buildings."

34   Ben is defiant about the whole situation. He is now squatting on some land near Redstone and doesn't care who knows it.

35   The rodeo's last day was Sunday, with Ben Belanger announcing, and the crowd slightly smaller. Jack Palmatier won the three-hundred dollar saddle as best all-around cowboy, the most important award. On Monday morning the stampede grounds were deserted, dust settled: Panhandle Phillips, Lester Dorsey and William Billy Boy gone back to upland meadows to cut their winter hay. It seems an almost empty world, bright sun shining, the distant Itcha and Algak ranges snow-capped and silent.

36   Up in those high mountains there are landslides sometimes as sun loosens the binding blanket of snow. In the 60-below Chilcotin winter trees freeze with loud explosions, lakes and rivers crack and roar. Things that happen there, small deaths and the birth of spring— these are unknown unwritten local history in which the human animals are not participants.

Moose and grizzlies play their deadly game of hide-and-seek in the high country. Great wolves run in packs farther north. As we're getting ready to drive out, Tom and I are silent. The land itself overshadows everything else, a cold empire of mountains.

Al Purdy, "Boozy Saddles," *Maclean's,* May 1975: 78–80.
(With revisions made by the author for the present text.)

QUESTIONS

Subject
Purdy's story can be seen not only as the narration of a particular series of incidents that he experienced firsthand but also as an attempt to capture in prose a particular way of life. Explain.

Audience
Explain why a North American audience would have an easier time understanding and appreciating this story than an English-speaking European audience.

Purpose
Comment on the way of life that is being described and indicate how description aids the author in his purpose.

Structure and Style
(a) Comment on the way in which Purdy's diction helps establish the atmosphere of the essay.

(b) More specifically, comment on how the diction in paragraphs 14 to 21 helps create a sense of action.

(c) Comment on the effectiveness of the last paragraph. How does it suggest that a particular world has passed out of existence?

A Clear and Present Danger

Mordecai Richler

1   The most chilling image of the referendum campaign appeared on TV on October 25, the night of the big Yes rally in the Montreal suburb of Verdun. A young woman, eyes squeezed shut, held a little fleur-de-lis flag overhead, then began kissing it again and again as Lucien Bouchard thundered on stage. Any man who can arouse such all-but-orgasmic fervour in the young is a threat to the social order and would be more safely engaged at home honouring his own agenda, making "white-race" babies. Bouchard's summons to Québécoise women *pure laine* to bonk more productively did at least establish, in case anybody out there still had

doubts, that the imprint of the vile, racist cleric, the Abbé Lionel-Adolphe Groulx, still haunts the separatist cause. In 1922, elaborating on the theme of racial purity, Groulx published a pseudonymous novel, *L'Appel de la race*. Five years earlier, the monthly journal *Action francaise* had already preached *la revanche des berceaux* (the revenge of the cradles). *Plus ça change*, as my grandmother used to say, *plus c'est la même chose*.

2   Groulx's racist vitriol, rising out of a spiritual sewer, also touched something in Jacques Parizeau, separatism's second banana. In 1917, Groulx observed that Canada's soul was menaced by "cosmopolitan European immigrants." And, by Jove, seventy-eight years later, as every television-watcher in the Western world now knows, an apparently sloshed, embittered Jacques Parizeau, addressing the faithful after their defeat in a referendum squeaker, blamed the ethnics and the money, and talked of revenge.

3   Nobody booed and hissed. Nobody, so far as I know, walked out of the auditorium in disgust. Instead, responding to Parizeau's bile, the crowd began to roar, *"Le Quebec aux Québécois."* A chant, as I wrote in *The New Yorker* in 1991, that is tribal, and that does not include anybody called Ginsberg, or MacGregor, for that matter.

4   Parizeau's billet-doux to Quebec's racially impure was immediately endorsed by France's odious Front National leader, Jean-Marie Lc Pen. And a couple of days after the premier's talk of revenge, hooligans began to oblige. Somebody painted "FLQ" on the base of the statue of Queen Victoria outside the McGill Conservatory of Music on Sherbrooke Street. Then, on November 11, a brick, inscribed "Last Chance 101," was thrown through the front window of Café Books, and somebody, using black marker, had written on the window, "English Shit Go Home."

5   There had been an earlier incident, late on referendum night. The Parti Québécois's Rottweiler-in-residence, Deputy Leader Bernard Landry, entered the Inter-Continental Hotel, attempting to manage "le check-in," as they say in Paris, another French-speaking city. Landry turned on two hotel employees—one a francophone, the other of Mexican origin— and raged against immigrants, who had robbed the separatists of a triumph that their scrutineers had worked so hard to make good. A few days later Landry allowed that he had been "animated" but not abusive, and refused to apologize. Then he discovered that there was a video tape of the contretemps and, on second thought, he did offer an apology of sorts.

6   Landry, a stranger to irony, *Je me souviens* stamped on his forehead, had complained all the same that it was indecent of immigrants to vote "according to (their) grandmother's chromosomes." Grandmothers who, maybe sixty years ago, back in Poland, Italy, Greece, Haiti, or wherever, dandled grandchildren on their knees and told them, "Promise me when you grow up you won't ever eat with your elbows on the table, cheat at cards, or vote Yes in a Quebec referendum." Our grandmothers failed us. Had they been truly visionary, they would have taught us to make an acceptable referendum X, neither line crooked, neither too faint nor too dark.

7   Never mind. Landry, to give him his due, has always been good for some comic relief. In the absence of Mighty Mouse, wee Landry in the heat of the campaign wrote to the American Secretary of State, Warren Christopher, to warn him that Quebeckers would take it amiss if American officials continued supporting Canadian unity. "If victory eludes the Yes side by a slim margin, as is plausible," he wrote, "those who did vote Yes—a clear majority of francophone Quebeckers—will be tempted to assign responsibility to the United States for part of their profound disappointment. I do not know how many decades it will take to dispel that feeling." So far as I know, Landry is still waiting for a reply, possibly because he neglected to enclose a stamped, self-addressed envelope.

8   Parizeau's *cri de coeur* and Landry's vulgar outburst were both condemned in the French-language press, and Lucien Bouchard promptly disowned the slur made by his increasingly embarrassing sidekick. Mind you, this did not inhibit Sheila Copps, the Liberals' parliamentary fishwife, from rising in the Ottawa monkey house and pretending that Bouchard had been silent on the issue.

9   It should also be noted that those separatists who truly believe in territorial rather than ethnocentric independence of a sort were horrified by Parizeau's gaffe, and said as much for the record. Parizeau was denounced by Jean-Marc Biron and other prominent Jesuits. They wrote in the Montreal *Gazette* that Parizeau's remarks "do not represent the sovereignty movement." I'm afraid I disagree. The PQ, as Don MacPherson wrote in *The Gazette*, is "a political party founded by old-stock French-Canadians to address their own grievances and advance their own interests.... As a government, it has often advanced francophone interests at the expense of non-francophone ones. The most obvious example is the French Language Charter, also known as Bill 101.... At worse, [the PQ] has treated non-francophones as scapegoats or a threat against which francophones must be protected—by the PQ or sovereignty, of course."

10   Although some in the PQ insist that the term "Québécois" embraces all those who live in the province, that concept is, to my mind, a public-relations fib. A chimera. Going back to René Lévesque, never mind the Abbé Groulx, there has been too much damning evidence to the contrary.

11   When Lévesque appointed Robert Boyd head of Hydro-Quebec, he hastily pointed out to the faithful that, in spite of his Anglo-sounding name, Boyd was a bona fide Québécois, that is to say, of *pure laine* origin. When he introduced Bill 101 to the National Assembly in 1977, the ayatollah Camille Laurin ventured, "The English in Quebec is like a fox in the hen coop."

12   In April, 1990, Pierre Péladeau, the bumptious publisher of the tabloid *Journal de Montreal* and an ardent PQ supporter, put on his thinking cap and said, "I have a lot of respect for Jews, but they take up too much space."

13   More recently, the ineffable Pierre Bourgault warned that there would be trouble in store if the non-francophone vote deprived "real" Quebeckers of independence, a sentiment endorsed by the former Tory cabinet minister Marcel Masse.

14   In February, 1995, the Bloc Québécois MP Philippe Paré accused "immigrants" of getting in the way. "Couldn't they, if they don't want to contribute to the Quebec solution, avoid putting on the brakes by voting against us?" Another Bloc backbencher, Gilbert Fillion, declared, "Who's to say that at some point two years from now, they won't wind up in Toronto, those people?" And the Bloc MP Suzanne Tremblay snarled at Joyce Napier, a Montreal-born reporter, that, judging by her accent, she probably wasn't "a Québécoise at the start."

15   The truth is, the goodwill of pure-of-heart separatists notwithstanding, the separatist movement is essentially xenophobic, and, judging by the unsolicited mail, abusive phone calls, and death threats I have received, still tainted by anti-Semitism. An independent Quebec would not be a healthy environment for non-francophones, and many of "those people" would leave on any account, a flight that would not displease too many Péquistes, Gilbert Fillion obviously among them.

16   Immigrants to this country, whether Norman peasants, dispossessed Scots, Irish fleeing the potato famine, *shtetl* Jews, poor Ukrainians, Greeks, Italians, Chinese, Koreans, or Portuguese, came to these shores to escape tribalism and discrimination. Our grandparents or great-grandparents, wherever they came from, were mostly dirt poor. Or, looked at another

way, if anybody's blood in this country is blue, it's not owing to our progenitors but is a consequence of the climate. And that includes the *pure laine*. Together we eventually forged a civil society where everybody was equal, at least in their democratic rights. But now, after all these years, tribal conflict is threatening to undo us; and, to the amazement of people in less fortunate lands, this incomparably rich, still nearly empty country, everybody's second chance, may soon self-destruct, splitting into two acrimonious parts. And if that happens, there will certainly be another mass exodus from Montreal, and the only "ethnics getting in the way" will be the poor and the elderly.

17   In fact, three or four years from now, when Bouchard, adding up his humiliation points, pronounces it time for Referendum III, the separatists could win by default. Since the first referendum, in 1980, at least 150,000 of *les autres* have quit the province, and over the next few years another 50,000 unwelcome anglophones and ethnics, maybe even more, could easily vote with their feet. The PQ's policy of genteel, nonviolent ethnic cleansing may yet win them a country with a depleted but uniform population, where the only English-language signs would read FOR SALE.

18   That young woman at the Yes rally, kissing the flag in such a state of ecstasy, strikes me as a metaphor of Quebec now. This province, once church-ridden, has embraced a new faith: nationalism. And now it also enjoys the presence of *un chef*, the strong man the Abbé Groulx once longed for. A veritable Dollard des Ormeaux redux. In a lecture he delivered in Montreal in 1919, *"Si Dollard evenait...,"* Groulx sang of the pressing need for a leader of men:

19   … Arise, Dollard, and live on your granite pedestal. Summon us, with virile charm, with a hero's accents…. Together we shall work for the reconstruction of our family's house. And should you command it, O Dollard, O powerful leader, we are ready to follow you to the supreme holocaust for the defence of our French tongue and our Catholic faith.

20   But as things stand, the PQ, now Bouchard's chariot, is not so much a political party, its members sharing an ideology beyond independence, as it is an umbrella of convenience that would splinter into three or more parties following separation. These would range from the far left to the extreme right. The irresponsible left, tied to the unions, would promise daycare, full employment, whopper pensions, winning lottery tickets, in fact, a ring-a-ding francophone utopia, although there is no candy in the store. On the extreme right, we could count on enduring the nutters of the St-Jean-Baptiste Society, those luvvies who, in 1938, delivered to Parliament a petition signed by nearly 128,000 of its members opposing "all immigration and especially Jewish immigration" to Canada. Today the St-Jean-Baptiste Society is made up of such linguistic zealots that it would surely call for a limit on the number of English-language TV and radio stations serving Quebec, and possibly even seize any cans of alphabet soup that failed to include *accents graves* and *aigus,* and ban thinking in English.

21   Something else.

22   Right now the largely Jewish-owned clothing industry employs something like 50,000 people in Montreal, but, even as I write, some manufacturers are already looking at other sites for their factories in Ontario and Vermont. The day after a Yes vote in Referendum III many of them would pack up, swallow their losses, and move on to more hospitable climes. This could cost Montreal, already *Time* magazine's nominee for the poverty capital of Canada, at least 30,000 jobs. And then union leaders would surely complain that *les maudits Juifs,* who prospered in the city, were deserting the new state. Certainly they wouldn't acknowledge that it was Jewish energy that helped create a viable economy in Montreal, and departed only after Jews began to feel unwelcome in the city that had once been their cherished home.

23   And so, should separation come, I do expect a revival of racial strife in Quebec, where, as demonstrated by Parizeau and others, it has never lurked far below the surface.

24   The separatists in Referendum II did not have to cope with Pierre Elliott Trudeau, whose scorn they justifiably feared. Instead, there was only Jean Chrétien at home in Ottawa and a Liberal front bench made up of footnotes. And, oh, yes, there was also Preston Manning and his band of bumblers. In an I'll-show-those-bastards Rambo mood, a Reform Party stalwart advocated that MPs belt out *O Canada* every day in the House. Alas, this might have necessitated the lyrics being projected on a screen, so that his bunch could follow the bouncing tennis ball, as in the community singsongs featured in the cinemas of my childhood.

25   The federalist campaign, even before it was overcome by panic in the final week, was astonishingly inept—the indefatigable Jean Charest, doing his Canadian-passport shtick here, there, and everywhere, a shining exception to that rule.

26   Charging cocksure out of the starting gate, the federalists began to fumble and contradict each other, tripping over their bromides, once Lucien Bouchard, having disposed of Parizeau like a used Kleenex, geared the separatist campaign into overdrive. Clearly, whichever ad agency was responsible for the federalists' TV spots ought to be tarred and feathered and driven out of Ottawa on a rail. Their lack of verve and imagination was beyond belief. Instead of ducking Bouchard, they should have tackled him. They could have, for instance, shown footage of that latter-day Messiah who, after his swearing-in as a Tory cabinet minister in 1988, said, "I don't like the word 'separatist.' You know it is a loaded word. It's not the reality. You know many people voted 'Yes' [in the 1980 referendum] for negotiation.... I feel since Quebeckers have decided in a democratic way that their future was within the federation ... it is the duty of the francophone Quebeckers to make it work.... I am very proud to be a Canadian. I showed the flag in Paris for Canada.... I proved it is possible to be a committed Canadian and a Quebecker at the same time."

27   They might have flashed on screen every night, without comment, a live wiggly lobster being plunged into a pot of boiling water. They should have played my favourite Parizeau TV sequence. In an effort to remake that pompous man's image, he is shown on his estate near Knowlton in the Eastern Townships. Not so much habitant as squire, Parizeau, wearing a snazzy tweed cap and stylish topcoat, is seated unconvincingly on his tractor with modishly attired farmerette Lisette. He turns the key in the ignition, pumps the pedal, and smiles lamely as the tractor won't start. This, with the caption "Separatism is a Non Starter," would have appealed to Quebeckers' sense of humour. Instead, the what-Canada-can-do-for-you TV spot that turned up again and again showed a man being rescued from drowning at sea by a helicopter, hardly a Quebecker's typical experience.

28   And then, whichever adviser allowed Chrétien to appear on national TV, which meant that Bouchard, the far more capable advocate, had to be granted equal time, ought to be strung up by his thumbs for a week. Chrétien's broadcast to the nation was a disaster. Looking sickly, a loser, he appeared not as Canada's champion but like a supplicant. And he emerged from the campaign a diminished leader who panicked in the last week, making nebulous promises to Quebec of distinct-society status and a renewed veto on constitutional changes. Back to square one. Back to the discredited Mulroney's Rube Goldberg constitutional fiddles, which would have rendered Canada a pretzel rather than a country.

29   CBC-TV's "The National Magazine" also let us down. Mind you, I have a problem with Hana Gartner. Whenever she appears on "The National Magazine," fidgety, twinkly, her direct, wide-eyed stare into the camera somewhat crazed, I automatically retreat a couple of feet lest she actually leap out of our TV set to demand my attention; and then along came her interview with Bouchard.

30   Rarely have I seen such an inadequate, ill-researched, no-brainer interview with such an extremely vulnerable politician. Bouchard, posturing as Mr. Clean, was not asked about the millions his sponsor Mulroney had manured his Lac St-Jean riding with in 1988, in order to ensure Bouchard's election in time-honoured Duplessis style. He was not questioned closely about how it was that a former Conservative cabinet minister could be born again a social democrat, conveniently, just as the separatists were desperate for union support in the referendum. There was no suggestion that a man who had been a Liberal, a PQ member, and a convincing Tory before founding the Bloc Québécois in his own image might be a hustler with his eye on the main chance or, to be kind, a tad confused. Bouchard wasn't asked how a man born into a working-class family in the boonies, who had risen to become our ambassador to France, an MP, a cabinet member, and leader of Her Majesty's Loyal Opposition, could parade as a victim of anglophone prejudice and feel humiliated every day before dusk. As Bouchard went on to say that French Canadians were a people, unlike the rest of us, and that it was therefore natural for them to have a country, I waited and waited for Gartner to enquire if Bouchard also favoured nationhood for the Corsicans, the Basques, the Scots, the Welsh, never mind Quebec's very own Cree, who are also a people. I thought surely, at one point, she would put Trudeau's proposition to him: "If Canada is divisible, Quebec should be divisible too." But no. Instead, at any moment, it seemed the adoring Gartner would ask Bouchard what his favourite flower was, and had he given Audrey chocolates for Valentine's Day.

31   On the other hand, Bouchard's free ride on "The National Magazine" was nothing compared to the idiocy of Gartner's chitchat with the CBC's national reporter, Francine Pelletier, the evening after Parizeau's bons mots about ethnics and money. Harold Pinter would be hard put to outdo the following dialogue of obfuscation:

32   PELLETIER: Jacques Parizeau is not a racist. I know everyone wants to call him a racist. It's the thing to do often in terms of—

33   GARTNER: No, people aren't calling him a racist. They're saying what he said was racist.

34   PELLETIER: Yes, well, very often they mix up the two.

35   Me, I don't mix them up. *In vino veritas.* If you talk like a racist, you are a racist pure and simple.

36   Following this exchange, Gartner and Pelletier really sailed off into cloud cuckooland.

37   PELLETIER: Jacques Parizeau has been around for thirty years … and that first generation of nationalists … when they got up to fight for this, there were no ethnic minorities to speak of.

38   GARTNER: So he's out of touch.

39   PELLETIER: Yes … Because if Quebec had remained the *pure laine*, uniform society it was thirty years ago, they probably would have won it by now.

40   Actually, it's Pelletier, who has covered Quebec politics in the past for both Radio-Canada and *La Presse,* who is out of touch, and Gartner who knows nothing about Montreal. In 1965, the population of metropolitan Montreal was 2,109,509. Far from being a uniform society this figure included 101,466 of Italian origin, 73,062 Jews, 377,625 from the British Isles, 26,347 Polish, 27,873 Germans, and 11,849 Asians, not to mention 462,260 anglophones.

41   On an earlier segment of "The National Magazine," Pelletier ventured that Parizeau was an honest man. Tell me the *Reader's Digest* is a cornucopia of original ideas, say you

would buy used furniture from Brian Mulroney without doubting Mila's price tags, but don't pretend Parizeau is a man of honour. A wily old pol, yes, an enormous ego, certainly, but honest, no.

42   A trained economist of undoubted intelligence, Parizeau, a couple of years back, assured Quebeckers with a straight face that independence would cost each of them no more than the price of a couple of cases of beer a year. Just when the sovereignty campaign started to falter in the early going, Parizeau, elbowed by Bouchard, suddenly advocated the offer of a partnership with the rest of Canada. However, in a TV interview released after his resignation, he revealed, "For a long time, I have started from the principle that that thing would never happen."

43   Parizeau has been known to suffer other lapses into candour. *The Globe and Mail*'s Graham Fraser reported after the referendum that Parizeau had once said privately, "We are elected by idiots. In Quebec, 40 per cent are separatists and 40 per cent are federalists— and 20 per cent don't know who is prime minister of Canada. And it's that 20 per cent that makes and breaks governments."

44   Actually, thirty per cent is more like it. For, according to consistent poll data, that was the percentage of Quebec Yes voters who believed they could become "sovereign" and still remain Canadian, continuing to send MPs to Ottawa and to enjoy other federal benefits. Or, put another way, our country came uncomfortably close to being undone by the votes of village idiots.

45   What with the polls predicting just about an even split in the vote in the days leading up to the referendum, dread was rampant in Montreal. Rich and middle-class people, francophones among them, emptied their bank accounts and safety-deposit boxes and transferred their savings and stock portfolios to Ontario. As the Canadian dollar teetered, there was a stampede to convert into American currency. Even the poor in the Eastern Townships, where I live, were scared. Snowplough drivers, house painters, and barmaids of my acquaintance lined up at banks in Mansonville and Knowlton to withdraw their meagre savings and stuff them under a mattress. Of course, currency speculators did make money out of our misery. And prominent among them was the politically motivated Caisse de dépôt et placement du Québec, *la machine à milliards*, which bought Canadian dollars on the cheap, propping up the buck, and came out ahead by a declared profit of $7-million.

46   In the last days of October, confusion was the rule in some quarters. Item: The troubled CEO of a Montreal factory that makes train wheels, CN its major customer, told me that he had spoken to his workers, explaining that if the Yes side won, their jobs would be at risk. The plant would have to move. One of the men on the floor corrected him. "He held up his pay cheque," said the CEO, "and pointed out the deductions for provincial and federal tax. 'If the Yes side wins,' he said, 'we will no longer have to pay federal tax. I will take home a bigger pay cheque.'"

47   On referendum eve, old people stood in line for hours to claim Canadian passports, lest their citizenships be withdrawn on November 1. Many of us thought they were overreacting, but, astonishingly, it turned out their apprehensions were justified. Pushy little Landry, that compulsive pen pal, had sent notes to all the embassies in Ottawa, advising them, "When the Quebec National Assembly will have proclaimed the sovereignty of the new state the moment will have come to recognize it, without putting in peril good relations with the rest of Canada." A Bloc MP wrote to francophones in the Canadian armed forces instructing them that they should be ready to transfer their allegiance to Quebec. And, according to

my information, federal customs officers at Quebec borders and airports were told to be ready to withdraw and be replaced within twenty-four hours. Put plainly, we were on the verge of a minor-league putsch. This, is in a country where, in many cities, you can still get a ticket for jaywalking.

48   Post-referendum Montreal is deeply depressed and ridden with anxiety. Interestingly enough, René Lévesque never frightened anybody here, but the perpetually seething Lucien Bouchard has some people terrified. The man whom separatists celebrate as a saint and possibly their Messiah, many of *les autres* fear as an irresponsible demagogue. A twister. And a clear and present danger to this province's already severely tested, fragile social fabric.

49   Item: In Toronto, after the referendum, I ran into a friend from Montreal. "I was born here," he said, "of Greek origin, and I've never been so scared stiff in all my life. I'm fifty-five years old. Fluently bilingual. So what? You work and you work all your life and suddenly everything I've managed to accomplish is at risk. The day after the vote I phoned our real-estate agent in the Laurentians and said I wanted to put our cottage up for sale. She burst into tears. 'I've had forty-five calls today,' she said, 'from people who want to sell, and I haven't got a single buyer on my books.'"

50   A real-estate agent I ran into in Winnie's, my favoured watering hole in Montreal, claimed that just about every house on the West Island is up for grabs. "In Westmount," she said, "people want to sell their homes, move the cash out of the province, and rent an apartment, while they hang around to wait and see." Then she said that she had closed a Westmount sale with a two-tier contract. "The price was six-fifty, but if the Yes side won, it was five-fifty."

51   An insurance broker I know told me that many of his clients have acquired 800-numbers in Ontario and pieds-à-terre in Alexandria or Cornwall, so that they can easily shift their business addresses out of Quebec. "Meanwhile," he said, "everything is on hold. Nobody is investing."

52   The separatists tried blackmail. In the early running, long before the official campaign had begun, Finance Minister Jean Campeau warned that if the No vote won, he would be obliged to increase provincial sales tax by a percentage point. Next it was intimidation, the charming Messrs. Bourgault and Masse threatening trouble if the racially unclean frustrated the wishes of the *pure laine* Québécois. They tried to win by stealth, contriving a murky question with the intention of confusing, not daring to ask Quebeckers outright, "Are you for independence, Yes or No?" because they already knew the answer to that one. They first bowdlerized, then hid, their own damaging studies, commissioned by the Restructuring Minister, Richard Le Hir, at a cost of $5-million, because they clearly indicated the punishing economic cost of separation. Upon taking charge of the foundering campaign, Bouchard said, "I don't want to hear anything about the Le Hir studies. Those are not my studies. Those are M. Le Hir's. That's the past for me. That's the past campaign."

53   Then there was the vote itself. The separatists had failed to send out ballots to many Quebeckers temporarily resident in the rest of Canada, the U.S., or overseas, who had proved that they were entitled to vote. And scrutineers worked to rule in advance polls in anglophone or allophone districts of Montreal. All too typical was the experience of an old friend of mine, now confined to a wheelchair, who had to wait two and a half hours to vote and finally returned home without filling out the ballot. You can take the Union Nationale out of Quebec, but you can't take Quebeckers out of the Union Nationale. Which is to say, scrutineers, all of them appointed by the PQ, were instructed by their coaches to cheat shamelessly at the polls in Montreal, pronouncing thousands of No votes spoiled.

54   They threatened, they lied, they cheated, and still they didn't win, although they did come nerve-rackingly close. And now four, maybe only three, years down the road, we're going to have to endure Referendum III, and no doubt another question calculated to confuse. Next time out, however, whatever ethnics or money that remain here should insist on international observers from more advanced democracies to oversee the shenanigans. Observers from, say, Nigeria, Haiti, or Bosnia.

Mordecai Richler, "A Clear and Present Danger," *Saturday Night,* February 1996: 51–55.

QUESTIONS

Subject
To what degree is Richler's persuasive essay marred or enhanced by inflammatory rhetoric and emotion?

Audience
To what class of readership is Richler's essay supposed to appeal?

Purpose
Comment on Richler's use of the developmental strategies of illustration, definition, and cause and effect to support his purpose.

Structure and Style
(a) Although a sometimes angry author in this essay, Richler uses humour or satire to help prove his point. Indicate examples of humour/satire in the essay and point out how such humour works.

(b) Comment on Richler's use of hyperbole or exaggeration in this essay.

(c) What is the point of Richler's characterization of Sheila Copps and the federal parliament in paragraph 8?

The Story of Grey Owl

Colin Ross

1   Once upon a time there was a pervert called Grey Owl, who lived in the Canadian woods. He is famous because he came to Canada and learned how to imitate the Indians—he wore a disguise and grew his hair long. The white people in Canada know so little about Indians, and about their own woods, that Grey Owl fooled them all for a long time. But even after they found out that the famous Indian was really only Archie Belaney from England, even then they still respected him. Canadians have so few heroes that they decided to have Archie Belaney for a hero—they said to themselves, "Old Archie sure fooled us, didn't he? What a great man he was, to be able to fool us all, and live like an Indian."

2   Archie was only like an Indian on the outside though. That's why the Canadians liked him, and made him a hero. They wanted to have a hero who played little boy's games in the woods, and made friends with the animals just like in a story book. Canadians don't like Indians, on the outside or on the inside. That's why they liked Archie so well, and still do—they know that he's just a pleasant Englishman on the inside, just like them. When they know that, then they can love his Indian clothes and his Indian canoe, and even think that maybe his Indian life is very beautiful. When it's only harmless old Archie Belaney inside that Indian costume, then the Canadian ladies have nothing to be afraid of. Why *there's* an Indian who would just *love* to talk to them, and tell them about his friendly animal pets in the woods.

3   The Canadian ladies may live in Canada, but they don't like Canada—they don't like the cold, they don't like the bears, they don't like the lonely prairies, they don't like the forest. They're afraid of all those things and places. They don't have to be afraid of Archie Belaney—he writes nice books for them, that sound just like Henry Williamson, and other nice Englishmen who love nature. Archie Belaney had a very big heart, not like Indians—if the Canadian ladies ever tried to talk to an Indian, that Indian's heart wouldn't like them. They wouldn't like the Indian either.

4   All the Canadians are very grateful to Archie Belaney. His books are such a relief for them. When they read his books then they're not afraid of nature anymore—Archie makes them feel that nature is tame and friendly and safe. The only difference between Archie's life in the woods and Mrs. Smith's life in the city is that Archie has beavers for pets. Mrs. Smith, and her neighbour Mrs. MacKenzie, both keep budgies. The Canadian ladies are *very* grateful to Archie for keeping beavers for pets. Beavers seem like the best symbol Canada could have, when you think of Archie Belaney's friendly pets. All those Indians care about is killing the poor beavers, and selling their skins.

5   "Yes sir, those Indians are awful," says Mrs. MacKenzie. "Why if they came to our city they'd probably eat my budgies. Those poor friendly beavers and rabbits that live in our beautiful forests, the Indians hunt them and kill them. And Indians never write lovely books like Grey Owl does. Isn't it a shame that they never learned how to write!"

6   "Quite a shame," says one of the ladies.

7   "Yes," says Mrs. Smith. "You know, we should form a club to help those poor Indians. They have no books and no shoes, and all they ever eat is rabbits and wild things. We should help them. It's a shame. They're people too you know, just like us. Let's gather up some money and give it to the Indians to buy food and clothes. It would be *such* a good thing to do."

8   "Very good," says another one of the ladies.

9   The bridge party was at Mrs. MacKenzie's house that day. Mr. MacKenzie wasn't feeling well so he was at home. Mr. MacKenzie is a fireman. Mr. MacKenzie was serving the ladies tea and cakes—he had gotten up too early to bake them.

10   Mr. MacKenzie is very proud of being a Canadian man. He's very tough. He fights fires in the city, and in the fall he takes his holidays and goes hunting just like an Indian. Just like Grey Owl. Mr. MacKenzie spoke up and said, "The Indians were good people. They only killed the friendly animals in the woods because they needed them for food and clothes. They couldn't let their children go hungry. The Indians were good people, and very good hunters. They just weren't very smart, that's all—they weren't quite as high up as we are in the family tree of man." Mr. MacKenzie was talking to his wife, explaining about Indians to her. All the other ladies were listening.

11   "As a matter of fact," continued Mr. MacKenzie, "we're at the top. Yes, ladies, it's true. Now if the Indians had been able to build cars and houses like us, then I'm sure they

wouldn't have killed so many of the poor animals in nature. They would have loved them just like you love your budgies."

12   The ladies knew Mr. MacKenzie was a very good fireman, and they listened to what he said with a great deal of respect. Mrs. MacKenzie knew her husband went hunting in the fall though. She didn't like the poor dead wild animals he brought back, and she wondered how he could ever bring himself to pull the trigger. But Mr. MacKenzie is so tough and strong that he still has hunting instincts just like a real Indian. Just like Grey Owl. You can't expect him to stop hunting just because of the Canadian ladies. After all Mr. MacKenzie loves nature in his own way, and who is Mrs. MacKenzie to say his way is wrong?

13   The Canadian ladies are *very* grateful to Archie Belaney. They had some bad feelings about nature, and about Indians, but after they read his books they felt all right. The bad feelings went away. After the Canadian ladies read Archie's books they felt that the woods and the Indians were safe and friendly after all. And Archie Belaney was so concerned about his animal friends he went *all* the way to England, just to talk about them. Wasn't that a great thing for Canada!

14   Mr. MacKenzie doesn't have much time for books. But his wife and the other ladies have said such nice things about Grey Owl that *he* admires Grey Owl too. Mr. MacKenzie would never call Grey Owl just old Archie Belaney. If he did that then his wife's bad feelings about Indians might come back. That wouldn't be nice.

15   Mr. MacKenzie and his friends were so grateful to Archie for making the bad feelings go away that they got together. They made Archie into a hero, and promised never to call him anything but Grey Owl. If they called him just old Archie Belaney, then he might seem like just another Englishman.

16   Yes, it was a good day for Canada when Archie Belaney came over here and started pretending to be an Indian. There was quite a mystery to his life you know, not like the Indians, who just sneak around in the woods in a bad mood killing things. Let me show you what a nice guy Archie was—here's some of his writing. This is from his wonderful book which he called *Tales From an Empty Cabin:*

17   There was a wood-chuck, a special chum of mine, who year after year made her home under the upper cabin, where she had every Spring a brood of wood-chucklets, or whatever they are called. She was an amiable old lady, who used often to watch me at my work and allowed me a number of privileges, including the rare one of handling her young ones. But if a stranger came, she would spread herself out so as to quite fill the entrance to her domicile, to keep the youngsters in, and when the stranger left she would emit a shrill whistling sound at his retreating back, very sure that she had frightened him away. She too has gone, her time fulfilled, and another has taken over her old home; a well-built, very trim young matron who stands up straight and very soldierly before her doorway and tries to look in windows.

18   Old Archie sure was a tame Indian wasn't he. *Isn't* Mrs. Smith grateful for that? When Archie Belaney left his three aunts in England and came over to Canada Mrs. Smith really felt good. She loved nature then. "Good!" she thought to herself. Mr. Smith and Mr. MacKenzie were so grateful they gave Archie a place to live in a special park, and paid him for the rest of his life just to keep on playing games with animals. They never paid any real Indians.

19   When Archie writes a book, he writes just like an Englishman. That's the nicest way. He makes the woodchucks sound just like the ladies who read his books. Archie Belaney dressed up like an Indian and pretended to be one himself. The Canadian ladies loved him for that. But inside Archie was all the time an Englishman who called the woodchucks his chums.

Archie had lots of friends. Some had feathers. Some had fur. Some wore hats to church. They were all one big happy family, Archie and Mr. Smith, and Mrs. Smith, and Mr. MacKenzie, and his wife, and Mrs. Woodchuck and her woodchucklets. Archie sure had a nice time in nature. Wouldn't it be beautiful to live like an Indian too?

20   Indians are really very lovable people. If Mr. MacKenzie was an Indian he would be able to say wonderful things about nature too. Just like Archie and Geronimo. Archie Belaney was brought up by his three aunts in England. This was bad for little Archie— there were too many ladies around all the time. So when Archie got the chance he decided he'd *really* show his aunts he didn't need them. He'd go over to Canada and be a wild Indian, and no aunties would tell *him* what to do. Archie Belaney was one guy who sure was tough. He didn't need a bunch of aunties to take care of *him*. He was a wild Indian who lived by himself in nature and showed everybody. After he showed them real good, he came back to England.

21   Yes, Archie came back to England as an Indian, and gave speeches and went to dinners. He even went to dinner with that white man the King, and he sure didn't show *him* any respect. How could you expect a wild Indian to stand up when the King walked in the room? Boy, Archie really showed his aunts that time, when he went back to England.

22   Even when Archie was a little boy living in England he used to play at being an Indian. But he couldn't play Indians in England and still live with his aunts when he was thirty or forty. Everyone would laugh at him. Archie was smart. He went over to Canada and played at being an Indian over there. No one laughed at him in Canada; in fact he fooled them all and played the game for the rest of his life. Trouble was, he wasn't really an Indian on the inside. Inside Archie Belaney was an Englishman who got lonely for his aunts. What do you think he did? Well, he made friends with all the animals, then he never got lonely again, not for the rest of his life. When he wrote about his animal friends, in his books, he used words like "domicile," "chum," "youngsters," "matron" and maybe even "auntie."

23   The Canadian ladies are *very* grateful. They were worried about living in this country. But Archie helped them. He wrote books, and in his books he showed the Canadian ladies that all the wild animals are really just as warm and friendly as an aunt or a grandma. Wasn't that wonderful! Mr. MacKenzie and Mrs. Smith were grateful too. All the Canadian people loved Archie Belaney for doing this great thing, and promised *never* to call him anything but Grey Owl. And that's just what they did.

Colin Ross, "The Story of Grey Owl," The Compass, 5 (1979): 79–83.

QUESTIONS

Subject
How does the word "pervert" in the first sentence both differ from the tone in the rest of the essay, and yet provide a base from which to interpret that tone rightly?

Audience
Who is Ross's target here? How do you know?

Purpose

How can Ross's purpose be said to be argumentative? How do satire and irony take the place of conventional argumentative reasoning?

Structure and Style

(a) How does Ross structure his piece like a fairy tale? To what end?

(b) Ross uses repetition to very good effect. Analyse the repetition in paragraph 3.

(c) What is the effect of the small dramatic vignette at Mrs. MacKenzie's home?

Canadian Culture: Colonial Culture

R. Murray Schafer

1 I am going to speak the words of this lecture loudly. I want people to hear them. They are not very far away, these people. They are cultured, or want to be; but this does not mean they are very intelligent or inquisitive, and in fact their indifference to the cultural topic I have elected to discuss tonight is really quite astounding. I can hear them snickering already; but I also hear their teeth chattering as I prepare to cut into their favourite prejudice.

2 The job of the artist is to tell the truth. It is one of the few honest professions left. Once it has been formulated the truth is quite simple (it always is) but it is never easy to formulate. To raise a dimly-perceived intuition to the level of consciousness and action needs sharply chiselled words. This is how I must focus my thinking if I am going to pierce the minds and senses of the people I want to reach.

3 Our subject is Canadian culture. Both the adjective and the noun are emotional, and so they should be. They can't be objectified; they are under our fingernails, under our skin, fed by the heart. And yet, they are not, like our blood, a part of us, but are artificial concepts which someone else prepared for us to inhabit. I am a Canadian by accident; but I did not receive my birthright like a telephone number; I inherited with it a complex nucleus of habits and sensations that trigger mixed emotions. I love my country, but I despise it also. I love its natural beauty, but I weep for the destruction of it. I recognize the molds that have shaped it but I agonize to reshape them. And I know that this is possible, even though I often wonder just what effect my efforts are having.

4 Culture is the *prima materia* for shaping societies. It is a strong weapon, a terrible weapon sometimes, but it is always at hand. The moment you pick up a fork you have it. It can be used to civilize and to barbarize. It is quite amoral. It can be used to strengthen pride and self-confidence or it can be used to weaken these qualities. What I have to say here is as much concerned with how culture can weaken as with how it can strengthen: hence the second part of the title. A colonial regime strengthens itself by pushing out from centre to margin. It makes raw materials from the extremities and ejects finished products from the centre. It would be wrong to think that this is a balanced exchange, for as the economic historian Harold Innis showed, the central producer always attempts to maintain control over his suppliers by paying cheaply for raw goods and in an exchange medium that will guarantee

dependence. The same is true for culture. A colonial regime can never adjust its sights to recognize valuable cultural assets in the margins of the empire. Either the margin is a wasteland, or it is full of impediments that must be exterminated—as the Indians were exterminated in North America by the European colonialists. To the extent that culture in Canada is still colonial, we are concerned with the position of victim. To the extent that the victim is still alive, things can change.

5   When I mentioned to an American that I was now more interested in the development of Canadian culture than I was in his, and that I intended to write something about it, he said: "What are you a goddamned fascist?"—which shows how the cultural invader can be as paranoid about this subject as the threatened. The only way I can justify nationalism is to see it as a way of regulating what goes in and what goes out. I would like to see a balance in this exchange, nothing more. But it is a sign of how in control foreign interests are in Canada— I mean *mentally* in control—that every time we call for an accounting they accuse us of tribalism pointing towards another holocaust.

6   What I am concerned to express is an attitude that leads to maturity, not immaturity. I will put my contention quite simply: unless you let your culture mature, *you* will never mature; you will always remain someone else's clone. By failing to resist the inflow of foreign influence in Canada we have prevented this growth, which is natural and necessary for any human community. Maturity works from the inside out and cannot be plastered in like glitter on a ceiling. Yet this is precisely what the custodians of culture all across Canada are attempting to do. This activity is carried on in the highest places. I intend to name names and give examples as far as my personal factfinding energies have permitted.

7   A note: This personal investigation is partly the odyssey of my own thinking on this subject over the years. If I speak of music it is because this is the field I know best. But what I shall say applies *mutatis mutandis* to the other arts too; and I know that there are many artists in other fields who feel the same way as I do.

8   About 20 years ago I was asked in an interview: "Is there or ought there to be a distinctively Canadian music?" I responded: "There isn't and there oughtn't." I was reminded of this recently by another interviewer who detected that I'd changed my mind. There is no inconsistency here, merely the lapse of twenty years. Let me tell you how I felt then so that you can understand the inclination of my thoughts today.

9   Thirty years ago we young composers were very conscious of the desire to move out internationally. It was the great era of the United Nations, the unity of the world and the harmony of all peoples. We were also more than vaguely aware of the dummy culture which then burdened this country, with a British organist in every cuckoo nest. We wanted to seek our own level in an expanded world order. It was more a question of getting "away from here" than of going to any place in particular. We left home and the years of *wanderlust* commenced. Most of us went to Europe, a few to the States. The international *esprit* that was then in the air seemed most detectable in those places, specifically in New York, Paris or London, which is where most of us ended up. We found our mentors in those places; they taught us how to create in an acceptably international idiom. We took heart in the fact that artists in Madrid and Buenos Aires and Stockholm and Tokyo were also working in recognizable languages. We believed that soon the whole world would turn this way. McLuhan's global village concept later gave a boost to these expectations.

10   It was a pardonable sin. It took us half a lifetime to learn that what we had perceived as internationalism was really a new parochialism, spawned and carefully guarded by a few large centres in which the cultural industries were most highly developed. It would have been

nearly impossible to rise to the top in these centres without certain advantages which we innocently lacked. What was wanted was copies, not originals. Our duty which was implicitly laid in our heads by our teachers was to extend the international style to the peripheries, centre to margin, that is, from New York to Toronto, Paris to Montreal, London to Vancouver. This is a role we willingly played without thinking of it in those terms any more than patrons at the National Arts Centre or listeners to the CBC think about it today. Nor probably have many of my colleagues of those years begun to think about it yet. They returned to satisfying jobs in universities or in other ways barricaded themselves from certain realities.

11   I began to think of this seriously for the first time when I moved to the country in 1975. That is when I wrote *Music in the Cold,* a little allegory about authentic and counterfeit Canadian culture, which I sent out to numerous friends as a Christmas present in 1977. The best response I received was from a Swede, who translated and published it in Scandinavia where there seemed to be a greater understanding of what I was talking about. Canadians seemed indifferent to it; only about 100 copies of it have been sold since.

12   The basic argument of *Music in the Cold* is that culture is shaped by climate and geography, that as the product of a northern territory Canadian art has a wildness and vigour not evident in the hot-house effusions of more civilized centres. I tried to show that the essential difference between Canadian and European landscapes is that ours are not peoplescapes and that the viewpoint (i.e., the painter's position) of a Canadian landscape suggests hardship (cold, rough terrain, black flies, etc.). I tried to show how the real culture of the North is tough in this way, and that to appreciate it takes special techniques which are unknown to the aesthetes and hearties of hotter tropicalities.

13   I wanted Canadian music to develop in ways that recognized what some of our best writers and painters have known for some time. I did not want this to be its exclusive feature but rather to emerge as a trait against which other identities could be measured. Eventually the speculations of *Music in the Cold* took form in *Music for Wilderness Lake* and ultimately in *The Princess of the Stars,* which are the two most authentically Canadian pieces I've written. Typically, each of them has only been performed once, though I know that they touched a sensitive spot in many people, particularly those who witnessed the dawn performance of *The Princess of the Stars* on Heart Lake in 1981. With musicians positioned around the water and spectacularly costumed actors and dancers in canoes in the centre, an autumn ritual was enacted in which real birds intersected with singers and dancers imitating them, the sun-god appeared at the precise moment of sunrise, and the legendary substance of the plot sought in every way to unite the fate of characters in the drama with environmental changes in and around the water on a late-September morning.

14   This was not a piece which could be performed in New York or Paris or Vienna and that is precisely why I wrote it that way. To witness it one would have to make a pilgrimage to a Canadian lake—which reverses the rule that art can only be transmitted from the centre. The relationship with Indian mythology was neither consciously sought nor avoided. Both the music and the text were my own; but the setting and to some extent the context related this quite new work atavistically to something from the collective tribal history of all humans.

15   Now that I've given you some idea of the passage of my thinking over the years, let me return to the question of Canadian music. Is there a distinctively Canadian music? The question dissolves into its own answer when we begin to see products that could best be described that way. Time is always turning interrogatives into affirmatives with the accumulation of data. We do not ask whether there is distinctively German or French or Japanese

music; we acknowledge these matters as demonstrated. Yet when we go deeper into the subject, we see that distinctively German music is nothing but a miscellany of many pieces in many different styles by many different composers. Yet the impression of coherence is confirmed because we keep hearing these pieces over and over. A recent survey of the 15 top orchestras in Canada showed that Beethoven was performed by every orchestra and that Mozart's music accounted for nearly 10% of the total programming of all orchestras combined. If the Canadian musical style is not evident it is because it is not allowed to countervail. I shall demonstrate the extent of its neglect in a moment; on the basis of these facts it would seem strange that anyone, *anno* 1983, would have *any* opinion on Canadian music whatever. When a piece of mine is performed it is fairly certain that the conductor is doing it for the first time, the orchestra has never played it before, the audience has never heard it, and the programme annotator knows nothing about it. From this adumbration of an event the critic is supposed to extract some vital truth for the national newspapers.

16   We are rather in the position of the Polish, Czech and Hungarian composers of the 19th century, who also had to fight to establish their identity. If you regard Dvorak—just to pick a figure—from the point of view of the 19th century German musical hegemony, he comes off as an inferior Brahms; but if you put that question aside and ask what he accomplished that Brahms didn't accomplish, he becomes a Czech hero. Now you could listen to Canadian music this way. You might detect English or Scandinavian influences in the music of Harry Somers or claim that Serge Garant orchestrates like Boulez, but if you consider how their music *differs* from these models, you perceive something quite new. That newness is Canadian—it can't be anything else; and if we had any musicologists in this country who weren't trained in Princeton or Oxford, they would now be busy pointing this out.

17   I am reminded of a story Istvan Anhalt told me about how he first became aware of the Canadian style of music. When he arrived from Hungary he wanted to see the country, so he took a train from Halifax to Montreal. All day he travelled through the woods of New Brunswick, seeing nothing but trees. Here and there he passed a grubby clearing with perhaps a sawmill or a gas station and a few squat houses, then more trees. When he first heard the music of John Bechwith his mind connected back to that experience. Here were bars of repetitious *ostinatti* followed by a sudden wild modulation, then the relentless repetitions again. The music and the forest were companions; they intensified one another.

18   A very civilized Japanese lady came to visit me in Bancroft. When I took her back to the bus station, it was crowded with local men, dressed traditionally; red hunting caps, open tan-coloured boots, tied halfway up, with jeans so low on the hips that the crotch was somewhere around the knees. "They're a bit rough," I said. "Yes," she replied, "I like."

19   Perhaps only the foreigners can appreciate the Canadian artifact or animal without prejudice, though it requires a particular mental attitude to do this. Such curiosity is seldom mustered by the post-colonial set whose models are always in another country.

20   To get back to Istvan Anhalt: when he wrote *La Tourangelle*, a scenic cantata based on the life of the immigrant nun, Marie de l'Incarnation, partly in his new home in Kingston, which looks out on a giant and ancient stone church, his own work became beautifully Canadian in the expression of a subject which probably only an immigrant could handle.

21   I am mentioning these things as inevitabilities. The list of authentic Canadian works is growing. But will you hear them in the National Arts Centre or on the CBC? Not for 50 years unless a lightning bolt hits the heads of the programmers for these institutions. So what fills their programmes at the moment? We shift into the analytical mode to find out.

22   First of all, CBC radio. By way of preface let me mention that all Canadian performers and composers of serious music who have been in the business for 10 to 30 years know that little by little CBC has reduced their employment possibilities. Gone are the house orchestras, gone are the commissions for composers, gone for the most part are the recitals for solo performers. In the survey I am about to present, which covers the first month of a new season, the CBC did not initiate a single musical programme; the few that are live were picked up as remote broadcasts of events under other sponsorship.

23   What I did was take the *CBC Radio Guide* for September 1983 and list all the names of musicians for the programmes on the stereo network (the main music network) by nationality. There are 630 foreign composers and performers listed compared to 82 Canadians. If we were to include those programmes which do not list their contents (*Stereo Morning, Off the Record,* etc.) the Canadian presence shrinks to near invisibility. For instance, a week-long (September 12–16) survey of all the music played during the 20 hours *Stereo Morning* is on the air showed these results:

24   Canadian composers 0

     Canadian performers 4

     Foreign composers and performers 140

25   A week-long (October 3–7) survey of *Off the Record* produced these results:

26   Canadian composers 0

     Canadian performers 0

     Foreign composers and performers 114

27   These are the results for 30 hours of actual broadcasting, from which it must be clear that Canadian musicians are being slapped off the air in those meandering programmes of recorded music, while announcers lick the boots and polish the halos of their foreign favourites. A sampling of remarks:

28   "Nifty Neville, one of the busiest men in the world"—after playing six recordings of Pommy ace Neville Marriner.

     "The towering, basic essential classics"—in reference to the Mendelssohn Violin Concerto.

     "Let's return to that marvellous Swedish baritone"—reference to Hagen Hagegard.

     "We have some delightful English Baroque today."

29   Returning to the printed listings we should now see where the foreigners come from. We discover that the largest block of composers by far is German/Austrian (94) followed by French (46) Italian (25) British (25) and Russian (21). There are 13 Canadian composers in the listings. Almost all of these can be credited to one programme, *Two New Hours,* but since this programme is especially designed to present unfamiliar music by young and unknown composers, the Canadian group is not particularly representative. Of the more established figures, only the name of Harry Somers appears. No Weinzweig, Freedman, Beckwith, Garant, Anhalt, Tremblay, Prevost, Papineau-Couture, Pentland, Willan, Champagne or MacMillan for the month of September.

30   Among the performers, the largest single contingent is British (111) followed by American (79). Only then come Canadians at 69 then German/Austrian (53) French (23) and others (33).

31   There is a cliché going around that music is international. Of course it isn't, but, like all culture products, is the expression of a particular people at a particular time. As such it may or may not be intelligible to other peoples at other times. If the CBC was really trying to educate us internationally we would be hearing music from Rajasthan or Iraq or Manchuria or the Tuamotu Archipelago. We don't, so we assume that *détente* is not their business. What is it? To endorse colonial loyalty by demonstrating that this smart music, which socially upward-bound Canadians should learn to appreciate, did not originate here but comes to us from the eight or ten great lands of our forefathers (i.e., some of them). As a recent policy paper from the National Arts Centre put it: "We yearn for our Mozarts, our Shakespeares and our Picassos. Nation-building is a matter of establishing links; and to the extent that the Great Artist is lacking, Canadians face the problem of a missing link." In other words, if God had intended Canada to have music, Mozart would have been born in Regina. The fact that he was born in Salzburg is supposed to be incidental. As a matter of fact, Mozart wore a perfumed wig and lace panties and his music sounds like it. I am not raising issue with this any more than I do with Beethoven, whose music often reminds me of Vienna sausage; I am merely pointing out that any art exudes a variety of regional smells which are unavoidably packaged along with the product; and that when your *Stereo Morning* host opens up his programme with another piece of Mozart a little unvented miasma from Austria reaches our nostrils.

32   As John Weinzweig said, "Mozart is a pop composer." This makes him a perfect candidate for any station specializing in classical Mooze, which is what CBC stereo has become, as a survey of the repertoire could easily demonstrate. Not only do we have here a concentration of music from six or eight favoured countries, but we also have a shrunken repertoire in which the same peewee classics (viz. Respighi's *Ancient Aires and Dances*) are played a dozen times a week in the manner of all pop stations. Pieces are broken apart and thrown together by announcers and producers who have little care for integrity, form or gracefulness in programme building. This is all in keeping with "abbreviation radio," a characteristic of most contemporary broadcasting. I don't want to get into the question of what radio could accomplish if it became in itself an art form (I've dealt with this in my article *Radical Radio, CF,* Dec./Jan. '82, 83), but I will say a few words about how it could assist in centring Canadian musical culture without drastic changes or additional expenses.

33   There is quite a lot of Canadian music. We even have dead composers. Heaven knows we have enough of undisputed innocuousness. There is also a good deal of interesting material from the 19th and early 20th centuries which no one knows about. Years ago for *10 Centuries Concerts* we revived a quite satisfactory 18th century opera, "Colas et Colinette," by Louis Quesnel, the equal of a good many European products of its type. John Beckwith has extended this work in the reconstructions he has made of old pieces for the festival at Sharon. There is a prejudice that Canadian music consists exclusively of unpleasant noises made by misfits like Schafer, which needs readjustment. The annals of Canadian music history are strewn with works which should be heard again, if only in order to make a final evaluation of them. I am speaking now of works by Leo Smith, W.O. Forsyth, Guillaume Couture, Rudolphe Mathieu, Herbert L. Clarke, Claude Champagne and Sir Ernest MacMillan. When I look at the 25 British composers (as compared with 13 Canadian) in the CBC stereo listings for September and see the names of Arnold Bax, E.J. Morean, Roger Quilter, Eric Coates, Arthur Benjamin, *inter alia,* I do not consider that group in any way superior to the Canadians I have mentioned.

34   The CBC has never attempted to record any of this material. A long-standing policy of recording some contemporary music seems to have been abandoned in favour of recording major Canadian orchestras in exclusively European repertoire. What I am trying to say is that the spectrum of Canadian material is exceedingly broad and makes numerous appeals, some of which may not be inconsistent with present offerings. Of course I would like to see a policy that goes well beyond this, but since the CBC may not be able to appreciate my wilder enthusiasms, I will for the moment not press them forward. In any country but Canada, this kind of material would have been recorded long ago and presented frequently enough to have worked its way into the marrow of national consciousness. It is unbelievable that a public broadcasting service that plays such a large role in the recording industry should be able to avoid it. When it is instituted there will be two important residual effects: the DJs will be forced to purr as thrillingly about "us" as they do about "them," and the performing rights money for these works will stay in Canada.

35   Every time a copyright work by a foreign composer is played in Canada, money is collected and shipped out of the country to the country in which the work originated. Can you imagine, on the basis of the figures I have presented, how much performing rights money is being sent out of Canada—for instance to Britain—as a result of the policies of our public broadcasting system? Haven't we a right to demand that more of it should remain here to assist those who are building our own culture, and especially to demand it of a public corporation which has avowedly the same intention?

36   The discouragement of Canadian music on Canadian radio had been intentional and systematic. The aspirations of Canadian composers and performers have been blocked by a colonial administration that is blind and gutless and which, like all things colonial will have a temporary evanescence before it is overturned, perchance violently. I have given you some facts and thoughts on one aspect of the CBC service. You can think about what is happening on the other services. If you do, or rather when you do, you may feel like standing up and making some demands of your own.

37   I could go on to show how the patterning of all large organizations is similarly colonial without in any way impeding their abilities to grasp by far the largest share of public money made available for the arts—how, for instance, the Canadian Opera Company (which I indiscreetly point out is directed and managed by Americans) has not produced an original Canadian opera since they did Harry Somers' *Riel* in 1967,—how in 1984 they will be given $1,250,000 to produce an opera by an Englishman while Comus Music Theatre was given $60,000 to produce a Canadian work of infinitely greater complexity,—how the Toronto International Festival turned down both *Ra* and *Apocalypsis* and God knows how many other Canadian offerings to bring the Met to Canada,—how the Stratford Festival spends its millions on plummy British plays and squirts its music budget into Gilbert and Sullivan,—yes, I could go on for quite a while about all this but you know the tune as well as I do.

38   The dimensions of the monster who has been set up to devour us are of great magnitude. He appears very benign; he is on a decorated leash held by fistfuls of government administrators and doting heiresses; he speaks all the mittel-European languages; he knows how to purr when petted and he has beautiful well-kept fingers. But if you're a Canadian artist, he's out to strangle you and his mistresses will kick your carcass into the gutter as they parade him joyously across the country to the applause of punch-drunk audiences for whom he has become the Redeemer of Boredom and a narcosis for their lazy lives.

39   I've described the problem and I've given enough facts to release it from the charge of personal idiosyncrasy. I've limited my analysis to the field of music, because I know it best, but I also know it is not unique to this field. What we are really concerned with is a mental attitude which I have called colonial because that seems to be the most appropriate way to describe the insecurity which downgrades the local and elevates the alien without seriously evaluating either. This is a Canadian habit and while it may be weakening in some areas, in the aristocratic field of classical music it is hardening into a canker. If we can't lose this habit our culture will remain sick, and despite all establishment smugness, will look sick next to the presentations of independent people anywhere, whether black, white, yellow or red. How do we achieve independence from the scourge of colonialism? Radical changes of thinking are necessary and these are what now must be discussed.

40   Task number one: forget where you came from; only then will you find out where you are. Ask an Englishman where he came from and he'll say England; ask a Frenchman and he'll say France; ask a Canadian and he'll say Buffalo, or my mother came from Poland, or my grandfather sold rugs in Armenia. I told you that in *Music in the Cold* I tried to describe the Canadian experience from the point of view of one who was in harmony with the climate and the land. That is when I finally forgot where I came from and found out where I was. It was a good feeling: a feeling of strength and confidence. When you finally realize you come from Canada (with no strings attached) you find yourself brother and sister of the Indians and the Inuit. All your life you had denied this possibility on ethnic grounds—it's what our teachers taught us; now you discover that it is right and inevitable.

41   You must know that I am not merely speaking here of the rehabilitation of native culture. But if you are going to define Canadian culture, that is where you must start. Then the revolution will follow from a plenum, rather than a wasteland—the colonial contention. But if we don't do this, everything will always be out of alignment.

42   I mentioned at the beginning that a colonial regime was one with a strong centre and weak margins, or rather that this is the centralist perspective on it. Therefore if we are going to rid ourselves of colonial attitudes, our second task must be to abandon the centre-margin view of culture. And this should apply nationally as well as internationally. Culture in New York is no more significant than that in Toronto any more than that in Toronto surpasses in interest that in Kitchener or Bancroft. It is a matter of appropriateness. What makes central culture *apparently* more interesting is the way it is fanned about by the culture industries. This is the Maya of our age, the illusion, and we must learn to see through it. The warnings Schumaker gave in *Small is Beautiful* apply to culture as well as to economics.

43   I have dealt here with the subject of serious music because it concerns me most; my life depends on it. The situation is particularly serious because the whole system is exogenous and has been imported for the amusement of the social elite. Perhaps if I'd taken theatre or dance or film I would have had to retouch my arguments; but my friends in these professions assure me they are confronted with the same opposition.

44   It is time to sum up. I could follow academic practice and conclude that everything has now been said but since no one paid attention I'll say it all over again. But this would be doing you a disservice, because I think you have heard quite clearly what I have been saying and recognize truths in it despite whatever might have irritated you in the delivery.

45   And so my second last line is to you who have listened. I feel the pulse in your fingers and on your throats and I know that at last you are ready to come with us into the future, ready to listen to our songs and poems and look at our pictures and read our stories, because they

are about you, and through them you will know yourselves, and behind them are the trees and the lakes and the snows of Canada, and behind them are the Indians, your ancestors, and behind them are the animals, and behind them is the myth, and without a myth the nation dies.

46   At the opening concert in Thomson Hall, sandwiched between inevitable major compositions by an Englishman and a Frenchman, were two short Canadian works.

47   I was told to keep mine to 8 minutes. One piece on the concert got bravos. "They're cheering Canada," my wife said, and she was right.

48   My final line is to my fellow artists. Continue to weave your magic spells, on street corners, in the little theatres and houses of creation, on the empty roads and in the quiet of the night. They are getting sick of the old diet. The country belongs to us now. Tell them so.

R. Murray Schafer, "Canadian Culture: Colonial Culture," *Canadian Forum,* March 1984: 14–19.

QUESTIONS

Subject
Schafer's title offers a definition of Canadian culture. What are the defining characteristics of a colonial culture according to Schafer?

Audience
Through a consideration of paragraphs 1, 37, 44–45, and 48 sketch the range of Schafer's audience.

Purpose
Paragraph 2 outlines something of Schafer's purpose. How do his metaphors here carry over into his argumentative strategy later?

Structure and Style

   (a) What is the function and effect of the "analytical" section in paragraphs 22–37?

   (b) Schafer characterizes himself at one point as a "misfit" making "unpleasant noises." How do certain aspects of his essay live up to this billing?

   (c) Paragraphs 36, 38, and 48 diagnose the need for radical change. How does Schafer's use of figurative language-metaphor, image, etc., bring us on side?

Saving the Marbles

Jim Stirling

1   Around a campfire in the mountains of British Columbia's south Cariboo, Dave Eyer explains to his 19-year-old son Travis, why he's working so hard to preserve this landscape. "I don't know if we're doing the right thing," he says, "but we're trying to do something."

2   Eyer hopes that these mountains will be much the same when Travis brings his children or grandchildren here to swap fireside tales. He and others from the Clinton area have asked the B.C. government for permanent protection of the Marble Range, an ancient geological oddity northwest of Clinton, between the Fraser River and Fraser Plateau.

3   B.C.'s Commission on Resources and Environment (CORE) established in 1992 has been studying the sustainability of the Cariboo-Chilcotin region. The idea is to find a balance between keeping jobs and preserving the environment. The challenge is to sustain both a lifestyle and an economy based on the natural environment. Clintonites, an independent-minded lot, didn't want outsiders making land use decisions for them, so they formed their own unofficial planning group to ensure a say in what happens in their own backyard.

4   "We involved everyone with a stake who was interested," says Eyer. "We had our share of harsh words and impatience, but we stuck at it, working together for something positive." It was a juggling act, an exercise in common sense and compromise. In requesting preservation of the Marble Range, the group told the commission it wanted buffer zones around these mountains to protect them from development. As they await CORE's recommendations, there are hints that their lobbying may have been successful.

5   Eyer runs a silver-fox farm on the western flanks of the Marble Range, 45 kilometres northwest of Clinton. As the group's representative for fish and wildlife concerns, he talked with local hunters, trappers, guides, and biologists. "The main thing was they all shared a deep concern about wildlife habitat and how to preserve it," says Eyer. Together they identified critical seasonal ranges and migration corridors for moose, California bighorn sheep, and deer.

6   Representatives of forest companies with cutting rights in the area were also involved. It was a learning experience for everyone, observes Eyer, and now there's an established nucleus of people who care about how the land is used.

7   Known as "The Limestones" by Clintonites, the Marble Range is like a next-door neighbour with 230 million years of family history. Only 32 kilometres long and half as wide, they run northwest-southeast between Highway 97 and the Fraser River northwest of Clinton. An ancient thrust of upper Permian limestone, the range consists of pale grey, trowel-smooth ridges linking occasional castellated peaks. Forests cloak the lower elevations where the Fraser twists through a deeply dissected valley. Above it, sage dry benchlands are punctuated by emerald patches of irrigated soil. The land rises steeply, from about 275 metres at the Fraser to the towering 2,243-metre peak of Mount Bowman in The Limestones, all within a span of six kilometres.

8   Though side by side, the Marble Range and Fraser Plateau are dramatically different. The plateau is underlain by basaltic lava flows about 13 million years old. They're strikingly visible in the horizontal rock layers of Chasm Provincial Park, about 22 kilometres northeast of Clinton, where a 1.5 kilometre-long gash in the landscape is 120 metres deep. Ranchers once used this box canyon to winter cattle.

9   When the Pleistocene ice retreated 10,000 years ago, it sculpted a landscape scattered with glacial drift. Drumlins—hummocks of glacial gravel—were formed beside flowing ice. Sinuous gravel ridges, or eskers, were dumped by ice streams while meltwater scoured channels. The land is a pastiche of shallow lakes, meadows, and forests. Large ice-deposited rocks are strewn around the countryside.

10   Mitch and Daphne Henselwood operate Circle H Mountain Lodge on the range's west side. It's a warm, rustic place: no nightly television; clocks are inconspicuous, baking is always fresh. Guests here ride horses along wooded trails up into The Limestones. One of

B.C.'s prime guest-ranch regions, it draws visitors from various countries. But for those who operate the ranches, these mountains are more than mere business. "Local people have an emotional stake in The Limestones," says Mitch. "We ride in the mountains and enjoy them in a non-consumptive way."

11   Behind the Henselwoods' corral, a murder of crows squabbles for roosting rights atop a ponderosa pine. The largest and loudest bird prevails, scattering the remainder in noisy caws of protest. That may work for crows, but the Henselwoods became involved in the CORE process because they didn't want the future of The Limestones similarly decided.

12   The loudest voice, with the most potential political clout, is the forest industry. Near the Henselwoods' ranch is a reminder of recent encroachment by the industry. New trees are "greening up" in a clearcut logged 10 years ago to salvage timber from an infestation of mountain pine beetles.

13   Kelly McCloskey claims it's neither fair nor accurate to cast the forest industry in the villain's role. He's the industry's spokesperson in CORE negotiations concerning the Cariboo region. "In the last five years, there's been a real change in how the public wants the forests managed and how they've become involved in the process. From the forest companies' perspective, the industry gets what's left after other interests have been accommodated." McCloskey says licensees and the Clinton group can develop trust by determining together the amount, type, and location of future log harvesting.

14   Brian Gunn hopes so. Five years ago, he unshackled himself from a high-pressure engineering career and moved to the Cariboo to fulfill his dream of running a horse ranch. His Big Bar Guest Ranch lies within the quintessential rolling Cariboo grasslands, with the Marble Range rising abruptly behind it.

15   "It's peace and tranquillity we're selling," declares Gunn. Visitors don't want or expect their views marred by clearcut logging or their stillness marred by the racket of logging helicopters, the roar of unmuffled machinery, or the buzz of chainsaws, he says. "British Columbians have always been hewers of wood and drawers of water, but people in the Clinton area see that being eroded away. We should manage the land in a way that's beneficial to all parties."

16   What's happening around Big Bar Lake characterizes land-use pressures. The lake lies northeast of The Limestones on the Fraser Plateau's southern tip. It's only about six kilometres long, but it is one of the area's largest and most attractive lakes. And one of the most sought after—Big Bar Lake Provincial Park occupies 330 hectares around the northwest corner, an 80-lot residential subdivision lines the north shore, and rumours of future lakeshore development abound.

17   Recreational properties throughout the Cariboo are being snapped up by small numbers of large companies, including some offshore owners. It's a disturbing trend to Julian Demaerschalk, who owns a secluded property on the lake and believes that enough is enough. "The peace will be gone. When the blacktop arrives, I move."

18   But Peg Marriott plans to stay put. Born in 1900, she came to the south Cariboo from Vancouver as a young teacher. "I wanted the open spaces. And I wanted a man with a horse—the horse first." She found Harry Marriott (and his horse), a transplanted Englishman and Gang Ranch worker. Harry's book—*Cariboo Cowboy,* reprinted this year—is required reading for anyone interested in the area's pioneer history.

19   Harry died in the mid-1960s. Peg was eventually persuaded to sell their Big Bar Ranch and fishing lodge to the developer who put in the 80-lot subdivision. She kept a two-hectare

lakeshore enclave. "I sold for what's probably the price of one lot today," she says, "but nobody's got a nicer place than I've got. I've been selfish for years. I don't mind them (the subdivision newcomers) as long as they don't bother me."

20   On the plateau side of the Marble Range the eskers add a different riding dimension for visitors to the Cariboo Rose Guest Ranch, maintained by Karl Krammer and Teresa Hobot. The couple train their own horses and specialize in riding lessons for small groups. Krammer, a tireless member of Clinton's CORE group, staunchly believes a vigilant watch is essential to protect the area's qualities. A management committee, he feels, with representatives from every interest in the region, should remain in place to form a consensus on proposed changes.

21   No one around Clinton has watched the changes more closely than James Robertson. He's been here nearly all of his 103 years. Back in 1910 he started working at the old Foster general store, a "temporary" job that lasted 44 years. Ranching and credit went hand in hand in those days. Ranchers fattened their cattle on the rangelands all summer and settled up with the store after selling the beef in the fall. "It was a simple life," Robertson recalls. "Everyone knew everyone else. There was no need to lock doors."

22   Robertson remembers when The Limestones were mined for cement and whitewash, and soda was cut in frozen blocks from nearby alkali lakes and sold to the Royal Crown Soap Works in Vancouver.

23   But that was then. "I don't live in the past," insists Robertson, "I never have. All some people can remember is what happened 50 years ago. I don't dwell on that. I try and keep up with the times."

24   Ironically, the big issue in Clinton is to keep something from the past. To Clintonites, The Limestones are not only a geological link with bygone eras, but the heart of a lifestyle, both industrial and recreational. If Dave Eyer and the others working toward their preservation are successful, that lifestyle is something that won't change here.

Jim Stirling, "Saving the Marbles," Beautiful British Columbia, 36:3 (1994): 13–19.

QUESTIONS

Subject
What are the threats to the Marbles as outlined in the essay?

Audience
Does the author's audience possess expertise in the subject or is it a general one? Give evidence for your answer.

Purpose
Give reasons to show that Stirling's exposition attempts to present both (or all) sides of the issue.

Structure and Style
(a) Look up the word "anagram" in the dictionary and find an example of one in the essay.

(b) Explain how the structure of the essay is based largely on personal anecdote.

Better Dead Than Read?

Paul Stuewe

1   There's a familiar bogey astir in the land. Cry "Censorship!" in a crowded theatre these days and you'll be trampled to death by liberals manning the battle stations of editorial opinion and engaged reportage. What's all the fuss about? Mainly it's about a few groups of concerned parents in mostly rural areas of Nova Scotia, New Brunswick, and Ontario who have begun to take an active interest in what their children are being encouraged to read in school. Furthermore, they have had the temerity to suggest that certain books are unsuitable for impressionable young minds.   └ lack of respect.

2   The most recent censorship crisis has occurred in Huron County, Ont., an agricultural area about 120 miles west of Toronto. William French of the *Globe and Mail* has diagnosed a "strange mood" infecting the Huron County population with a desire to keep such books as *The Diviners, Catcher in the Rye* and *Of Mice and Men* out of the hands of local high-school students. Curious about the psychology of any group foolhardy enough to go up against both the teaching *and* intellectual establishments, I paid a visit to Huron County and found that the realities are rather different from the picture presented by the national media.

3   After reading press coverage of the controversy, I had expected to be confronted by crazed bands of Bible-waving fanatics burning books in the town square and extracting oaths of moral purity from local high-school teachers. Instead I found that the pro-censorship forces are led by two capable spokesmen whose arguments have a high degree of logical and moral force and are firmly grounded in community traditions at least as old as the notion of Canada itself.

4   One of these spokesmen is Elmer Umbach, a pharmacist who operates his own drugstore on the main street of Lucknow, a town on the northern edge of Huron County. Umbach represents the more intransigent wing of the fundamentalist, evangelical Christian opposition to the books in question, and his first words to me are: "I want you to insist that what I'm saying is a *declaration of truth,* and I am not interested in discussing or dialoguing with you." A finger stabs at me in emphasis. "It's available to anyone else from the same place I got it—the Bible. It's the only source of successful moral living, and the only system that has ever proved to work for everyone's good."

5   This unpromising beginning has taken place in front of several customers and staff at Umbach's drugstore. But later over coffee in the secluded back room of a neighbouring restaurant he unbends a bit and expands on his involvement with the pro-censorship movement. Umbach is not married, and thus has no children in the local school system; but he is active in community religious groups, and when some of his fellow churchmen became upset about the kinds of books being taught to Huron County students, he was asked to be their spokesman.

6   For Umbach and his associates, the salient fact of the controversy is that children are involved, children for whom their parents are morally responsible until they reach adulthood and children who are in danger of corruption from those who are supposed to be setting them a sound moral example: "Teachers now believe that students won't be well-rounded unless they study books such as *The Diviners* and *Catcher in the Rye,* but we don't agree. We believe that a child is not mature until he is physically mature, at about the age of 21.

Until then he is not able to handle things like sex, and should not be exposed to them." He stresses that it's the protection of children that requires such strong action: "As far as adults are concerned, they can go ahead and destroy themselves any way they want to."

7   As a pharmacist, Umbach sees some of the nastier consequences of a decade of sexual revolution. The number and severity of cases of venereal disease is increasing rapidly in his hometown. Where a liberal would argue that this calls for more sexual education, he draws just the opposite conclusion: "Young people get venereal disease because they practise free love the way Margaret Laurence and such writers advocate. But when they get it they don't go to her for help—they come to me, which is what they should have done in the first place."

8   This raises, albeit obliquely, one of the thornier issues in the controversy over book censorship: Does the reading of books actually influence behaviour and what are the consequences of the possible answers? A common liberal response is some variation on, "There is no evidence that anyone ever did anything simply because they read about it in a book." This (a) is untrue, since there is some social-scientific evidence to the contrary, although it is by no means unequivocal, and (b) tends to diminish radically the significance of reading. If books don't influence behaviour, then there would be little point in preferring one book over another for classroom use and school boards could save money by using a book already in most students' homes—and in the case of Huron County, the Bible would certainly qualify.

9   The problem here is the double-edged nature of the liberal response. By denying that books encourage certain specific activities (sexual ones, usually), it lays itself open to the more serious charge that books are, at most, entertaining diversions. If the tactical reasons for this are understandable—no one in their right mind would want to have to tell a group of Huron County parents their children were reading a book containing sexual incidents, that these were presented in a positive way, and that their children were likely to take them to heart—the thorough-going spinelessness of the position is still unacceptable. Does anyone reading this doubt that there are connections between reading and our social behaviour? We may not know exactly what the connections are, and we certainly don't want to say that reading about something necessarily entails doing it; but within these common-sense limitations, I suspect that we can all bring to mind examples ranging from direct emulation (I know that reading Norman Mailer's "The Time of Her Time" led to my first important sexual experience) to more diffuse effects (I'm sure that reading Proust as a teenager made me into something of an aesthete, although there's no way of proving it). To argue the contrary is to reduce reading to the level of twiddling thumbs and scratching itches, and if you've read this far I doubt that you're that sort of person.

10   And if it may be objected that proponents of book censorship don't argue at such a sophisticated intellectual level, let me introduce you to a Huron County man who proved quite able to do so when I talked to him. Lloyd Barth, a retired schoolteacher, moved six years ago into the small community of Blyth, where he does a bit of gentlemanly farming and keeps an eye on the passing scene. Barth is an intelligent and articulate spokesman for the local pro-censorship forces and his story sheds a great deal of light on the issues and circumstances involved.

11   Barth and his family, which includes two children who attend a local high school, moved to Blyth for certain specific reasons: "The people we met here impressed us as good people and good Christians, as being industrious, friendly, and of high moral standards." He experienced the kindliness and consideration of his neighbours when his home burned to the

ground during the busy growing season a year after he arrived. Local farmers dropped what they were doing to help the Barths save what they could and begin to rebuild.

12   In a community imbued with such mutual concern and shared values, the position of school teacher is seen rather differently than it is in more fragmented urban societies. As Barth puts it: "We've always thought of teachers as *dedicated,* a spiritual word meaning that they offer themselves up for the good of the children. For us, teachers came right after God, ministers, and parents, and were always pure in thought and action; and teaching was a *profession,* which means to speak out the good that is in you."

13   Thus Barth is perturbed by some recent developments in the practice of teaching. The notion that teachers might strike, for example, is repugnant to him; it suggests that what was once a noble profession now has become merely a job. He sees his children coming home from school with an apparently endless series of fact-gathering projects and worries that they aren't learning anything about principles and morals. And when his children were required to read books he considered filled with blasphemy and obscenity, this naturally quiet and contemplative man felt compelled to become a social activist.

14   Two points must be emphasized here. First, much of the opposition to *The Diviners* and similar books is aroused because students are either required or encouraged to read them in school. Barth and fellow members of a group called "Concerned Citizens" know that there are many people who enjoy this kind of literature and while they are not happy about that fact, they have no plans to muzzle Margaret Laurence, boycott McClelland and Stewart, or even remove the 18 copies of the book in the Huron County library system. They just don't want it being forcibly injected into their homes, and that's quite different from advocating the sort of prior censorship exercised in totalitarian societies. Second, they are even more outraged by blasphemy than they are by obscenity—not least because many of them are farmers whose awareness of the sexual facts of life is rather more direct than that of most town-dwellers. Their concern with obscenity is largely a matter of context, and emerges only when what they would define as "immoral" sex (infidelity, prostitution, perversion) is being described. But Barth argues that "blasphemy is *never* in context." So the group is more concerned about God's name being taken in vain in such books as Steinbeck's *Of Mice and Men* than it is by the overt sexual content of *The Diviners.* Both these points should be kept in mind the next time you read something about the "sexually repressed fascist" many liberals identify as the typical proponent of censorship.

15   The strength of groups such as Concerned Citizens is grounded in a shared perception of a threat to the values of their community, and even to the sanctity of their very homes. There are no large funds, no outside agitators, no Canada Council grants inflating a minority gripe into a public issue. In his canvassing of area parents, Barth finds that he need only show them the books in question to arouse their energetic wrath. Where outsiders have been involved, as when the Writer's Union sent a delegation to Huron county in June to defend the books under attack, they have succeeded only in swelling the ranks of the local opposition. (Concerned Citizens was formed in July as a direct result of what was interpreted as an invasion by alien elements with no stake in the community and an obvious vested interest in promoting books such as *The Diviners.*) Let me repeat, if I haven't made it clear already, that people such as Lloyd Barth are not dummies, or hicks, or pathological mental cases. They believe that everything that is important to them is under attack and are fighting back with all the power they can muster. And as long as their opponents continue to treat them with condescension, their numbers and influence will continue to increase and multiply.

16   Concerned Citizens achieved its initial success in late August when the Huron County Board of Education voted to remove *The Diviners* from the list of books approved for study in its five high schools. (It seems that the trustees are more upset by "obscenity" than blasphemy). Before this decision, Lloyd Barth had canvassed all 16 trustees, and had again found that, in most cases, he had only to show them certain passages from the books under fire to win support for his arguments. By that time Concerned Citizens had shaken down to a hard core of active members, following what Barth describes as "Stalin's principle of decreasing the numbers and increasing the power," and was also able to bring pressure to bear on some of the trustees. It was a classic exercise in community organization tactics: define the issue; recruit those willing to commit themselves to it; and use every avenue of public and private influence available.

17   The word "community" keeps cropping up because it is essential to a proper understanding of what is going on in Huron County. There it connotes an integration of social and family life that just doesn't exist in big cities; urban residents accept a much higher degree of disjunction between their public and private selves. Many Huron County people have been aroused to the point where they intend to exercise control over what happens in their community in the same fashion that urban social activists proposed in the 1960s and early 1970s, and anyone planning on opposing them will have to operate in the same context and with the same methods as groups such as Concerned Citizens.

18   The moral issues involved here are not simple ones. If I ever have children, and they attend a school where they are required to read a book that is repugnant to my most deeply held beliefs, I hope that I will have the fortitude to not interfere with their experience of a world that I know to be composed of good, evil, and indifference. But if it were a book that glorified war, or advocated the right of the strong to exploit the weak, I am also sure that I would, at the very least, be tempted to have it proscribed. Those without convictions of any kind may cast the first stones.

19   But what about the significance of events in Huron County for the Canadian community as a whole? My view is that they have been blown out of meaningful proportion, and that there are the more serious threats to liberty than those discerned by liberal commentators looking for red-necks in the woodpile. Viewed objectively, the people who live in Huron County are for the most part on the receiving end of social forces over which they have no effective control. If they do succeed in removing certain books from their high schools, these books will still be available commercially and in public libraries; and if they should succeed in removing them from the community entirely—a position on which groups such as Concerned Citizens are unlikely to reach a consensus, from my observations—this would not affect the existence of the books; and would have only the most minimal impact upon the processes of their production and distribution. If a large number of such communities acted in concert, then the alarm might well have to be raised. But that isn't happening and isn't likely to happen, given the localized nature of the conflicts involved and the absence of anything resembling a national ban-the-books movement. No, as things stand the pro-censorship forces in Huron County have about as much chance of affecting Canadian literature as they do of converting the rest of us to their particular religious beliefs.

20   The real threat to freedom of expression in Canada will come, as such threats have always come, from those who wield centralized power without fear of check or control. The 1970 War Measures Act was the most effective censorship ever implemented in Canada;

periodicals were seized, the press was muzzled, and it became impossible to exercise what we had come to think of as our natural political rights. Big government has big powers— and it still has them: at the moment the editor and publisher of the Toronto *Sun* are being prosecuted for printing secret RCMP documents; and amendments are being proposed to the Criminal Code that would broaden the legal definition of obscenity to the point where almost any serious work of literature could be judged obscene. The new definition would make obscene anything of which "the dominant characteristic of the matter or thing is the undue exploitation of sex, violence, crime, horror, cruelty or the undue degradation of the human person." If you consider the potential vagaries of interpreting "dominant" and "undue," not to mention "sex, violence, crime…" and so forth, I suspect you'll agree that this is one bogey that does call for protest on the widest possible scale.

21   Thus while the media have been diverting us with tales of attempted censorship in the boondocks, the people and institutions with real power have gone about their traditional tasks of making laws and regulations conforming to the requirements of power, secure in the knowledge that what little opposition there is is laughably ineffective. If some of our national political and cultural leaders possessed the sort of moral conviction exemplified by Lloyd Barth and Elmer Umbach, they'd be righteously upset about that. They'd probably even try to do something about it. (I would like to thank Deanna Groetzinger for her help in the preparation of this article.)

Paul Stuewe, "Better Dead Than Read?" Books in Canada, October 1978: 3–7.

QUESTIONS

Subject
On the strength of your reading, would you say that the author is in favour of or opposed to censorship? Or would you choose to put the question in a different way?

Audience
Comment on the effect the following sentence has on the reader: "To argue the contrary is to reduce reading to the level of twiddling thumbs and scratching itches, and if you've read this far I doubt that you're that sort of person."

Purpose
Describe the relationship between the expository and argumentative modes in this essay.

Structure and Style
(a) Explain how the second-last paragraph of the essay demonstrates the author's abhorrence of censorship of a particular type. Does his view here contradict what he has said earlier about the subject?

(b) Look up the following words in the dictionary: "red-neck," "fundamentalist," "fanatics." Explain how the connotations of these words as used in the essay are similar.

A Planet for the Taking

David T. Suzuki

1   Canadians live under the remarkable illusion that we are technologically advanced people. Everything around us denies that assumption. We are, in many ways, a Third World country, selling our natural resources in exchange for the high technology of the industrialized world. Try going through your home and looking at the country of origin of your clothes, electrical appliances, books, car. The rare technological product that does have Canada stamped on it is usually from a branch plant of a multinational company centred in another country. But we differ from traditional Third World countries. We have a majority population of Caucasians and a very high level of literacy and affluence. And we have been able to maintain our seemingly advanced social state by virtue of an incredible bounty of natural resources.

2   Within the Canadian mystique there is also a sense of the vastness of this land. The prairies, the Arctic, the oceans, the mountains are ever present in our art and literature. This nation is built on our sense of the seeming endlessness of the expanse of wilderness and the output of nature and we have behaved as if this endlessness were real. Today we speak of renewable resources but our "harvest" procedures are more like a mining operation. We extract raw resources in the crudest of ways, gouging the land to get at its inner core, spewing our raw wastes into the air, water and soil in massive amounts while taking fish, birds, animals and trees in vast quantities without regard to the future. So we operate under a strange duality of mind: we have both a sense of the importance of the wilderness and space in our culture and an attitude that it is limitless and therefore we needn't worry.

3   Native cultures of the past may have been no more conservation-minded than we are but they lacked the technology to make the kind of impact that we do today. Canadians and Americans share one of the great natural wonders, the Great Lakes, which contain 20 percent of the world's fresh water, yet today even this massive body of water is terribly polluted and the populations of fish completely mixed-up by human activity. We speak of "managing" our resources but do it in a way that resembles the sledgehammer-on-the-head cure for a headache. On the west coast of Canada, Natives lived for millenia on the incredible abundance of five species of salmon. Today, the massive runs are gone and many biologists fear that the fish may be in mortal jeopardy because of both our fishing and management policies. Having improved fishing techniques this century to the point of endangering runs yet still knowing very little of the biology of the fish, we have assumed that we could build up the yield by simply dumping more back. But it wasn't known that sockeye salmon fry, for example, spend a year in a freshwater lake before going to sea. Millions of sockeye fry were dumped directly into the Fraser River where they died soon after. In Oregon, overfishing and hydroelectric dams had decimated coho populations in the Columbia River. In one year, over 8 million fry were released of which only seven were ever caught. No one knows what's happening to the rest.

4   We act as if a fish were a fish, a duck a duck or a tree a tree. If we "harvest" one, we renew it by simply adding one or two back. But what we have learned is that all animals and plants are not equivalent. Each organism reflects the evolutionary history of its progenitors; in the case of salmon, each race and subrace of fish has been exquisitely honed by nature to return

to a very specific part of the Pacific watershed. Similarly, in the enormous area of prairie pot-hole country in the centre of the continent, migratory birds do not just space themselves out according to the potholes that are empty. Scientists have discovered that the birds have been selected to return to a very restricted part of that area. And of course, our entire forestry policy is predicated on the ridiculous idea that a virgin stand of fir or cedar which has taken millenia to form and clings to a thin layer of topsoil can be replaced after clear-cut logging simply by stocking seedlings into the ground. How can anyone with even the most rudimentary understanding of biology and evolution ignore the realities of the complex interaction between organisms and the environment and attempt to manipulate wild populations as if they were tomato plants or chickens?

5   I believe that in large part our problems rest on our faith in the power of science and technology. At the beginning of this century, science, when applied by industry and medicine, promised a life immeasurably better and there is no doubt that society, indeed the planet, has been transformed by the impact of new ideas and inventions of science. Within my lifetime, I've seen the beginning of television, oral contraception, organ transplants, space travel, computers, jets, nuclear weapons, satellite communication, and polio vaccine. Each has changed society forever and made the world of my youth recede into the pages of history. But we have not achieved a technological utopia. The problems facing us today are immense and many are a direct consequence of science and technology. What has gone wrong?

6   I believe that the core of our 20th century dilemma lies in a fundamental limitation of science that most scientists, especially those in the life sciences, fail to recognize. Most of my colleagues take it for granted that our studies will ultimately be applicable to the "big picture," that our research will have beneficial payoffs to society eventually. That is because the thrust of modern science has been predicated on the Newtonian idea that the universe is like an enormous machine whose entire system will be reconstructed on the basis of our understanding of the parts. This is the fundamental reductionist faith in science: the whole is equal to the sum of its parts. It does make a lot of sense—what distinguishes science from other activities that purport to provide a comprehensive "world view" is its requirement that we focus on a part of nature isolated to as great an extent as possible from the rest of the system of which it is a part. This has provided enormous insights into that fragment of nature, often accompanied by power to manipulate it. But when we attempt to tinker with what lies in the field of our view, the effects ripple far beyond the barrel of the microscope. And so we are constantly surprised at the unexpected consequences of our interference. Scientists only know nature in "bits and pieces" and assume that higher levels of organization are simply the expression of the component parts. This is what impels neurobiologists to study the chemical and electrical behaviour of single neurons in the faith that it will ultimately lead to an understanding of what creativity and imagination are, a faith that I don't for a moment think will ever be fulfilled (although a lot of useful information will accrue).

7   Physicists, who originally set this view in motion, have this century, with the arrival of relativity and quantum theory, put to rest the notion that we will ever be able to reconstruct the entire universe from fundamental principles. Chemists know that a complete physical description of atoms or oxygen and hydrogen is of little value in predicting the behaviour of a water molecule. But biologists scream that any sense that there are properties of organization

that don't exist at lower levels is "vitalism," a belief that there is some mystical life force in living organisms. And so biochemists and molecular biologists are intent on understanding the workings of organisms by learning all they can about sub-cellular organization.

8   Ironically, ecology, long scorned by molecular biologists as an inexact science, is now corroborating physics. In studying ecosystems, we are learning that a simple breakdown into components and their behaviour does not provide insight into how an entire collection of organisms in a natural setting will work. While many ecologists do continue to "model" ecosystems in computers in the hope that they will eventually derive a predictive tool, their science warns of the hazards of treating it too simply in management programs.

9   At present, our very terminology suggests that we think we can manage wild plants and animals as though they were domesticated organisms. We speak of "herds" of seals, of "culling," "harvesting," "stocks." The ultimate expression of our narrow view (and self-interested rationalizations) is seen in how we overlook the enormous environmental impact of our pollution, habitat destruction and extraction and blame seals and whales for the decline in fish populations or wolves for the decrease in moose—and then propose bounties as a solution!

10   But Canadians do value the spiritual importance of nature and want to see it survive for future generations. We also believe in the power of science to sustain a high quality of life. And while the current understanding of science's power is, I believe, misplaced, in fact the leading edges of physics and ecology may provide the insights that can get us off the current track. We need a very profound perceptual shift and soon.

David T. Suzuki, "A Planet for the Taking," *Canadian Forum*, February 1985: 6–8.

QUESTIONS

Subject
Does Suzuki's title adequately reflect his subject? If so, how? If not, what aspects does it not sufficiently take into account?

Audience
While scientists may be a subset of Suzuki's audience, they are not his primary target. What aspects of the essay allow us to conclude this?

Purpose
Is Suzuki's purpose primarily expository or argumentative? Explain your answer by considering his audience.

Structure and Style
(a) Cause and effect is a central developmental strategy for Suzuki. Identify at least three ways he employs it.

(b) What role do paragraphs 3 and 4 serve in the essay's structure?

Jungle Fever

Jamie Zeppa

1   The doors of the Paro airport are thrown open to the winds. I stand shivering in line at the visa desk. There are no luggage carts or conveyor belts, no pictograms showing this way to the women's toilets, this way to a taxi, this way to food and drink. There are no signs at all. Outside, people are tossing suitcases off the little plane onto the tarmac. I am watching for my three strained bulbous hockey bags containing ninety kilograms of things said to be unavailable in Bhutan: novels, a dictionary, *The Norton Anthology of English Literature;* conditioner, tampons, dental floss; chocolate, coffee; Extra Strength Tylenol, antibiotics, a lifetime supply of immodium.

2   All around, the mountains rise and rise, pale gold and brown. The sun slips into the crevasse between two hills and the afternoon is over. The line moves slowly, and I am the last one at the desk. The visa officer carefully inspects and then stamps my passport. My hockey bags are lying alone on the pavement outside, beneath furiously snapping flags. I haul them in. I have arrived.

3   "Well, I hope you know what you're doing," my grandfather says, shaking his head. "I hope you know what you're getting yourself into."

4   I know. I have gone to the library, I have looked things up. I have studied all the documents given to us at a week-long orientation session in Ottawa; the Country Guide, the Briefing Kit, the List of Things to Bring. I know that Bhutan is a small Mahayana Buddhist kingdom in the Eastern Himalayas. I know the capital is Thimphu. I know the national language is Dzongkha, which is related to classical Tibetan, and the national sport is archery. I know that modern economic development started in the 1960s. Before that, there were no roads, no banks, or telephones. I have talked to a returned volunteer. I know things will be difficult in the first few weeks. I am going to a small village in an isolated district of a remote country that has been closed to the outside world for centuries. I have studied the maps. I know how far away I am going.

5   Why there? people ask. Why not? I shrug. For the experience, I say. I've never been anywhere. I'm tired of school. I want to do something different. I want to travel. The opportunity just came up. I don't want to be a tourist. It sounds fascinating. I don't know.

6   In Thimphu, there is more orientation with other volunteer teachers, Canadian and British and Australian. Some of them have taught in Nepal, Costa Rica, Zimbabwe. Everything is funny to them. The power blackouts, the icy hotel rooms, the cockscomb in someone's chicken curry. The session on health, "from scabies to rabies," they call it. The stinking local bus becomes the vomit comet, the dubious-looking dumplings are dysentery Danishes. They tell horror stories with glee. The man who loses all his bottom teeth after getting a simple filling. A woman with tapeworm cysts in her brain. A Canadian in Tashigang cracks up, is found running around the prayer wheel in the centre of town, naked; he is taken out in handcuffs. Typhoid, paratyphoid, hepatitis A, B, and C, TB, cerebral malaria, meningitis, Japanese encephalitis. They make up a little song. "I don't find that funny," I say, but no-one hears me. They cannot stop laughing.

7   I cannot eat meat. I cannot eat much at all. I use bottled water to brush my teeth and wipe the droplets of unboiled unfiltered water out of my glass before filling it. Victoria, who will be my nearest Canadian neighbour, frowns. "I don't think we have to be *that* careful," she says.

8   A young woman comes to give us lessons in Sharchhop, the language of Eastern Bhutan. It has no script. We cannot hear the difference between *b* and *bh*, *d* and *dh*. I cannot pronounce *tshe* or *nga*. The grammar is incomprehensible. The verb must dangle its legs off the end of the sentence. Progress is slow. After two weeks, I can count to eight, ask *where are you going?*, and have two possible answers to *are you a cowherd?* (No, I am a teacher; no, I am a nun.)

9   I am learning another language as well: lateral road, hilux, land cruiser; out of station, posting, in the field; expat, consultant, vol; UNDP, FAO, ADB. *Are you a consultant? No, I am a vol. Where are you going? I am going to the field. Are you taking the vomit comet? No, I have a ride in the FAO hilux.*

10   We are told to buy supplies in Thimphu, because "things" are not available outside the capital. I walk through the tiny shops. Things are not so available in the capital either. We buy kerosene stoves, jerry cans, plastic buckets, hot-water flasks, quilts, noodles, peanut butter. Victoria, an artist and a vegetarian, goes off in search of dried beans and sketch paper. We both buy large square tins with lids. Against the rats. I spend the last day in Thimphu packing and repacking my luggage. I put chocolate, raisins, cashews, almonds, Smarties, coffee, and a small flask of Cointreau into the square tin. *Where are you going? I am going to my posting.*

11   In the morning we are told the passes are blocked with snow. We cannot go to our posting yet. We will have more orientation in Thimphu. We will visit the temples, the National Library, the Painting School. I do not want to go. I want to stay in bed. I want to go home. I tell Victoria I am coming down with something, and lie in bed and wish for things: a *Cosmopolitan* magazine, a bagel with cream cheese, a ride on the subway. Loblaws, pizza, the Eaton Centre two days before Christmas.

12   The passes are clear and we are driving across the lateral road. I eat nothing but crackers and Gravol. The road twists and writhes and burrows through forests. The hilux grinds its way up to passes eerie with snow and silent white mist lying over the withered trees and the drip of water on black rocks, then descends into valleys, tangled green and warm. Monkeys scatter as we turn a corner. Grey langurs, someone says. We stop at a small shack. "Foodings and lodgings," the sign says. We climb out, stretch, and yawn. Inside, from blackened pots on a mud stove, a woman serves plates of steaming rice and small bowls of mostly bone soup. "Aren't you going to eat?" the others say. I shake my head and sip bottled water. They exchange glances. I know what they are thinking. They are thinking I won't make it. I won't last two years, I won't even last two months. I should never have come. Why have I come? What did I expect? Later, when I have gone home, they will tell stories about me. Remember that girl from Sault Ste. Marie, what was her name, she'd never been anywhere in her life? oh, yeah, she was afraid of everything, remember? is that the one who only ate crackers? what was she thinking when she decided to come here? what did she expect?

13   It takes three days to reach Tashigang, a tiny town tucked into the crook of a mountain. Tashigang is warm, subtropical. Bougainvillea erupts over doorways and races along the tops of stone walls, and elegant eucalyptuses bend over the river that runs through the centre of town. Tashigang reminds me of a little medieval town, pictures from a grade-twelve history book; we sit on a bench outside a shop and watch the traffic—horses carrying sacks of rice, people laden with bamboo baskets, children chasing a dog with a string of red chillies around its neck. We spend the night in a guest house, a stark, unwelcoming wooden cabin above the town.

14   In the alley below, dogs bark hysterically. I throw open the window and search for something to hurl at them, but can find nothing except the batteries from my Walkman. I fling them out into the night, and the barking continues uninterrupted.

15   Victoria and I are the last to be dropped off. I help Victoria unload her luggage, two suitcases, one large, one small, her tin box and hot-water flask. A young man appears, introduces himself as the headmaster, and leads us to his house, where we sit stiffly on hard benches. A small boy brings a wooden bowl of rice crisps and two cups of tepid tea. "Do you think the water was boiled properly for this?" I whisper to Victoria. Victoria stares straight ahead, scowling, and drains her cup in answer. Then we are taken to her quarters, a tiny whitewashed cottage with a wooden bed frame, a desk, a chair. We stand at the doorway, peering in. Even Victoria looks unsettled. It is so empty, so far from home. We promise to visit—"It's only three hours up the road," we tell each other. "We'll hitchhike, we'll keep in touch." I get back into the hilux and turn to wave goodbye, but Victoria has gone inside and the door is firmly closed.

16   It is the third day of school, and I am standing in front of Class IIC. There is no blackboard or chalk. There are no books. No crayons, scissors, glue. There are, however, five students. The rest are "coming, Miss." They have been coming, Miss for three days. The headmaster says it will take a week for the teachers and students to arrive. "And the books?" I ask. "A little longer for the books," he says, smiling. I don't know what to do with them, the five who spring to their feet each morning and shout, "Good morning, Miss." I tell them to go out and play, and they tumble out of their seats and burst out of the classroom, shrieking, as if it were the last day of school.

17   At lunch, I walk across the field to my house. It is cavernous, dark, the concrete walls stained with smoke and grease and handprints. I turn on all the taps, but there is still no water. I have not unpacked. I have not cooked. My diet has not changed. The Gravol helps me sleep, but I am almost out of crackers. My neighbours, a Keralan couple, also teachers, have invited me for supper three times; each time I say I am having stomach problems. Standing at the bedroom window, I look out over the verdant confusion of the Pema Gatshel valley. It makes my head hurt, looking down the green steepness, looking up into the empty sky. There are long moments when I cannot remember where I am.

18   I pick up the letter I started yesterday to my family. Dear family, I have written apathetically. I crumple it up. The headmaster says that a landslide has blocked the lateral road. It will take a week or three to clear. There will be no mail. It's just as well. What would I write? Dear family, I am fine, I am settling in, I am getting used to my new life here. What would I write that is not a lie?

19   I sit at the table until the sun drops behind the mountains. Outside, the dogs begin to bark. Hark, hark, I say out loud, and eat a cracker, an orange-cream biscuit, another cracker. I wish for cappuccino, I wish for roast chicken, I wish for raspberry cheesecake. I wish to go to sleep and wake up in Canada. My legs are covered in flea bites, and I scratch them until they bleed. What am I doing here? What did I expect? Am I going to cry? Then I remember the tin. The tin, the tin, the square tin with the round lid, the rat-proof tin, the treasure box, the Christmas chest, the store of all goodness. I pry open the top and reach in and pull out another package. Dried beans. Lentils. Split peas. A package of origami paper. A box of charcoal pencils. It is Victoria's box. I have Victoria's split peas and origami paper and she has my Cointreau and chocolate. Now I *am* going to cry. I sit on the floor and cry and cry, and when I have finished, I have decided: I will go home in the morning. I have made a

mistake, but it can be rectified. I will send a wireless message to Thimphu. I will say that I am sick. Physically sick, mentally ill, pregnant, and in need of an operation. I will lie. I will cry, I will beg. I will throw myself on the floor and scream. They cannot make me stay here! They cannot make me stay!

20   But the next day there is a letter for me. It has come from Tsebar, a village across the valley and up another mountain, from Jane, a British teacher. *I heard you were there,* she writes. *Why don't you come and visit? I'd walk across but I sprained my foot washing clothes in the creek.* A likely story.

21   She has drawn a map. It's only a three- or four-hour walk. Only. Only!

22   I decide to go. I cannot go home until the roadblock is cleared. I will go and visit this Jane across the valley, and on my way back, I will go home, I will pass this house and the fields and the school. I will pass the gate, the crooked shops, the little white temple, I will keep going, straight home.

23   I take my sleeping bag, bottled water, the last of my crackers, a mini medical kit of antibiotics, Tylenol, iodine tablets, and my copy of *Where There Is No Doctor.* Down the valley path I go, stumbling under the bright, sharp afternoon sun against rocks and the roots and bones of trees. I stop, panting, at a stream. Why is my backpack so heavy?

24   You shouldn't have brought *Where There Is No Doctor.*

25   Are you crazy? What if something happens out here? I'll need it.

26   The only thing that's going to happen is you're going to collapse under the weight of it.

27   You can't be too careful.

28   Yes, you can. You can be too careful unto craziness.

29   Caution is not crazy. Singing a song about tapeworm cysts in the cerebellum is crazy.

30   Carrying a medical book into the jungle is not crazy. Coming here in the first place was crazy.

31   Look at this narrow little path. This path is crazy. What if I get lost?

32   You won't get lost, you have a map.

33   No, I don't, I left it on the table with Victoria's kidney beans.

34   It doesn't matter, you don't need a map. This is the path, you just have to follow it.

35   I'd better go back and get the map.

36   It's too late, it's already close to evening. Just keep going. How many paths do you think there are down here?

37   What if this is the wrong path already? It looks like the wrong path. It's too small.

38   Are you kidding? It's the 401. Keep going.

39   I keep going. The sun has disappeared and there is no sign of Tsebar. There is no sign of anything. I am already exhausted, and my water is finished. I practise my Sharchhop in my head. *Where are you going? I am going to Tsebar. Are you a nun? No, I am a teacher.* Shadowy thoughts of wild animals begin to solidify, taking the shape of bears. There are bears in Bhutan, I read it in a library book. *The Himalayan black bear: small black bear with characteristic white V on its chest.*

40   *Are you a teacher? No, I am a coward.*

41   The way up is exceedingly steep, and my legs ache and burn and shake. I stop, gasping, and rub my stinging eyes. The path bifurcates around an enormous mango tree, one route continuing sharply up, another levelling off into a dense forest. It levels off because it leads to a settlement, I reason, and take it. Forty-five minutes later, it plunges into a pool of stagnant water and does not come out on the other side. I sit on an exposed tree root and stare into the shadows, trying to determine the most reasonable thing to do. Everything

seems reasonable. I should go back to the mango tree. I should go back to Pema Gatshel. I should spend the night here. I should go on and look for the other end of the path. I should scream for help.

42   Everything seems possible: I will find the path, I will find a village, I will find Tsebar, someone will find me, no-one will find me, I will be lost in the bush and die of starvation. My stomach feels like a huge, hollow, echoing drum, and I have run out of thoughts. I have reached the end of something, but I do not know what it is.

43   Twigs snap behind me and there is a cow. A reddish-brown bulk with a bell. Another cow, black with a bent horn. A calf. A boy with a stick. He looks surprised to see me. A man bent under a load of wood and a woman with a basket come up behind him. The cows drink from the green pool, and the man and woman stare at me.

44   "Where are you going, Miss?" the boy asks me.

45   "I'm going to Tsebar."

46   The boy raises one eyebrow. "But Miss," he says, "Tsebar is not this way."

47   "Which way is Tsebar?"

48   He gestures. Back and up.

49   "Thank you," I say. "I'm a teacher at Pema Gatshel. Across the valley. Do you know Pema Gatshel?"

50   "Miss," he says with great patience, "I'm in your class."

51   Karma Dorji is also going to Tsebar with his aunt and uncle. I follow them back to where the path splits, and we sit under the mango tree. It is almost dark now, but I feel strangely light. I came to the end of something and passed through it. I do not know what it was. "Tsebar is not far," Karma Dorji says. "We always take rest here." He pours clear water from a cloudy jerry can into my empty water bottle. The aunt and uncle unwrap three small, round baskets. They pass one to me, and Karma Dorji helps me pull it open. Inside large chunks of meat, red chillies, and onions are embedded in a mound of rice. Karma Dorji and his uncle are going to share a basket. They are waiting for me. His aunt is saying something.

52   "She is telling our food is not that very good, but please don't mind." Karma Dorji translates. "She is telling please eat."

53   "Thank you," I say, and eat the meat. It is delicious.

Jamie Zeppa, "Jungle Fever," *Saturday Night*, May 1996: 77–78, 81–82.

QUESTIONS

Subject
On the surface of it, this essay tells us an interesting story about someone's experience in a foreign country. But there is more to the story that this. Can you argue that the journey is one that focuses as well on a journey into the self?

Audience
Discuss ways in which the author wins audience interest even though none or very few of the essay's readers would have made the same physical journey as the author.

Purpose

Comment on the way the title, "Jungle Fever," helps explain the essay's narrative purpose.

Structure and Style

   (a) Explain the significance of the repeated phrase "I know" in paragraph 4 and the effect of the final sentence in paragraph 5, "I don't know."

   (b) In paragraph 10, the author uses a sentence fragment "against the rats." Explain the appropriateness of this phrase which appears to be a clear violation of a grammatical rule.

   (c) To whom is the author speaking in the short sentences beginning at paragraph 24? Decide whether this "dialogue" fits the purpose of the essay.

   (d) Pay attention to the emphasis in the story on food and eating. Explain how the final paragraph focuses on the resolution to the crisis through the use of eating.

This page constitutes an extension of the copyright page. Every reasonable effort has been made to find copyright holders. The publishers would be pleased to have any errors or omissions brought to their attention.

J.H. Anonymous, "Pinocchio Street," *The Literary Review of Canada,* December 1996.

Margaret Atwood, *Survival: A Thematic Guide to Canadian Literature,* Toronto: Anansi, 1972. Used by permission, McClelland & Stewart, Inc. *The Canadian Publishers.*

Black's Photography advertisement published in *This Country Canada,* 1:1 (1992).

Clark Blaise, "A North American Education," *The Narrative Voice,* Ed. John Metcalf, Toronto: McGraw-Hill Ryerson, 1972. Copyright © 1973 by Clark Blaise. Reprinted by permission of the author.

Clark Blaise, "To Begin, To Begin," *The Narrative Voice,* Ed. John Metcalf, Toronto: McGraw-Hill Ryerson, 1972. By permission of the author.

Jeb Blount, "O Dirty Canada," *The Idler,* May/June 1989.

Harry Bruce, "The Alchemy of Sailing," *Maclean's,* July 1973. By permission of the publisher.

Dalton Camp, *An Eclectic Eel,* Ottawa: Deneau, 1981. By permission of the author.

Dalton Camp, "The Decline in Public Morality," *Saturday Night,* January 1981. By permission of the author.

Emily Carr, *Growing Pains: The Autobiography of Emily Carr,* Toronto: Clarke, Irwin, 1946. By permission.

Ann Charney, "The Monument," *Saturday Night,* January 1987. By permission of the author.

Nancy Miller Chenier, *Reproductive Hazards at Work: Men, Women and the Fertility Gamble,* (Ottawa: Canadian Advisory Council on the Status of Women, 1982).

David Coburn, "Patient's Rights: A New Deal in Health Care," *Canadian Forum,* 60.699 (May 1980). By permission of the author.

John Robert Columbo, "Recipe for a Canadian Novel," *Abracadabra,* Toronto: McClelland & Stewart, 1967. Reprinted with permission of the author.

Matt Cohen, "Hannukkah," *Canadian Geographic,* November/December 1995. By permission of the author. First published in *Canadian Geographic,* 1995.

Commissioner of Official Languages, *Annual Report, 1985,* Minister of Supply and Services Canada, 1986. By permission of the author.

Neil Compton, "Broadcasting and Canadian Culture," *Commentary,* 38 (November 1964).

Stanley Coren, "Sleep Sliding Away," *Saturday Night,* April 1996.

Robertson Davies, *A Voice From the Attic,* Toronto: McClelland & Stewart, 1960; reissued, 1972. With permission of Pendragon Ink.

Marg de Villiers, "Too Many Guns," *Toronto Life,* August 1975. By permission of the author.

Ken Dryden, *The Game,* Toronto: Macmillan of Canada, 1983. Reprinted by permission of MacMillan of Canada, A Division of Canadian Publishing Corporation.

Howard Engel, *The Suicide Murders,* Harmondsworth: Penguin, 1985. First published by Clarke, Irwin, 1980. © Copyright Howard Engel from *The Suicide Murders.*

T.E. Farley, *Exiles and Pioneers: Two Visions of Canada's Future, 1825–1975,* Ottawa: Borealis, 1976. By permission of Borealis Press.

Timothy Findley, "Better Dead Than Read? An Opposing View," *Books in Canada,* December 1978. By permission of the author.

Allan Fotheringham, "Dan George's Last Stand," *Maclean's,* July 1971. By permission of the author.

Barbara Freeman, "'Every Stroke Upward': Women Journalists in Canada, 1880–1906," *Canadian Women Studies,* Fall 1986. By permission of the author and the publisher.

David Frum, "Why She Needs the Bomb," *The Idler,* May/June 1989.

Northrop Frye, *The Educated Imagination,* Toronto: CBC Enterprises, 1963. By permission of the author.

Robert Fulford, "Charter of Wrongs," *Saturday Night,* December 1986.

Ellen Gabriel, "Kanesatake: The Summer of 1990," in *Nation to Nation: Aboriginal Sovereignty and the Future of Canada,* Eds. Diane Englestad and John Bird. (Concord: Anansi, 1992). Reprinted with the permission of Stoddart Publishing Co. Limited.

Ian Gentles, "Rethinking Death with Dignity," *The Idler,* Summer 1993. Ian Gentles teaches history at York University's Glendon College and is Research Director of the de Veber Institute for Bioethics and Social Research.

George Grant, *Lament for a Nation,* Toronto: McClelland & Stewart, 1965.

Peter Gzowski, *The Morningside Papers.* (Toronto: McClelland & Stewart, 1985). Used by permission, McClelland & Stewart, Inc. *The Canadian Publishers.*

Roderick Haig-Brown, "The Nature of Estuaries," *Fisherman's Fall,* Don Mills: William Collins Sons, 1964. Published by Douglas & McIntyre, © 1964 and 1975. Reprinted with permission.

Rosa Harris-Adler, "Pictures of an Exhibitionist," *Saturday Night,* July/August 1996. Rosa Harris-Adler is a writer and editor.

Ralph Heintzman, "Liberalism and Censorship," *The Journal of Canadian Studies,* Winter 1978–9. By permission of the publisher.

Patricia Hluchy, "Teenage Wasteland," *Maclean's,* 19 February 1996.

A.Y. Jackson, *A Painter's Country,* Toronto: Clarke, Irwin, 1958; reprinted, 1964. Courtesy of Dr. Naomi Jackson Groves.

"Japan car sales," *The Globe and Mail,* 7 August 1987.

Ann Dowsett Johnston, "Introduction," *The Maclean's Guide to Universities,* 1996.

Janice Kennedy, "L'affaire Richler-Abley: A Classical Confrontation," *The Ottawa Citizen,* 14 July 1996.

John Keyes, "These 22 Minutes Take Hours," *Canadian Living,* October 1995.

William Kilbourn, *Canada: A Guide to the Peaceable Kingdom,* Toronto: Macmillan, 1970. By permission of the author.

Paul King and Barbara Fulton, "Charlevoix, Naturally Quebec," *Leisureways,* June 1996.

Mark Kingwell, "Not Available in Stores," *Saturday Night,* July/August 1996.

Mark Kingwell, "The Goods on the Tube," *Saturday Night,* March 1996.

Marcia Kircher, "Nicaragua: Revolution Plus One," *Canadian Forum,* 60: 703 (October 1980).

Margaret Laurence, "The Greater Evil," *Toronto Life,* September 1984. By permission of the Estate of Margaret Laurence.

Margaret Laurence, "Where the World Began," *Maclean's,* December 1972. Excerpt from *Heart of a Stranger* (Toronto: McClelland & Stewart, 1976).

Ross Laver, "Plugging into the future," *Maclean's,* 29 January 1996.

René Lévesque, "Heartbread," *Memoirs,* Trans. Philip Stratford (Toronto: McClelland & Stewart, 1986). Used by permission, McClelland & Stewart, Inc. *The Canadian Publishers.*

Jack Ludwig, "The Calgary Stampede," *Maclean's,* July 1975. © Jack Ludwig July 1975. Originally published in *Maclean's* July 1975.

David Macfarlane, "On Days of Yore," *This Country Canada,* 1:1 (1992).

Martin Martin, "We, the Inuit Are Changing," *This Country Canada,* 1:1 (1992).

Michael McCordie, "Modern Monuments," *Canadian Forum,* 58: 681 (May 1978).

Liz McKee, "A Woman's View of Liberation," *Canada and the World,* 40 (December 1974).

Carol Milstone, "Sound and Fury," *Saturday Night,* March 1996.

Brian Moore, in [Silver] Donald Cameron, *Conversations with Canadian Novelists, 2,* Toronto: Macmillan, 1973.

Farley Mowat, *And No Birds Sang,* Toronto: McClelland & Stewart-Bantam, 1979. Used by permission, McClelland & Stewart, Inc. *The Canadian Publishers.*

H.V. Nelles, "Creighton's Seminar," *Canada Forum,* 60: 702. By permission of the author.

Toni Onley, "The Longest Night," *Saturday Night,* February 1985. By permission of the author.

Kim Pittaway, "Sex Offenders: What You Need to Know," *Chatelaine,* March 1995. Copyright Kim Pittaway. Originally published in *Chatelaine* magazine.

Al Purdy, "Boozy Saddles," *Maclean's,* May 1975. By permission of, and with additions by, the author.

George Randwanski, *Trudeau,* Toronto: Macmillan, 1978. By permission of the author.

Mordecai Richler, "A Clear and Present Danger," *Saturday Night,* February 1996.

Mordecai Richler, "Going Home," *Notes on an Endangered Species,* New York: Alfred A. Knopf, 1974. Reprinted by permission of International Creative Management.

Spider Robinson, *Mindkiller,* New York: Berkley Books, 1983; Holt Rinehart, 1982. By permission of Holt, Rinehart and Winston.

Eve Rocket, "Some Like It Hot," *Chatelaine,* May 1996. Author of *Life In The Runaway Lane: Recapturing The Spirit of Childhood Through Adventure.* Published by Doubleday Canada.

Colin Ross, "The Story of Grey Owl," *The Compass,* Winter 1979. By permission of the author and publisher.

Lionel Rubinoff, "National Purpose and Ideology," *Notes for a Native Land,* Ed. Andy Wainwright, Ottawa: Oberon, 1969. Reprinted by permission of Oberon Press.

R. Murray Schafer, "Canadian Culture: Colonial Culture," *Canadian Forum,* March 1984. By permission of the author.

Robin Skelton, "O Canada!" *Notes for a Native Land,* Ed. Andy Wainwright, Ottawa: Oberon, 1969. Reprinted by permission of Oberon Press.

Victor C. Smith, "Lumbering, Pulp and Paper, and Forestry," *A Vast and Magnificent Land,* Eds. Matt Bray and Ernie Epp, Thunder Bay: Lakehead University; Sudbury: Laurentian University, 1984. By permission of the Ontario Ministry of Northern Affairs.

Edna Staebler, *Food that Really Schmecks,* Scarborough: McGraw-Hill Ryerson, 1968.

Jim Stirling, "Saving the Marbles," *Beautiful British Columbia,* Fall 1994. Reprinted from *Beautiful British Columbia* magazine by Jim Stirling.

Paul Stuewe, "Better Dead Than Read?" *Books in Canada,* October 1978. Paul Stuewe is the former editor of *Books in Canada*, and author of five books, most recently the mystery novel, *This Dark Embrace* (Mercury Press, 1996).

David T. Suzuki, "A Planet for the Taking," *Canadian Forum,* February 1985. By permission of the author.

Scott Symons, From *Place d'Armes,* Toronto: McClelland & Stewart, 1967. Copyright © 1967 Scott Symons. With permission of the author.

Margaret Visser, *Much Depends on Dinner,* Toronto: McClelland & Stewart, 1986. Used by permission, McClelland & Stewart, Inc. *The Canadian Publishers.*

George Whalley, *The Legend of John Hornby,* London: John Murray (Publishers) Ltd., 1962.

Richard B. Wright, *The Weekend Man,* New York: Farrar, Straus, and Giroux, 1970. Excerpted with permission from *The Weekend Man* by Richard Wright copyright © 1970 by Richard Wright. Published in Canada by HarperCollins*Publishers Ltd.*

Jamie Zeppa, "Jungle Fever," *Saturday Night,* May 1996.

Index